HEIDEGGER'S

Being and Time

A READING FOR READERS

HEIDEGGER'S

Being and Time

A READING FOR READERS

E. F. Kaelin

University Presses of Florida

THE FLORIDA STATE UNIVERSITY PRESS
TALLAHASSEE

University Presses of Florida is the central agency for scholarly publishing of the State of Florida's university system, producing books selected for publication by the faculty editorial committees of Florida's nine public universities. Orders for books published by all member presses should be addressed to University Presses of Florida, 15 NW 15th Street, Gainesville, FL 32603.

Library of Congress Cataloging-in-Publication Data

Kaelin, Eugene Francis, b. 1926
   Heidegger's Being and time: a reading for readers / E.F. Kaelin.
     p.   cm.
   Bibliography: p.
   Includes index.
   ISBN 0–8130–0865–4 (alk. paper)
   1. Heidegger, Martin, 1889–1976. Sein und Zeit. 2. Ontology.
3. Space and time. I. Title.
B3279.H48S46627   1987
111—dc19   87–18624
                                                        CIP

Second printing, 1989
© 1988 by the Board of Regents of the State of Florida
∞ Printed in the U.S.A. on acid-free paper.

CONTENTS

To JOOP DORMAN,

itinerant Dutch mathematician,
who first showed me
there was something there.

PREFACE

WHEN I FIRST CAME TO KNOW HIM, JOOP
Dorman was a graduate student in mathematics, formally matricu-
lated at the University of Wisconsin for the purpose of writing a
dissertation in intuitionist mathematics. One would have supposed
that were his vocation. Those of us who got to know him well,
however, were soon to realize that the time spent on a vocation, in
his case, was not commensurate with a true life's calling. He had
three loves in his life that left little time for mathematical speculation.
In apparent order they were philosophy, in particular that of Martin
Heidegger; dramaturgy and the cinema, in particular the films of
Ingmar Bergman; and lastly, his wife, Minnika.

To say that his wife came third in the hierarchy of these interests
is, perhaps, to overstate the case. He would go to a Bergman film
alone because she couldn't stand to sit through the same film twice,
or three times, as she would have to, if it were possible for him to do
so in continuous showings. Yet she seemed to understand his drive
to come to grips with the majestic symbolism of the ponderous Swede.
To be open to the influences of artistic communication was the only
way Joop could understand his being in the world. The very concept
of a world devoid of created significance, as of a proof that was only
mechanical, beggared his imagination. As a consequence the reality
of his world—and there are as many worlds as there are imaginations

to produce them—seemed to take precedence over the formal demands of the real world. There, in his world, was a place to be, alone or with his wife. And whether the one or the other, the situation was much the same: if he were alone, he felt her absence; if she were there, she merely enlivened his world, and the importance of the surrounding world seemed to be reduced to nothing. When they were together one could sense the complicity of the one in the action of the other that betokens a silent conspiracy of the loving couple against any incursion of the external world.

How to understand this being with another that lets the other be what he or she will? That, I think, is what motivated Joop's interest in the Heideggerian philosophy. Asking the question was simple, since its exigency was felt in the daily events of his life. Answering it was another matter.

From his previous readings of Heidegger—in particular *Being and Time*—he had learned that asking the question is itself a form of being in one's world, and that finding an answer necessitates making an interpretation of one's own interests, desires, one's own accomplishments or failures, and that, however this interpretation be made, it can only be expressed in a language that is one's own. What does one do when one becomes convinced that every question honestly felt must be turned into a quest for personal fulfillment? One might be excused for dropping an interest dictated by a past decision or imposed upon one by another. When the quest for being—for personal fulfillment—becomes tinged with enthusiasm, the enthusiasm rightfully replaces the original object of awareness, one's prior being, into a questionable state.

The language does not come easily. How can one talk of traits and states without supposing the existence of someone, some thing, some substance that possesses that trait, that state? But what has happened in reality? As a pragmatist would say, one has merely felt unsettled in a situation. Finding oneself so situated motivated a question, indeed was the object of the question. Any attempt to settle the question is an act that generates enthusiasm as it approaches success. The original doubt, dismay, curiosity, or awe, as the case may be, has betrayed one way of being in the world; it has been replaced by another, the search for fulfillment; and as a possible success becomes announced in the inquiry being made, there is still a third, which I have noted as enthusiasm. Jean-Paul Sartre was famous for saying that between these three moments of conscious awareness there was nothing at all. Transcendental nonbeing he called it; but I shall attempt throughout this work to avoid the jargon of Germanic philosophy, even while commenting on one such text. Joop Dorman communicated his enthusiasm by inviting a few of us to share in the quest. It was 1963, I think, when we began our seminar.

Having been through the text before, Joop served as coordinator. Bill Hay consulted a Spanish translation; Bill Baumer, then a graduate student, and I struggled with the German text. All of us made translations into an English that in retrospect would have to be called barbarous. Since that beginning I have introduced generations of students to the subtleties of the same text—a task that became infinitely easier with the general availability of the Macquarrie and Robinson translation.

The text of the commentary is being prepared during a sabbatical leave from the Florida State University, in the calendar year of 1984. In order to view my past and my more recent commitments from a position of removed neutrality, I have taken up residence on the eastern shore of the Iberian peninsula. Spaniards are friendly people, and open to this kind of invasion of their culture. At any rate, it is comforting to be writing in a place where the expression *un ser humano* makes perfectly good sense; and if *el ser humano* remains ambiguous, the comfort of being surrounded by *seres humanos* is at this moment a welcome change in my life.

To make this reading I availed myself of the eighth unchanged edition of the German text (*Sein und Zeit* [Tübingen: Max Niemeyer Verlag, 1957]), not because it is any more authoritative than any other edition, but because it was the only one accessible to me. For points of clarification, when the ontological reversal boggled my mind, I sought further corroboration of my reading in the translation of Macquarrie and Robinson (*Being and Time* [London: SCM Press, Ltd., 1962]). In every case, I have reserved the right to differ with a given translation; for example, I have rendered *Dasein* by *human being* and suggested *an existential* as a more suitable rendering of *Existenzial* than *existentiale*, whose plural form is rendered by Macquarrie and Robinson as *existentialia*. The reason for such reserve is in every case the improved readability of my commentary and not an eccentric pursuit of originality.

Campello,
Alicante,
Spain
March 1984

INTRODUCTION

THE QUESTION WILL NOT BE POSTPONED.
Why write a commentary on a text first published in 1927 and since rejected by the majority of English-speaking philosophers as one of the monumental errors in the history of philosophy? A closer and perhaps more critical look at the recent history of the discipline, including the part played by the various interpretations of the text, may give a clue toward an appropriate, if not quite satisfactory, answer.

Sixteen years after the first publication of Martin Heidegger's *Being and Time*,[1] Jean-Paul Sartre published his own *Being and Nothingness*.[2] The year was 1943, and the new text was perhaps the most thoroughgoing interpretation yet given the Heideggerian philosophy, in Germany or abroad. The world was at war, and no one had yet heard of existentialism, either as a philosophy or as a literary style. Sartre had spent an extended period of time in Berlin, in the calmer thirties, studying the philosophies of Husserl and Heidegger. He was aware of Heidegger's adaption of the Husserlian phenomenology into a fundamental ontology, the purpose of which was to recover the firstness of first philosophy. But the readers of Sartre's text called themselves existentialists; and he was above all a practical, even humble, man. Once written, a text belongs to its readers, and not to its author.

1

In the European mode of philosophizing, a text is important insofar as it has useful social or institutional consequences—a fact called to mind by Merleau-Ponty's remark that philosophy is the conscience of history.[3] Although the earliest French "existentialists" were referred to by an offended bourgeoisie as *rats de cabaret*, because as young students they spent more time in (heated) cafés than in (unheated) university lecture halls, they tended to show as much good faith in adopting the term for their philosophical views as they had good sense in preferring heated to unheated places to study. Because they believed that human values were created by human acts, they acted in such a way as to criticize the dominant values of their society that had led them into war. And if they bathed too little and too badly, that too was an effect of the war.

Sartre had chosen the dilemma of social commitment to illustrate the essence of his "existential" thought.[4] In a time of war or occupation does an able-bodied male stay at home to take care of his invalid mother or join the forces of opposition? Nothing—neither the will of God, nor social approval, nor any prior personal decision—guarantees that one mode of conduct is superior to the other.

But we must remember that *Existentialism is a humanism* was a lecture delivered by Sartre to an audience curious to know what *Being and Nothingness* was all about, to learn the mere essence of this philosophy without having to read it. That personal commitment, freedom, and responsibility should constitute the main themes of his popularizing lecture[5] comes as no surprise to anyone who has actually read the treatise. What Heidegger found displeasing in that lecture was a reference to himself as an "atheistic existentialist," in a class with Nietzsche and Sartre himself, as opposed to that line of theistic existentialists created by Kierkegaard's opposition to the scholastic Hegelianism of his day, and which claimed proponents in both Germany and France.

Sartre, he maintained, had misinterpreted his position. The predicament of the existentialist rats possessed no more than an ontic significance, which as experienced was real enough, but which could hardly be explained ontologically by the Hegelian concepts of being-in-itself and being-for-itself that Sartre had used in the place of his own existentials *(Existentialien)*. That too would not wash!

Although Sartre had all but quoted Heidegger verbatim in stating that "being has not been given its due,"[6] and further stated his agreement that it is always possible in our philosophical investigations to "go beyond" the existent to its essence, or meaning, and then to go beyond that to its being, the passage from object to being-in-itself and from consciousness to being-for-itself seemed hardly enlightening to the person looking for a true ontological reversal. Sartre's proof for the transphenomenal existence of being and absolute nothingness was as weak as the original proof offered by St. Anselm for the existence of God. The move from the statement "I am conscious of something" to "There is something of which I am conscious" seems as innocuous as Descartes' deductive move from the existence of a thought as attribute to that of a thinker as substance. And in both cases the error was the same: an uncritical attention to the categories by which being—or existence—in its most general form gets expressed in language.

Besides the example alluded to above, Heidegger found Sartre's supposed ignorance of the difference between the German "Es gibt" and the French "Il y a," both of which are translated into ordinary English as "There is," symptomatic of his failure to understand the ontological reversal it is necessary to perform in order to develop a truly fundamental ontology. It mattered little that one had to be human—a man or a woman—in order to perform the reversal; the meaning of that necessary connection—between a person and the thoughts one harbors about oneself—had to be worked out. Sartre had done nothing in his lecture other than to dramatize the depths of feeling implicit in being bound in times of stress to choose a personal mode of action. As we shall see, choosing such a mode of action is called "authenticity," in the usual mode of translating Heidegger's *Eigentlichkeit;* but as Macquarrie and Robinson admit, the qualities of a self expressed in the act of choosing get lost in this translation.[7]

To be or not to be—to be at root one's own person—is the question whose meaning had never yet been made absolutely clear, because the categories for determining the clarity of the question had yet to be explained. That, indeed, was one of Heidegger's purposes in writing *Being and Time*—to distinguish between the ontological categories applicable to the things of nature and, because they are applicable only to human beings, the "existentials" by which we can understand the structures of our being human.

Heidegger's letter *Über den Humanismus,* elicited by one of his French students, Jean Beaufret, explains the difference between his own philosophy and that of Sartre but in a manner perhaps no one would understand if that person had read only the two ontological treatises. The term *existentialist* that was imposed upon both was accepted graciously by Sartre and denounced as a barbarism by Heidegger. Heidegger continued to maintain that he was an ontologist; and Sartre could continue to be what he wanted to be. Later, in *Question de méthode*, Sartre referred to his existentialist period as only one "ideological" moment in the history of the movement opened up by Kierkegaard in the nineteenth century. Although the remark was intended as an explanation of his newer Marxist phase of philosophizing, which was necessitated by a change in dialectical methods, to a historian of the movement it represents a positive riposte to Heidegger's criticisms. Nowhere in Heidegger's writings, as far as I know, had he ever acknowledged his considerable debt to that melancholy Dane. And in spite of his denials, even in Germany Heidegger was better known as the philosopher of *Angst* than as the ontologist who would destroy the history of ontology.

History has treated this affair with some amusement. Sartre went on to be awarded the Nobel Prize for literature, which he refused, because accepting it would have constituted an approval of bourgeois values, while Heidegger spent the greater part of his later years in his mountain retreat "shepherding Being"—as the wags insisted— and affording an occasional audience to a select group of disciples.

In the meantime, existentialism as a postwar philosophical movement refused to die. Departments of philosophy in American universities as early as the 1950s began hiring tokens of the species, who communicated with each other mostly through the newly formed Society for Phenomenology and Existential Philosophy, which continues to flourish as of this writing. With the foundation of *Man and World*,[8] a journal dedicated to phenomenological and existentialist topics, and with the almost heroic effort of the Northwestern University Press[9] to publish translations of the principal texts of the European founders of the movement, the philosophy seemed safely institutionalized, if not in the mainstream of American philosophy.

Curiously enough, the case was different for theology, psychoanalytic theory, and literary criticism. Heidegger's insistence upon interpretation as a method of understanding found support in theology, a discipline that had considered itself "hermeneutical" since the humanism of the Renaissance. After two world wars in thirty years theologians turned from the earlier dogmatic readings of Scripture and traditional metaphysics to a study of the human values implicit in the relationship between men and their fellows, as between men and women, for a deeper understanding of the old Christian adage that God is love. Bultmann in Germany[10] and Tillich in Germany and the United States[11] brought different aspects of the Heideggerian philosophy to the new theology. In Germany "demystification" of religious belief flourished as a postwar theology; and Tillich brought his brand of systematic theology to America, where he was perhaps better known for his *Courage to Be*.[12] For many of its readers *The Courage to Be* was almost a primer of Heideggerian "existentialism," part theology and part a newer type of depth psychology.

American readers were introduced to the new psychology by Rollo May,[13] student of Medard Boss and Ludwig Binswanger, the two Swiss psychotherapists most influenced by Heidegger. Boss has recorded what he interpreted to be an instantaneous conversion on reading Heidegger's *Being and Time*.[14] In Austria Viktor Frankl, who loved to change the accepted names of things, chose the expression *Daseinsanalyse* in preference to Heidegger's *Daseinsanalytik* to name his therapeutic methodology. Heidegger's term, of course, was intended to designate the philosophical methodology of the only portion of *Being and Time* as yet to be published. But if *Daseinsanalyse* is a method of analyzing self-alienated patients, *Daseinsanalytik* is its methodology. Rollo May's introduction to the new methodology bore the simple title *Existence* and constituted a tribute to its foundation in the Heideggerian philosophy.

Of the new "humanistic" psychologists in America, perhaps only Carl Rogers followed Heidegger in preferring the term "being" as the object of his concern for his patients. But here, once again, the difference seems so minimal as to be negligible. Whether one is interested in one's patient's existence or being, one way of getting at this subject is to ask "How are you?" or "How do you feel today?" Since the question in German is "Wie befinden Sie sich (heute)?" Heidegger referred the question to a state of being he called *Befindlichkeit,* in English, our affectivity, which betokens a relationship between ourselves and our worlds.

No fewer than three journals of existential psychotherapy were created to open the modes of communication among practitioners of the therapeutical techniques derived from existential philosophy.[15]

As for recent literary criticism and cultural history, the same phenomenon is apparent, with a slight change in the order of the program. As far as I know, there is no "existentialist literary criticism."

Before he had accepted the designation as philosophical existentialist, Sartre had written some very perceptive essays on a number of American novelists, including John Dos Passos and William Faulkner.[16] Sartre's analysis of Faulkner's use of varying concepts of time in *The Sound and the Fury* was both sound and brilliant. One could only have wished that he had chosen Faulkner's *As I Lay Dying* for the same purpose, since in that novel the author chose to represent the events in real time or history indirectly via the direct representation of passing and intersecting moments of the conscious events being lived by his fictional characters. Rather than experiencing fictional temporalities *in time,* as the reader does in reading a naturalistic novel, in Faulkner's greatest moments the reader is immersed in the temporalities of each of the characters whose being is expressed in stream-of-consciousness prose. The difference between time and temporality—objective and subjective time—which gives point to the Faulknerian narrative is also the point of "existentialist" philosophy. Faulkner too was awarded the Nobel Prize for his achievement.

As an existentialist activist, Sartre was personally more interested in creating a new form of literature—he called it "total literature," which was to be a political action of the novelist rather than the occasion for displaying one's analytical skills. The psychological analyses of a Marcel Proust, we recall, were derided by Sartre as bourgeois vanity.[17] But that was in a literary manifesto. Literary criticism is of a different nature.

Sartre's principal critical works spanned the various changes of his philosophical orientation. His studies of Baudelaire, Jean Genet, and Gustave Flaubert were exercises in what he called "existential psychoanalysis,"[18] the principles of which were outlined in *Being and Nothingness,* but which were put into practice only in these essays and represented in fiction as the methodology used by the hero of Simone de Beauvoir's *The Mandarins.*

The essay on Flaubert, depicting its subject as "the idiot of the family," was perhaps the last large-scale work produced by Sartre. Contemporary criticism has, for the most part, rejected these exercises in depth psychology on the grounds that "biographical criticism" misses its mark—the work itself of the author—whenever the object of critical discourse is removed to the author himself, whether the reason for that removal is grounded in an insight into the newer humanistic depth psychology or only in a run-of-the-mill understanding of the classical theories of psychoanalysis.

More to the point was Sartre's suggestion in his literary manifesto that "the new novel" reflects the conditions of the new philosophy, and that plots exhibit the contingencies of natural and political situations in which the characters act so as to define themselves, creating a value by their activity of projecting significance within the scope of the possibilities presented to them by their environments. The idea itself was hardly novel: realists had always maintained that the characters and events of their novels should be "real"; and naturalists, that they be "natural." That the personages and events of an "existentialist" novel should be consistent with the descriptions of a human world given in existentialist philosophy gives testimony only to the fact that a metaphysics in general becomes embodied within a literary work as a literary technique, that is, in the novelist's manner of depicting his fictional world.

Heidegger's criticism, on the other hand, was directed mainly to poets, as an example of the "dialogue" between philosopher and poet. Hölderlin, he told us, both explained and exhibited within his poetry on poetizing that a poet's task is "the creative naming of the Gods."[19] And in his often cited work *Der Ursprung des Kunstwerkes* we are given an explanation of what might be called "an ontological criticism." A work of art, we are told, in the struggle between its earth and its world, allows being to come to a stand.[20] But none of these metaphors, I am convinced, can be understood without a prior reading of *Being and Time*, since the interpretive context, the "forestructure of the understanding" as it is called there, is first made clear in that text. On this, more is to be found in the text of my commentary.

Although Heidegger's personal brand of criticism took the form of a dialogue between an author and himself, "Heideggerian" criticism came to America in another form. Taking their point of departure from an essay on the historical epoch of building world images— one way of "doing" metaphysics in the cosmological mode, by which the metaphysician creates a theoretical picture of the real world— "postmodernist" critics have proclaimed with Heidegger the death of "modern" metaphysics; and, along with this death as a historical circumstance in philosophy, the postmodernists announced the passing of modernist, read "formalistic," criticism. The circumstances were not gratuitous.

Heidegger's invective against modern cosmological metaphysics formed a part of his crusade against the traditional metaphysics it was his purpose to destroy. It was that destruction that permitted his return to a dialogue with the pre-Socratic philosophers for a rediscovery of our Western quest for an understanding of being. But in the hands of such literary critics as Professor William Spanos and his colleagues at *boundary 2*,[21] the change in metaphysical orientation necessitated a change in our conception of a literary work of art. Upon the gratuitous assumption that a novel, for example, was the representation of a particular world view drawn from fixed concepts used to describe the events of nature constituting the "real" world—which, indeed, it never was—it was propounded that to become postmodern a novelist must abandon the traditional metaphysics for a more up-to-date narrative technique.

That the suggested technique should correspond to the distinction Heidegger sought to perpetuate between an ontic and on ontological analysis, that is, between the portrayal of a world view and the being of the beings living in such a world, seemed natural enough. Since the meaning of our human being is our temporality, in Heidegger's postmodernism at least, it came as no surprise that "postmodernist" literary criticism took the difference between time and temporality to be the clue for interpreting contemporary literature. Such a move, if I may be forgiven for saying it, puts Descartes before the horse, since it is deductive, and merely replaces one world view with another, presumably more accurate. Rather than looking for any truths in its representation, however, one must still approach any text of any author open to what *it*—the text—intends.

So the case has been poorly argued. Postmodernism came to us as a diatribe against the new critical formalism. Had the postmodernists heeded the difference between formalist and structuralist criticism, the case might have been different. If a novel never was merely a representation of a fictional world, what indeed is it? Two answers are possible, and they eventually merge into one.

First of all, besides being the representation of a fictional world, a novel is a literary creation. When Heidegger asked the question "What is at work in a work of art?"[22] his famous answer was "the strife between earth and world." His metaphors seem on second reading to be transparent: the world is composed of that network of images, represented objects, and ideas that come to closure in the concept of the fictional world—*das Weltbild* of the modern tradition; the earth, on the other hand, represents the sensuous surface of the creative artist's medium, in literature the sounding of words. Even

Heidegger's ontology is rife with the expression "Das lautet wie [That sounds like]." And whoever says *Dasein* gives tone to *Sein*. The literary creation, on the other hand, gives tone to the world of the artist's expression; it brings to speech the tensions felt in the artist's being in the world.

Under this guise, the Heideggerian aesthetic—always to be differentiated, as he said, from the art of the pastrycook—is perfectly consistent with a structuralist criticism. But the linguistic theory upon which that criticism was built, Saussure's *General Theory of Linguistics*,[23] considered all uses of language to be structured relations of signs, themselves merely relational counters between a signifier and a signified. Literary works contained a text, a field of signifiers denoting or connoting a set of signifieds, which in their turn, in "symbolic" literature, could stand as signifiers to a higher level of signifieds. Unfortunately, from the Heideggerian standpoint, structuralism remained a scientific theory and, as such, an ontic explanation of the fixed relationships between structural signific elements, which constituted the laws of language and speech. Logocentrism, the charge that a metaphysics or a theory of knowledge depends upon the existence of such fixed essences or laws, constituted the battle cry of the poststructuralists against even the most successful of the structuralist critics.[24]

It was the poststructuralists, under the direction of the Parisian historian of philosophy, Jacques Derrida,[25] who created the most effective answer to my leading question, What is in a literary work of art in addition to a represented fictional world? The answer is cogent and stems from considering a literary work merely as a piece of writing, a text—indeed, a set of signs, not with an associated set of signified meanings, but a set of signs for which the reader of the piece of writing merely substitutes another set of signs, the critical text. These, too, to be "understood" must be interpreted, and so on *ad infinitum*. And if there is no ultimate meaning of a given text, there is likewise no initial structural relationship or essence that constitutes the source of the given text.

Heidegger, we recall, described the artist's being-in-the-world as the ultimate source of an artwork's working; and what gets expressed in that source is the human artist's opening to being, indeed to feeling, to interpretive understanding, and to the act of speech. But without a reader's interpretive response the artist's expression would be a "meaningless" gesture.

There are other points of comparison between Heidegger's planned *destruction* of the history of ontology and Derrida's technique of *deconstructing* a text,[26] but the question is too complex to be entered into here. Heidegger, says Derrida, was aware of the false logocentrism of the traditional ontology but was unable to escape the phenomenon in his own "fundamental" ontology. That indeed is a charge that must be examined in light of a reading of the Heideggerian text—as Derrida would have it, simply as a piece of writing.

Both these philosophers, moreover, Heidegger as well as Derrida, owe a great deal more to Nietzsche than either has ever admitted. We need only recall the cornerstone of the Nietzschean epistemology: "There is no truth, only interpretations." If the statement itself is true, not only can there be no thing-in-itself, as Nietzsche was arguing, but nothing like a metaphysics, an essence or *logos,* or even, for that matter, anything like a fixed text.

Within the more general area of cultural history, two other writers come to mind as owing a great debt to the Heideggerian methodology: Hans-Georg Gadamer in Germany,[27] and Paul Ricoeur in France.[28]

Ricoeur's career has been long and impressive. Early interested in the philosophy of religion, in particular in human attempts to symbolize the holy and evil both in rite and in expressive language, he has recently defended his personal style of hermeneutics against both those phenomenologists and those structuralists whose claims remained limited to the description of consciousness, on the one hand, and of signific relations, on the other. What limited the grasp of the phenomenologists was the depths of the subconscious, which Ricoeur rediscovered in Freud; and of the structuralists, the event of speech. His *Conflict of Interpretations* may be read as the epitome of French hermeneutics during the past thirty years. Having made the linguistic turn in philosophical methodology in pursuit of the mysteries of religion, he was well prepared to serve as interpreter of the continentals for American and English linguistic philosophers, a task he has performed at the University of Chicago for some years.

Although his own "arche-teleological" method remains foreign to his "Anglo-Saxon" peers, based as it is in both a Freudian analysis of the economy of desire and in a Hegelian dialectical drive toward a future state of expanded consciousness, his hardly veiled references to a simultaneous determination of the present moment of human consciousness by both past and future reveal an indebtedness to Heidegger, both early and late. Indeed, Ricoeur is one philosopher who has openly admitted that indebtedness[29] and has cheerfully defended the subtle German against both friend and foe. It is the mark of the true Heideggerian scholar, I think, that he or she recognizes the necessity to defend Heidegger against both his followers and his detractors alike.

Neither a follower nor a detractor, but a philosopher in his own right looking for a method of analyzing the truth of a historically evolving set of events, Gadamer accepted Heidegger's challenge to probe the difference between Dilthey's "philosophy of life," where life was considered as a whole that exhibited itself in significant *Gestalten* throughout particular moments of its career, and his own *Daseinsanalytik*, which considered care as the being of one's being human and temporality as its meaning. The difference, according to Heidegger, was between a frankly ontic study—a philosophical anthropology—on the one hand, and a fully conceived fundamental ontology, on the other. Gadamer's own problematic was to investigate the connection between a method of analysis and its expected results, or truth, when the object analyzed was linguistically expressed, whether it were a work of art or a piece of Scripture—and these could be the same—or a law codifying the intent of a lawmaker. Gadamer's insight was not so much to achieve the effect that he had envisaged, as to implement the process by which any hermeneutical method is to be tested.

It was on first reading Gadamer's *Wahrheit und Methode* that, upon reflection, I was brought to the understanding that Heidegger's *Being and Time* is an example of its own principal doctrine—understanding as hermeneutics—and that, to appreciate what it has to say, it is helpful to see it as exhibiting the structure it has because it had been written following the very process Heidegger describes in the text as the hermeneutical circle.

The claim is not being made here that Heidegger was right in describing the movement of the understanding as circular, and that *therefore* his treatise has the circular structure it has. That would be a vicious, not a hermeneutical circle; and there is a difference. To say that Heidegger was correct in his substantive claim and that therefore his book had to have the structure it has, since it too was the working out of an understanding, smacks too much of an illicit use of the a priori. The connection between method and truth, when the truth concerns what method must be used when, must be established *in actu;* and in this case that act was Heidegger's. My task, then, is to separate the question of method from the questions of its results.

As a system of signs in search of an interpretation, *Being and Time* in fact illustrates the structures of an interpretive understanding. I hope, in the main body of this treatise, to make this claim as evident to anyone else interested in seeing it as it seems to me. And should I succeed in this enterprise, readers of my text will find themselves in a position to reevaluate the claims made for a Heideggerian tradition in recent continental philosophy.

So far, so good.

If I am correct in my perception, and if in my commentary I succeed in transmitting that perception to my colleagues, then there are at least two reasons for taking on this task. First, the structure of *Being and Time* will have at least been made clear; and second, the historical influence of that text upon recent ontology, psychotherapy, literary and cultural criticism may then be evaluated.

If *Being and Time* is for us a text composed on the grounds of its own principles, it contains a guide for its own interpretation; and, by extension, a general methodology for reading any text at all. To read is to trace the path by which a text has been composed. That is why, in any attempt to grasp the "thought" expressed in a text, one is well advised to deconstruct it, to examine its structure with an eye toward exposing the hinges and turns of the argument, and, where necessary, supplying any missing connections.

One last *caveat lector.* If one enters Heidegger's heremeneutical circle, one runs the risk of being lost there. The same thing might be expected of any reading of Hegel. But where exiting the system of either thinker is difficult, Heidegger's case is still more difficult, since the very act of entering the system itself presents a problem. What are we to make of his project to create a "fundamental ontology"?

Philosophers have spoken of ontology as "the science of what is" from the first interpretations of the Aristotelian metaphysics. Indeed it was a bibliographer of the Aristotelian corpus that named the discipline of metaphysics as that text to be placed after the physics. Where the physics treated of beings qua moving or caused, the metaphysics treated of being qua being. This distinction has not been lost on Heidegger; indeed, he adopts it and refers to it as the "ontic-ontological" reversal.

In our own day, science deals with things, or their elements, and the relations obtaining between things or elements; and the end of the enterprise is the description of the general laws governing the relations of the things observed in nature. Mere ontics, all this, and as such, acceptable insofar as laws have been confirmed, and predictions of future events have allowed us to control the environment in living our natural lives. All sciences—physical, biological, behavioral—are general descriptions of the way things behave. Heidegger has no quarrel with this, until the categories used in scientific descriptions are brought into question. But questioning the metaphysical presuppositions of his science is no business of the scientist qua scientist. That is the task of the philosopher.

Heidegger enjoys this role tremendously. For, until the categories implicit in the investigations of the sciences have been submitted to ontological clarification, he claims, there is no fundamental understanding that results from any scientific investigation. Our faith in the method may just as well be judged by the accuracy with which our rockets hit their targets or by the ease with which we can construct computers to perform our mathematical and logical calculations, thereby relieving ourselves of the strain of performing these tasks. But going beyond the ontic to the ontological is not an easy project.

Aristotle's ten "categories" were elaborated to characterize being. The primary of these was substance: either that which needed nothing but itself to exist or that which is always the subject and never the predicate of an attribution. To substances and their attributes were eventually added modes; and all were eventually replaced, as David Hume had predicted in the eighteenth century, by a sound theory of relations.[30] Although relations are the new stuff of our computers, their substitution for substances, attributes, and modes has not been an unqualified success. When the metaphysical categories of the tradition were replaced, a distinctively scientific theory became possible. But since any purely scientific inquiry, qua scientific, remains purely ontic, studying the conditions under which observable phenomena interact in nature, the natural result of the replacement of metaphysics by science was the total elimination of metaphysics, not its epuration. Philosophy, according to Heidegger, entered into the slough of *Seinsvergessenheit*.

The problem created by the elimination of metaphysics did not become serious until the same methods of careful observation, symbolization, idealization, and prediction found in the natural sciences were applied to purely human subjects. Hume's very *Treatise,* we recall, was an attempt to apply the experimental method of science to "moral" subjects. And for over two hundred years we have continued to wait patiently for "scientific" results in the behavioral sciences. We were told the subject was too complicated, the variables too complex, for us to expect the kind of accuracy in predicting human behavior as our missile experts have attained in striking their targets.

Faced with the failure of the behavioral and social scientists to control human behavior for the betterment of humanity, Husserl had, in *The Crisis of the European Sciences,* attempted to evaluate the world view implicit in the contemporaneous "Galilean mathematization of nature." The concepts used by mathematical physicists to describe the course of natural events are, Husserl argued, derived from our common understanding of the events in our life-worlds. The concepts of mathematics are idealizations of observations made in our ordinary commerce with the things of our environment. Heidegger's purpose was to show that all scientific concepts are of this nature. He will explain, in *Being and Time,* that the concepts of space and time necessary to provide an understanding of the natural world derive in some manner or other from categories that are more primitive: such as spatiality, temporality, and historicity, which, as descriptive of human being in a world, are applicable in the first instance only to describe the ontological conditions of such a being. Whence the importance of the "existentials" elicited by Heidegger to replace the "categories" of traditional metaphysics.

How to get at such explicative notions is another matter, one more fitting for the body of my commentary than this historical gloss on the need for such a commentary.

In returning to the original motive for an ontic-ontological reversal, Heidegger thus found grounds for doubting the validity of the traditional metaphysics as an adequate explanation of *what is,* the perennial subject matter of ontology. His own ontology was to be fundamental, in relationship to other ontologies, as any ontology is to an ontic inquiry of any sort, in particular the methodology of the natural and behavioral sciences. It is for this reason, no doubt, that if philosophers could look upon the man as a crank and imposter, investigators in other intellectual disciplines, such as theology, psychotherapy, and cultural history, could find his work of momentous import.

So much for the fundamentality of Heidegger's phenomenology; and so much also for the ontic-ontological reversal it was his intent to exploit in the most fundamental way possible. Because he had such an intent and expected to be judged on the degree to which he had achieved it, he always maintained that he was no "existentialist."

His readers, friend and foe alike, may be excused for insisting otherwise, however, since the general explicative notions that had been historically called "categories"—ten for Aristotle, twelve for Kant—were amended by Heidegger to include *Existentialien*, the term I have consistently been rendering as "existentials," on the pattern in philosophical terminology of "universals" and "particulars," terms that are normally adjectives but were raised in traditional epistemology to the status of nouns, and therefore substances.

An existential is a structure in the existence of Dasein. The purpose of the analytic of Dasein is to elucidate such structures as possible ways to be in its world. The actual way in which a human being lives the tensions of its world is, of course, ontic; and so Dasein will be found to have both an ontic and an ontological dimension—and yet a third, the ontico-ontological, which the human understanding will have attained when the structures of the possibility of an existence are perceived in the actual conditions determining the existence of a human life.

The difficulty for my suggested translation for *Existentiale* (pl., *Existentialien*) is that Heidegger uses a correlative term for the ontic conditions of a real life situation, *existenziell*. Macquarrie and Robinson have opted for "existentiell" as the appropriate rendering. Since this term has no corresponding noun, as does the adjective *existenzial*, there is perhaps no difficulty in the translation. We need only remember that human existence has both an ontic and an ontological dimension, that the one intends a human being as an entity in the world and that the other describes the structures that constitute the possibilities for its being in any world at all. One could, in order to avoid the Germanicism of *existentiell*, render the term as "ontic" or "actually existing" conditions or entities.

Dasein is another matter. Macquarrie and Robinson leave the term as is, hoping the neologism will be understood as the technical term it is. The decision, I think, is as good as one could make. Certainly it is superior to Richardson's "There being,"[31] which the translator admits is awkward, even if literal. Richardson accepts the awkwardness of the expression in English to remind the reader that a technical term is intended and that this technical term has a peculiar ontological significance. But Dasein is the name of a kind of entity that may be analyzed in both an ontic and an ontological fashion. For an ordinary ontic analysis of a human being, "There being" is a bit much to accept.

Hofstadter, reflecting on this problem of translation, goes with "the Dasein."[32] He hopes to retain the technicality of the neologism but to indicate by the definite article that a specific kind of being is intended by the German term: not existence in general that might be attributed to any kind of entity but only that existence that a human being exhibits in its behavior qua human. That indeed was how Heidegger used the term, and by doing so, did constitute it as a neologism in German ontology. But the English article added to an ordinary German abstract noun substantive hardly makes an English expression; nor does it, alone, suggest the specific limitation intended in the use of the term.

As an alternative, in looking for something acceptable to an English reader, I found, paradoxically enough, Sartre's French, *réalité humaine.* The *réalité* captures the ontic-ontological ambiguity of the German; and the *humaine* makes specific just how that general ontic-ontological term must be qualified in order to grasp the force of Heidegger's neologism. Since *Dasein* is both an entity and one whose being lies in its *Existenz,* and since this latter is true only of human beings, I have opted for "human being" as an acceptable rendition of Heidegger's German.

In so doing, I have another purpose in mind. Since the proper study of the humanities is concerned with our being human in one way or another, and these ways become expressed in our languages, in our arts, and in our social institutions, we may, as is done for the most part, continue to pursue these studies in a purely ontic—even scientific—fashion, as linguistics, art history, or sociology; or we may look for another dimension of our being in the ontological structures given expression in particular instances of our using language, of creating and appreciating works of art, and of adjusting to or modifying the social determinants of our behavior.

Existentialism so conceived may yet be turned into a general methodology for humanistic studies. I shall in what follows try to demonstrate the case for literary criticism. Unfortunately, there is no alternative to a purely philosophical analysis of the concepts involved. I shall perform that analysis in the commentary that follows and then turn to the specific issue of criticism in the final chapter of this book.

PROLOGUE

1

Questioning the Meaning of Being

BESIDES THE "EXPOSITION" OF HEIDEGGER'S manner of questioning Being, which is developed under two heads, "Necessity, Structure, and Priority of the Question of Being" and "The Double Task in Working Out the Question, Method, and Design of the Inquiry," I include in my commentary the author's preface to the seventh German edition of the work and the brief, untitled foreword that immediately precedes the author's "Introduction."

First, the authorial preface. Heidegger notes that the original of his text was published in 1927 as part of Husserl's *Jahrbuch für Phänomenologie und phänomenologische Forschung,* volume 8, and simultaneously in an offprint version. The changes in the various editions were limited to quotations and punctuation; but in the seventh edition, he tells us, the words "Erste Hälfte" were removed from the *Daseinsanalytik,* since the second half was never published, and, after a quarter of a century, were the second half to be published, the first would have had to undergo massive revisions. Yet, posing his basic question is held to be necessary, "wenn die Frage nach dem Sein unser Dasein bewegen soll [if the question concerning Being is to stir our existence]." For the missing second half of the originally projected work the author refers us to his *Einführung in die Meta-*

physik, the published version of a summer semester's course given in
1935.

We know from sources outside the text why Heidegger had allowed *Being and Time* to be published with only part of the first half
finished. The offer of a job required a book-length publication, and
his former superior edited the journal that could guarantee its production. Such are the contingencies of history that color, if they do
not determine, the most authentic of self-projections.

The published text that was influential in procuring the job for its
author contained only two of the three divisions projected for its first
part; they are the preparatory fundamental analysis of human being,
and human being in relationship to temporality. "Time and Being,"
the missing division of part 1, was never published as part of the
treatise, although that title was given to a very famous lecture that
has subsequently been published not only in written form but as a
phonograph record as well.[1]

Part 2, which was to contain basic features of Heidegger's vaunted
destruction of ontology based upon the clues furnished by the formal
consideration of human temporality, never saw the light of day,
although two of the topics mentioned in the design of the larger
treatise did figure in other works of the author. Division 1 was to be
a treatment of Kant's doctrine of the schematism by which, in judgment, categories are related to percepts; and that topic seems exhausted in Heidegger's *Kant und das Problem der Metaphysik.* Division 3, an interpretation of Aristotle's theory of time as based upon
the phenomenon of passage and constituting one of the high points
of ancient ontology, forms a part of Heidegger's *Grundprobleme der
Phänomenologie.*[2]

On the basis of the evidence procured from works by Heidegger
published subsequently to the shorter treatise it is my task to comment on, latter day Heideggerians are intent upon reconstituting in
retrospect what Heidegger himself was incapable of constituting in
prospect. They could do so, I maintain, only if the design of the larger
treatise is accepted as the author's intent, and the intent is the meaning
of his projected work. Both these assumptions are critical errors,
whether committed by a literary or a philosophical critic. I do not
wish, in this place, to argue the point. All I need to do is refer such
system builders to Heidegger's own preface to the seventh edition:
there in his own words we read that should he have finished what he
intended to do, what he actually finished would have had to be
changed.

Although the author's intent may have changed over the years, there is no reason to suppose that the intent of the published text has changed; and that text is still available to us. In his preface Heidegger merely told us that the original text is useful in bringing human being to full self-consciousness, since it raises the question of the meaning of our being human as preparatory to considering the same question for any being whatsoever. His success in handling the question may be held open; only an insensitive human being can remain indifferent to the question itself. Obviously, no humanist can.

The foreword to the treatise has been with the text since its first publication. In it, the author cites Plato, *Sophist* (244a), where it was noted that the Greeks of his time were accustomed to use ʼόν, the participle of the verb *to be,* to designate beings, and that most assuredly they knew what was meant thereby, but that whenever one reflects upon the matter, one is no longer certain of the meaning. We recognize there St. Augustine's predicament meditating on time. Heidegger, reflecting in his own time and in his own language, notes that the question concerning the meaning of this participle still has not been answered, despite centuries of tinkering with the idea; and what makes matters worse, no one seems to have been perplexed by the question itself, nor, still worse, by the lack of a clear answer to it. It was his purpose, he tells us, to work out an interpretation of the ontological question in its most concrete form—and I interpret—on the basis of his own involvement with it. That the question of being should not remain an abstract consideration of first principles but rather become the personal quest of the author repeats the theme of letting the question stir us in our own existence.

Without explanation, Heidegger announces that his quest is to be guided by a provisional interpretation of time. He notes that St. Augustine had responded to time in the same way the early Greeks responded to beings, knowing full well what is meant by the concept until one is asked to state what is actually meant.[3] It is not unreasonable to assume, however, that his "provisional interpretation" is guided by his prior reading of the history of philosophy, beginning with Aristotle's *Physics* and ending with Bergson's *Données immédiates de la conscience.* That is the ground covered in division 2, chapter 6, the same field sketched out in reverse—from Kant, through Descartes and the medievals, to the ancient Greek ontology—in the second chapter of his introduction. Working in the reverse order, however, affords him the opportunity of foreshadowing the "destruction" of the history of ontology that was to have been the second part of the larger treatise. More on the destruction, later. The promise he holds out for us at this point in the development of his demonstration is that a careful provisionary analysis of the ontological concept of human being will make clear the connection between being and time. This he will do by focusing first on the being of the inquiring human and then, on the basis of that investigation, on the establishment of the "horizon" for an understanding of any being whatsoever.

Such indeed is the program of *Being and Time,* as the larger treatise was projected. We know that that work was never completed. The purpose of Heidegger's introduction was to give concrete reasons for adopting the aim of the inquiry described, to delimit the investigations necessary to achieve that aim, and to indicate the path to be followed in its achievement. Owing to the unfinished nature of the larger work, however, the statement of purpose, which forms the final paragraph of the author's untitled foreword, must be held as unfulfilled.

THE INTRODUCTION ITSELF is composed of two chapters and eight sections. Intended as an exposition of what is involved in formulating the question of the meaning of Being, the introduction attempts to justify the "necessity, structure, and priority" of the question of Being in the first place, and, in the second, to accomplish the double task of drawing up a method and outlining the design of the (larger) treatise which was to contain an answer to the question.

But why should this question be posed once again in the year of our Lord 1926? Heidegger's answer is simple and direct: the ontological question and an explanation of the categories necessary to explain it have been living issues in philosophy since its very beginning as a human institution. Plato and Aristotle have either been accepted or retouched for so long—from the patristic philosophers to Hegel—that the original phenomenon, which had initiated the inquiries of Plato and Aristotle, had become lost and its importance correspondingly trivialized. By the time of Hegel, indeed, the notion of substance had been replaced by the idea of an Absolute Subject. No longer resting on any observable phenomenon, the notion of Being became identified with the most universal and emptiest of all concepts. Being itself therefore was considered an indefinable; and in Hegel, at least, Being suffered the indignity of "passing over," by virtue of its total indeterminateness, into its own opposite. In such an identity of opposites the question of Being is surely superfluous, if not unanswerable.

To find grounds for restating the question of Being, Heidegger revisits the familiar presuppositions of the tradition concerning ontological investigations. Each of the presuppositions stems from the Aristotelian corpus, and each remains to this day unclear. They are: the universality of Being, its indefinability, and its self-evidence.

Aristotle's notion that there is an analogy by virtue of which all existing things are judged to be is the source of Being's supposed universality; but the alleged analogy of being remains unclear, in spite of the support given the idea in medieval and German expressionistic philosophy (Hegel). Being does not name a being, but only the "analogous" condition all beings share. It is the sharing of this condition that remains unclear.

As for its indefinability, that was the consequence of adopting Aristotle's method for giving definitions through genus and essential difference. Since there is no genus into which Being may be said to fit—and for this reason it was called a "transcendental" by medieval logicians—Being, of which we have at least a vague notion via the analogy pointed out above, remained indefinable.

But the same is true for individuals. Why this point is not brought out by Heidegger remains a mystery; for certainly the indefinability of the human individual is a consequence of the priority of existence over essence in his own as well as in Sartre's existential thought. Heidegger is content with pointing out that from the indefinability of Being only the conclusion that Being is not an entity follows, since it is the entities of the world that are classified into species and genera, and only these latter possess "essential" differences from each other.

The self-evidence of the concept stems from the necessity of using a cognate of the term in framing a definition for it. Moreover, all things, all natural objects and processes, all human beings, and all human behavior exemplify being. We ourselves are; our understanding is a way of our being related to other things that are. But rather than being "self-evident" in the sense intended by the traditional presupposition—as having no need of an explanation—the knowledge we have of our own being because we *are it* is only implicit. Some understanding of our existence is involved in all our daily acts; but that understanding is preontological, and stands in need of ontological clarification.

Although he does not stress the point until the next section of this introductory chapter, Heidegger has here found the grounds for a phenomenological investigation of (our human) being. The rest of his introduction will make this point clear.

In outlining the formal structure of the question of being, we may underscore a similar unstated proposition. Asking a question or performing an inquiry is a mode of human behavior and as such illustrates what ontological inquiry is about. We already know what asking a question involves, because we have already asked, and answered, many questions. Involved in any question, outside the activity of the questioner himself, there is something that is questioned *(ein Befragtes)*, something that is asked about *(das Gefragte)*, and something that is learned by the asking *(das Erfragte)*. Corresponding to each of these structural moments of a question, we have in ontological questioning an entity, its being, and the meaning of its being.

Whenever we ask a question, we are always guided beforehand by a knowledge of what will serve as an answer to our question; so likewise in posing the ontological question to entities we are guided in our questioning by what we expect to find. The access to Being (as what is asked about) is always through entities (which are questioned); and what is learned by the asking is the meaning of that being.

The only difficulty here is the selection of the most useful sort of entity with which to begin. And since no matter which entity we select, the reasoning would seem to trace a circle from the average understanding of what we are asking about to a full comprehension of its meaning (i.e., since ontological inquiry begins in and ends with an understanding of Being), the process would seem to be circular. But not to worry; the understanding we begin with is only implicit, and the understanding produced by the inquiry is to be fully explicit, if it is to be accepted at all. The "circular" move, which is a feature of all interpretation, is from an average, everyday awareness that we have called "a preontological understanding" of our own being to the anticipated, fully determinate, ontological characterization to be achieved in our inquiry. Rather than "a circle" at this point, Heidegger refers to a relatedness backward and forward: the act of inquiry points in one direction to its beginning and in the other to its completion. Paul Ricoeur, we recall, adapted this feature of hermeneutical inquiry as his own "arche-teleological" methodology.[4]

If the formal structure of the question of Being exhibits a distinctively circular path, it has as yet to be decided which entities are to provide the best access for answering the ontological question. Although it should seem obvious that our preontological comprehension of being is more securely grounded by our own being, in our handling or perceiving the objects of our environments we likewise possess some vague understanding of the being of such objects. To establish the priority of our human being for ontological inquiry, in section 3 Heidegger goes through what might be considered an aside at best, an irrelevance at worst.

The section is entitled "The Ontological Priority of the Question of Being [Der ontologische Vorrang der Seinsfrage]." Since the question of Being is the ontological question, what can the "ontological" of the title mean? The question is answered by the context. In this section Heidegger is at pains to show that ontology takes precedence over other forms of inquiry, in particular over the specific scientific investigations into the nature of things. As he sees it, the particular sciences are devoted to "areas of Being," the phenomena of nature as grouped into foundational classes. Chemistry studies the properties of matter, and physics, of energy; and so on. So many specific sciences, so many regional ontologies, as Husserl was wont to say.[5]

The pattern of scientific investigation, however, displays its concern with entities and their relationships, and as such remains ontic. Although it has been supposed that one might construct a world picture out of the results of scientific investigation, and thereby constitute an ontology for the events pictured in the diverse sciences, the historical development of the sciences indicates that they tend to periods of crisis, when the degree of systematization permitted by the originary concepts seems achieved, yet leaves a residue of incommensurate phenomena.

Even within the area of formal ontologies, such as the mathematical sciences, such crises have been evident. Formalists and intuitionists do not even agree on what is to count as proof in mathematics. And within the material ontologies (so called by Husserl), the development of relativity physics, which produced the reduction of matter to energy, called into question the so-called law of the conservation of matter. In biology, the mechanists confronted the vitalists, thereby calling for a reformulation of the concept of an organism, environment, and life, likewise a matter of relativity, to which we apply the name "ecology."

For their part, the human sciences were pursued, in the main, historiologically, but in a trivial way, since historiology itself went ontologically unclarified.

Finally, theology, which had been based upon the ancient metaphysics, changed character in modern times as theologians approached their subject from the point of view of human behavior as motivated by religious belief. Although Heidegger would never have admitted it—"Gott ist, aber er existiert nicht"[6]—even some of our professional theologians have since moved from this point to the conclusion that God, as the Lord of Ages, has simply passed away.[7]

In sum, the particular sciences have developed from a few basic, central concepts. These concepts derive from a metaphysical view of nature itself. Metaphysics is therefore the foundational science for the other, purely ontic, sciences. Its "logic" is to be productive of new ways for investigating nature, rather than "limping after" the sciences in an attempt to construct a coherent world view based upon their findings. This notion was not new; Descartes, in the beginning of the modern age, held the same view. What was new was Heidegger's example. Consider the case of the historiological sciences. They develop from an ontologically grounded historiology, which is not itself a scientific theory, nor yet a methodology of concept formation, nor even a theory of history as an object of study. It is, basically, an interpretation of authentically historical entities (such as human beings) with respect to their historicality; as such, historiology is concerned with the mode of being of historical entities.

To generalize, the question of the being of the objects investigated in the sciences takes precedence over the discoveries of these sciences and over any "regional" ontology which may have generated their central concepts. And the reason for this priority is that a fundamental ontology describes the a priori conditions necessary for the development of such areas of specified knowledge. Thus, the fundamental ontological question into the meaning of Being in general takes precedence over any specific ontology and over any particular science developed therefrom.

The only difficulty in accepting this ordering of the sciences of Being, from the ontic to the regional ontological to the fundamentally ontological, is that *Being and Time* is itself Heidegger's attempt to provide the fundamental ontology that is to take precedence over all other ontologies. And since his case depends upon a projected "destruction of the history of ontology" that is not a formal part of the text under discussion, it can never be established that his point has been proved. As we shall see further along, the best that could be expected from this abbreviated version of his original project would be further elucidation of the ontological clarification of historiology based upon the meaning of human being as temporality.

IF THE FOREGOING gives some idea of grasping the reason why the question of being takes precedence over any regional ontology, there remains the question of the "ontical" priority of the question of Being. On the face of it this new priority is as baffling as the preceding. Why is the ontological question—that concerning the meaning of Being—given an ontical "priority" here? Once again, the answer must be gleaned from an examination of the context.

Here the clue is the question of Being. It must be asked, and when it is, a particular human being—in this case, Heidegger—expresses its concern in given historical circumstances. Such a being is ontically distinguished, that is, from other entities conditionally existent, by the fact that for it its being can become an issue. That means that in living we can, and do, become concerned about the conditions of our lives and initiate inquiries into the status of our being. Such is the ontic priority of the question of Being. Here the "priority" is not a precedence over other forms of investigation, but of the grounding of our "preontological understanding of our being" in the here and now of everyday existence.

At this point in his inquiry Heidegger first introduces his notion of existentiality. Just as, before, historicality was the object of existential analysis (an "existential," as a matter of fact), whose ontological elucidation was to ground historiology as the study of human history, so existentiality, the a priori structure of a human being's existence, will ground the behavioral sciences. Human being, we will be told many times, lies in its *Existenz,* that is, in its projection upon possible ways of being. The ultimate of these possibilities is to be or not to be oneself. Since the answer to the question of which it is must be determined by the actual conditions of one's personal life choices, it must be found in a study of such conditions. All studies of actual conditions are ontic, or as Heidegger says, *existentiell.* All scientific inquiry is of such a nature.

Yet the ontic conditions of our everyday lives may be understood in a right and in a wrong way. The wrong way is to consider the human personality as if it were a thing in the world, an effect of a cause, or the resultant of a set of contributing causes all of which impinge upon it from without. The right way, he suggests, is to interpret the context of its *Existenz*, its existentiality understood existentially, that is, in terms of the categories fitting the subject; and when this is done, the analyst is describing a state of Being of those entities, and only those, that exist as projections upon their possibilities. Given this technical use of the term, it should now be apparent that only human beings can be said to exist in this sense.

The behavioral and anthropological sciences deal with human beings as if they were only objects in the world of nature. They can do this, of course, but human beings in such a condition behave only pathologically. The world that is definitive of a human being's existence is a creation of that being. Heidegger hyphenates the expression *In-der-Welt-sein* to indicate the concreteness of the relation between a self and its world. Being-in-the-world is definitive for a human being's existence, since that world is created by that being's unique self-projection.

But the understanding of the entities found within its world is likewise a mode of a human's being in the world. Any ontology of such entities, however, would depend upon the fundamental ontology Heidegger is about to elaborate. Since any knowledge of the being of nonhuman entities is founded in the ontic relations of the historical human existence—upon human history, indeed, the ontology which is adequate for human being will comprehend the regional ontologies formed by the particular areas of scientific investigation heretofore undertaken in history. For this reason, to achieve a fundamental ontology that would give sense to any particular ontology one would have to develop an existential analytic.

If these claims sound extreme, we should remember that the case has as yet not been made; that is to follow. We can, however, anticipate the analyses to follow and point out that the scientific concepts of space, time, and history derive their meanings from human spatiality, temporality, and historicity, each of which is an "existential," or structural component of human existence.

In summary, of the priorities to be assigned the entities that might be investigated to grasp the meaning of Being in general, human being is found to possess a threefold precedence. First, it is ontically prior, since existence is determinate for it, and the most fundamental ontology is the expected result of an existential analytic. Next, it is ontologically prior, because as it exists ontically, *it is* ontological, that is, possesses a preontological comprehension of its own being;

and the working out of a full ontological understanding is itself a mode of its existence. And, finally, it is ontico-ontologically prior in that it understands itself as existing in a world as it is related to other things. And this is the condition necessary for the working out of any ontology whatsoever.

The fundamental ontology sought would result from a simple "radicalization" of an essential tendency of our own being human. In some sense, we all know what it means to be, because we exist. But what it means to exist as yet remains unclear, and that it is the gravamen of the published text.

CHAPTER 2 of Heidegger's introduction contains an explanation of the method he is to adopt and an outline of the larger, unpublished text. Since the design of the fuller project has already been explained in these notes, I proceed to the question of method.

Section 5, which begins chapter 2, takes up where the author's discussion of the priorities of human being as the first object of ontological inquiry had left off. How is it to be understood that an analytic of our human being *(Daseinsanalytik)* will yield a "horizon" for an interpretation of the meaning of Being in general?

An answer may be found in considering the function of a natural horizon, the limit of our visual field. For Heidegger, all explanations are given from a particular point of view—our place in a world, from which we project an anticipated state of closure on the basis of what we already understand about our relationship to the objects of that world. As in our visual field, the "horizon" for an interpretation is the furthest point of projection; and all "meanings" must be detected between the here and the there of the projection. Thus, when Heidegger states that an analytic of our human being will lay bare a horizon for determining the meaning of Being in general, he means to call to our attention the fact that temporality will be found to be the meaning of our human being as caring, and that it is in respect to that that we may find the grounds for explaining the being of any entity whatsoever. Indeed, the proposition follows from the description of the ontic-ontological priority of human being described in the preceding section.

We start with human being simply because we are human beings. Ontically, our human being is what is closest to us. Consequently, it is the point from which we make all ontological projections. We attempt to let this being show itself, just as it is. Once the meaning of our being is clearly understood, we are in a position to explain the being of other kinds of entities, those which form a part of our familiar worlds. And since there is no being which is not the being of some entity, we need proceed no further with our projection in order to accomplish our task of formulating the meaning of Being in general—or so it is claimed.

The moves to be performed are as follows. First, the preliminary and provisional analysis of human being based upon our preontological comprehension of what is meant by "our own being." This analysis will establish the connection between being and temporality. Then we shall be in possession of a new vantage point: our preontological comprehension of our being as background for the projection will be replaced by the ontological comprehension of the provisional results. Where in the first phase of the inquiry the move is from our human being to temporality as its meaning, in the second, the move will be from temporality to Being in general considered as presence, the old-fashioned *parousia* of Aristotle.

The rest of this section and all of section 6 explain these anticipated connections. The first thing to be kept in mind is that *temporality* and the terms *spatiality, historicality, existentiality,* and the like refer to existential structures of human being; these concepts are not mere abstractions on the characteristics of entities found in our worlds. We ordinarily say, for example, that certain of these entities are temporal as being part of nature or history, and that such entities must be held apart from nontemporal entities such as numbers, geometrical figures, and the like. *Temporal* here is understood as being-in-time, and this notion is taken as self-evidently understood. The point of our inquiry is to make the concept ontologically understood; and for this we must return to the phenomenon of time, to let it appear as it is, so that the being of entities may show itself within the "horizon" of our human being's basic temporality existentially understood.

So far, then, what we have is an explanation of the two divisions of the first part of the larger treatise.

Section 6 contains the first projection of "the destruction of the history of ontology." We are warned that the object of such a destruction is not purely negative (to bury the dead past), but positive, that is, to dissolve the concealments thrown over the basic concepts of being or time by centuries of loosely appropriated "tradition." It is the same process that ordinary mortals call "reading history backwards" to discover the historical antecedents of an accepted idea. And there is a subtlety here sometimes missed in the exposition of Heidegger's plan. The history of ontology is already the history of a part of our human being in that ontology is a formalization of our understanding; and our understanding, of whatever nature at all, is a mode of our being.

In the order of descent from the ontological, the lowest of the hierarchy is ontical history, because it is a temporal ordering of events. To understand the highest of the relevant concepts, historicality, we must already possess the idea of temporality gained in the provisional inquiry. It is a human being's historicality that is displayed in the manner by which it "historizes" itself. In some sense of the term a human being always is what it already has been; that is its continuity in time. But the significant particular history it creates for itself results from its projection into a future: from the state of what it was as an actuality to what it might be in the time to come. Human institutions, in particular political constitutions, exhibit the same historizing process.

"World history" is the context in which lived traditions are created, preserved, or transformed by the continual self-projection of the individuals, living under their influence. For there to be a science of history or "historiology," which does not cover up what tradition transmits to us, the historicality of our human being, it must form its central concepts from the ontological understanding of human being's existentiality.

Finally, "history," as we read it, with its series of events with causes and reasons pretentiously exposed for our appreciation, contains nothing but the ontic and contingent events of a life of a people.

In order, then: historicality, historizing, world history, historiology, and then written histories.

When we merely fall back upon a tradition, or take our conventions for absolute truths, what actually gets transmitted by the tradition, our historicality as historized under particular circumstances, gets covered up in our historical accounts, and our appeal to self-evidence is an admission of our ignorance concerning its true nature. Fortunately, however, all traditions may be discovered, preserved and studied out of our understanding of world history. What we must do is to develop the technique for returning to the sources (of history) in a positive manner. Such is the aim of the "destruction of the history of ontology."

There is even a mapping here of how such a destruction would be worked out. The details are sketchy, but the moves are clear. We proceed once again by reading history backwards, beginning with Kant.

For Kant, time was the form of the inner, as opposed to the outer, sense, whose form was space. As forms of the sensibility, both space and time were universal and necessary conditions for the possibility of the sensuous experience. The knowledge gained in such experience was composed of intuitions, interpreted through concepts given meaning by the twelve categories of the understanding. Between the categories, on the one hand, and the intuitions, on the other, and for the purpose of relating the one to the other in an act of perception were the schemata of the imagination. For each category there was a formal schematism making it fit the materials of sense; and for each schema of the imagination there was a structural determination within the temporal, or inner, sense of the perceiving mind.

The problem Kant was addressing was the possibility of establishing a relation between categories, as forms of the understanding, and intuitions, as formed by the outer and inner senses. His insight was to have noted the intimate connection between time, perception, and the human spirit; but since he was interested in establishing a critical epistemological basis for a metaphysics of nature, he tended to ignore the problem of Being as such and thus failed to provide an ontology of human being. His "I think," which was said to accompany every act of perception and to which he gave the name "the transcendental unity of apperception," merely repeated Descartes' *cogito* argument for the existence of a perceiver for every act of perception, and so remained traditional in the conventional sense of the term.

Descartes himself, assigning the notion of a *res cogitans* as the meaning of the *sum* in his argument, assumed that there could be no attribute without a substance, but he failed to establish that thought was an attribute of anything. The perdurability of any thinker was caused by the properties of substance, the primary of which was to need no other thing in order to exist. As we know, however, Descartes hedged on this bet, by distinguishing between the finite substances of extended and thinking things on the one hand, and the infinite Substance of God on the other. In doing so, he merely brought forward the tradition of the medieval metaphysicians and theologians, who distinguished in the same way between created and uncreated substances.

The medievals, in their turn, brought forward the ancient ontological doctrine of substance as that which was always the subject
and never the attribute of a predication. This was the Aristotelian
ousia in all its unclarity; *ousia*, or substance, could be either primary
or secondary—either an individual thing or a definable form, such
as a species or genus. The distinguishing mark of a substance, however, was its presence *(parousia)* to some perceiver.

Since the time of Aristotle, then, *substance* referred to those entities
grasped in their Being as presence. Hence the notions of substance
and time have been linked throughout the philosophical tradition of
the West. What remained unclear was how substance or being remained a mode of time and how time itself was related to human
temporality.

In Heidegger, of course, temporality is the meaning of human
being as caring. For Aristotle, however, and for Plato, as well, time
was interpreted as an entity—as passage, as that which was measured
between the before and the after—and so was given only an ontic
explanation. How was time known? For Aristotle, through the specialized mode of understanding he called *aisthēsis,* the simple, sensuous awareness of entities present to our senses. It was for this
reason, Heidegger supposes, that Aristotle no longer needed the
Platonic interpretation of *legein* as a dialectical "seeing" of what lies
transcendent to individual things. For Aristotle, *legein* was equivalent
to *noein,* which was knowledge of the universal, and with respect to
substances, fitting only the secondary kind, that of a species or genera.

Aristotle's superiority within the tradition stems from his having
abandoned the Platonic dialectic for a more down-to-earth theory of
knowing, according to which perceivable things are said to present
themselves as they are to our senses, rather than as signs of something
other than themselves.

At this stage in his demonstration, Heidegger has illustrated what
he intended by the "destruction of the history of ontology." And, in
the same stroke, having ended up with Aristotle's ontic account of
our knowing primary substances as being both necessarily temporal
and intimately connected with the phenomena of perception, he has
found the transition to his own consideration of phenomenology as
a method for ontological investigation.

That consideration is given in section 7 of the text and reverses
the destructive pattern of the prior section. Here the attempt is to
show how the phenomenology of Husserl, abbreviated into the

expression "Zu den Sachen selbst! [Back to the things themselves]," marks the retentive renewal of the ancient Greek theory of knowledge. Working through the retention will illustrate "what is living and what is dead" in the tradition we have inherited. The moves are etymological and are not given a full, ontological explanation. What they foreshadow, however, is Heidegger's later appeal to "speech" as one of the modes by which human beings disclose themselves and to language as the depository of meanings created in human self-projection.

Modern phenomenology, after Husserl, became a method for doing philosophy. The name was not like those of geology, theology, biology, and the like, appropiately applied to an area of things to be studied. Rather, says Heidegger, it was to be applied to how such things are studied. Insofar as ontology has Being as its area of study and phenomenology may be adapted to it as a method, the aim of phenomenological ontology would be to make the Being of entities stand out in full relief against a horizon constituted by the meaning of human being itself, temporality. The need for this horizon and the central position of human being within the inquiry has already been explained.

The explanation of the applicability of modern phenomenology to the central problem of ontology is outlined in three phases: the root meanings of *phenomenon* and *logos* as established in the tradition, and their unification into a single description of the method for doing ontology. I consider them in their order.

First, *phenomenon*. We are accustomed in our own day to distinguish a phenomenon from a semblance, and both of these from a "mere appearance." But in order to differentiate between a true phenomenon and a semblance in the first place, it is useful to consider what the term meant for the Greeks. *Phainomenon,* we are told, is the noun derived from the verb, *phainesthai,* which means "to show itself." Accordingly, the phenomenon is that which shows itself, or the manifest. The verb is a middle-voiced form of *phaino,* "to bring into the day," or "to put into the light." This verb bears a relation to *pha-* and *phos,* the light, the clear. For this reason, says Heidegger, we should understand *phenomenon* as that which shows itself, or is made manifest, in itself and from itself.

A true phenomenon shows itself as it is. But when something shows itself under the guise of what it is not, then we are faced with a semblance, or a seeming. In such an occurrence, there is a "phenomenon" that gives itself off as something else; for example, a *phainomenon agathon,* something good which looks like, but which actually is not, what it gives itself off to be. Not being able to differentiate between these two senses of phenomenon, when applied to the detection of edible mushrooms, can be fatal. But even so, if the error has been committed, there is still a phenomenon in the positive sense of the word: something showed itself; something was made manifest—not those properties calling for a stomach pump but those which seemed to announce the presence of an edible food.

It is tempting in the above to use "appearance" to make the above distinction stick; but Heidegger warns against this loose usage. A true phenomenon and a semblance both are distinctive ways something gets encountered; on the other hand, an appearance in any of its possible forms is a structural, referential totality. In an appearance there is something, for example, a disease, which *announces* itself through a set of symptoms, at least one of which is of a truly phenomenal nature. For example, an infection in the body is announced through a fever, and the fever through a rise in temperature, which is registered either on a thermometer or in a change in the coloration of the skin.

A "mere appearance," on the other hand, would be a set of observable symptoms falsely interpreted as announcing a disease. A false light on the subject's body may appear to be the effect of a fever, and the fever to announce an infection; but the initial visual impression was a mere appearance. A mirage is a mere appearance because what is announced through it cannot under the perceptual circumstances given even be made manifest. If the water of a heat mirage were present, then the appearance of the rays of heat would not exist. Even so, however "mere" an appearance may be, something shows itself—the symptom, the indication, the interpretable phenomenon.

Since the multitudinous senses of *appearance* listed by Heidegger on page 30 of his text are not germane to his argument, I shall skip over them. The point of his demonstration was merely to indicate that the true sense of the term *phenomenon,* as that which is self-manifesting, is needed whether we are concerned with true phenomena, with semblances, with appearances, or only with mere appearances. In all cases something is self-manifest. The aim of a phenomenology will be to make its objects manifest in the same way.

But like any other intellectual discipline phenomenology must use language to do so. Whence the second composite term for our discipline—the *logos*. We have already indicated the verbal source for this term in Plato and Aristotle: *legein*, gathering together. The *logos* is correspondingly what gets understood by a gathering of evidence, dialectically for Plato, and perceptually for Aristotle. Subsequently, the term has come to stand for discourse, judgment, concept, definition, ground, relation. How?

First, by restricting *discourse* to an act of making manifest what is discoursed upon, the object of the discourse; in this, its most general form, *logic* is discourse in which a meaning is revealed. As speech *(phone meta phantasias)*, the sounding of the discourse lets something be seen, and the logos becomes related to our senses. It becomes *synthesis*, when what is let be seen is something in its togetherness—with something, as something. And because it is synthesis, discourse may be true or false; that is, the entity spoken about may be taken out of its hiddenness *(aletheia)* or get covered over in a confusion of meanings. False discourse *(pseudesthai)* covers up its object. In true discourse, however, what gets talked about becomes revealed *(apophainesthai)* and becomes open to our simple, sensuous grasping as *aisthēsis*, a seeing, hearing, perceiving. *Logos* as synthesis, and as possibly true or false, permits something to be seen as something.

The purpose of reason *(logos)* was to permit entities to be perceived as they are; reasoning that did this was an instance of *legein*. The object of the reasoning *(logos* as *legomenon)* is constituted by that which gets exhibited in the discourse, the ground for discoursing in the first place. And lastly, the discourse that is logical makes something manifest in its relatedness as self-constituted, in its concept, according to its definition.

How these two terms, *phenomenon* and *logos,* are to be related so as to give a preliminary conception of our methodology may be understood if only we can perceive the sense of Husserl's directive "Back to the things themselves" in the etymological derivation of the term he uses to designate his methodology. Phenomenology is, as said in Greek, *legein ta phainomena,* discourse on phenomena, but precisely performed in such a way as to let these phenomena be made manifest *(apophainesthai ta phainomena).*

The aim of the discourse that is truly phenomenological, then, is to let that which shows itself be seen from itself in the very way in which it shows itself from itself. The strangeness of this description seems to be due more to Heidegger's desire to be exact than to the uncharted semantics of his enterprise. Since what phenomenological discourse allows us to see is Being, and this is what for the most part gets covered up in ordinary, scientific, or any other discourse that deals only with entities and their ontic conditions, phenomenology is to become under Heidegger's hand a universal ontology.

We have already seen that human beings are privileged entities for ontological discourse. They give us a point of departure, an access to the phenomenon of being (through their preontological understanding of being), and a trajectory to follow: from *Daseinsanalytik,* the analysis of human being, to its meaning, temporality; and from there to the ontological grounding of all historiological sciences.

The direction to be followed in this trajectory varies from paragraph to paragraph. When Heidegger tells us that his techniques are to be hermeneutical, that is, interpretive of the relationship between human beings and their worlds, he recalls the point of departure and the reason for adopting it. But when he defines his interpretive method as a special way of working out in a concrete fashion the conditions on which the possibility of any ontology depends, he imputes another ultimate aim to the inquiry.

Beginning with the analytic of the existentiality of human existence, therefore, we may move on to settle the question of the meaning of Being in general—or merely to furnish the central concepts for an ontologically clarified methodology for the humane, historiological sciences. This is in effect what Hans-Georg Gadamer has done in theory, and Paul Ricoeur in practice.[8] No one, as far as I know, including Heidegger himself, has ever "moved on to settle the question of the meaning of Being in general." At least it is safe to claim here that the question is not settled in the published portion of *Being and Time.*

Being, Heidegger tells us in his introduction, is the transcendent pure and simple. Our phenomenological discourse is to let it show itself. But a final caveat is in order. For any discourse to make Being manifest, since there is no accepted dictionary or grammar for the terms used in discoursing upon Being, a phenomenological truth must be expressed in odd-sounding language. In this way Heidegger lets us know that his language will be strange, perhaps even more so than has already been apparent, but he tells us that we might understand his difficulty in composing his text if we compare the ordinary Greek of Thucydides in narrating a historical event with the equally odd-sounding ontological language of Plato (*Parmenides*) or of Aristotle (*Metaphysics,* 7th book)!!

Section 8, the last of the introduction, continues to give the full sketch of the larger treatise, including the two halves, each of which is divided into three subdivisions. The entire second half is missing and was never published as such; and the third section of the first half, "Time and Being," is also missing.

WHAT IS the reader to make of all this?

Of the three aims set forth in his introduction—re-posing the question of the meaning of Being, undertaking the "destruction" of the history of ontology, and constructing an analytic of human being—only the third was achieved. What does exist of the other two intended projects was never achieved by the method described in the introduction, nor, in my view, could it have been. How could human speech, even on the basis of analyzing temporality, the meaning of its being, allow Being in general to show itself from itself as it is in itself? The very concept of Being in general, which is not the being of a human nor yet of a nonhuman entity, has never been made clear. If being is always the being of some entity, what is that Being which, in its generality, may be attributed to any entity? And by virtue of what is any such attribution to be made—an Aristotelian-like "analogy"? If so, we would not have progressed in ontology, and our destruction of the history of the discipline would merely have been its reinstauration. So many questions, so many doubts. But we need not settle this issue here. Suffice it to restate that the promise of Heidegger's introduction went unfulfilled in the text we have to read.

Even so, none of the doubts that could be felt in connection with the meaning of Being in general, including the total denial of the possibility of establishing any such meaning, can detract from what was actually achieved in Heidegger's analytic of human being. And it will stand or fall by virtue of its results.

Consider: the published version of *Being and Time* generated a new movement in the history of philosophy, albeit repudiated by Heidegger himself; and his text has stimulated the only significant developments in both depth psychology and theology in the past fifty years. It has also called for a similar development in one of those "historiological sciences" that still stands in need of such a stimulus.

Despite the sometimes furious activity undertaken in the name of "literary criticism," and despite the very postmodern criticism already written under the banner of Heideggerian philosophy, the connection between the *Daseinsanalytik* and *literary* criticism has yet to be made clear. If I can succeed in making that connection clear, the intellectual discipline we call "the humanities" may be given a new foundation, and one not so far away as all that from the original Renaissance attempt to rediscover humanity through the interpretation of the ancient and, sometimes, sacred texts.

From this point on, therefore, I shall pursue my commentary with this aim in mind. If Heideggerian literary criticism is to be ontological, *ontological* cannot refer to the being of those worlds represented in works of literary art, which would therefore contain a world-picture *(ein Weltbild)*,[9] but to the working of those works as their surfaces and their depths constitute a world of their own, and come to form a part of our own worlds as we write or read them.[10]

2

The Interpretation of Human Being in Terms of Its Temporality, and the Explication of Time as the Transcendental Horizon for the Question of Being

THE TITLE OF THIS CHAPTER IS THE ONE given by Heidegger to the first part *(Erster Teil)* of his larger projected treatise. The first division of that part *(Erster Abschnitt)* is entitled "The Preparatory Fundamental Analysis of Human Being." How this topic gets further subdivided shall be of primary concern to us here. The sketch for his preparatory fundamental analysis is laid out in a single introductory paragraph outlining the six chapters by which it is to be completed. In sum, then, two heads, and a paragraph of outlining material.

The material is found between sections 8 and 9 of the original text, where the paragraph and the two headings occurring above it take up less than a page.[1] As if following the contingency of this matter's being placed between two sections of the text, Macquarrie and Robinson's translation of the material is found, apparently isolated from the developing argument, on a single page of their text.[2] Rather than emphasizing Heidegger's partitioning of the subject here, I shall be interested in tracing out the implications of the method he has used as a guide for reading the remainder of his text. If reading is an activity that consists of following an exposition or a narrative from a beginning to an ending in which a sense is to be understood, it seems necessary to follow the lead of the textual development and to allow the "substance" of the argument to appear as we ourselves perform the moves required by the author's methods.

Although in any philosophical treatise method and substance are integrally related, in this text one might say without exaggerating that the method is the substance. To understand the claim, all we must do is remember that making an inquiry is a way of behaving, a way of being human, and that the behavior of human beings is the starting and the projected ending point of the inquiry to be made. In order to grasp the significance of Heidegger's beginning, therefore, let us begin ourselves by backtracking for a moment and rereading the title of this chapter.

Rather than the name of the projected first part of the longer treatise, it is in effect, from our own vantage point, the name of the entire published treatise. The naming is accomplished by designating the two tasks to be carried out in the published text: that is, the interpretation of human being on the basis of temporality (division 1), and the explanation of time as the transcendental horizon for the questioning of Being in general (division 2).

If we remember, as well, that these two tasks were to be carried out under three heads—the preparatory fundamental analysis, human being and temporality, and time and Being—the last of which is not part of this text, the two "divisions" of the published text *(erster und zweiter Abschnitte)* correspond roughly to the last two tasks designated in the title of the first part of the treatise as originally projected.

Both divisions of the published treatise contain introductory materials. Comparing page 41 with pages 231–35 reveals some similarities and some differences. The most striking difference is that pages 231–35 contain all the material of section 45 of the text, whereas the introductory materials of page 41 are placed between two sections of the text. An accident, an oversight, an intentional ploy? It matters little which. In both sets of materials there is a sketch of the plan to be followed in the respective divisions, following a brief account of what one already knows about the subjects to be analyzed.

Technically speaking, the difference in the lengths of the two sets of introductory materials may be explained by the difference in the hermeneutical situations in which the author found himself. Since "the hermeneutical situation" is indeed explained as the "forestructure" of the human understanding involved in working out any interpretation whatsoever, and this explanation occurs along with that of the other structures embedded in the same source, all going to make up the "disclosedness" of our being in the world, this material could not function in the introduction to the first division of the text. In part, it is the subject matter to be developed.

Since the constitutive structures of human disclosedness all stem from the same source (in a manner to be described), they are called *gleichursprünglich* by Heidegger. An interpretation is the way an understanding gets worked out; and understanding, feeling and discoursing are the three constitutive structures of our human disclosedness, that is, three possible ways of disclosing the significance of our being-in-the-world.

All interpretations are made with respect to some context. And the context by which an interpretation is made is called by Heidegger the "forehaving" *(Vorhabe)* of the interpretive forestructure; it is constituted by the background of secured information from which point of view the interpretation is made.

The "forehaving" of the interpretive structure Heidegger brings to bear upon the meaning of our human being is not absent because it is not mentioned in the part of the text under discussion; it is merely presupposed, and foreshortened into a simple repetition of the salient point of the overall introduction to the text: "Das primär Befragte in der Frage nach dem Sinn des Seins ist das Seiende vom Charakter des Daseins [The first entity interrogated in the question concerning the meaning of Being is that having the character of a human being]."[3]

We were told in Heidegger's discussion of the threefold priority of human beings over other entities for ontological inquiry that in its existence a human being is ontological in that it already possesses a (preontological) understanding of its own being and can express its concern for itself and its world by making an inquiry into that being.

The first "forehaving" for any ontological inquiry is the preontological understanding we already possess. As our implicit knowledge of our own being becomes explicit through the stages of the interpretations we make of our own involvements with our worlds, the results of preceding analyses constitute a new "forehaving" and a new context for further interpretation.

Since any human being possesses the necessary preontological understanding of its own being because it is that being, any human being should be able to follow the analyses. In order to make sure of the fact, however, Heidegger will usually divide his subject into its essential parts, beginning not with the simplest, as did Descartes, but with any of the constitutive structures of the whole to be interpreted, selected for the purpose of further illuminating the whole. That in general is the process of the Heideggerian hermeneutics.

Return once more to the German sentence quoted above. It recalls the structure of questioning as a human behavior. Besides the questioner himself, there is something questioned, something to be questioned about, and something to be learned by answering the question. So much for the structural whole serving as a context for understanding the various elements found in any questioning situation. That much is a part of our preontological forehaving. That the questioner and the entity questioned should be the same for the pursuit of ontology is, for Heidegger, guided by the ontic and ontological priorities of human being. That much was added to our initial forehaving for having read Heidegger's introduction.

The content of the preparatory fundamental analysis of human being is to be an interpretation of the being of human beings in light of their essentially temporal character. Due care must be expressed here, however, to distinguish the ordinary, or ontic, sense of *temporal*, as taking place in time, from the intended ontological sense of the term, which denotes an essential structure of human existentiality. How to move from the ontic to the ontological, from the *existentiell* to the existential, is a problem to be considered later in this chapter. It is the same question as how to perform the ontic-ontological reversal, which is usually referred to by Heidegger and Heideggerians as "the ontological difference."

Heidegger's division of his topic has the following six components: chapter 1, the differentiation between an existential treatment of human being and the other, merely ontical, treatment it receives in the behavioral sciences; chapter 2, setting out "being-in-the-world" as the originary and fundamental structure of human being; chapter 3, the worldhood of a human being's world; chapter 4, being-in-the-world as being-with-others and being-oneself; chapter 5, being-in as such; and chapter 6, the indication of a preliminary conclusion: the being of human being as care. Heidegger even makes an error here (p. 41) that was never corrected. He states that the "existential meaning" of the being of a human being is care; but when he gets to the topic on page 180 of the text, he gives the correct title as "Die Sorge als Sein des Daseins [Care as the being of human being]." The anticipated meaning of human being is, of course, temporality.

Reflection on this division of the whole first part of the printed text produces a number of problems whose solution may make the reading of that first part a little easier. I present them as a series of related questions.

Q$_1$. What is meant by referring to being-in-the-world as the (first) fundamental structure of human being?

Q$_2$. What is meant by calling being-in-the-world "a priori"?

Q$_3$. How does the whole (being-in-the-world) afford ways of looking at its constitutive structures, e.g., being-in, being-with, being-oneself?

Q$_4$. What aspect of caring (being human) gives the clue to the interpretation of its meaning as temporality?

After considering the answers received to these questions, I shall select the existential structures of "being-in" as definitive for any hermeneutical inquiry of the Heideggerian type. In so doing, I hope to show how the ontic-ontological reversal in metaphysics has implications for epistemology; how *Being and Time* contains a methodology which prescribes how it is to be read; and, even if I should fail in these two aims, how to read *Being and Time* with more profit.

Q$_1$. What is meant by referring to being-in-the-world as the (first) fundamental structure of human being?

The first question concerns a methodological point of inquiry, which upon expansion will be found to yield information of a substantive nature.

As mentioned, the introduction to division 1 announces the topics to be covered in the preparatory fundamental analysis of human being; and following a basic description of the differences between human entities and the objects of nature that are merely present to our perceptual apparatus, all the chapters are devoted to structures of human existence. Existentiality is itself a structure of human being, an "existential" understanding of what it means for a human being to be. Such understanding is a mode of human behavior and, in consequence, a part of being to be explained by the inquiry. It is precisely this characteristic that distinguishes the existential analytic from the ontic sciences studying man.

Biology, anthropology, and psychology, for example, treat of human behavior as if it were simply a matter of interacting objects found in nature as elements of the positive world. Of such a world considered as a whole one has only an abstract or conceptual grasp. A fundamental ontology and the existential analytic upon which it depends differ from the positive sciences in that they investigate the very meaning of the concept world from the point of view of the decisive manner in which a person is in its world—ultimately as a projection upon its own possibilities. Such a world is lived concretely, through the self-projection. We simply cannot wait upon the future development of the behavioral sciences for an understanding of the world (of nature), since the clear conception of the entities involved and of the world wherein they are conceived to interact already presuppose the existence of a unique structure, a human being, whose behavior is to be explained. So much for the importance of the existential analytic.

Why should it begin with being-in-the-world?

Readers have two ways of answering this question, and most of Heidegger's readers have used both. The most obvious is, perhaps, to look forward, to the results of the analysis. Human being is a special mode of being-in; knowing, feeling, understanding, and dis-coursing are so many ways for a human to be in his or her world. But readers who take this primarily pragmatic tack find in Heideg-ger's descriptions of a human being's disclosedness precisely those structures that return them to the point of departure, Heidegger's description of the three "priorities" of human being for any ontology. His hermeneutical effort is indeed circular.

Whenever anyone asks an ontological question—such as the "Where now? Who now? When now?" of Samuel Beckett's *Unnamable*[4]—one is always already in a world. This "always already" phenomenon is a fact of every human existence. Whenever we question our existence we merely find ourselves already in a world. The factuality of such a fact is first labeled *facticity (Faktizität)*,[5] that structure of our being by which we are "thrown" into or given over to our worlds, so that later the same structure will come to be called *Geworfenheit* (thrownness or abandonment).[6]

Because it is always already in its world, and because it always possesses a preontological comprehension of its own being, a human being knows itself as tied to that world. In a word, being-in-the-world is the first ontological structure to be elaborated because a human being is factually tied to its world even as it is ontologically concerned for itself and for the other entities of its world while living out the conditions of its ontic existence. And being-in-the-world is fundamental, in that its analysis will yield a point of view on the various substructures by which it becomes expressed in the lives of particular human beings: worldhood, being-with, and being-in.

If one were to be purely pragmatic in attempting to answer this first question, one would be tempted to say that being-in-the-world is the first fundamental structure of our inquiry because expounding it is the most propitious way available for entering the hermeneutical circle, and because upon reflection everyone already knows what it means to be in the world. The process is amazingly simple: our forehaving is the preontological comprehension of our own being; from that we sight out our being as what we ourselves are (the foresight) and project it upon our foreknowledge (the foreconception) of what it means to be in a world.

Q₂. What is meant by calling being-in-the-world "a priori"?

One of the mysteries of modern philosophy, since Kant's *Critiques*, is how the adverbial Latin expression *a priori* has become a common qualifying adjective. At least one author has argued that Kant always used the expression in its borrowed form, that is, adverbially, so that what it properly modifies is a verb rather than a noun.[7] The difference is sometimes hard to perceive in German because the same vocable may be used either as an adverb or as a noun; and translators have not always been sufficiently careful in their examination of the context of use to determine the exact meaning of Kant's borrowed term.

The same problem of interpretation may be said to exist when the term is extended from its normal adverbial use, the specification of a way of acting (e.g., judging, or knowing), to the qualification of the end or the conditions of the same sorts of actions. As a method, *the a priori* denotes a set of techniques of analysis by which the acceptability of certain statements is determined independently of any empirical grounds of verification. Empirical statements are *a posteriori*, that is, true or false, depending upon an observed set of affairs recorded in them. And here the same confusion is apparent: empirical statements are a posteriori because their truth is determined a posteriori. Analytical statements, on the other hand, are a priori because their truth or validity is determined a priori, that is, before or independently of any facts whose knowledge depends upon our observations.

Heidegger uses the term, in the twenty-six or more occurrences within the text,[8] in both ways; and sometimes in completely nontechnical, but related, ways, as when he says that the self-evidence of Being in its traditional interpretation only shows that in every comportment of a human being toward being—in its own being-toward entities as such—there lies, a priori, an enigma ("a priori ein Rätsel liegt") that must yet be solved.[9] Here the expression is used adverbially, to be sure; but it is most probably better rendered as "already" or "beforehand." The understanding of the comportment in question depends upon the prior understanding of something else; to wit, the preontological understanding we have of our own being.

A similar example of a nontechnical use of the term is its use to indicate that one state of affairs has occurred prior to another. Such is the case when Heidegger states that human being has already encountered "space" as a region—in the stretch from its facticity in the past through its transcendence in the present to one of its own future possibilities—before any attempt to measure the exact placement of objects in the natural world.[10]

Both these uses have obvious relations to the "always already" phenomenon of the existential structures of human being, as explained in the previous question.

But what is one to make of the question, "Is it obvious a priori [*a priori selbstverständlich*] that Dasein [a human being] is always right when it says most vehemently 'I am the one who . . . '?"[11] An adverb, once again; but this time modifying an adjective. Obvious, without consideration of the facts? Obvious, only after an analysis of the structures of human being? Or, in general, "must we assume that . . ."? All the interpretations fit; but the use seems purely nontechnical in this context.

Some of the occurrences of the term listed in Macquarrie and Robinson's *Index of Latin Expressions*[12] give the reader an insight into the history of the term.

Descartes, it is said, grounded the philosophical use of the term as a presupposition.[13] *Extensio,* he claimed, is a presupposition for every other characteristic of bodily things; because the definitive attribute of a bodily substance is its extension, an understanding of extension is required, a priori, for an understanding of all other characteristics of extended or corporeal objects. Although the horrific errors of the Cartesian physics soon became apparent, its author had established within his metaphysics a "way of understanding an *a priori* [(*ein*) *Verständnis eines Apriori*]." Here the term appears as a noun. So be it. For Descartes, whatever was presupposed by an inquiry was itself known a priori.

The "content" of the a priori discovered by Descartes was, according to Heidegger, further elaborated by Kant.[14] That elaboration, we all know, was of the subjective conditions that were necessary for the actual existence of human knowledge, ultimately the transcendental unity of apperception, or its ideal counterpart, the noumenal Self. The forms of sense, both inner and outer, the categories of the understanding, and the Ideas of reason all are known a priori; and taken together, they make possible the elaboration of our knowledge into a metaphysics of nature.

When Kant established knowing a priori as the theme of his critical epistemology, he posited (presupposed) the existence of an ideal subject, whose faculties of knowledge were structured in a certain way.[15] Heidegger accepts the procedure of justification by presupposition. Philosophical knowledge is and of right ought to be ontologically prior to scientific knowledge. Ironically, indeed, the "is" portion of the last statement is on the Heideggerian interpretation itself an analytical statement, and hence has a claim to validity that may be established a priori. Since ontology is a description of the structures of being implicit within the determination of particular entities as they are studied by the positive sciences, it deals with something that comes before, and as a necessary condition of, the particular events of nature.

The differences between Kant and Heidegger are likewise apparent to every student of modern philosophy. In the context cited immediately above, Heidegger criticizes Kant's notion of an ideal subject as a fanciful creation—established by a transcendental deduction rather than by phenomenological intuition, which allowed Kant to miss the "a priori character" of a merely factual subject. The notion of *facticity,* indeed, awaited the future development of phenomenology by Husserl as a method for describing the "subjectivity of the subject." Heidegger admits his debt to Husserl,[16] from whose earlier studies he had learned that "possibility stands higher than actuality" and is, in consequence, the first order of business in any intellectual effort to cognize the events of nature on the basis of their ground. If one were to deny the existence of the Kantian "pure I," or of consciousness in general, one would not necessarily deny the possibility of a priori knowledge; one would merely deny the validity of the transcendental deduction.

Consider the case of contemporary mathematical physics.[17] In projecting the concept of nature onto a mathematical grid, contemporary physicists have disclosed something—matter or energy—that reveals a prior projection of a state of Being. It is not the mathematics of modern physics that constitutes its a priori character; it is the presupposition that something is always already present-at-hand, and that this "substance"—matter or energy—is understood before any determination of its current state. Within the region of this projection, particular motions, forces, and locations may to some extent be observed and predicted. If Heidegger is right on this matter, mathematical physics illustrates the same kind of a priori illustrated in the Cartesian physics. The difference in the degrees of success in the two physics—the Cartesian and contemporary mathematical—is neither the accuracy of measurements nor the exactitude of the calculations; first and foremost, it lies in the horizon opened up by the originating a priori concepts of the two disciplines.

It seems obvious, on the basis of these examples of the uses Heidegger makes of the term, that the a priori is a set of necessary conditions for the existence of an actual event; that these conditions describe "structures of Being" that make possible the factual occurrence of entities of whatever sort; and that these structures and conditions are "always already" implicit within the determinate condition of a human being, its existentiality; and that in consequence they have an existential, rather than a categorial, determination.

All we need recall to understand this set of attributions applied to the area of the a priori is that human being has a threefold priority over other entities for the development of a fundamental ontology—the ontological, the ontic, and the ontico-ontological—and that nonhuman entities are described in categorial terms, while human beings are described in existentials.

Moreover, the validity of any category, including the Aristotelian, to characterize the being of any nonhuman entity depends upon our prior understanding of the existentials constitutive of human being; that, indeed, had been established in Heidegger's description of human being's ontico-ontological priority. As we shall see further on, the principal Aristotelian categories grounded in our preontological understanding of our own being are "where" and "when," rather than "substance," which is an idea whose time has long since passed.

Q₃. How does the whole (being-in-the-world) afford ways of looking at its constitutive structures, e.g., being-in, being-with, being-oneself?

Rather than a substantial self, whose existence had been presupposed within the dialectical structure of Descartes' *ego cogito* argument, and which had been denounced as a "paralogism" in the rational psychology of Kant, Heidegger's closest corresponding notion, human being *(Dasein)*, will be interpreted as a process having both an ontological and an ontic determination.

The "priorities" possessed by human beings as entities to be interrogated in an ontological investigation guarantee both a starting point for the inquiry and the necessary foreconception for characterizing the object of specific intent isolated by a particular foresight into the general context with which the investigator is already familiar. Indeed, the general context *(Vorhabe)*, the particular intent *(Vorsicht)*, and the foreconception *(Vorgriff)* constitute the structural moments of the hermeneutical situation Heidegger refers to as "the forestructure of the understanding," and the human understanding is itself a structural moment of human disclosedness, of a human being's being-there—in its world.

So, as we have met the problem of the relationship between analytical whole and constitutive parts before—in the analysis of the questioning attitude, in the hermeneutical situation, and in human disclosedness—we shall meet the phenomenon in our discussion of *Gleichursprünglichkeit,* or groundedness in the same source. Macquarrie and Robinson translate this expression as "equiprimordiality."[18]

Whether we refer to such structural relationships as grounded in the same source or of having equal primordiality, the idea seems clear. None of the constitutive elements exists without others; nor the whole without its substructural moments. What grounds every such analytical whole is the appearance of the phenomenon in question—not only those mentioned before, but many as yet to come: for example, the structural totality of a human being's being-in-the-world, with an approximation of which Heidegger begins his inquiry (worldhood, being-with, and being-in); the structural totality of human being as care (existentiality, facticity, and forfeiture); the three ek-static dimensions of temporality (future, past, and present) as the "meaning" of the previously delineated care structure.

The movement of the argument (and, in consequence, the growth of the text) is from the simplest approximation of a primordial structural whole: *from* the isolation of a human being as an entity projected upon its possibilities of being, as this being is revealed to it in its facticity—always already there—*to* its being (care), which is projected upon temporality and its structural constituents as the meaning of its caring.

The whole of the published text, then, is laid out in a series of expanding hermeneutical moments each possessing the tripartite structure of the interpretive understanding. And, if one may be forgiven for pointing it out, the expanding hermeneutical moments of the text are themselves constitutive elements of the text considered as a whole. We have seen that it is divided into two parts—the preparatory analytic of human being, and human being and temporality—and that these two divisions correspond to the characterization of human being as care (or caring) and the meaning of this being as temporality. We shall have to move from division 1 to division 2 because the preparatory analysis of the first division was not "primordial" enough.

Heidegger explains: since the preparatory analysis dealt with human being as it is found every day and on the average, its descriptions were of humans as they are not themselves, as they behave for the most part as everyone in their circumstances behaves. What is missing in the first division, in hermeneutical terms,[19] is an account of a human being's potentiality for being its own person, for being a whole and not just stretched between birth and death, and for developing in time according to its own historicity.

Heidegger is more precise yet: an ontological interpretation will have achieved complete primordiality when

1. the structural elements of the hermeneutical situation are secured by a phenomenological intuition;
2. the whole of the entity it has taken as theme has been brought into the forehaving (the originally understood context);
3. the unity of the structural elements of the whole foresighted in the analysis is perceived as such;
4. the anticipated meaning (foreconception) is demonstrated in the concrete, i.e., in the ontical conditions under which we live our very lives.[20]

If we have followed his reasoning carefully enough, we can easily understand that the medieval question as to which was prior, being or knowledge—which has traditionally been posed in terms of a *ratio essendi* and a *ratio cognoscendi*—has been completely obviated by Heidegger's selection of human beings, whose knowledge is a mode of their being, as the primordial theme of his ontology. As we proceed, indeed, knowledge, considered ontologically, will constitute the access to being-in-the-world interpreted existentially.

Worldhood, being-in, and being-oneself are all structural moments stemming equally from a human entity's being-in-the-world. The hyphens in these expressions signify the concreteness of the relations between the structural elements of this whole; and Heidegger will not rest his case until the primordial totality of a human being's constitution *as articulated* has been made clear.[21] At this stage of our own inquiry it is not clear whether this is a promise or a threat.

Q_4. *What aspect of caring (being human) gives the clue to the interpretation of its meaning as temporality?*

Announced as early as Heidegger's introduction to *Being and Time* as the anticipated meaning *(Vorgriff)* of human being as care, temporality represents an ontological-existential conception that must be run through the complete hermeneutical process. It is announced as the meaning of human being almost dogmatically:

> Als der Sinn des Seins des Seienden, das wir Dasein nennen, wird die *Zeitlichkeit* aufgewiesen.

> Temporality will be exhibited as the meaning of the being we call human.[22]

The dogmatism of the claim is not surprising, since the author is explaining the moves to be expected in working out his theme. He had just stated that the first division of his work is provisional, but that it would isolate the phenomenon of human being as care. The next step would be to show or exhibit the ontological structures of temporality as the meaning of that being.

We are now in a position, however, to evaluate this contention in light of the preceding description of the hermeneutical understanding. It would be impossible to work out the significance of our human being in terms of temporality as an existential or ontological structure, unless under the obvious ontical conditions of living out our lives, this ontological structure were somehow implicit.

The expression "living out our lives" already gives a clue to the ontic interpretation of the connection between our being and time; but the other expressions are still more dramatic: expecting, plan-

ning, doing, deciding, forgetting, remembering, or just plain waiting—for whatever or whomever. One of Samuel Beckett's finest plays
is structured on the ontological difference between time and
temporality.[23]

The idea seems simple enough: how we spend our time constitutes
our being; it is both who and what we are. Searching through our
"forehaving," in particular our knowledge of the history of philosophy, may give us the clue for making the right interpretation. If we
are not substances, for example, what are we? What we do and how
we do it seem appropriate substitutes for our lost "souls" or animate,
thinking substances.

In section 6 of the text Heidegger had gone through a sketch of
the history of ontology from the transcendental unity of apperception
of Kant to the Aristotelian presence *(parousia)* of things to our
perceiving consciousness to find the clue for a reinterpretation of the
meaning of Being in general. Although the second part of his treatise,
which was to produce the destruction that was not a destruction but
a reconstitution of the history of ontology, was never completed,
projecting such a plan in itself illustrates what is talked about—as a
real-life project of a real-life thinker, it could not come to be without
the structures of temporality.

What was lacking in the history of ontology was phenomenological rigor: the move from ontic access to a primordial, ontological
explanation and back to an enriched ontic existence was not heretofore achievable, according to Heidegger, because the history of our
ontological thinking had never before reached the level of primordiality that would ground a return of knowledge to its source.

Testing a hermeneutical assumption, or anticipated meaning, however, is no different from testing any other kind of hypothesis. Whatever its source, it must do more than merely generalize the conditions
of past observations; to be accepted as workable, it must be verified
by a newer and independent set of observations. Traditionally, the
metaphysical hypothesis positing the existence of substances was a
failure since it did not allow for verification of its claim. The new
ontology, which was to be so fundamental that it would ground all
other ontologies, could not suffer the same consequences. For this
reason, the descriptions of the a priori structures of being must be
brought to phenomenological intuition. The phenomenon, as it is,
must be allowed to appear in the entities it is claimed to structure.

In order to achieve the feat, we shall have to use words; but using words, putting tongue to thought, is itself a mode of our being, a constitutive structure of our disclosedness, i.e., of a distinctive habit, possessed by all human beings, of defining themselves by projecting a world of unique significance. We can do this by merely expressing our disgust at the weather or by writing a novel explaining *How It Is*.[24] The trick here is to move from the ontic to the ontological and then back again. We may pity the misguided plutocrat who first exclaimed that time is money, even smile at the claim that time is of the essence. In Heideggerian terms it is much more revealing to claim that temporality is embedded in existence, and that how this is so is precisely what is to be shown. In the words of the prime minister, at the present time, we shall just have to wait and see.

Answering a series of questions for the purpose of illuminating a text is an exercise in making explicit what lies implicit in our knowledge of the text at the moment we pose the questions. When the answers to the questions are secured in a prior reading of the text, as those composed above were, we have an evident illustration of the hermeneutical process, including the specific technique of "bringing into our forehaving" the concepts necessary for understanding how an element is focused on for analysis and connected to an anticipated meaning. Obviously, the interpretive process corresponds roughly to what is described as "clarifying what we already know"—and, indeed, as an "ontic determination of the state of our own questioning being."

How do we move from the ontic to the ontological demonstration? I propose to do so by following Heidegger's moves into chapter 2, division 1, of his text. I shall reorder the steps in his argument, however, in an effort to make the hermeneutical process more apparent and to provide for a smoother transition to the ontological analysis of the constitutive structures of human being's being-in-the-world. As before, I am not doing violence to the text, but merely making what is implicit at one moment explicit in my own demonstration. Anyone can do this who has read a book twice.

Consider: Being-in-the-world is the fundamental, a priori structure of human being. Constitutive of that structure are worldhood, being-with, being-oneself, and being-in. Heidegger considers these constitutive substructures in that order but gives an example of how his own analyses differ from the ordinary—scientific—accounts of human life, along with an overview of the structural totality of being-in-the-world; he then selects being-in as the one substructure most useful for making the total structure clear.

One way to be in a world is to know something of that world. Indeed, upon analysis of what is involved in our knowing, we shall be able to progress from the self-assurance of our own preontological understanding—a form of knowing—to a full, ontological comprehension of our being-in as constitutive of our being-in-the-world. The same hermeneutical process we detected in the whole of the text is repeated here in the part.

If my prediction is true, we should move from merely being-in as having some knowledge of worlds to an explicit understanding of what it means to be-in; and from there to use this knowledge in all further acts of being-in our worlds. This is the same process, by the way, which allowed psychotherapists to adapt Heidegger's methodology to their own therapeutical purposes.

Knowing, Heidegger tells us, is a founded mode of our being-in. The term "founded mode" is borrowed from Husserl,[25] whose *Fundierung* most probably served as model for Heidegger's notion of constitutive and fundamental structures. A mode of existence *is founded by* another when both are parts of the same whole and neither can exist without the other. All truly correlative terms (such as *cause* and *effect,* as referring to events within nature) are names for such founded modes of existence. And so are *subject* and *object.*

As traditionally interpreted, subject and object are relata, neither of which can exist without the other in a relationship of knowing. But subject and object are ontically defined, and it is Heidegger's purpose to adduce the primordial evidence for clarifying the being of the entities that may be either the subject or the object of an act of knowing. Epistemology, he claims, must be grounded in ontology, not ontology in epistemology.

We may begin to make our evaluation of this claim by engaging in a historical destruction of our own—this one, of epistemology. There are three current non-Heideggerian views of the knowledge relation.

First, the causal, by which objects become known as they impress themselves upon the sensory apparatus of some living subject. The relationship may be envisaged as being created by the object. See figure 1. This causal theory of perception is the basis for most em-

$$S \longleftarrow O$$

Figure 1

pirical theories of knowledge. It was most staunchly defended by John Locke in the seventeenth century.

The second version is found in all those theories of knowledge that treat the acting subject as creating the true object of knowledge. Husserlian phenomenology is a case in point, even if, by virtue of the phenomenological reduction, the existence of the object is "bracketed" out of relevance along with rest of the world. According to this theory, the following may represent the relationship between subject and object (prior to the first reduction). See figure 2. In this figure, the arrow represents the act of intending, an activity of consciousness.

$$S \longrightarrow O$$

Figure 2

The difference between the two theories, according to the two figures, is the origin and the direction of causal efficacy exhibited in the relationship. But there is a similarity in the two theories that gets lost in the diagrams; it came to be expressed in American pragmatism as "the spectator theory of knowledge."[26] It makes no difference whether the causal force originates from outside the subject and is impressed upon it, or from inside and becomes expressed as a force in nature as in Hegel's phenomenology of mind. Both the impressionistic and the expressionistic theories of perception treat the subject as a spectator, either of the external world or of its own inner states.

The alternative to the two preceding theories approaches Heidegger's notion of being-in as a mode of a human being's existence founded upon its relationship to a world. According to this theory, knowing is not a matter of acting or reacting, but of an interaction between subject and object defined in a continuous ongoing process. It may be diagrammed as shown in figure 3. In Dewey, of course,

$$K_r \longleftrightarrow K_n$$
$$K_{ing}$$

Figure 3

this process is naturalistic and is given a purely ontic explanation. Knowing, for him, is one way a human organism has to interact with its environment.

All that Heidegger has done—after excluding biology and anthropology as proper explanations for the primordial structural relatedness exhibited in human knowledge—is to show that what epistemologists have always called "knowledge" is, from the point of view of his own ontology, a primordial grounding in the structures of being-in-the-world. The justification here is once again by presupposition, but with this difference from the Kantian and Cartesian, that the a priori structure presupposed be further grounded in hermeneutical clarification. And for that we need worldhood, being-with and being-oneself, and being-in.

I shall save the definitive analysis of being-in for my next chapter. In what follows immediately, a few preliminary considerations are in order.

Let us begin by asking: How can a human being be in its world? The most obvious answer is the ontic characterization already given: a human being is abandoned to its world, thrown there by the factual conditions of its existence. Corresponding to the fact is the previous ontological explanation: facticity and abandonment are structures of our being in a world. The explanations here, as elsewhere in the text, begin with the observation of the factual conditions, and then proceed to show the primordial "ontological" structure that makes possible such conditions.

But being-in is a complicated structure, requiring an act of bringing into our forehaving what has already been revealed in the ontic and ontological priorities of human being. Consider: as a factual condition of a human being's existence there is always the possibility of questioning the meaning of that existence. This is the ontological question. And the answer to that question is always found in reference to one's *own* being:

Das Seiende, dessen Analyse zur Aufgabe steht, sind wir je selbst. Das Sein dieses Seienden ist *je meines*.[27]

The entity to be analyzed is always ourselves. The being of this entity is ever mine.

What is involved in this *Jemeinigkeit?* Far from being an appeal to a solipsism of the present moment, the statement "The being of this entity is always mine" states a double universality—covering all those moments when the ontological question arises and all those subjects to whom it occurs. "Ever-mineness" is an existential, that is, a structure of a human being's being in a world, indicating the possibility of posing the ontological question and opening up the field of investigation for possible answers.

That a human be in such a way that its being is a question for it has, says Heidegger, a double consequence: first, according to the answers discovered by the ontological questioning, the "essence" of a human being lies in its having yet to be what it is *(in seinem Zu-sein)*. But posing questions and answers in the traditional categories—e.g., essence as opposed to existence, which is attested to by factual presence before some observer—may lead the investigation astray. Strictly speaking, a human being has no essence and no existence that is limited to the observable properties of a body or the effects of one's behavior. It is for this reason Heidegger uses the term *Existenz* to characterize human being. The same difference is intended here as was noted earlier between a categorial and an existential determination of the being of an entity.[28] As for the second consequence, what a human being is to be is determined by its own decision to act.

Again, two consequences: existentials are structural components of a human being's existentiality, the more primordial phenomenon of being-in-the-world: and second, *Existenz* is attested to in fact by the possibilities being expressed in every ontic situation. That curious sentence, which owes its curiousness to the maintenance of the traditional and the existential terms for being, as well as to the triple occurrence of a term indicating being, should no longer harbor any ambiguity: *"Das 'Wesen' des Daseins liegt in seiner Existenz [The essence of a human being lies in its existence]."*[29] The indicated translation maintains the ambiguities of the text. To eradicate them, try "The way a human being exists is as a projection toward future possibilities."

As we continue, there will be other nonstandard translations. For example, "Who I am depends upon my possibility to choose and to become what I am" expands Heidegger's notion of *Eigentlichkeit* (authenticity). And the equally determinate possibility "to forego normal choice and to adopt those offered me by the world or other people" captures the kernel of his *Uneigentlichkeit* (inauthenticity). Such are the conditions under which I am abandoned in my world—

to be one or the other. Existing in the present is a self-projection into the future.

Ever mine, as a projection forward, my existence opens up a world. But the choice of possibilities must be kept an open context; otherwise upon analysis we shall fall back on a purely ontic characterization of our lives in terms of the factual conditions of a given moment rather than opening up the ontological basis for an existential determination of our being as directed toward its possibilities. For this reason, Heidegger needs and offers a second pair of existentials (as opposed to categories). Our being bound over to and projected toward the world of our possibilities must be described as it is on the average *(Durchschnittlichkeit)* and as an any-day occurrence *(Alltäglichkeit)*.

The indifference of the time and circumstances of the occurrence, along with the average understanding we possess of our being at the moment we actually question its meaning, guarantees the openness to the future ontological determination we seek. We begin, therefore, not with a specific choice, nor even those which are most our own *(eigentlich)* but with our indifferent status of being open first and foremost *(zunächst und zumeist)* to the choice of *some* possibility.

Heidegger gives an account of the reigning humane sciences— anthropology, psychology, and biology—with an excursus through traditional metaphysics and theology, to indicate that an ontology of the human person could not eventuate from such investigations, since, given the ontico-ontological priority of human being, an understanding of that being is presupposed by these investigations.[30]

So far, then, we have learned that our analysis is to be existential, and not categorial, and that our techniques are to be hermeneutical. With facticity, human being discovers its connections to a past; with existentiality, to a future. The next move is to bring forward an anticipated meaning for the present moment in which any decision is to be made. The prior elucidation of our being-in as facticity and existentiality, abandonment and self-projection, calls for, literally, the third dimension of its temporality.

To make his point, Heidegger borrows from Jakob Grimm's philological research.[31] *In,* Heidegger tells us, is a preposition deriving from an older German verb, *innan,* "to reside"; and is related to the Latin, *habitare,* sometimes translated into the current *sich aufhalten.* In a related sense, *sich aufhalten bei* may be translated into English as *to dwell on.*

The *an* of *innan* translates the Latin *colo,* I take care of, in the related senses of *diligo,* I cherish, and *habito,* I inhabit. All these senses seem to indicate that the "in" of our being-in is "where we feel at home." The entity that feels itself thus at home is precisely the one I myself am; so *ich bin,* "I am," "is connected with *bei"* and indicates an existential involvement with my world: in existing, I dwell alongside (at or with) the entities of my world.

Thus, at the same time I am abandoned to it, and projected to my possibilities in it, I reside alongside those entities of my world that absorb my attention *(sich aufhalten bei).* But here too caution is in order: *in* and *alongside* must be given existential, and not categorial, interpretation.

Heidegger's further determination of a human being's present existence in its world bears close attention. It assumes an understanding of "facticity," "existentiality," and "average everydayness."

He begins by mentioning fourteen ways a human being relates itself to the entities of its world: having to do with something *(zu-tunhaben mit etwas),* producing something *(herstellen von etwas),* attending to something and looking after it *(bestellen und pflegen von etwas),* making use of something *(verwenden von etwas),* giving something up, letting it go *(aufgeben, und in Verlust geraten lassen von etwas),* undertaking *(unternehmen),* accomplishing *(durch-setzen),* evincing *(erkunden),* interrogating *(befragen),* considering *(betrachten),* discussing *(besprechen),* determining *(bestimmen), und so weiter* (to supply the ellipsis).[32]

All these ways of behaving, and many more, including some that seem negative—leaving undone *(unterlassen),* neglecting *(versäu-men),* renouncing *(verzichten),* and taking a rest *(ausruhens)*—all are either positive demonstrations of our everyday concerns or deficient modes of our concernful dealings with the things of our worlds. The general term that may be used to cover both the positive and the deficient modes of human concern is *besorgen,* "to concern oneself with," by carrying out something, getting it done, or straightening matters out.[33]

The existential structure that gets expressed in these various ontic determinations of the ways in which we can express our concern is *care.* And so, the final answer to the question of how a human being exists in its world is "by caring." Beginning with the entity we call distinctively human, we isolate its being as care, which has the structure of facticity or abandonment in a world, as a projection upon its possibilities, its *Existenz,* while existing carefully alongside the entities of that world.

In this "care-structure" we begin to see more clearly the structures of temporality that constitute its meaning. How are we in our worlds? Always already, ahead of ourselves, alongside and with other entities.

Our hermeneutical expansion has moved up a notch.

PART I

3

From Worldhood and Significance to Spatiality and Space

IF THE PREVIOUS CHAPTER OF THIS COMMEN-
tary gives a sketch of the entire scope of *Being and Time* as we know
it, emphasizing the hermeneutical method by which it had been
worked out, this and each of the following chapters will be dedicated
to the continued expansion of the initial structural existential, being-
in-the-world. But it would be a mistake to assume that since the
whole treatise is divided into two parts one should expect two simple
interpretive projections.

True, the first division contains a single preliminary analysis of
human being as being in a world. That interpretation is given in
terms of our "average" and "everyday" manner of existence, and
will have to be repeated for a fuller explanation of one's being a
whole person, as being integral, and as developing within the time
of the world. Correspondingly, the phenomena of death, conscience,
and fate (or destiny) will be traced out in Heidegger's continual search
for primordiality of ontological significance. Indeed, significance is
itself a phenomenon associated with the structures of our personal
worlds and will require its own ontological interpretation, to be given
in the sequel of this chapter.

In the second division of his work I find at least three more
"projections," three more attempts to bring into our forehaving the

ultimate meaning of our existence. And, following an evaluation of the cumulative effect of these approaches to the ultimately primordial existential, human temporality, I shall supply a fifth projection of my own—a description of our being-in-a-literary-world, still based upon the existential structures laid out in division 1 of the text, beginning with "worldhood" and "significance."

WORLDHOOD, as should be expected, is an existential, and not a categorial determination for the being of a human being's world. The existential-categorial distinction is nothing new; nor is the ontico-ontological distinction used by Heidegger to mark off the differences between the facts of a human existence and the a priori structures defining the possibilities realized in every human existence. Indeed, combining the two sets of distinctions, besides illuminating the ordinary uses of the word *world,* will give us access to the connection between worldhood and significance it is my purpose to demonstrate. What corresponds to this notion of "worldhood," and how is the phenomenon of worldhood revealed in a purely linguistic analysis?

Worldhood is the worldliness *(Weltlichkeit)* of the world. Although the negative connotations associated with *worldliness* in English suggest an attitude of false sophistication or an outlook limited to the here and now of a current situation, the positive and neutral senses of the term recommend it as the proper rendering for the German. For the neutral sense, try "what pertains to a world"; for the positive, as applied to subjects, "having one's feet on the ground," or, exactly as Heidegger intended with his description of knowledge as a founded mode of our being in a world, "knowing where one is, and being at home there." All the negative senses of the term stem from the smugness that usually accompanies the realization that one knows where one is.

There seem to have been at least two prior indications that worldliness should become our theme. Besides the clue indicated by knowledge as a founded mode of our existence, there was the discussion of the "structural totality" indicated by the hyphens in being-in-the-world. The structural totality is composed of constituent moments, each equiprimordial with the others and stemming from the same source. From this point of view, worldliness calls for a future ontological determination of our being-with-others and of our being-in as such. But each of these existentials has its ontical counterpart from which all existential analysis begins and to which it must eventually return if the ontological claims it makes are to be verified. We return, then, to the basic ontic senses revealed in the ordinary uses of the term *world*.

First, the natural world. The world of nature is filled with things: houses, trees, people, animals, mountains, stars; and with events, or what happens to houses, trees, people, and the like. Traditionally, as things existing within the world, the components of nature have been determined ontologically as substances; their being is their presence *(parousia)*. Unfortunately for the traditional metaphysics, however, neither the collection of things nor their categorial substantiality discloses a world as a phenomenon. Moreover, both things and people are found in the world of nature; so why should their natures differ? If all sciences reveal the structures of the same world, then why, considered *grosso modo,* do their results differ so much?

Consider further. If the ordinary ontical sense of *world* is the totality of natural entities, everything that is the case as Wittgenstein has told us,[1] and if, ultimately, the being of such innerworldly entities is the presence or fitness for perception they exhibit, then the being of the world, of the collection, is neither accessible to us, since it cannot be perceived, nor adequately described as presence, since the very idea of a world is that of a mathematical summation across an indeterminate set of individuals. In this sense, there are mathematical worlds, worlds of pure possibility; and physical worlds, biological worlds, cultural worlds; as many different kinds of worlds as there are ways of grouping similar phenomena. But none of these worlds is capable of showing its face.

The second ontical sense of *world* is a reference to the "place" wherein human beings dwell. It may be entirely idiosyncratic, as the private world of any conscious person; or shared, as a public environment. Even these may be multiple in that one culture may differ from another by the ways they furnish an environment to the persons living therein. It is this ontic sense of (a human) world that must be made to exhibit its character of worldliness, that is, to appear as a phenomenon, to show its face, and just as it is, if the existential-ontological analysis of such things is to succeed where the traditional metaphysics has failed.

We begin once more with human being in its everydayness. Reflecting upon our facticity, we always find ourselves in some environment; things exist around us and in space. Aroundness and spatiality form the new constitutive moments for still another existential—environmentality *(Umweltlichkeit)*. If it too is an a priori structure of our human being, then it too must be given its hermeneutical expansion.

That expansion begins from a familiar starting point, the ways in which human beings concern themselves with the entities of their worlds—the ways of taking care or of bringing something off. To open a door, says Heidegger, I have to use the latch.[2] And doors and latches are not mere things but pieces of equipment for attaining something. We are here at the point of switching the analysis from the ontics and the ontology of the things of nature to those of culture. Where a simple thing is known for what it is by its presence to us *(Vorhandenheit)*, equipment or tools are what they are because of their utility or handiness *(Zuhandenheit)*.

Although the Greeks used the word *pragmata* to characterize the things used in their practical concerns, the ontological status of these "things" was still determined by their presence, rather than by the work performed in the Greek *praxis*. What, indeed, is a tool? And how do tools, in their functioning, yield an insight into the nature of a human being's world? Anthropologists and archeologists have paid attention only to the ontics of distinct cultural worlds.

Everyday human being consumes itself with caring for its projects, using tools to accomplish its purposes. But strictly speaking, no tool simply "is" ("Ein Zeug ist strenggenommen nie"). Insofar as a tool functions, its being is to function, along with other tools, for a specifically projected purpose. True, something is made to serve; but that thing, in the concernful practice, gets referred to something beyond itself.

To abstract the "totality structure" of equipmentality, we have the relation, "something in order to [etwas um zu]." The serviceability of the tool is apparent in its being referred to an end; and, as such, its being is to be handy. But the handiness of the tool is primarily grasped in its very use. The handiness of the hammer is in the action of hammering—a nail, through wood, to fix and join, to produce the object—a room that itself is a tool for living or the boots that are for walking. What is first and foremost the object of our practical consciousness is the world to be produced. The tool along with its handiness makes its appearance in the activity producing the work.

Handiness, or serviceability, differs ontologically from presence as functioning tools differ ontically from mere things, as cultural worlds differ from the natural. It would be impossible, even though what comes to serve as a tool must be provided by nature as materials for production, to deduce the nature of the tool by a simple inspection of the visual aspect of the things of nature ("das 'Aussehen' von Dingen"). The purely "theoretical" insight into things as such misplaces the object of understanding from the handiness of the tool to the presence of the material. For this reason, Heidegger claims that the knowledge displayed in our being able to use tools or to adapt to the life-enabling equipment of our cultures is not gained by inspection but rather by circumspection, by a human being looking around for itself as it is abandoned and projected toward continued existence rather than at the things in the world of nature.

Circumspection, the peculiar seeing proper to the acting person, unites the reality of the past to the possibilities of the future. In the referential totality of the equipmental structure the human being assigns itself as that for which all other assignments have been made: human beings are themselves the users of the things of nature, as well as of those entities for the production of which tools are used.

In sum, then, using materials for human purposes constitutes a context in which something like a human world (or culture) announces itself. In that context something is used for something by someone; or something is made for someone to use for his or her purpose. In the first instance, we gain a glimpse of a private or personal world; in the second, of a public world. It is to either of these, and not to the world of nature, that the preontological comprehension of our being directs us, given the founded nature of the relationship between knowing and being-in-the-world.

The ultimate, or most primordial, meaning of cognition is established by the fact that when we question our being we find ourselves as having already been related in the structures of our being to an equipmental or use complex. For this reason our knowledge of the natural world is embedded in the cultural; that is to say, performing a scientific investigation is something we do, once we have perfected a technique for inspection. But our knowledge of our own cultural worlds is not embedded in the natural.

Rather than drawing out the consequences for a general philosophy of science at this juncture, Heidegger proceeds, in section 16 of his text, to show how a change in attitude on the part of tool-users has produced the knowledge of the two worlds of every human being, that of culture and that of nature.

That a human being's world is said to have "announced" itself in the equipmental context of human action should remind us of Heidegger's earlier discussion of the differences between a phenomenon in the strictest sense of the term and an appearance, with which it is often confused. A specific world is announced by the structure of its equipmental complex in the same way a disease is announced by the structure of its phenomenal symptoms. But our analysis has not yet allowed the worldliness of a human world to appear as a phenomenon. We have indeed characterized what that world is ontically, but our language has not as yet succeeded in letting the being of such a world appear as it is. Although handiness and presence describe the being of the entities of the two kinds of worlds, and something like a human world announces itself within the equipmental complex of our cultural worlds, our analysis has yet not achieved its aim.

Two preliminary steps are necessary prior to the attempt. The first is the further discussion of the manner in which a world is announced in a use structure, and how circumspection is modified into inspection on the basis of a failure in a use structure; the second is an analysis of reference, signs, and involvements in the determination of significance.

First things first. How does an environment, which is a purely ontical concept, announce itself as worldly, that is, as expressing an ontological structure? The question amounts to our asking how, in concerning ourselves with the things closest to us in our environments, the tools with which we work out our concerns, we become expressly aware of the environment itself, rather than of the things that surround us. The discussion though sometimes dense is never unwieldly, and thus, in a sense, illustrates what is being talked about, since the text we are interpreting forms a part of our intellectual environment.

When our worlds are "worlding,"[3] when we are pulling things off, as it were, the entities we find handy to our concerns are inconspicuous, unobtrusive, and pliant. Their functioning as tools to accomplish our ends discloses a world that has already been "understood" in the circumspection by which the totality of one's involvements has been understood in the first instance. If our worlds are announced in the totality of these involvements, how does the environment come to announce itself?

By a failure or a fault in the use complex. A broken pencil or pen point calls attention to the tool as nonfunctioning; to an examination as unwritten; to failing grades; to unhappy parents, etc. But even this sheer unusability of the writing instrument does not reveal that in-strument as a merely existent object. What happens in the failure of a tool is that the tool lights up the cultural environment in a negative way: what was inconspicuous in itself because of our familiarity with our worlds now has become conspicuous—not just the tool itself, but the totality of our involvements with it.

Similarly, a tool may fail simply by being missing; or our worlds may fail because something stands in the way of our using the tools we do possess. Impediments must be removed; missing tools must be supplied. Our cultural environments show themselves thematically as the formerly familiar worlds now become unfamiliar and distant; the failure of our equipmental or use complexes brings forward a peculiar awareness of the unhandiness of certain of our tools.

This procedure may be summarized as follows. The Being of equipment as handy possesses a structure determined by assignments: "something in order to"; a togetherness of this with this for that. Ordinarily, these assignments go unthematized because our concern is with the whole work. But given a disturbance in the system of assignments, which are already understood by our circumspection, notice is brought to a specific dysfunctionality. Where before the world announced itself through the totality of the equipmental con-text, as "seen" circumspectively and therefore as understood non-thematically, after the break circumspection comes up against a noth-ingness. The acting person may then step back, allowing in their proper order the environment and "merely existent" things to appear. Stepping back and looking again is the basis of all scientific inspection of the reality of innerworldly things. But this is the first sense of *world,* a world that is constituted by perceivable entities, whose being is characterized by their presence to our observational capacities, by their perceivability, either in reality or in principle. Indeed, the wrong world.

So, the foregoing discussion of a human world as referential to-tality that constitutes the handiness of an equipmental context calls for further analysis of the difference between references and signs.

According to the prior analysis, every tool exhibits in its being a referential structure. But not all tools indicate. Although it is assigned the task of planting nails, a hammer, for example, does not indicate what is to be joined to what; wood, leather, composite materials of various sorts may allow us to understand the reference totality of hammering. A sign, however, is a special tool with the specific purpose of indicating something. The directional signal of an automobile, for example, is for the purpose of indicating the intention of a driver to turn one way or another, an ontically concrete relation with the environment that is communicated to other drivers or pedestrians, with whom we share our worlds.

If, ontically considered, the concern with one tool differs from that with another, the difference must be understood in our circumspection, by which we initially understand our relationship to our worlds. A sign, like any other tool, is not a mere thing standing in relation to other such things; its use raises an actual instrumentality complex into circumspection in such a way that the worldly character of everything serviceable within our environment is announced. As they function, signs indicate to us and to others who can read or interpret them what we are at any given time, since they reveal where and how we live, what sort of involvements we have—in short, ontologically considered, the "wherein" of our concern.

How does this come about? The question is asked in section 17; to answer it properly we must bring forward the results of the prior analysis concerning the reversibility of ontic and ontological concerns.

We become aware of the worldly character of our worlds through an act of circumspective foresight into the equipmental context of our environments. So it has been shown; to be circumspect, ordinary languages tell us, is to act with care. The entities within our environments reveal themselves as being serviceable to the end of our continued living. When a useful object, whether tool or more specifically a sign, becomes conspicuous (as being unusable, missing, or blocked), the object serving as tool or sign is not thereby reduced to the status of mere thing. The malfunctioning tool gets its sense from the prior circumspective foresight and not from the material that is referred to some use. For a tool no longer to function properly something had already to have been assigned a position in the use structure. That is what is accomplished in the circumspective foresight.

The south wind, for example, at least in the northern hemisphere, is a sign of rain—to farmers who need it to water their crops. To insist that such winds were always there and that they were usually accompanied by rain is to misunderstand how signs get taken as such. Wind as a sign of rain may very well be conspicuously there, but it receives its conspicuousness from the inconspicuousness of the equipmental totality associated with crop husbandry. The handiness, the serviceability, of this sign is obvious in an everyday agricultural world.

The lack of a proper wind may result in drought and in reduced harvests; but the changing of one's attitude from circumspection to scientific inspection is likewise a possibility of human ingenuity, itself serviceable as a tool for survival. Seeding clouds may be an alternative cultural means for attaining the same natural end, the procurement of sufficient food. All these phenomena indicate how one's concern for one's world must be understood in terms of the worldly character of that world.

In summary, what we take as signs are tools that indicate the specific nature of our worlds. The indicating of the sign makes concrete the "toward which" of something serviceable, the end toward which a means is employed. In so doing, it reveals as implicit the equipmental structure of the "in order to" relating means and ends. Indicating is likewise itself the equipmental character of something that lies close to our hand—whatever is taken as a sign—and hence belongs to the totality of equipment constituting the context of assignments or references with which we may become involved in our daily concerns.

For this reason, the being of a sign is to be characterized by its serviceability to indicate the environment of our circumspective involvement in our worlds. Ontically, signs serve to indicate the things holding a place in the context of our involvements; ontologically, they exhibit the structures of an instrumental complex. These instrumental complexes are referential totalities, such that when we are capable of "reading" them we come to possess knowledge of the world of the makers and users of such signs.

Finally, the ontological function of signs is to allow us to understand how the worldhood of a world in general is to be understood. At any rate, it is not with tongue in cheek that I note the sign character of the written word and that once again Heidegger's text both explains and exhibits our being-in-the-world.

How involvement, significance, and worldhood are related, and how significance (of our existential-ontological worlds) may be modified into the mere signification of objects of our natural world constitute the themes of the next section of this chapter.

SECTION 18 of Heidegger's text contains material compelling interest for two reasons. First, his argument reaches a culminating point in his description or interpretation of the worldliness of a human being's world; and for this reason, second, readers have the first opportunity for judging the degree to which Heidegger has made good on his claim that his method is to use words in such a way as to make the phenomena of human existentiality actually appear. A word on each of these interests.

For Husserl phenomenology was the description of the events occurring in the world insofar as a subject was aware of them; his technique was to reduce the world to phenomena as they occurred to a consciousness and to use language to describe what appears in this way to the attentive consciousness. For Heidegger, there is no distinction between consciousness and body given with any degree of apodictic certainty. Interpreting is a way of understanding what is given in our preontological understanding of our own being. The phenomenon we are interested in revealing must be disclosed in our act of discoursing upon our relationship with our worlds.

In this section, Heidegger discourses upon the worldhood of a purely human world as that existential structure is implicit in our being-in-the-world. To test the validity of Heidegger's methodological claims, therefore, we must judge how his use of language has permitted us to understand our own being-in-the-world. If the worldliness of our worlds is revealed through his descriptions, then he will have made good on his claim.

The first culminating point of Heidegger's preliminary analysis of our being-in-the-world is his description of worldhood, considered as a constitutive structure of human being. The title of the section is rendered by Macquarrie and Robinson as "Involvement and Significance; the Worldhood of the World."[4] To understand the connection among these three concepts, a short summary of the prior section is helpful. And, as always, when it is necessary to adjust the tensions in the forestructures of our understanding in order to make an interpretation, Heidegger obliges by giving the necessary summary.

Whenever anything appears to us as being handy to our purposes, a world and an understanding of it are already there. But the understanding we possess of our own worlds is merely implicit and is not thematically developed until we have made our ontological interpretations.

Prior analysis has interpreted the world as that in terms of which the serviceability of our tools is made apparent through the instrumental totality of our equipment. Since the world has merely *an-*

nounced itself within the contextuality of the instrumental context of our concernful living, however, we must continue our interpretation until our descriptions of the structures of our worldhood allow it to appear as a datum of our ontological understanding. So far, we have been led to understand our equipment through serviceability; once our tools have been freed from our tacit, ontic involvements in the events of our daily lives, we can reflect upon them as functioning in those involvements.

How has the serviceability of the tools constituting our personal involvements been freed for interpretation? Through reference, or assignment of value within a specific act of purposing. The utility of a tool is not a property of some physical matter; the tool is appropriate for some action, for some attempt to appropriate something. Upon analysis, therefore, a tool is revealed as an entity that has already been assigned to a specific purpose. We are reminded here that coming explicitly to know the worldhood of our worlds always presupposes an implicit awareness of what is involved in those worlds as the locus of our actions. In its attempt to make explicit what is only implicit in our everyday worldly knowledge, phenomenological analysis has merely called attention to our tools in their serviceability and therefore to our tools as entities that have already been assigned as the entities they are.

Letting the things of our environments be involved in this way Heidegger calls a "perfect tense a priori"[5]—an apt description of the "always already" phenomenon I have already discussed.[6] What matters here is the effect of the ontological analysis to set free the ontological structures—the existentials—from their insertion in the context of an everyday act. As entities that have been revealed as those always previously assigned to be what they are, tools exhibit a new structural totality, that of our involvements with them as directed toward something else. In ordinary pragmatic terms, our tools reveal a continuum of means and ends.[7]

Some words of caution concerning the translation of *Bewandtnis* are in order. The verb *bewendenlassen* means to let something go as it is, and it is general enough to cover such acts as allowing something to run its course or letting it go in the double sense of permitting it to go on as is or of dropping our interest in it. The object of the verb always seems to be something in process of determination. For this reason, the associated noun, *Bewandtnis,* may be a condition, a circumstance, or a set of conditions or circumstances. Macquarrie and Robinson opt for "involvement,"[8] which is perhaps as well as one can do. Nothing is lost by translating the term one way or the other, however, since Heidegger gives an analysis of the ontological structures the term is used to name.

As an existential construct, an involvement (Bewandtnis) takes place within a larger context, a Bewandtnisganzheit, or system of relatedness among tool, tool-user, and task accomplished in the use of the tool. A tool is still found within its etwas um zu ("something in order to") context. Although this reference to another end is ontologically definitive for the involvement of our tools, in any given purposive act, under prevailing ontic conditions, we merely take the reference for granted. What is the ontological structure revealed in the reference of means to ends?

In a purposive act of concern with the things of our environments, we are ourselves "involved" (no pun intended; this is one of the meanings of bewendenlassen) with our tools to accomplish our ends. The "toward which" (wozu) of the equipmental context implies a "with this" toward that, toward that, toward that, in a hierarchy of progressively higher ends; but this ongoing linkage between means serving ends that become means for still further ends is not open-ended. An initial assignment of value within the referential scheme is made on the basis of an ultimate "for the sake of which."

That for the sake of which an action is performed is the acting being itself, indeed, a human being that has an understanding of its being as a constituent of its being. It is with respect to this prior, preontological understanding of its being that a human being can discover in its purposive actions that something has already been involved. The letting something be involved is the decision to use this rather than that as the means to attain our ends.

The phenomenon has two interpretations, the one ontical and the other ontological. Ontically, letting our tools be involved is to let something serve our purpose, so that it might be the tool it is. In this sense, things get worked on, improved, or merely smashed to pieces— so that something else may be done. Every homeowner knows that a plumber will begin by destroying the wall to get at the pipes that need replacement. Ontologically, letting things be involved itself involves a previous freeing of something for serviceability within our immediate environment.

The system of our human involvements is therefore not deter-mined, conditioned, or allowed to be what it is as some kind of world-stuff or substance that has been glossed over with some mysterious predicate, usefulness; the property of such stuff always exhibits its previous freeing—from a human being's prior, primordial understanding of itself as being-in-the-world.

The context of equipmentality shows the following relational totality: (1) the basic fact of reference or assignment of value to this or that indicates the "with which" and the "in which" of the serviceability context; (2) the ultimate "toward this," the end for the sake of which an action is performed, closes the system and makes a unity of the equipmental context; (3) as that for the sake of which its actions are performed, a human being is revealed as having assigned itself as the connecting link between the initial "with which" and the ultimate "for the sake of which" an involvement has already been made.

On the basis of this structural totality Heidegger offers the following description (interpretation) of a human world: a world, in the second sense of our term (as opposed to the natural), is

Das Worin des sichverweisenden Verstehens als Woraufhin des Begegnenlassens von Seienden in der Seinsart der Bewandtnis.

The wherein of the understanding that has assigned itself as that for the sake of which entities are allowed to be encountered as a context of involvement.[9]

Worldhood, or the worldly character of a human world, is in consequence the structure of the system of involvements in which a human being has always already assigned itself.

Figure 4 may serve as a graph for a human world. In figure 4 we recognize figure 3,[10] which was intended to characterize knowing as a founded mode of our being-in-the-world. That preontological understanding of our being has merely been brought forward and related to the entities that in their equipmentality, in the assignments

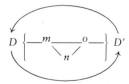

Figure 4

of means and ends values within a system of involvements, allows a personal world to appear.

Worlding is a process. We come to understand it ontologically from the moment of finding ourselves abandoned in a world, at D, and projected to a possibility, at D'. Projecting itself from D to D', a human being creates its world; and it always discovers itself in a world it has already created. Significance (*Bedeutsamkeit*), like worldhood, has a preontological and an explicitly ontological explanation.

Preontologically significance is felt; it is the understanding we have of our own being because we are that being. But we are always in a world. So significance is what gets interrogated in the ontological questioning of our being in a world. How this significance gets traced from a purely affective state to full, discursive understanding befits a discussion of being-in as such. That is a topic of my next chapter. Here Heidegger merely shows the relationship between significance and worldhood, reading off a human being's understanding of its worldliness in reverse order to that exhibited in his analysis or worldhood.

Once again, all points of the analysis may be read in figure 4. We begin with the preontological, that is, a human being's ordinary understanding of how it is to be in its world: we see its projection. Upon reflection, we recognize that humans always exist understandingly in their worlds: we can recognize their points of departure in facticity and themselves as the ends of their projections; that is the process they are said to live and thus to understand. What is signified in the structure of this tacit significance? First, that a human being knows itself as that for the sake of which assignments of value are made; this "for the sake of which" constitutes an end for the "in-order-to" relation; and the in-order-to relation as a whole is composed of both means and ends—of "toward thises" and "with thises." The point of projection from the initiating "with which" to the final "toward which"—from D to D' in figure 4—reveals a relational totality of significance: the wherein of an understanding that has assigned itself as the end of an action. The structure of this world, of this wherein, is a human being's "worldly" character. And when we question it, we have always already understood it, at least as a feeling.

To understand how significance is related to signification, however, we must trace out the process whereby a basic ontological structure gets modified depending upon whether our understanding is of the tools of our cultural worlds or the things of our natural worlds. The significance of our human worlds becomes in a purely ontical analysis of linguistics the counterpart of significations, the things referred to by linguistic expressions.

Looking upon words as signs for designated meanings becomes possible upon the basis of some prior use. The actual use of a word or words constitutes a contextual totality that reflects significance in the worldly sense of the term. Once a meaning has been established by use, one can overlook the worldly significance expressed through language as a tool and inspect words as objects possessing a signific function, that is as referring to other objects in the natural world. The change in analysis is the same as from circumspection to inspection; from the significance of worldliness to signification; from equipment to merely present things. Whatever its power to express human feeling, language as a tool for that expression is based upon significance as an existential state of human being.

On this, much more is to be found later.

ONE OF THE advantages of a phenomenologically clarified humanistic world is the possibility of further contrasting the traditional ontological interpretation of the natural world with the sense we possess of our lived worlds, and finally of contrasting the scientific notion of space with the spatiality with which we are most familiar in our everyday concerns. In order to exploit this advantage, I shall devote the next two sections of this chapter to the indicated topics.

First, the contrast between lived worldly significance and the world interpreted as an infinite "container" of corporeally extended things. The interpretation is Descartes', and we are best reminded to recall his intuition of extension as the clear and distinct property of bodies, either that of his hand, as analyzed in the first *Meditation*, or of a piece of wax, in the second. By gradually stripping away those ideas of an external body which are first of all not clear, and then the idea of color, which is clear, but not distinct, Descartes arrived at the intuition of extension as a simple idea—this, after attempting to show that the defining property of a human soul is its thought.

Heidegger is, of course, killing two birds with one stone in his excursus into Cartesian ontology. He really means to throw more light upon his interpretation of a human world by contrasting it to the Cartesian description of the natural world; but, as will be apparent in both halves of my commentary, having a body—a function of a human being's spatiality—and having a mind—a function of its temporalized spatiality—will be shown to be a faulty description of human being. Bodies and minds are functions of our worlding experience; as studied in the physical sciences of anatomy and physiology or the behavioral sciences of psychology, anthropology, and sociology, they will not be treated in such a way as to reveal the nature of the human worlds we live in. The reason, of course, is that such sciences are ontic descriptions of phenomena, qua natural; and, as such, they are pursued without regard to a possible metaphysical foundation.

The case was not the same for Descartes. For him, things were extended substances; and minds were thinking substances. The external world was itself a plenum of the infinitely extended three dimensions of space. Within this plenum there was an infinite number of bodies existing *pars extra partes* with each other and containing segments in the same way. The piece of wax, we recall, was reduced from its brute appearance to its primary qualities, which were all functions of three-dimensional extensionality. Division of whole into part could be measured by number; and figure and motion, as measured by change of place, were likewise primary qualities of things.

But hardness was not. Hardness was a function of the relative motion of two things; and as measured by the touching of two moving bodies, was not properly speaking the attribute or property of any single body. If a hand and a thing it touches, for example, moved in the same direction and with the same intensity, there could be no tactile perception of hardness, and nothing would get touched.

Now, although the primary qualities of all physical bodies may change, along with their hardness, there is something persistent that does not change. And this persistence through change is one definition of the substantiality of physical substances.

But there is another definition of substantiality in Descartes: what is conceived through itself and therefore what exists independently of whatever cannot be so conceived. Both bodies and minds, he claimed, were independent substances relative to each other; but since both were creations of the infinite and truly independent substance, God, their independence seems to have lost some of its luster. Bodies existed extended, and minds thinking, because God made them that way. Their being was created and depended upon the being of the most perfect being, who left his impression upon us when he made us in his image.

And this ontological account of minds and bodies as natural events was borrowed by Descartes from the medievals, who detected an analogical sense for the term *being* as applied to God and the entities he had created. But they too were merely repeating what they had read in Aristotle, for whom being could "be said in many ways." Since there is an analogy in the concept of being or substantiality as that which could be conceived through itself or through itself as created by another, the basic meaning of the term was taken to be self-evident.

God's being was proved by Descartes either as the necessarily existing cause of our idea of perfection—which we as imperfect beings could not possess without that cause—or by the absurdity of the assumption that a perfect being could possibly not exist. This latter, of course, is the famous "ontological" argument.

But what about the substance of created things? It is not an idea we have derived from our senses; the substance of a thing is conceived, through itself to be sure, as that which possesses attributes. A thought without a mind, extension without a body, both of which may at least in some sense be observed, would represent a denial of the old metaphysical postulate that from nothing nothing comes. Detachable from their attributes only in thought, substances are not so detachable in reality. What is known is thought and extension—what is "presupposed" by their existence—is the substantiality of the substances they are really connected with.

As a result of the Cartesian analysis, says Heidegger,[11] the idea of substance remains unclarified; its gets passed off as being incapable of clarification, since it is presupposed as a postulate for the existence of attributes; and lastly, it is never directly connected with sensuous experience, except indirectly by the "real" connections between substantiality and the properties of particular substances.

What is one to make of the Cartesian world ontology? The kindest thing Heidegger is willing to say is that it fits one kind of world, and falsifies the other, more important world. The Cartesian *mathesis universalis* is applicable only to things having presence as their being, to merely extended things, the relations of whose parts may be symbolized in the abstract as "xRy," where R is a determinable spatial function. The assumption, in this mathematical methodology, is that the unchanging or essential properties of substances may be known, fixed, or determined with critical exactness; but it fails to understand that perception is itself an access to the truth of our worlds. If hardness is essentially resistance to penetration, then hardness is defined by the relative velocity and position of touching bodies; but then, the experience of tactility is lost as an access to our worlds.

In general, the Cartesian methodology accepts materiality in order to explain the behavior of physical objects, which are presumed to be given an added property of value by persons who deal with physical objects. This is an attempt to build up to an idea of the handiness of our equipment—as futile an attempt then as it is now, when it is attempted by those of our positive scientists who seek to explain the purely human world as the mathematical summation over an indefinite set of events. As Heidegger sees it, ontology comes before and lays the foundation for the positive sciences, not after, using the results of those sciences.[12]

THE FINAL THEME associated with worldhood is the derivation of the scientific concepts of space from our lived spatiality. The demonstration is given in three phases, following a summary of the conclusions derived from the Cartesian notion of spatiality. The problem concerns the nature of insideness (*Inwendigkeit*), which is not that of the contained in the container, both of which are three-dimensionally extended. A human being as an entity *lives* its being-in-the-world. What is the spatiality of a human world? The first part of the answer is given in section 22, where Heidegger treats of the relationship between the "aroundness" of the environment (*das Umhafte der Umwelt*) and the spatiality of the instrumental complex that had announced the existence of a specifically human world.

In the prior analysis of such a world, the spatiality implicit within the means-ends structural complex of tool, tool-user, and object produced was not yet made explicit. We began the analysis with what was closest to the circumspective concerns of the acting person, its equipmental complex. This closeness is not measured in terms of distances between existent objects, but rather by the calculative manipulating or using of the tools to accomplish one's purposes. Circumspective concern establishes what might be done and how best to do it in initiating an action. A tool has its place within a system of assignments. From the point of view of circumspective concern, it is the first entity encountered in an action; and it is always "close by" as being at hand for the action.

Once the world has made its appearance as a phenomenon, however, the placement of a tool has already been encountered within a context that has been set up; the system of references, following the indications of signs, has allowed an installation of equipment in which the various pieces of equipment have been arranged in the order indicated by the action. Generally speaking, the tool's placement is fixed with respect to a definite direction: there, relative to a certain here *(dort und da)* established by a human being's involvement of itself in its environment. The hither point and the thither point of the relationship create a region, which is the actual "whither" of the human involvement in its world.

This relationship may likewise be read from a slightly modified figure as shown in figure 5. Instead of reading the projection of *D* to

Figure 5

D' as the self-projection of a human being (which, however, it still is) from a present state of actuality to a future possibility, in which the passage is mediated by an equipmental context through which a significance is revealed to the acting person, we may assign *D'* the value of the "there" and *D* the value of the "here." In being stretched between its being here and there, a human being is opened to its world, which now reveals itself as a region. In this way, the thither and the hither are united into a single, stretched openness, the whither of human action.

We must remember, however, that we are translating *"Dasein"* as "human being," and are thus covering up the etymological suggestion for the determination of a human region contained in the *Da*. That term is marvelously ambiguous in German, indicating both "here" and "there." A human being, in its activities, is always stretched between a there and a here; it is, indeed, neither here nor there as these loci are determined within the space of the natural world, but always in-between. Time, of course, is what both separates and unites the moments of a human action within the region of its world; but that description is left to the second half of the text. Here, a region is created by the openness of a human being appropriating its own being-in-the-world.

A region has direction—from there to here and from here to there—and a range within which a tool is allowed to function. The actual use of a tool shows that it has already been oriented toward something and within something, the region that has been set up by the projection of a human act. When, in speaking of a human world, we referred to the aroundness of the equipmental complex set to rights ("eingerichtet") in a human purposive action, this is what was meant. The equipmental complex reveals a region that is constructed of a multiplicity of "places," which is definitive of all possible "wheres" of the acting being's concerns. Inside a building, we say "above," and we mean "on the ceiling"; "below," and we mean "on the floor"; "beyond," and we mean "outside." In short, a region is oriented to the usual and the preferred mode of human action.

Regions are thus not constructed out of objectively three-dimensional objects and their relations, nor are they merely subjective, in the sense of having been arbitrarily arranged by some conscious person. They are determined by human concerns, to be sure, as these become displayed in a full-bodied action of relating means and end in a context of equipmental use. The sun is used by architects to determine the sunny and shady sides of a house; the one is better for planting, the other, for sleeping. And it has been used in religious symbolism as well to determine the placement of church and churchyard, the place of living worship and the place of final repose for the dead. In all such cases, of course, the degree of involvement necessary for determining the being of human beings is at issue in an ontological inquiry.

The analysis here is similar to that given for the derivation of significations from significance. Whenever there occurs a break in the familiarity of a use-context experienced as the felt significance of our worlds in the preontological comprehension of our own being, the inconspicuous familiarity breaks down into a conspicuous visibility; the region, as the transparent locus of our concerns, reveals itself as an object of possible inspection by which we can determine why our tools have failed us. In the failure, some entity is found out of its accustomed "place." That is how regions, which carry the germ for a concept of space, get broken up into a multiplicity of places.

In sum, the worldliness of a human world, first experienced as significance in the context of the interinvolvement of acting persons and the equipment of their environments, is the primordial existential source for the conception of space as an empty container, as a dimension of the beings found in the natural world; but only because of a conspicuous failure to pull something off. In order to show the derivation of the scientific concept of space, we must therefore elucidate the spatiality proper to a peculiarly human world. This, we recall, is what Descartes is charged with having failed to do. Heidegger takes on the task in section 24.

IF ENVIRONMENTS are not first experienced as three-dimensional expanses, the reason is that circumspective concern has already arranged them into organized regions when our ontological questioning first brings attention to them. Regions are themselves given internal structure by virtue of human activity. If we had to, we could draw another figure, this one number 6, projecting the direction and range of a region into the "stretch" and the directionality of an intended action.

The stretch phenomenon Heidegger called "Ent-fernheit." Macquarrie and Robinson translate the German word into "de-severance," which may leave some intuitions blunted.[13] I myself prefer "de-distancing." Whatever English expression suits our fancy, the original term meant "making a farness vanish," or "bringing something close by." Since what brings objects close to us is our concern for our environments and since we use tools to procure what is needed to continue our projects, our tools are environmentally the "closest" to us. They are always at hand, that is, handy even when not being used. And in some way or another most of our purposive activity is directed toward bringing something closer to us. Acts of cognition, for example, reduce the mystery surrounding the objects of our environment; and current equipment for travel and telecommunications has reduced the size of our immediate worlds. Television, for example, brought the Vietnam War right into our own homes, without the least disturbance to our dinners.

In all this "bringing close," of course, there is no explicit estimation of distances; that is a later phenomenon, one of metrics. Instead, the language we use to interpret the distances that separate us from our goals sounds hopelessly inexact. From here to there is "a good walk," but a quicker, hence shorter, ride. Something close is "a stone's throw away"; and an estimated "half hour to the house" may be measured by "the length of (the time it takes to smoke) a pipe." Even "a short bit" ("ein Dauer") may be used to communicate the distances of our circumspective concern. What become "de-distanced" in the art of bringing something close are the elements of our equipmental complex—those "with whiches" and "toward whiches" that go to make up our structured worlds.

As with the range and directionality of an environmental region, the de-distancing of the objects of our concern is neither a purely objective nor a purely subjective phenomenon. Subjects and objects fill the natural world. So little is the phenomenon a functional relationship of the things of the natural world that what is closest and what is furthest in our regions are completely invertible. The glasses on our noses are further from our attention than the objects they bring into our vision. Only when our glasses are dirty, and for that reason fail to function, do they become conspicuous in their presence, just as when we cannot find them, they are conspicuous in their absence. The same possible inversion may be found between the street under our feet and the destination to which it may lead. To be close by, then, for the objects of our environmental worlds, is to be within the range of what is serviceable for our circumspection.

In summary, de-distancing the objects of our environments takes place within the range of our regions: in the whither between hither and yon. A human being is not where its body is in three-dimensional space, it is always "there," with the objects of its concern. The "space" occupied by a human being is the de-distanced stretch between its tool and its objectives, which have been arranged by circumspection into a region of concern in advance of its action. When our tools are yonder, they must be brought hither; and what is already here has significance only insofar as it serves to make some other remoteness vanish. Wherever a human being goes, there is a distance traced in a world, which is the result of its own being structured spatially as de-distancing activity.

Human spatiality is thus the existential structure revealed in de-distancing behavior directed toward the objects of our environments. Assignments and references may change, but the range of a region will never be reduced to nought; as long as our concerns continue to have significance, we shall live the conditions of reaching out to bring something close by. All distinctively human activities are directed toward an end, and this directed character belongs to the de-distancing function of an action. The intent of an act is toward a region from which our de-distanced entities are brought close—to us. Consequently, to our de-distancing activity belongs a necessary directionality.

Special signs are developed, as tools, for indicating direction: an arrow, or a vector, serves nicely to illustrate the point that movements are directed toward objects of circumspective concern and from there back once again to the sign-reader himself. Certain tools, such as gloves, considered as equipment for warming or protecting the hands, cannot be used unless they are oriented in parallel to a human being's spatial orientation to right and left, whereas others, such as hammers, need no such orientation. In each case, however, the prospective use determines the orientation.

Finally, an office or a private room oriented and arranged in such a way as to allow one set of living habits to be expressed becomes something quite different when, unbeknownst to its owner, someone else rearranges the objects within it. The reason: a world having been outfitted in accordance with the exigencies of one's own circumspective concern has lost both directionality and de-distanced spatiality. Such a world is both confused and confusing and is in need of repair.

How is the scientific concept of space derived from one's lived spatiality? The answer is composed in three stages, but only two of them interest us here. Heidegger's contrasting of his own version of a priori reasoning with those of Descartes and Kant—which provided an objective and a subjective accounting for space, respectively—adds little to the demonstration. Heidegger's first meaningful step is to review our knowledge concerning human spatiality; and the second, to show how our knowledge of lived spatiality is converted into the sciences of space, through the modifications of an attitude as our practical concerns are changed.

First, the summary. Whenever it poses the ontological question concerning its own being, a human being discovers that it is already living in a world that is revealed in the totality of its involvements. The world itself is disclosed as a structural totality from which entities have been freed for involvement, that is, have been assigned a position within a use-structure. In its self-projection within the world, a human being discovers a region defined by its concerns, in which entities serviceable for its purposes have been de-distanced and directed toward the unique end of that being's continued existence. In the directed de-distancing of the equipment in its world a "space" is co-disclosed with the entities themselves.

This "space" is not the three-dimensional world of Descartes but the structure of the human being's organized region. De-distancing and directionality give form to the region, the "whither" of the pulsating thither-hither tendencies of human action. The entities permitting such action belong to a total structure of referential assignments ultimately closed by the human being itself, for the sake of whom the action is undertaken. As these entities are de-distanced and given direction, space is announced in the lived spatiality. With respect to their placement in the instrumental complex, room is made for and space is given to the functioning tool. Because there are regions of concern, things may be moved around, out of the way, or set into place.

When spatiality becomes a theme for cognition, however, circumspection changes into inspection. Some tool has failed in its functioning; what was familiar, but inconspicuous, has become strange and conspicuous. Things out of their assigned places cause confusion, which forces the change in attitude. As the very term *geometry* indicates, calculation and measurement have historically preceded the purely formal science of space. Early geometers surveyed and marked boundaries, as, for example, one kind of *géomètre* still does in France.

As we know, surveying, calculating, and measuring were at first purely practical arts and not cognitive sciences. Our cognitive sciences arose when, in inspection, a human being could merely look at the region in which the malfunction occurred. "Placement" gave way to the concept of "place," which was definable without regard to the tool's or the object's having been assigned its proper place in a system of involvements. The concept of a homogeneous space became possible with the abstraction of the thing from its placement; things became figures on a homogeneous ground, which, in itself, formed a multiplicity of positions for the placement of random things.

But there was a corresponding ontological loss. The significance of the original human world given to circumspection was reduced to a region, itself inconspicuous within the totality of one's initial involvements. The structure of these involvements revealed entities serviceable as tools; and in the failure of one or more tools, these entities lost their inconspicuousness and became idle, mere things occupying an inert space.

As a scientific construct, space becomes a basic parameter for determining the nature of the purely natural world. This same space, defining the possibility of an infinity of relative positions, had already been announced in the human world of involvements but was merely not taken as a theme for abstract awareness. The exactness or the precision of the spatial sciences—plane, solid, and analytical geometry and trigonometry—derives from this abstraction from a humanly felt significance.

But the question remains: just how exact do our measurements have to be for there to be a human world? And the answer is still blowing in the wind—as exact as some task requires. Human worlds were human before any attempt to measure distance, be it from there to here, or from hither to yon.

For anyone sneaking into such a place, the next question is, "Who goes there?"

4

The Who and the How of Being-in

A HUMAN BEING ALWAYS FINDS ITSELF EXIST-
ing in a cultural world. So much has been established by the phenomenological analysis of worldliness, significance, and the spatiality and
space of those entities capable of understanding their involvements.
Outside the earlier reference to the "my-ownness" that guaranteed
an ontic access to the ontological structures of the thinking human
being, little has been said about human subjectivity, and, surprisingly,
practically nothing at all about consciousness.

Along with the reversal of the Cartesian notion of space into
existential spatiality, however, it should come as no surprise that
there should be a corresponding reversal in the notion of a soul-
substance Descartes had brought forward from the Christian Middle
Ages. Both Cartesian substances—the extended things of the natural
world and the coexisting thinking things—suffer the same ontological vagueness. For example, if the soul is considered as a perdurant
identical something capable of taking on changes of inessential or
accidental properties depending upon the physical circumstances of
its placement in the world through its relationship to its body, it is
still known by its presence to self in an act of reflection. A thinking
self is both subject and object of cognition. That indeed was the force

of the *cogito* argument. Although as substance it was an a priori, by experience we could know only the contingent circumstances of our embodied souls.

Moreover, as that which was thought to underlie the contingent experiences of the human animal, the soul-substance was considered as subjacent to those experiences and as constituting the basis for our being subjects. But a subject is not necessarily a self. That notion came from another property of substances—that of maintaining selfsameness (identity through change), however great the changes might be. But the selfsameness of the thinking substance was likewise a postulate of the *cogito* argument. Personal histories, which are likewise selves, offer little of the necessary properties established in the Cartesian deduction because, tied to worldly events, their only necessity is to be contingent.

In order to reground the ontology of the ego, knowing subjects, and personal selves, we must answer two questions here: What existential structures are to replace the outmoded categories of substance and attribute? And once this question is posed, the old familiar one must be asked: How can we gain access to the knowledge that would constitute a successful answer? Given the forestructure of interpretation already established, we shall not be asking what an ego, a subject, or a self is, but: Who is in the world? and: How?

The clue for the reversal is to be found in the contingency of our personal histories. In Heidegger's world, contingency is the mark of an ontic situation. Ontically, we always find ourselves already in a world; that is our facticity. And facticity is a structure of human being that, ontologically considered, is always mine. That is one way in which an "I" may be given; but like any other purely ontic condition the givenness of even my own ego, for the very fact that it is my own, stands in need of ontological clarification. Descartes' analysis of the indubitability of the ego's existence gives ample proof that we can be mistaken concerning the ontological significance of an act of our own thought. What would be the case if the human being I am is in fact not I-myself?

The question is asked in section 25 of the text, because in a later section Heidegger explains just how it is possible to act in such a way as not to be oneself. Indeed, on the average our everyday existences exhibit no other structure than that of not being ourselves. How can this be understood? First of all, by a change in the basic conception of a human subject. If we take the sense of the word *I* to be automatically given, whether in the manner of Descartes or Kant or of our ontic familiarity with our own being, the resulting intuition is only a formal indicator of a subject of possible experiences. Does such an ego correspond to what is disclosed in our everyday concerns with the objects of our environments? Not necessarily. The *I* may be, in the words of Arthur Koestler, "a grammatical fiction."[1] And in its abstraction of content it may indicate quite the opposite of a subjective self, as has been argued by Sartre in *The Transcendence of the Ego*.[2] A purely psychical self may be an object possessing dispositional properties, such as states and traits, and expressing itself in its acts. As a result of such a conception, the self as object of (impure) reflection, the acts attributable to the subject of experiences are still referred to a perduring substance. The ontology of reflection within the self as both subject and object needs further elucidation.

We may begin that elucidation with a reminder that no human being exists in a cultural world alone. An "I" without reference to others is without ground even in contemporaneous studies of social psychology, which treat of the self as a social construct.[3] The reason is quite simple in Heideggerian terms: no human being exists outside its (cultural) world, and no cultural world exists for a single individual. The clue for the interpretation of various cultural worlds lies not in the essential determination of a being that may become acculturated but in the fact that a human being's constitution is determined by its manner of existing in a world it already shares with other human beings. If to have an ego is constitutive of human beings, then our being someone rather than another must be given its existential interpretation.

Heidegger begins his case in earnest in section 26, which is on existing with others and our everyday being-with. The description begins with recalling the structures of significance within the framework of human worldliness. Our everyday being-in-the-world is a context of significance established within an environment by a system of signs and references. In such worlds, acting entities are what they do:

Im umweltlich Besorgten begegnen die Anderen als das, was sie sind; sie *sind* das, was sie betreiben.

In the world of our environmental concerns others are encountered as what they are; and they *are* just what they do.[4]

Although the quoted sentence opens the next section, it is given as a conclusion to Heidegger's discussion of being in the world with others.

ON THE AVERAGE and in an everyday manner we tend to encounter other human beings, whether or not they are physically present within our field of action, as participants in the world of our concerns. If we work, we produce something for use—write a book, something for someone to read. If we need something, we go to the nearest shop where it may be bought. Ships, automobiles, planes, rockets—all indicate others in the way a sign designates an object. True, the other so indicated may not be actually present to us; and it is never, ethically speaking, a tool to be exploited for our own purposes. Neither are they, as Sartre would have it,[5] a transcendence to be transcended, or another self with whom I may enter into conflict, although both these behavioral patterns are possible.

Other subjects are freed from a system of involvements much in the same way a bare tool may be freed from a system of involvements. But this is only to say, once again, that they have already been encountered environmentally in my circumspective concern. A true solipsist can have no nationality and most certainly could never have been born. Since an acting person knows itself through its acts, in what it does, needs, expects or avoids, it knows itself in the context of its environing world wherein it may propose actions over which others may have the final disposition. No one goes into the world alone.

Attempts such as the one by W. von Humboldt[6] to explain the significance of the personal pronouns by reference to locative adverbs (I, here; you, there; he, yonder) remain controversial; such attempts find formal reference points within an act of conversation but fail to give the ontological clarification necessary to understand conversation as a phenomenon of a human region wherein the here and there are reversible. Others are revealed within a region of human spatiality but as that region is structured into a system of involvements—of whatever nature. No one need be present, as in a conversation, for someone to be aware of another person. The absence of a loved one is more strongly felt than an occasional or perfunctory presence of the same person. But someone may be missing only on the basis of a preontological understanding that others share our worlds. Being-with, therefore, is a component structure of worldhood.

Along with this additional structure, Heidegger adds distinctive modes of concern and a variation on the theme of circumspection as fitting our awareness of the existence of others.

If *besorgen* is translated as "taking care of" or "being concerned with" the entities of our environment, the proper term for our concern for others is *Fürsorge,* translated by Macquarrie and Robinson as "solicitude."[7] The term in ordinary German may be used as widely as simply "caring for," as a mother cares for her child, or as "social welfare," by which a state cares for its citizens. Ontologically, the term names a way of being in the same world with others.

Heidegger notes two opposed ways of expressing our solicitude for others. We can jump in for another and assume the responsibility for the actions of that person. We do this as parents for our children and as teachers for our students. The unfortunate result of this mode of caring for others is to produce dependence on the part of the cared-for and a possible domination on the part of the caring individual. But children learn to assume their own responsibilities, and students sooner or later learn to think for themselves. In such cases, we are said to leap in ahead of them, for the purpose of giving back to the objects of our solicitude a responsibility that is all their own. In our counseling, we do not choose for the other, we limit our action to pointing out the alternatives for a personal choice, insofar as we ourselves are capable of perceiving them.

Circumspection, with respect to the existence of others within our worlds, is either considerateness (*Rücksicht*) or forbearance (*Nachsicht*), each of which indicates a way in which the existence of another has been viewed. Both have their opposites, and both have deficient modes. Thus, inconsiderateness of the wishes of another and perfunctoriness in the performance of a duty are found on the other side of an evenhanded indifference to the rights or wishes of another.

In our everyday being-with others, indifference to those others is as good a "proof" for the existence of other persons as the knowledge we are supposed to have by empathy. "Feeling ourselves into" the situation of another is hardly a proof for the existence of other minds. I may see a body in my visual field acting in a certain way, and I may recall myself acting in similar ways. What follows therefrom? That the observed body is guided in the way I felt myself guided in similar circumstances? Hardly, although that is what the theory claims.

Heidegger's objections are posed, as would be expected, on ontological grounds. First, that human beings relate to themselves in an act of reflection is an assumption without ground. Our being toward others is an autonomous and irreducible characteristic of our being in a human world; and this is understood preontologically, not in an act of premeditated analysis. Finally, the empathy theory seems to have been invented to overcome the deficiencies of certain of the modes of our being with others in a common world of culture: it is as much a prescription for overcoming the moral effect of indifference as a description of a way for knowing others.

What, then, is the proof that there are other minds? The question is badly posed. Other persons are not disembodied minds; and, as entities freed from a system of involvements, they have already been constituted as structures of our worlds. As such, they need no proof, only phenomenological description, and that has been amply supplied.

Heidegger's excursion into our being with others is not primarily given to show that one need not argue with a solipsist. Rather, it is a step in his attempt to show that one may be concerned with the things of one's world in such a way as not to be oneself. Others are met in our worlds, as cited above, by what they do. They help us; they hinder us; or they are indifferent to our very existence.

In our everyday actions, although we too are what we do, we never meet ourselves in the same way, precisely because we project ourselves as that for the sake of which our actions are performed. To be self-conscious always has its negative effect. As a modification of our being in the world with others, to be concerned for ourselves is to be concerned with our difference from others who are not ourselves and represents an action that covers up our being with others in anxious solicitude. In this way, concern for self is characterized by an existential distantiality ("Abständigkeit").

But to insist upon one's distance from the other—be it that of "above" or "below" or merely "equal to" the other in a social arrangement—is a way of subjugating oneself to the other. The mechanism is simple: if the I is not the Other, then we can know ourselves only as a function of that other or those others, without our being able to state just which other person is the cause or the reason for our subjection. For the most part, the others are those who are there, with us, in our worlds. Who they are is an irrelevant question:

Das Wer ist nicht dieser und nicht jener, nicht man selbst und nicht einige und nicht die Summe Aller. Das "Wer" ist das Neutrum, *das Man.*

The who is not this one nor that; not oneself nor some others, nor even the sum of them all. The "who" is neuter, the indefinite, impersonalized subject.[8]

Under the force of convention, for example, everyone acts as "one" acts; to do otherwise is to make a show of oneself. One merely says what everyone says in a similar situation. "I feel fine," for instance, when I actually feel rotten, because I know the person who asked me how I am is not asking for a report on the state of my health, but merely acknowledging by his question my presence in his world. Acting conventionally in this way, as we all must in the average social situation, we act in such a way as not to be ourselves.

But we do act; and in accordance with the principles of the indefinite, impersonalized subject, in a world stripped of any personalized significance. Such a world is average, in which everything to be known is already known, and nothing is of primordial concern to anyone in particular. Everyone does what "one" does, says what "one" says, is what "one" is.

As a result, the everyday world of the conformist becomes leveled down to the rule of the average. Possibilities of being outside the range of the prearranged are merely not considered, as they are not called for, not needed for continued social action.

The three characteristics of the impersonalized world mentioned above—distantiality, averageness, and leveling down—constitute a fourth: publicness. As being the property of everyone, the public world becomes that by which everyone's existence is interpreted. Since no one questions the meaning of a "rule" of the conventional world, no one gets to the bottom of anything.

Moving on the surface only of such a world, everyone feels the disburdening effect of no longer having to make a personal decision; for in this world there is neither counselor nor counselee. Personal responsibility is lost and therewith the right to be oneself.

Lastly, following the least tendency to let things go as they may, the average person lets himself or herself be accommodated by the impersonal subject, which nonetheless exacts the price of continuing its dominion over the individuals it has absorbed.

In the world defined by such a subject "Jeder ist der Andere und Keiner er selbst [Everyone is the other and no one himself]."[9] And such are the conditions, indeed, by which anyone at all can act without being oneself. They are the ontological determinants for the "who" insofar as that existential is exhibited in our customary, everyday behavior. First and foremost reflecting the conditions of the impersonalized world, our everyday behavior is not our own ("eigentlich"); and we are not independent of the others, who for the most part are as dependent upon us as we are upon them.

Yet the existence I exhibit that is not my own is not merely negative; it is a positive feature of my everyday behavior, as I constitute myself in my acts. Like worldhood, significance, and spatiality, it is a primordial phenomenon of my being human and living in a cultural world.

The problem is therefore not one of explaining how I can act in such a way as not to be myself, but how I must act to recover the self I have lost by living in the world of the other. Beginning with the experience of everyday events, traditional ontology allowed the self—the true self—to be covered up by a concern for the things of the average world—the natural world that is the same for everyone, where distances and influences are measurable, and where there are no selves either authentic or inauthentic. Contemporary psychologists help us make this point by studying the maze behavior of rats.

To get out of the maze that is not of our own construction but into which we are thrown as surely as the rats in the psychologist's maze, we must be able to modify our behavior. If living in the world of the other, by the other's rules, is an essential structure of individual existence, then to be oneself a different form of behavior is indicated: from being lost in the world of the other, we must project a world of particular significance to ourselves. Indeed, we must insist upon our right to be creative. Being a true self, being one's self truly, is such a creative projection, an *existentiell,* or ontic, modification of the world in which we merely find ourselves every day.

And on this subject, much more is to come later. For the present it suffices to point out, against Descartes, that instead of constituting a substantial ego held to be identical throughout a series of changes, a true self manifests its selfsameness only on the basis of a gap, on the possibility of recovering itself from being lost in the world alongside the objects of no one's concern.

AS WE TURN from the "who" of everyday being in the world, the argument continues against Descartes' version of the human soul. Instead of being attributes of a substance that underlies them, thinking, feeling, and speaking are manners of being-in as such. In this way, being-in is to be demonstrated as a structural component of human being on all fours with being alongside the entities of its world (concern), being with others (solicitude), and being or not being oneself (who). Like these other phenomena, the new existential must be revealed as a constitutive characteristic of the human world we have already brought into our forehaving.

Indeed, it is in these sections that forehaving is first brought into explicit discussion. I have introduced the notion earlier, the better to follow the method of my author and to permit my readers to view his text as the specific application of the methodology of hermeneutics detailed in section 32. In this way, I was able to claim that the book contains an explanation of a set of methodological procedures by which the text was written and a prescription for reading it. There is no mystery here: interpreting the significance of one's world is one way of being in it.

Perhaps no further mention need be made of the fact that the term *in* of *being-in* does not indicate a relation between mere things of the natural world, each of which is capable of including or being excluded by the other. We must keep our attention on the humanness of the human world and on the difference between the way a thing of nature is *there* for our perception and the way an existing human being projects itself from here to there, opening a region within which to be.

The *da* of *Dasein,* the German word for existence or human being in Heidegger's restricted sense, we are reminded in section 28, is ambiguous, meaning both "here" and "there." In projecting itself from one factical situation into a possibility of being in another, the existent human being opens itself up to a new significance, a new world. This openness, from the German word *erschliessen* (to open, unlock, disclose, conclude, infer, and the like), gets translated as disclosedness, because an essential characteristic of human spatiality is its *Unverschlossenheit,* its not being closed in upon itself.

Always open in its self-projection upon new possibilities of being, a human subject discloses itself within its characteristic spatiality as a clearing that lights up the "places" established within its system of involvements. The "sight" this clearing permits is none other than our basic "circumspection" *(Umsicht);* and all other seeing, whether ontological or merely ontical, whether "looking after" others in solicitude or merely using our eyes to inspect the objects of nature, are behaviors made possible by this existential structure.[10]

Heidegger uses the metaphor of a clearing ("die Lichtung des Da"), extrapolating from the context of forestry. Woodsmen clear a forest by removing the more spindly trees, along with any undergrowth, to allow the more vigorous trees to achieve maximum growth. Fewer trees allow more light to penetrate the forest. What gets removed in the existential sense of clearing, as a human being projects a novel significance, may not be luminously clear itself, unless it be the objects of the always present real world of nature, the removal of which opens up a region of truly human action. However this may be, the clearing of an original self-projection is the basis for the natural-light metaphor used to explain the ontic effects of being conscious.

If there is a "natural light of reason" by which a rationalist, such as Descartes, could come to prove his own existence, the light of that reason is only an ontic reflection of a human being's ontological openness. That openness is called disclosedness because the being exhibiting it discloses itself as already understanding its essential connection with a world of significance. That, we recall, was the "preontological comprehension" we all have of our own being and without which there could be no fundamental ontology.

In the remainder of this discussion of the "how" of our being in a world, there shall be three lines of development: (1) human disclosedness as affectivity, understanding, and discourse; (2) discourse, affectivity, and understanding in the everyday world of "one's" being there; and finally (3) forfeiture and thrownness.

1. Human disclosedness.

Heidegger begins his discussion with an analysis of *Befindlich-keit*.[11] Macquarrie and Robinson render the term as "state-of-mind," which is certainly close enough, but which leaves open the suggestion that Heidegger's ontological conception of human being is concerned with bodies and minds, as was Descartes'. "Affectivity" is less specific in its application to minds as opposed to bodies; so I shall use it.

A human being is always in some mood; happy or gay (merry), sad or in a blue funk, even only bored. In its moods, the human being feels how it is, or knows how "things" are going: well or badly. Feeling the mood, not just having it, is a way of being delivered over to its being here and now, in every purely ontic situation. We may even be in a mood the whence and whither of which remain totally in the dark. But the point of ontological analysis is not to discover causes or reasons for behaving as we do; that is the work of empirical psychologists, whose characterological or typological charts, treating of human beings as if they were things in the natural world, must here be beside the point.

Ontologically, a mood accompanies our being thrown into our worlds, of our already being there when someone asks us how we are or how we feel, or when we ask ourselves the question of who we are. Our facticity is to find ourselves delivered over to some world. Whence, the source of the German term, *Befindlichkeit,* from the usual question into our being: *Wie befinden Sie sich?* The translation "How are you?" gets to the ontological core of the matter but fails to reveal the fact that we know how we are (if we do in fact) by the mood in which we find ourselves at the moment of the question. *Befindlichkeit* is affectivity; as such it is the tone, the qualitative feel, of being thrown into a world.

Certain moods are interpreted as threatening; they induce flight, an evasive turning away, which may avoid the sting of one mood only to throw us into another. We are told we must master our moods, especially the "bad" ones. Why is anger usually referred to when we claim someone is in a bad mood? Boredom is an all-engulfing mood, so terrible in its essence that Baudelaire could get out of it only by writing a poem depicting it. A "moody" personality is one given over to quick changes in its moods.

Any mood reveals the whole of our being-in-the-world. With respect to the context of our worldly involvements, a mood will yield possibilities for directing ourselves to the specific tools functioning or failing to function at a particular moment. The serviceability of our tools and their resistance reveal how our worlds turn and in consequence how we feel. We may even live in constant fear that someday our worlds will no longer turn. How we are touched by the things of our worlds reveals what matters to us.

In a word, our bare moods reveal to us the nature of our worlds in a way no theory of human behavior can. What we have a sense for, what cuts to the bone, what leaves us flat, is revealed through a mood. To develop a theory for such things is merely a deficient mode of letting the world matter to us, a positive attempt to escape what really we cannot help but be, because we feel it so.

The philosophical treatment of affect and feelings, says Heidegger, has not been improved upon since Aristotle's *Rhetoric.* The reason, we might surmise, is the connection Aristotle points out between a context of linguistic expression and an affective tone communicated through it. Our surmise is based upon the connection Heidegger asserts between affectivity, understanding, and discourse. *The Rhetoric,* of course, is a purely ontic consideration of *pathe,* as was Descartes' *Treatise on the Passions.*

What improvement there has been on Aristotle's handling of the public management of feeling through discourse would appear to be, in Heidegger's opinion, *Being and Time* itself. For he says,

> Die phänomenologische Interpretation muß dem Dasein selbst die Möglichkeit des ursprünglichen Erschließens geben und es gleichsam sich selbst auslegen lassen. Sie geht in diesem Erschließen nur mit, um den phänomenalen Gehalt des Erschlossenen existenzial in den Begriff zu heben.

> Phenomenological interpretation must make it possible for a human being to disclose its world primordially and at the same time to interpret itself. It enters into this disclosure only in order to raise the phenomenal content of what has been disclosed to a conceptual level, and this existentially.[12]

Whatever his personal intent, these words obviously apply to the intent of his text. But they apply equally well to the recent developments in humanistic psychotherapy; to the works of some aestheticians, who have not lost their taste through the effects of a bad theory; and to a possible methodology for literary criticism. The move from an Aristotelian rhetoric to a Heideggerian methodology of literary criticism is compelling but as yet has not been clearly worked out, although the problem has been broached by Paul Ricoeur.[13]

One of the reasons for this phenomenon, of course, is that Heidegger goes on his merry way with the analysis of fear as a distinctive but inauthentic way of being in the world. The other apparent reason for this text is that few of our contemporary critics have grasped the connection between human disclosedness as existentially interpreted and the writing and reading of a literary text. I shall attempt to fulfill this need in the final chapter of this text, after all the dead trees in the forest have been cleared away.

Heidegger chose fear as his example of affectivity because it is common and easily analyzable, and because it has certain affinities with anxiety, which is less common, but which nonetheless is definitive for an authentic mode of feeling our being in the world. The contrast between fear and anxiety will be made in the sequel.

The tripartite structure of fear comprises confronting that which we fear, the fearsome; the fearing itself; and that about which we express the fear.

The fearsome may be anything within a human world, as long as it is viewed as threatening. It may be something merely present, something possibly useful, or another human being; in each case we already possess the explanation of how such entities are isolated from the environment: by inspection, circumspection, or solicitude. Whatever it is, the threatening thing is seen as detrimental to our system of involvements, since it is viewed within a definite range, near to or far from the fearing subject. The region is well known, since it is given in circumspection and established in the totality of the subject's involvements. It is distant, not yet in striking range; yet it seems to draw closer as the fear grows in strength. The fact that it may still pass over, like a threatening cloud, makes the detrimental object all the more fearsome since the indefiniteness of the outcome with the fearsome object enhances its fearsomeness.

The fearing, our experience of the fear itself, may root us in a spot or force us into evasive action. Since the fear is our apprehension of the fearsomeness of the detrimental object, it is circumspection that discovers the detrimental qua fearsome. In a bygone day and in another idiom, the fear would be called the "subjective correlative" of the pattern of detrimentality in our system of involvements. Self-confidence in the face of such a chain of events would not be bravery, but foolhardiness, a deficient mode of caring for oneself. When one is a Trojan, one has the right to fear Greeks, even when they arrive bearing gifts.

Lastly, what the fear is about is the being of the fearing subject or, as in the case of the Trojans, the sanctity of their institutions, symbolized by the solidarity of their beloved city's walls. But alas, fear is always private; the prophet's words went unheeded. Her fear was for her being-with her fellow citizens, and they remained self-confident, while she suffered the second indignity of becoming the mistress of Troy's conqueror.[14]

Fear has numerous variations: alarm, a sudden onset of fear accompanying a modification in circumspective concern; dread *(Grauen,* not *Angst),* which is felt in the presence of an object that is both threatening and unfamiliar; terror, or alarmful dread. Other feelings with marked affinities to fear are shyness, timidity, misgiving, and startled surprise. Apprehensiveness, the monkey on Woody Allen's back, is not always funny, but it is common and sometimes incurable.

Fear, like any other feeling, gives us something to understand—about ourselves and about our worlds. Understanding, indeed, stems from the same source as feeling, the opening of an existent being to its world. We are not talking here of a specific human faculty persons may possess and use with more or less skill in constructing explanations for observable situations; that sense of the term is derivative and is obtained by a series of ontic modifications. We are still talking about a structure of a human being's openness to its world.

A human being finds itself thrown upon possibilities of being, as that for the sake of which a complex of involvements has been elaborated into a world. Worldhood and significance appear simultaneously as the integrated structure of the involvement complex bounded only by the here and the there of the cleared region. Finding itself thus thrown upon its own possibilities has both ontic and ontological explanations.

Ontically, we say that someone understands his world when he is able to pull something off, or is "up to" the performance of a feat, or competent in his relations with the entities of his world, both those that exist and those that are merely possible in the sense of "conceivable." Ontologically, these ontic conditions are permitted by the existential determinants of human being. "Doing something," "living a choice," or laying out a possibility by projecting it as the future eventuality of a living present—such possibilities are not merely conceived as non-self-contradictory; they define a human being's immediate self-projection. In this sense a possibility, too, is an existential, a structure of human existence and of it alone.

The significance of a purely human world is the result of human choice. As that for the sake of which a world has been elaborated, the human subject is delivered over to a world in which it must act. Whenever it reflects upon its situation, it is always already *there*, within the region of its burgeoning concerns, disclosed to itself both as mood and as the (preontological) understanding it has of its own being, as having to be what it already is as a possibility. It can, of course, go astray, fail to recognize itself, and act in such a way as not to be itself.

Living in the world of the impersonal subject—as "one" does for the most part every day—is to fall into the state of not being one's self, a condition Heidegger calls *Verfallenheit*. We read, with Macquarrie and Robinson, "falling"[15] as a condition of the human being whose persistence as a self has deteriorated in the way I have described.[16] Even acting as a self that is foreign to itself, however, a human being is in a world.

Our understanding of that world is of a totality of the possible interconnections within the instrumental complex from which the entities, in their serviceability, usability, or detrimentality (as in the case of fear) are freed for possibilities of continual or modified involvements. How is this to be understood ontologically?

The analysis is as follows: an understanding is a projection (*ein Entwurf*) by which a significance comes into being. The projecting (*Entwerfen*) is the activity of a human being that has found itself abandoned to its world, whose significance is felt as a mood. In the mood that determines its being so abandoned, the human being projects itself toward a possibility of being that it already is, qua possible. In this understanding self-projection, the choice of an action lets the possibility be; and that is the only way an action can be called human rather than caused by some external nonhuman cause. In this way, a human being is always more than a mere phenomenon of the world of nature; but at the same time, it is never less than what it is not yet as a matter of fact.

It is for this reason, too, that self and world are correlative notions; as that for the sake of which a projection has been made, the human being discloses itself at the same time its self-projection lights up a world. The "light" here again is not the natural light of reason but the clearing—the primordial *lumen naturale*—by circumspection, solicitude, and the other forms of "seeing," that are equivalent to understanding. The person who suddenly exclaims "Now I see!" is not necessarily a blind man suddenly cured of his blindness nor a sleeping man who suddenly opens his eyes; the terms also mean in ordinary English, "Finally, I understand."

But what do we understand, when we are reflecting on the ontological conditions of our own existence? Heidegger answers the question in the final two paragraphs of section 31. In the immediate self-projection of a human being, being itself gets understood, either the being of the world of involvements or of the self as the ultimate for the sake of which involvements are made. The connection between self and world is revealed in a mood, but that mood need not be interpreted ontologically.

Indeed the preontological comprehension of our own being, which was dogmatically presupposed at the beginning of Heidegger's inquiry, by the hermeneutics of the question, is here revealed as involved in any instance of self-projection by which a human being "lights up" its world, that is, by which the phenomenon of significance as the peculiar mood of a particular world allows itself to appear—and the appearance is to the self-projecting self.

Having a mood, a human being sees possibilities and understands them as determinant of its own being. Its most peculiar possibility, qua human, is to be delivered over to its thrownness, its necessary connection with a world. That is what is disclosed in the spatiality of its region, in its own being, stretched between a here and a there (*Da!*). How this understanding gets interpreted in a concrete case of ontological analysis is the subject of section 32 of the text, but it is also an example of the methodology exposited therein, a fact long noted, but not yet assimilated, by literary critics.

Interpretation in German is *Auslegung*—a laying out of the possibilities brought into sight by a human being's self-projection. By its mood it has found itself in its world, feeling the significance (*Bedeutsamkeit*) of the world brought to light by its directedness toward the future. In this way, both affectivity and understanding, as constitutive moments of a human being's self-disclosedness, and as given in the preontological comprehension of its being, stand behind every act of interpretation. Circumspection discovers a world already understood; it is this world, co-disclosed as a phenomenon with the human self-projection, that gets interpreted in an act of interpretation.

Interpretation makes explicit what circumspection has already found implicit in human being. The involvements lit up by the self-projection as a chain of somethings "in order to . . ." may be laid free and viewed as a series of moments, each illustrating or isolating the "in order to," which becomes an "as" of interpretation. The meaning of this "as" may eventually be generalized into a way of "seeing" something as anything at all; but with respect to the meaning-giving event that is the worldliness to the human world, it is always a connection previously established in a context of involvements. The "as" of interpretation merely makes clear what has already been experienced as the significance of a world in an act of circumspection. That is, the interpretation only makes the implicit connection of a system of involvements an explicit element of human knowledge.

But making explicit what is implicit is itself a constitutive element of human disclosedness. A statement of the connection between a subject and a predicate, such as "That hammer is too heavy," merely expresses what has been made explicit in a prior act of concern with one's working environment. The tool is not first simply there as something to which a putative purpose has been added; one has already been engaged in an act of practical concern when the tool is found to be too heavy for the job at hand. Instead of saying to his helper, "The hammer is too heavy," a do-it-yourself carpenter or plumber might express the same content by saying, "Not that one, the other." The world of practical concern is primarily that of the tinkerer, who ready-reckons his way about his world, and not that of the engineer who manipulates the mathematical formulae expressing the laws of the natural world. What gives sense to the "as" of interpretation in the practical world of bricolage?

We have known the answer to this question from the beginning of our inquiry. Human understanding is a circular structure by which what is given as a preontological comprehension, and therefore as only implicit, gets laid out into a system of explicitly understood ontological connections. The entire progress of this commentary has been built upon this assumption, now being made the object of analysis. Behind every interpretation is the forestructure of understanding.

This forestructure, as pointed out in my introduction, consists of a forehaving *(Vorhabe)*, a foresight *(Vorsicht)*, and a foreconception *(Vorgriff)*. The English translations of each of these terms sound strange until they are related to the ontological analysis of worldhood given above.[17] Both *Vorhabe* and *Vorsicht* are used to express an intention, but *Vorsicht* adds the implication of premeditated care; and the *Griff* of the *Vorgriff* is not so much a full-fledged concept as it is an anticipated meaning already understood, prior to any act of conceptualization.

The *Vorhabe* expresses a field of general intent; at its most basic ontological level, the context of involvements "understood" as a mood in a human being's necessary connection with its world. Once that context has been analyzed, however, the results of the analysis will have been reintegrated into the context, with a resulting adjustment in what the investigator has before him.

The *Vorsicht* is a particular intent by which a tool that has been freed from a context of involvements gets separated from its "in order to." The *x* so separated is therefore seen in circumspection as having been connected with, yet is interpreted as being separable from, its function. Its use-value may be predicated of it, but is already "seen" in advance of any specific act of predicating, as in the example of the hammer above. The particular intent, or foresight, picks out something in its connection with something else. This connection is the existential hermeneutical "as." As such, it is always given in advance of a particular act of interpretation.

The *Vorgriff* is the anticipated meaning by which what has been sighted out of the initial context is understood. To understand something by interpretation we project it upon the totality of our involvements, indicating its "place" therein. The "as-structure" of interpretation merely repeats the "forestructure of the understanding" in a particular ontic situation.

How can we be sure of their interconnection? By the mediating term *meaning (Sinn)*.

When it is called upon to make an interpretation, a human being already has a complete forestructure, grounded ultimately in the preontological comprehension of its own being and the mood by which it understands the significance of its world *(Bedeutsamkeit)*. Entities disclosed in a human world are said to have meaning *(Sinn)* in that they may be projected upon what is already understood as significance.

What is understood in this projection, however, is not strictly speaking the *meaning* of an entity but the entity itself or its being, depending upon whether the analysis is ontic or ontological. The meaning is the fittingness of the entity into the scheme defined by the totality of involvements; it is that which maintains a certain quality of intelligibility *(Verständlichkeit)* and which ultimately can be disclosed in an articulation of this intelligibility.

The forestructure of the understanding supplies the ground for any such articulation. A particular object is seen as fulfilling or not fulfilling a specific purpose. That is what gets expressed in the sentence, "The hammer is too heavy," which merely gives expression to the meaning already laid out in an act of interpretation.

Expressions *(Aussagen)*, which are a derivative mode of interpretation, have their own as-structures, called "apophantical" by Heidegger, pursuant upon his interpretation of the being of a phenomenon. The apophantical as-structure of expressions still precedes any account of "minding" as a form of discourse. The distinction between expressions and sentences corresponds roughly to that between judgments or propositions on the one hand and statements on the other. Heidegger rejects the notion of a judgment as being too idealistic to convey what he intends by *expression*. A statement is a string of words by which one claims to state a fact; the facts stated in the claim, as understood, are the propositional content of an expression. The content of an expression, however, always derives from a prior act of interpretation, which reflects a human being's openness and therefore its connection with its world.

Expressions are known, by what they assert, according to their structural form. They point something out, for which reason they are called "apophantical"; they predicate something as a property of what they point out; and they communicate the linkage between subject and object of predication to someone else. As a result, an expression is defined as an act that points something out and communicates it as having a definite character.

This total structure, like that of the interpretive as-structure to which it is related, is projectable onto the forestructure of the understanding. It requires a forehaving of whatever is disclosed in the assertion—the subject of attribution; the predication aims at, or specifically intends, a sighted predicate given in the foresight; and the predicate is conceived beforehand by virtue of a familiarity with the significance of the context.

Expressions, then, exist prior to any purely linguistic statement or even a logic to determine their proper form. They have meaning because they exhibit the forestructure of the understanding and not primarily because they come to be stated in well-formed formulae. Ordinarily, the foresight of an expression aims at (intends) the material of the tool that has been freed from a context of involvements—the hammer, for example, inspected as a mere thing—and characterizes it. This characterization, by virtue of a foreconception, is the ontological basis for the linguistic notion of a predicate, as well as of the physical notion of a property.

To understand this move from the forestructure of the understanding to the apophantical-as of an expression, however, it is necessary to recall how an original circumspective concern, which reveals a structured instrumental environment, is modifiable into an attitude of attentive inspection of the properties of the things merely present before us in a deficient mode of environmental concern. Expressions are here viewed as the activity by which this modification has taken place.

Within the tradition, both Plato and Aristotle are said to have misunderstood the function of expression as apophansis. For Plato, the structure of the logos was exhibited in two sets of real objects, a string of words and an order of facts each reflecting the meaning of the other. Aristotle, it is claimed, discovered the ambiguous function of the "is" in an act of predication, as both relating the subject and predicate terms of the expression and as affirming the truth of their relation. He also noted that the *synthesis* and *diaeresis* stated in affirmative and negative judgments respectively are involved in both kinds of judgment; but he could not, of course, relate these peculiarly linguistic phenomena to the structure of intelligibility based upon the being of a human subject, since his categorial system had no place for the being of an instrumental complex experienced as a world. As a result, Aristotle's theory of interpretation is expressed in categorial rather than in existential terms; and substance took precedence over human activity as the grounding principle for the interpretation of interpretation itself.

DISCOURSE *(Rede)* is the articulation in language of what has been given structure in an expression, and like affectivity and understanding before it, it constitutes a manner for a human being to be in its world. The means of discourse is language, the totality of words and their preestablished significations in which the discoursing human being has its innerworldly being.

Language is something we are all born into, a phenomenon of our being-with others in a single cultural world. Its being is as a tool for communicating with ourselves and others, and involves both speaking and hearing. But our speech is not limited to acts of predication; commands and wishes likewise communicate something of our shared worlds.

Speech manifests the same tripartite structure as the forestructure of the understanding, the as-structure of interpretation, and the apophantical-as of expression: what is talked about *(das Beredete)* is what we have before us; what is talked to *(das Angeredete)* is what has been sighted out of the context of our worlds; and, finally, what is said *(das Gesagte als solches)* is the anticipated meaning of our words, relating the "subject" and "predicate" of the expression given in anticipation. Upon inspection, "the hammer" is "heavy," and that is what is revealed in the sentence itself.

What gets communicated in the process of speech is the significance of the world initially brought to light by our being in it. The traditional metaphor for speech as the externalizing of something that is internally felt or understood perpetuates a metaphysical distinction between bodies and minds not corroborated in this ontology. When a human being expresses itself, what it shares is a characteristic of its world; and its means are not limited to the conventional words and significations of its inherited language. In order to express itself, and not just what pertains to every person in a given culture, it disposes of the whole panoply of rhetorical devices: intonation, modulation of the voice, tempo, and characteristic manner of exposition. Poetry, which makes maximum use of these devices, is the means *par excellence* of communicating one's personal existential possibilities, and not the least, in its lyrical form.

Since the usual ontic treatments of discourse, from logic and linguistics to the philosophy of language, deal with speech acts, expression, symbolic forms, and the sentences exhibiting speech acts as a way of comprehending the ways of life portrayed through them, the ordinary ontic treatments of linguistics give us only a partial treatment of our worldly knowledge; a truly ontological treatment of knowledge, which had as yet only been called for by the failures of history (including the attempts of Plato and Aristotle, who had no concept of language at all outside that of the *logos* itself), will attempt to fill in the continuity of human disclosedness from affectivity to discourse, following the structures of the hermeneutical whole herein completed. It will include such behaviors as hearing, hearkening, speaking, and keeping silent.

Who talks too much, for example, communicates nothing; a taciturn person, on the other hand, may communicate the very essence of his being. The difference is, once again, between a talking subject who is not himself and one who is capable of revealing the significance that attends his being in a world. That indeed is what talk should be about. To understand speech as a co-disclosure of a manner of being in a world perhaps there is no better model than poetry, whether lyrical, narrative, or dramatic.[18] Poetry at its best is authentic discourse; reading it allows us to share the authentic characteristics of a truly personal world.

2. *Disclosedness in our everyday worlds.*

Having just laid out the structures of a human being's openness to its world, Heidegger can run through the characteristics of our everyday existence very quickly. He dedicates one section each to discourse, affectivity, and understanding of the self that is not itself.

Compared to the discourse of the poets, that of the plain person is idle talk *(Gerede)*. *Gerede* is chatter, but it is not meaningless; for it reveals the average understanding of plain talk. What comes to be revealed in such discourse is still a way of being toward what is talked about, the forestructure of an understanding that just happens to be average. And what is said, as such, the anticipated meanings of the language used, does not result from a projection of a foresighted element upon the structures of an authentic world. Instead, "meanings" are presented as they are fixed in dictionaries, untied to the exigencies of a unique context of significance. As a result, circumspective concern has given way to a partial revelation of the qualities of isolated elements.

The communication of such information is gossip, merely passing the word along about what everyone already knows. In this way, everything may be claimed to be understood in our idle talk, but the sophistication that usually accompanies such a claim wears off as quickly as the alcoholic effects of the cocktail parties at which such discourse abounds. The effect of idle chatter is to close us off within the conventional rather than to open up a significant new world.

The conventional use of language nevertheless gives something to be interpreted. If poetry must be read to be understood, conventional prose is capable of depicting a world that everyone can come to know. Such is the world of nature, revealed through the significations of ordinary or scientific languages. That world too needs interpretation and reinterpretation, as the state of the arts by which we relate ourselves to that world change following the discovery of something new.

Heidegger says of all average understanding:

In ihr und aus ihr und gegen sie vollzieht sich alles echte Verstehen, Auslegen und Mitteilen, Wiederentdecken und neu Zueignen.

In it, and out of it, and against it all genuine understanding, interpretation and communication, all rediscovery and any new appropriation is performed.[19]

For this reason, no doubt, to communicate the mere results of an experiment is to engage in intellectual chatter and to communicate the significance of those results is to relate them to the conditions under which they were discovered and to the new possibilities they may portend for a useful life in the future.

This requirement for a true understanding of what gets communicated to us in dictionaries, scientific encyclopedias, and the like, reflects the ontological preconditions of any understanding whatsoever, what Heidegger called the forestructure of the understanding that results from being in a world. If such a connection with our worlds is lacking, what gets talked about in intellectual chatter may be anything at all considered in any light at all.

Conventional discourse is idle because it is ungenuine discourse, leaving those who engage in it unrooted in a meaningfully shared world. The groundlessness of any claim to knowledge that leaves a human being unrooted in its world can only be overcome by heeding the call to criticism. And that criticism for Heidegger bears the name *fundamental ontology*.

Parallel to discourse as idle talk is affectivity as curiosity. The talk that is about everything everyone already understands expresses a very human state of mind, here intended as such, the eagerness for the new by which *curiosity* gets translated into German as *Neugier*. The curious person, like the cat with eight lives to lose, is avid to see everything. Sight, of course, is a privileged way of knowing, associated with both the ontological structures of a human being's clearing a world for itself and with its ontical tendencies surveying the nature of its world in continuous acts of perception.

It was no idle talk of Parmenides to have pointed out that knowing (perceiving) and being are the same thing; nor of Aristotle to have stated that all men by nature desire to know; nor of Augustine to have noted the more universal employment of the verb *to see*. Each of these traditional philosophers was calling attention to a human being's basic disclosedness.

What everyone had failed to note, however, is that once circumspection has been freed from involvement with the instrumental complex of our purely cultural worlds, our concern comes to rest, since it lacks the limitations set upon it by the goals of work. But the "resting" circumspection retains its de-distancing properties of its existential spatiality, so "seeing" is in this form a manner of distraction; the purpose of any looking is just to see. Instead of tarrying alongside the entities of its world, therefore, the curious human being allows its attention to drift everywhere its desire for the new directs it, that is, to nowhere in particular. And what it sees in this attitude gets expressed in idle chatter.

Idle talk and an unbounded curiosity make it impossible to have a true understanding of human worldliness. The understanding they do engender is therefore ambiguity (*Zweideutigkeit*). The two possibilities of interpreting the curious world of idle chatter reveal the following dilemma: either, by the effects of conventional wisdom, everything already seems said and therefore understood, and yet is not because we are curious to see something new; or, by our curiosity, everything does not seem understood, yet is because all we can say about what we discover is what has already been said by someone else. A vicious paradox, indeed.

The self-defeating character of our "openness to the everyday world" is likewise apparent when we realize that what everyone says is what we are impelled by curiosity to find out. But once that happens, there is no longer any room for surmise. Not only are the genuine and the new already out of date when we come upon them, but "one" already understands and has stated what the result of any investigation has to be. And whether we are talking of events or of other people, gossip and surmise are taken for reality.

Camus's *The Stranger* illustrates beautifully the degree to which an unconventional person may be estranged from the world of conventional wisdom, tyrannized by the society closed in upon itself, and ultimately dying in the name of its laws, because he could not understand the necessity of living by them.[26]

3. Falling (forfeiture) and thrownness.

With the disclosedness of the impersonal subject in the everyday world Heidegger's account of the relationship between a human being and its world approaches the point of summary, which is given in section 38 of the text. He notes once more that a human being is always thrown over or abandoned to an actual situation, by what he had earlier termed "facticity," or the "factuality of the fact of human existence," which understands its destiny as being tied to the being of the entities that surround it. This understanding of its "being in the throw," however, remains a structure of the disclosedness by which a human subject *is* its there—as a projection upon possibilities.

These possibilities may be the possibilities offered by the conventional world, in the projection toward which a person is not its own self; or they may be those of a uniquely significant world: the creation of a self that is its own. We recognize again the initial existential alternatives of being or not being oneself. Whichever is the nature of the self expressing itself, a world is revealed in the action. The acting self feels its thrownness and understands itself as the projection it is. Between the past of its having always already been thrown and the future of an as-yet-unrealized possibility that it may become, the human subject finds itself in a present. When this present is disclosed in the manner of our everyday being-there, our ontological condition is said to be "Falling" (*Verfallenheit*).

The language is clearly metaphorical and conjures up some purely ontic interpretations that must be shunted aside. Existential falling is not from some prior state of grace that can no longer be recovered, nor from some expected millenium that we might attain if only we change our behavior. The fall is indeed from something—a world revealed in idle chatter, curiosity, and ambiguity. Such a world, we have seen, is without ground; it comprehends everything, which is to say, anything at all; and it allows the human beings inhabiting it to be everywhere, which is to say, nowhere at all.

Heidegger refers to the activity of falling from one's true self to an identification with the objects of an impersonal world—or from an authentic understanding of ourselves into the duplicities of ambiguity—as a "downward plunge" (*Absturz*). Recall the characteristics of the impersonal self: distantiality, averageness, leveling down, publicness, disburdenedness, constantly accommodating. Experiencing our being-with-one-another in this impersonal way, we enter the plunge into the world of Everyman.

The characteristics of our *Falling* are similar to those listed above. Being in such a world is *tempting,* owing to our being disburdened by adopting the attitudes of an impersonal self; it relieves us of any personal responsibility. Second, since nothing in this world is not understood, we become *tranquilized* by the removal of all doubt and personal anxiety. Third, since it is doubt that motivates the ontological questions such as "Who am I?" "What am I doing?" "Why?" and these are obviated by the first of our two characteristics, the condition of falling becomes exacerbated until the acting self is *alienated* from its own true possibilities. Fourth, since the alienation of self from self closes off the authentic possibilities for human action, the fall becomes *entangling*. And fifth, since there is no ground for the world into which one is falling, the fall of the self into an essentially foreign world is *turbulent*.

Is there an escape? Yes, the very turbulence of the downward plunge is a fact of human "thrownness," and may be felt as disturbance, an affective condition that calls for a liberating understanding—as one bored guest said to another at a cocktail party: "Let's go to a quiet bar and have ourselves a beer!"

AND ON THAT note our forehaving is prepared for a new interpretation. Having begun his analysis with being-in-the-world and moved on to its constitutive structures, worldhood, the who, and being-in as such, Heidegger moves next to bring back into foresight once more the total structure of our being. Being-in-the-world as constituted, even on the basis of an everyday understanding, is care. Whoever goes there into a purely human world goes there caring.

How do we know? Asking the question itself is a form of caring. And once again it is not the what, but the how of the behavior that counts.

5

Care and Caring

Die Sorge TRANSLATES AS "CARE." WHY THEN
the gerundive in my title? The difference is small, perhaps, but real.

Having divided the basic constitution (*In-der-Welt-sein*) of human
being (*Dasein*) into three structural moments—worldhood, selfhood,
and being-in—each enjoying the same level of primordiality as the
other, each stemming from the same source, Heidegger becomes
aware of a problem of narration in his phenomenological account of
our being human. Have we become lost in the composite details of
the overall structure? And if so, is there a way to pick up the thread
for an account of the whole? The total structure is not something
that can be understood by a process of summation; it was for this
reason, we remember, that the world of nature cannot be experienced
as a phenomenon. The totality of a human existence is not, moreover,
anything that may be definitively described in this first part of the
treatise, which contains only a preparatory analysis, based upon the
average and everyday character of a human life.

The whole we are seeking to describe is not to be constructed of
elements, since it is qualitatively different from the sum of its parts.
To be understood, it must be given, as a phenomenon is given, as a
whole. For the same reason, we are given no clue for an interpretation
of the whole from the perception of the events of the natural world:

116

the ontology of human beings is fundamental and prior to that of the things of nature. Nor, lastly, can the being of human beings be deduced from an anthropological conception of humankind; that would be to deduce the ontological from the ontical.

Although Heidegger uses the term *care* to refer to the phenomenal whole he is seeking to describe, without due care on our own parts we may be looking for a static summation, a blindly enduring condition, as life is a blindly enduring condition of a human animal undergoing a series of experiences from the moment of its birth to its death. If we recall that the significance of a life is in its living, we shall have no difficulty with my substitution of the gerundive for the substantive. Caring is something we do, not something we must suffer. Heidegger, of course, agrees, as when he says:

> Daß Seiendes von der Seinsart des Daseins nicht aus Realität und Substanzialität begriffen werden kann, haben wir durch die These ausgedrückt: *die Substanz des Menschen ist die Existenz.*

> That an entity existing in the manner of human beings cannot be conceived on the basis of reality or substantiality has been expressed by the following thesis: *the substance of man is existence.*[1]

At the very beginning of his treatise, where the pronouncement came as an item of dogma, *"Das Wesen des Daseins liegt in seiner Existenz* [The essence of human being lies in its existence],"[2] he had said the same thing, only interchanging the categories of the tradition to make his point.

It was Descartes, of course, who, in his *Discourse on Method,* urged the solution of any complex problem by its division into simple components, each of which is to be solved on its own. Then, if only the enumeration is complete, by induction one might claim to have solved the initially complex problem.[3] Besides illustrating the quantitative bias of the Cartesian methodology, by which wholes are considered as merely the sum of their parts, this sketch of an analytical method may be found in practically every rhetorical exercise submitted by students of a French lycée, no matter what the topic. Perhaps for this reason the French are in a better position to understand the current predicament. What happens if the complex whole

I am seeking to describe is qualitatively different from the sum of its parts? And what if I can never be sure that my enumeration of its simple parts is complete?

The answer is simple. I merely change methods, even if this means abandoning the established metaphysical grounding that had been adduced to support the questionable method. In the case of Heidegger, whose method is phenomenological and whose analyses are hermeneutical, there is merely another application of the forestructure of understanding. The forehaving of an interpretation has undergone many a change from the initial preontological comprehension of our being as different structures of human existentiality have been sighted out for phenomenological interpretation. Each of the prior analyses has enriched our view of the human predicament, given us new concepts for describing the totality of our existence as simply "caring." Thus, with a slight shift in the forestructure, the narrative begins anew.

In its last condition of being in the world, we left human being falling, away from itself, toward the publicness of the impersonal world of everyone. In questioning the unity of this being, we are still interrogating its spread, its being laid open between a past, as always already having been thrown over to its condition—that is, its facticity, and a future which is as yet only a possibility defining what it might still become but toward which it projects itself—that is, its existentiality, even in the present moment of its falling. The average condition of a human being as it exists every day is therefore both falling and disclosed, thrown and projecting.

Even as an impersonal subject, however, acting as the self it is not, a human being projects itself upon its own potentiality of being that remains an issue for its ultimate ontological concern with both self and world. In the world it always finds itself alongside entities of one sort or another, either those of its circumspective concern or of its scientific inspection, and with other human beings in a culture shared by all. Such indeed is the picture of our human condition drawn in the preceding sections of the treatise.

Can this whole be grasped; and if so, how?

The access to the totality structure begins by recalling that an understanding of being belongs to a human being's disclosedness, here interpreted as affectivity and understanding in their equiprimordiality. Can the whole of a human existence in its fallen state be grasped? Yes, if there is truly a cognitive feeling for our attachment to our worlds, one which constitutes a ground phenomenon by which our care-structure is made manifest as both a whole and our own. That ground phenomenon is anxiety. But since our investigation is to be ontological, we must expend due care to avoid confusing anxiety with fear, or with other ontical states with which it is often associated. Fear has already been given structural analysis as the paradigm case of our being related by affection to the entities of our worlds. In section 40 of the text anxiety is similarly analyzed.

THE DEMONSTRATION begins with a new characterization of falling. Falling into the publicness of the impersonal world is a fleeing or turning away from a truly personal self. How in such a condition can a human being come to grips with its own personality? Sometimes, fearfully; as it shrinks away from those objects of its world or those of the impersonal world that appear threatening to it. In turning away from the threatening object, we find ourselves in the state of fear. But fear is still ontical, and derivative from the more primordial ontological condition we are seeking to describe.

At the same time falling is into a public world it is a flight from oneself as a self-determined entity. What a human being flees from in its falling is its ownmost potentiality for creating its own world, its being in the world as self-determined. Thus, unlike the case of fear, in which we flee from an entity of our world, in anxiety that in the face of which we are anxious is our own being-in-the-world.

The truth of the matter is that there is no "object" from which we flee. Ask the person feeling anxiety what the matter is, and you will receive the answer, "I don't know." Is there a reason for the feeling? None that is apparent. It merely engulfs one; its causes remain indefinite, being neither here nor there, indeed *nowhere*, as places are determined within the instrumental complex that determines the significance of an anxious person's world.

Still its being-in is disclosed in the feeling itself, and along with that disclosure, the insignificance of the world; that is, in our anxiety the world appears without its entities and without the structural relatedness of their significance. Nothing, no-thing, coming from nowhere within our world determines our anxious state. What we flee in the face of, in anxiety, is thus the bare world revealed as the condition of our own potentiality for being in it.

In sum, then, our anxiety is conditioned by a state of our being-in-the-world as thrown; and the turning away of our falling into the public world is from ourselves revealed in the uncanniness of the anxious feeling. So much for that before which we feel anxious.

The next step parallels the analysis of fear by indicating "that about which" we are anxious. But again, unlike the case of fear, we are not in anxiety anxious about any definite kind of being—as, say, the possibility of being hurt by an approaching car. Indeed, here once again nothing definite carries the burden of determining the anxiety, since the objects of one's world, the total instrumental complex, are without significance: only our possibility of being in a world and the necessity of making a choice for the kind of world we should like to call our own can bring us out of the tranquilized temptation offered by the familiarity of the impersonal world. Such is the second condition of our personal anxiety.

Falling and anxiety are related as the flight from self reveals what a true self must be: a possible being that will not be unless one chooses to accept responsibility for becoming that being. That about which we are anxious, in a word, is our being-in-the-world qua possible and qua our own.

To summarize, once again, in anxiety a human being is anxious before its being-in-the-world as thrown, about its being-in-the-world as projected upon its ownmost potentiality for being itself. Anxiety individualizes the human responsibility, since it reveals a way of being in the world when the nature of that world is yet to be determined and when the ultimate determination of that world must be made by a personal choice. No other person can make the choice of a self for me; nor as a moral subject will that self be determined by the things or processes of the natural world. Insofar as it reveals the necessity of my choosing, anxiety constitutes the most basic sense of the "solus ipse," that for the sake of which assignments of significance have always already been made.

Why, then, are there so few authentic personalities in the world? And why is this "distinctive determination of human self-disclosedness" so rare a phenomenon? To answer these questions there's a clue to be had by the everyday language—another form of human disclosedness. We feel "at home" (*zu Hause*) in the familiarity of the public world into which we are falling. Anxiety, which we flee in the forfeiture of our fall, is deeply disturbing or, as *unheimlich* is usually rendered, absolutely "uncanny." And the uncanniness of this feeling is accompanied by equally disturbing physiological effects: clamminess in the hands, aphasia, spatial disorientation, and the like.

What then is the precise relationship between falling and anxiety?

The feeling of uncanniness is merely the obverse condition of feeling at home in the tranquilized and familiar world of everyone. Ontologically, Heidegger claims, the not-being-at-home is more basic than the fallen state, because ontically the reverse is true. Sometimes it takes up to the third martini at a cocktail party before the uncanniness sets in; and then one cannot be sure if one is not merely drunk. Whatever is the case here, there seems to be no ontic explanation for the uncanny feeling, and the physiological components of the experience of dread seem to depend upon the feeling of the uncanny placement of the self before a future possibility.

THE RARITY of true anxiety has two explanations. First, the condition remains hidden in the ordinary state of fallenness; and second, its ordinary ontic manifestations—other than the physiological— reveal subtle modifications of the caring structure when it is one's own self, rather than objects, tools, or other selves, that is the object of the care. Before ourselves and on behalf of ourselves we can only feel anxiety.

Heidegger summarizes the condition in section 41. There we are reminded that anxiety and other affective conditions are manners of being in the world; and equiprimordially with this feeling there is an understanding—which before was preontological, but which now is ontological: the being of the care structure is now defined as a human being's concern for itself as both thrown-being-in-the-world and existing potentiality-for-being-in-the-world. Prior to ontological reflection this "understanding" is our feeling of the anxiety. In reflection, it is easy to compare the two conditions of the same self, that of being thrown into some world and that of being projected toward another. The original anxiety thus corresponds to our own sense of being free for determining our ownmost potentiality.

As existing, a human being is ahead of itself; but, as being in a world, it finds itself alongside other entities—tools and mere things— and in solicitude for others; and it does so knowingly, since when the ontological question occurs to it, it is always already factually related to some world. In sum, then, our being human is a simultaneous threeway stretch: as projected, ahead of itself; as thrown, already in a world; as falling, alongside entities of one sort or another. Since, ordinarily, we concern ourselves with the entities of our worlds rather than with our own precious selves, the basic human state of anxiety remains covered up.

To understand how this basic ontological feeling gets lost in ordinary concern and solicitude, we need only consult the modifications in the care-structure that make possible the obversion of familiar at-homeness into the uncanniness of anxiety. Heidegger considers four conditions, each of which brings the subject closer to, yet still at a distance from, true anxiety. He considers willing (*wollen*) and wish-ing (*wünschen*), addiction (*Hang*) and impulsion (*Drang*). I shall add a fifth, which gets a little closer yet to the subject totally ill at ease with itself for no apparent external reason: compulsion (*Zwang*). All these activities and states exhibit a distinctive care-structure.

In willing, for example, an entity is seized upon as projected upon its possibility—as being of concern or as something to be brought into being through solicitude. That is the something willed. But something can be willed only on the basis of ultimately being pos-sessed, which brings to the fore that for the sake of which the object is willed. This latter entity, which is the human being itself, has already been revealed in a prior disclosure, along with the world as the wherein of its being-already-there. The activity of willing is ac-companied by a feeling of expectation or fulfillment as the human being continues to project itself understandingly toward a future in which the entity willed is a possible object of concern. Expectation or desire is always ahead of itself, already in its world, and alongside the object, as the possibility that calls it forth.

Wishing is tranquilized willing, or willing in the mode of the public world. The accompanying feeling is less intense because the world in which the wishing person finds itself is less clear, its objects less considered. In this act, the subject still projects itself forward but with less conviction than the willing subject, since it has a weaker grasp of the factual possibilities inherent within the world. Indeed, it is possible for a wishful person not to know what it wishes; and in its completely fallen state, it gives itself over to a mere hankering after something (*nachhangen*), such as the pickles hankered after by pregnant women in the middle of the night.

Addiction (*Hang*) is another matter. In this modification of the care-structure, being-already-alongside the object of one's drive takes precedence over being ahead of oneself. One merely projects oneself as one has been. Instead of "living" its world, its world "lives" the human being.

Impulsion drives the human being one step closer to self-oblivion. Experiencing this *Drang* is a projection to a single possibility at any price, including the exclusion of all other possibilities. But the motive force comes from within, not from without the organism. In impulsion the ego is on a rampage but loses itself in its attraction to a single thing.

In compulsion (*Zwang*), the world wherein the human being dwells diminishes, along with its objects, into a mere theater for its own inner expansion outward. It still projects itself upon an object that forces its attention, but that attention is paradoxically a contraction into an outward tension. For this reason, compulsion is most strongly felt when an impulse to action is frustrated or delayed. In face of the deferment of the action or of the mounting tensions to complete it, one is forced back in upon oneself now known simply as an "I must." If wishing is tranquilized willing, then compulsion is a fanaticized impulsion.

Who can forget the rendition of the child murderer played by Peter Lorre, in the German film, *M* (for *Mörder*), bent in upon himself, hiding his face with his hands, and crying out from the depths of his lost self, to whoever would understand why he compulsively slew the children of his neighbors, "*Ich muß! Ich muß!*" (I have to! I have to!)? Indeed, in the depths of such a compulsion there is hardly a difference to be perceived between the "*ich*" and the feeling of having to do whatever it is that one feels one has to do. That feeling is simply the whole of the subject of the moment. And being caught in the act adds a measure of self-alienating shame to an already soul-wracking experience.[4]

THE QUESTION occurs at this moment why Heidegger sets up a gradual approach to a self completely exposed to its anxiety without making the last and most apparent step. Our everyday compulsions are as close as we can get to the uncanniness of a self existing in an alien world. Why did he refuse to take the step to consider them?

To understand the import of the question, consider his prior analysis of being-in-the-world as worldhood, selfhood, and being-in as such. When being-in-the-world becomes caring, and caring anxiety, the predicament of human being may be represented as in figure 6.

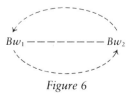

Figure 6

This is the same figure that started out as a diagram of "knowledge as a founded mode of being-in."

In this sixth projection of the relationships involved, Bw_1 represents human being as thrown, its always already being in the world; Bw_2 represents human being projected toward its ownmost possibility of being—this or that. I have left the two arcs and the straight vector in broken lines to indicate the abstraction of the authentic self from the attraction toward the public world toward which it "falls." In the "obverse figure" of the falling self, all the lines would be solid.

What is abstracted from, in figure 6, is the spatiality of a human being's region, its circumspective concern for its world, and the resultant clarity of its being defined as that for the sake of which assignments have been made in the totality of its involvements. The world sinks into the penumbral background of awareness when the familiarity of the public world gives way to the uncanniness of self-awareness as the feeling of not being a part of that world.

What then is left of human being's being-in-the-world? Answer: itself as thrown—always already there; ahead of itself—toward being itself, rather than an other; and now, no longer falling, but anxious to the roots before its being thrown and about its being itself.

But I must remind my readers that my addition of "compulsion" to the modified forms of the authentic care-structure was my own doing, motivated perhaps by the progressive degrees of awakening self-awareness suggested by the staccato beat of the linguistic progression, *Hang, Drang, Zwang*. In anxiety, the self is still in a world; but that world has been inverted into a frame within which an easy addiction may become an impulsion, and an impulsion a compulsion to realize oneself.

For this reason, Heidegger shows himself as a latter-day Columbus. Since he was out to grasp an answer to the question of the meaning of Being in general, he neglected to realize the value of his discovery of the self. Fearful in the extreme of being classified a "philosopher of existence," as is clear from his appraisal of the efforts of St. Augustine, Luther, and Kierkegaard to come to grips with the concepts of fear and dread,[5] he continued to pursue, without either humor or humility, his own relentless compulsion to grasp Being by its tail. That he thought he had done so is borne out by his explanation of caring as the "being" of a human being, whose meaning will be that upon which this newly foresighted structure is to be projected:

time. His project will come to a close, then, with a description of the temporalization of the human care-structure; or, as I prefer it, with the temporal modes of caring. To care is, in German rhetoric, a *Zeitwort;* it comes in all the tenses and, not being defective, is conjugated for all persons.

Relentlessly following his ontological reversal, Heidegger will continue to search out the meaning of this being, this entity that moves in mysterious ways, all the while calling itself human.[6] That we should be reminded of Columbus, who called the aboriginal Americans he discovered "Indians," may appear either just or unjust, depending upon our allegiance to his own ontological purposes or upon our admiration for his existential achievement.

His argument continues with the confirmation of his existential account of human being as care by a "preontological self-interpretation" of the phenomenon. The terms used to describe this move in section 42 of the text are not perspicuously clear in themselves. "Eine Bewahrung" is a confirmation all right, but how does a myth that was written in Latin and preserved as number CCXX in Hyginus's *Fables,* where it bears the title *"Cura,"* constitute a "preontological confirmation" of Heidegger's ontological analysis?[7]

If reading and writing are human modes of caring, then the composition of the myth, along with all its traditional interpretations, has as much right to the characterization "ontological"—in the sense of constituting an account of the being of an entity, in this case a human being—as Heidegger's own existential-ontological account as heretofore derived. Not so, says Heidegger. The myth is an "ontical," and in this sense "preontological," interpretation of human existence as care. But here we have to listen to the myth.

While she is crossing a river, Care notices some clay, with which she fashions an object. As Jupiter came by while she was contemplating her work, she asked him to breathe into it a spirit. And he did. But since Care had made the object, and Jupiter gave it the breath of life, each wished to have the object named for itself. Saturn, or Time, was asked to be the judge, when the Earth rose up to propose its name for the new creation; she had furnished the clay.

Since Time is the judge of all things, the unerring arbiter of what is good or evil, and Saturn therefore the wisest of the gods, it was agreed by all his decision was to be accepted. So, then, he decreed, let the creature be called man (*homo*), since his body was the gift of the earth as *"humus."* When it dies, its body shall be returned to earth; but Jupiter will receive its soul. As long as it lives, however, since Care has fashioned its body, man shall be delivered over to her. To each, his own; but only in its proper time. While it lives, the creature belongs to care.

Goethe uses the myth as he found it in Herder, according to one source, to structure the second part of his *Faust*.[8] Herder presumably found it in Hyginus. The fit between the ontic account of the myth and Heidegger's ontology was already suggested by Burdach, who was Heidegger's source. The personification of Care, in the myth, covers ambiguous attitudes, however: anxious exertion, on the one hand, and carefulness or devotion, on the other. These attitudes, claims Heidegger, represent the two aspects of a human being's being in the world, its abandonment and its self-projection, united in the cognitive affection of anxiety, as in figure 6.

The myth therefore contains a "preontological," read, "merely ontical," account of human existence. And, in a repetition of the pattern of relatedness between ontic situations and ontological possibilities, Heidegger explains that the ontological is no mere generalization over particular examples of caring, but an a priori structure of human being that makes possible experiences of one kind or another.[9] Every form of caring is a modification of the essential care-structure, whose meaning is yet to be determined by still another projection upon something we already understand—time, as grounded in our own temporality.

In this sense, of course, all ontological explanations that are not fully fundamental, as having their meanings grounded in the ontology of human being, would be "preontological." Heidegger continues to pursue his private India, answering the question of the meaning of Being in general, and so therefore digresses from the meaning of human being to discuss what he takes to be related topics—the "reality" of the real world, and the primordial sense of "truth."

Every student of philosophy recognizes these topics as old friends are recognized. It is for this reason I treat them in a chapter to themselves, under the title, *"Philosophia Perennis."* Except for these two topics, Heidegger's preparatory analysis of the meaning of human being is complete. Worldhood, selfhood, and being-in are equiprimordial moments of human caring, which reveals itself as falling or anxious, but in either way self-disclosed as abandoned in a world and projected upon its own possibilities of being, ultimately itself or not-itself.

What about the world? Traditionally, that is the question of reality. What about the truth by which we can determine the nature of self and world? Here too the tradition stands in need of confirmation or modification; reality and truth constitute two items for further analysis, two ways of caring, two ways of sharing our views of the world.

6

Philosophia Perennis

AS AN INSTITUTION, PHILOSOPHY HAS HAD the dubious distinction throughout the history of Western culture of being the first discipline to have been created for the purpose of investigating the nature of things. One by one, as the individual sciences gained greater insight and control over separate segments of their respective worlds—astronomy, geometry, physics, chemistry, and biology over the natural world, and most recently, psychology and sociology over the cultural world—there seemed less and less that could not be handled, at least in principle, by those specialists in positivistic thinking we have come to call by their specific name, when we wish to distinguish them from their fellows, with whom they share the honorific title "scientist." Thales, the first philosopher whose musings were recorded, was likewise an astronomer who dabbled with the question of the nature of things.

Physis, the Greeks called it; but if we were to translate the term as anything but "nature" as the Latin tradition did, we would most certainly fall into some well as deep and damp as the one that, according to some cynics, impelled Thales to proclaim that *physis* was water. His mistake was to have been looking at the stars just prior to his fall; and someone overheard his disgusted cry on surfacing, "All is water!"

128

When a theoretical problem has no specific "scientific" solution, it remains the possession of philosophers. For this reason, in spite of the increasing specificity of scientific progress, there are a number of problems that, being as general as they are, have no interest for scientists and so have remained the problems of philosophers.

It is often thought desirable to exposit these "problems" in terms of antitheses, since both sides of the questions have been steadfastly maintained by one philosopher or another in the past. The primacy of essence over existence, or vice versa; human freedom versus universal determinism; the relative worth of the substance of a scientific study as opposed to the method it must use to garner its results; man and his world; woman and hers—all may be trotted out at the drop of the question "Why this, rather than that?"

But if the questions of philosophy are perennial, the reason for their eternal recurrence need not be the inexactitude of their formulation, nor even the ineptitude of those who still take some pride in calling themselves lovers of wisdom. The love of wisdom remains the greatest of the intellectual virtues and, like all the others, seems beyond the scope of the scientific specialists' professional interests, if not beyond their ken as persons or citizens. Did not Thales himself very unwisely fall into that well while observing the stars?

Socrates—who was so great that the name given to the whole of philosophy practiced before him is *pre-Socratic*—was the first to stress the ethical issues of being in a world. He was the greatest of the Sophists, those vulgar rhetoricians of his day who accepted monetary recompense for instructing their students in the art of making the worse appear the better cause, just like any lawyer of today pleading a case. Socrates, of course, was condemned to die on this precise charge, along with that of perverting the youth by preaching the existence of an alien god that, upon inspection, turned out to be no other than his own conscience.

Heidegger will plead the case for conscience and human responsibility in the second portion of his treatise; here he indicates that reality is not only a problem of the "ontical" sciences but of philosophy as well. If, in falling in the well, Thales had fallen into ontology while engaging in one of the ontic sciences, the image is apt to represent the ontological difference Heidegger is seeking to perform. And from the time of Socrates philosophy has been an institution concerned with the cognition of the natural world and our rightful place within it.

Let us name a few of the philosophical questions that continually recur. Is it enough to appear to be just? Or must one really be just to live the life worthy of a human being? What then is justice? And what is the difference between merely appearing to be something and actually being it? Does the apparent progress of the individual sciences indicate that we are on the right track? Or do the recurring crises of our sciences indicate something seriously amiss? Questions such as these occur and recur, not because they are properly speaking not the business of the positive sciences, but because they are critical and reflective.

And they are critical in two senses of the term: first, as capable of defeating any intellectual enterprise, if they go unconsidered; and, second, as pronouncing a judgment on the appropriateness of any procedure of the positive sciences as fitting or not fitting the circumstances or the purposes of the investigation in question.

With the advent of phenomenology as a philosophical methodology, chiefly in the work of Edmund Husserl, Heidegger's mentor, philosophy became the study of the foundations for the physical and behavioral sciences. It is for this reason that Heidegger's "ontological difference" has been interpreted as it has. His fundamental ontology was to give a foundation for all purely "regional ontologies," Husserl's term for the specialized sciences. If space and time are dimensions of the natural world, then according to critical phenomenologists, those concepts must be given an ontological grounding.

We have already seen that space is grounded in (that is, its sense derives from) the spatiality of human being; and we shall soon have to show how time's sense derives from human temporality. We have also seen how signification derives from human significance, from the manner in which a human being is in its world; and knowing itself has been reduced to the founded mode of being-in-the-world. The philosophical questions occur and recur because questioning is itself a way of being in the world.

As long, then, as there are scientific claims to the truth about the natural world, there will arise anew those questions that meditate on the sense of our being situated in the world so described. The same questions in new circumstances generate new answers, and that is the reflective function of philosophical thinking. New answers generate differences between old concepts, and for this reason we no longer call physics "natural philosophy," nor psychology "moral philosophy," although these terms were current in the eighteenth century.

In sections 43 and 44 of his text Heidegger is merely taking into account the possibility of applying the results of his preliminary existential analysis of human being to clarify what is meant by the reality of the real world (studied by scientists), and what constitutes the truth of any scientific statement. So here again his study is philosophical in the sense of fulfilling the critical and reflective aims of the queen of the sciences.

I shall treat of reality first, and of truth in the sequel.

According to the tradition, the question of the reality of an external world, as well as of the things therein, encompasses the objects of perception, the tools of a cultural world, and the subjects for whom these objects exist. Stated from the perspective of the fallen kind of being a human being exhibits as it loses itself in the natural world, to be is to be present to some observing consciousness. And there is no difference in the determination of the reality of the things of the world and of those subjects who attempt to manipulate those things or merely contemplate their presence. What is real is present to our consciousness, either directly in perception or indirectly through an act of reflection, by which the observing self becomes an object to consciousness.

Three theses are conjoined in this traditional metaphysics: the ontological priority of substance over any of its attributes; the transcendentality of being, along with its convertible notions (e.g., thing, something, truth, and goodness); and the equivalence of mind and matter as processes of nature. The first is ancient, stemming from the Aristotelian doctrine of the categories; the second, medieval, as the continuation of Aristotelian hermeneutics; and the third, relatively modern.

At this point in his demonstration, Heidegger seems satisfied that his readers understand the difference between the ancient categories and his existentials, as differentiating the being of nonhuman from that of human entities, as well as the difference between any kind of entity and its being. For the medievals, we recall, being and its convertible notions were "transcendental" since they could not be defined as any natural species could be defined: that is, by being classified into a proximate genus and as possessing an essential difference from the other species of the same genus. Being, as the highest genus, cannot be fit into a higher proximate genus, and so could not be defined. For this reason, "reality," the ontological characteristic of things (*res*), was an indefinable notion. The reality of "real things" (this latter a redundancy) was established by their presence to some mind.

All this, of course, remains ontologically obscure; and Heidegger proposes to clarify the obscurities by a threefold analysis: (1) reality as an epistemological problem; (2) reality as an ontological problem; and (3) reality and human caring.

1. The epistemological problem.

Can the existence of an external world be proved? An examination of the question is sufficient to understand why the history of philosophy has suggested so many different answers. In what sense is the world external if not present to some consciousness? And, if present, whence the necessity for proof? But the world, in the sense of nature, is the sum of all natural events, both actual and possible, and cannot for this reason be present, qua world, to any natural consciousness, which is but a part of the world.

When such questions as these occur to consciousness, the "existence" of a world has already been established by the phenomenon of human worldhood, that is, by the significance established in the totality of involvements by which a human subject lives its relationship to its world. Knowing, we established above, was a founded mode of being-in a world. What, then, does the question seek to find out? It can only be posed by a human being; and every human being, in its disclosedness, already understands, implicitly, what it means to be in a world, at least preontologically.

Ontological analysis has revealed that a human being and its world are co-disclosed in every human action. The care-structure, which is the being of a human being, makes this eminently clear; ahead of itself, as a projection upon its possibilities of being, from its placement already in a context of involvements, a human being exists alongside the entities of its concern. If this is the way we all exist, then to ask for proof of an external world is a mental aberrancy.

Oddly enough, the attempts for such a proof have not been lacking. Consider Kant's refutation of idealism.[1] Kant maintained that the absence of the proof for the existence of the external world was a scandal for reason and attempted to remove the scandal in the context of his critical idealism. The "idealism" he is refuting is the naive notion that the objects of the world are mere congeries of "sensible ideas" as per Berkeley and Hume in the tradition of British empiricism.

Kant accepts the premises of these empiricists, that ideas of external objects occur to an observing consciousness, and that these ideas are observed by reflection to change through time. Time, as the form of the inner sense, yields a sequence of changing impressions of a "same" object, which remains what it is in spite of the changing impressions associated within consciousness as being of such an object. Space, as the form of the outer senses, constitutes the object as a pattern of coexistent points, which remain the same throughout the changes noted by the inner sense. The changes within and the permanence without fulfill the requirements of one definition of substance: that which perdures throughout a series of temporal or historical changes. Whence, then, the "proof" of the permanence of spatially defined objects? As always in Kant, by transcendental deduction. I am given the series of changing impressions through the inner sense of time. Since a change implies permanency in what undergoes the change, the permanency of the external object is the condition for the possibility of the changes undergone within me. And in this way, the permanency of the objects of the outer sense constitutes the very possibility of my perceiving the series of impressional changes occurring within me, as given to my inner sense of time.

But the argument is fallacious. What undergoes a series of changes in our perceptions of external objects is not the external form of the objects themselves, but my consciousness of that form. So, if we accept that change implies permanency, as Kant does, the most we would have shown is that the changes of my perceptions establish the permanency of my consciousness, which has had the perceptions. Nothing follows therefrom for the permanency of the external objects. Instead of refuting idealism, Kant's argument establishes one version of it.

According to Heidegger, Kant's argument fails because it assumes a concept of time that is ontologically unexamined. Since this concept of time can be established only through the functioning of the inner sense, it "proves" only that the events transpiring "in me" and those transpiring "outside me" are both present to my consciousness: those outside directly; and those inside, indirectly, through reflection. But two sets of events present to consciousness cannot establish the phenomenon of our being-in-the-world, which is already "under-stood" in our every act of caring.

Kant, of course, was fighting the skepticism of David Hume, who blithely admitted that the existence of an external world was something not susceptible of proof. When Hume was in his "closet," reasoning on human nature and our ability to know anything at all,[2] he was assured only of the impressions that "arise in our souls from unknown causes." But when he was seated, playing backgammon with his friends, he found it perfectly safe to take the existence of the external world on faith. Unfortunately, however, as Heidegger points out, to accept something as true on faith holds out for the possibility of an eventual proof. All that is established by our "animal faith" is the practical limitation it places upon our epistemological skepticism.[3] Besides, our animal faith is nothing more than our acceptance of the founded nature of "knowing" and being-in-the-world.

The same grounding is assumed for our knowledge of an external world by those who, like G. E. Moore,[4] claim that such knowledge is presupposed by the simplest of our actions. You say you doubt the existence of your hand (as Descartes did in the first of his *Meditations*, applying his dream hypothesis), but it's there: "See!" "It's there" and "You only need to look to see it" express with a degree of sanguine conviction unfounded by the circumstances, perhaps, the idea that every human being understands, at least preontologically, that it already exists, caringly, in some world.

Such is the grounding for the so-called realism of phenomenology. The thesis of realism—that natural objects exist independently of our perceptions of them—is upheld by the factual co-disclosedness of a human being and its world. No proof is needed for the existence of such a world because its ontological foundation is already clear when the question of a possible proof for it is posed. The scandal for human reason is not that a proof for the existence of the external world is still lacking, but that anyone should continue to think that such a proof is necessary.

Yet there remains some point to the "idealist thesis" Kant was attempting to refute. He was rightly disturbed by the "naive" idealism of Berkeley and Hume that ended in epistemological skepticism. But there is another form of "idealism" that is not irreconcilable with the realistic thesis explained above. There can be a reality only for an entity that understands, both itself and other entities; for the "reality" of an "external" object is its presence to an inquiring subject. Without some disclosing agent, nothing can be disclosed.

This argument does not claim that the real object exists only because it is observed; it claims only that the reality of the object, its presence to a subject, depends upon the existence of such a subject.

This second form of idealism one might call "ontological." It claims that being can never be confused with beings, and can never be explained by them; it is, rather, the transcendental limit for every possible entity. A thing is what it is, but its being (i.e., its presence) can only be understood by another kind of thing. For this reason, the idealistic thesis of Heideggerian phenomenology necessitates an inquiry into the being of that other thing we call a human being.

By now it is clear that this inquiry has been developing from the beginning—under the name of a fundamental ontology.

2. The ontological problem of reality.

If the phenomenon of human worldliness is basic to the understanding of any significance whatsoever, as Heidegger has maintained, then the ontological problem of the reality of the real world can be explicated only in terms of the care-structure by which worldhood, selfhood, and disclosedness have been synthesized into a single concept of human being. If reality is a problem, it is a problem for those human beings who attempt to cope with their relationship to a world already given in their every act of caring—either for themselves or for others or for the things they encounter through circumspection or inspection.

For the moment, Heidegger looks beyond his own theory in search for a precedent to begin the newer inquiry. Kant won't do here: things-in-themselves as putative structures of the real world have been bracketed out of the inquiry since the middle phases of Husserlian phenomenology.[5] That is, in order to ground his epistemology in the certainty of the phenomena of consciousness that show themselves as they are, it was necessary for Husserl to reduce consciousness to its acts (noeses) and its meanings (noemata), which could be inspected by a reflecting consciousness. In this process, the "real" world is bracketed out of relevance for determining the significance of any lived event. But this is to say nothing more than what phenomenologists have always claimed: phenomenology is a study of phenomena, and there is no good reason to suppose that there is some noumenal "something" beyond what actually appears to an attentive consciousness. In perception the objects themselves are given to consciousness.

The two followers of Husserl cited by Heidegger are Dilthey and

Scheler;[6] both phenomenologists he refers to as ontic theoreticians, that is, quasi-scientists, for the reasons which follow.

Dilthey, of course, is more interested in phenomenology as a philosophy of life, the basic phenomenon to be isolated and expounded, than in an ontology, or philosophy of being. It is for this reason that his work is called "ontic" and, as such, only a beginning for a more basic kind of analysis. Attending only to the phenomenon of consciousness, he states that an act of will and any inhibition to that act are given simultaneously in any feeling of frustration, and that the measure of reality—as opposed to the willing consciousness—is the resistance things (*res*) place upon our designs to manipulate them. Reality is therefore what resists human activity or opposes our will.

The positive portion of Dilthey's essay, says Heidegger, is his treatment of human experiences in both descriptive and analytical terms. Resistance is not something purely physical, as experienced in an act of touching, but "psychological" as well. What resists our volition is psychologically registered as an inhibition. This point had been made at least a hundred years before, by the French philosopher-psychologist, Maine de Biran,[7] but Heidegger fails to note the precedent. Instead he asks, what is the nature of this emergence in consciousness of the relationship between willing and being frustrated, however slightly? What, indeed, is it to be "inside" consciousness? Dilthey ignored these questions, since his stated "principle of phenomenality" limited him to a study of the effects of consciousness in the course of a life.

It was Scheler, primarily a moralist, who considered the phenomena of knowing in the fuller context from feeling to understanding. In effect, knowing something of the world is a relationship of being with respect to that world, and not primarily a judgment concerning the properties of objects encountered within that world. Although Scheler considers existence as an innerworldly phenomenon of being present-at-hand, rather than as a projection upon a future potentiality for being, his theory of existence is "voluntaristic" ("eine 'voluntative Daseinstheorie' ");[8] it claims, as did Maine de Biran, that I am because I will, and that objects are known as they resist my attempts to manipulate them. In this way, the being of external objects is given simultaneously with our drives and the working out of our wills.

Although he notes that the discovery of resistance is important for the history of phenomenology, granting that resistance is a basic phenomenon of living and that feeling the resistance of objects is a way of "knowing" them as being in our worlds, Heidegger is unwilling to let the matter lie there. What, indeed, is resistance?

From the existential point of view, a felt resistance is the encountering of an object in such a way as "not coming through" to an end we have proposed: a simple matter of our not bringing something off. But if this primarily negative function of an encounter is the resistance of innerworldly objects, then they must already have been disclosed by an act of circumspection in which the encounter had previously been intended. Ontologically, the care-structure always intervenes between our present awareness of a problem and any answer we may project for it.

Because it is a projection upon some future potentiality for being, a human being meets objects that may inhibit its trajectory. To experience a resistance as a factual occurrence, that is, as an ontic encounter, a human being must exist ontologically as disclosing a world. Finally, then, the ontic significance of any resistance felt to our inner drives is limited to the extent (as being more or less frustrating) or the directions of our concerns (as signifying a placement within an instrumental complex or our spatial region).

In sum, in addition to the purely ontic scope to which it had been applied by Dilthey and Scheler, Heidegger finds two limitations to the theory of resistance as a measure of reality. First, resistance is only one of the characters attributable to real objects, since in some of our projects we succeed in carrying out our ends; and, in these cases, frustration is replaced by some form of exhilaration. But this too needs an ontological explanation. And second, as explained above, an everyday experience of any resistance whatsover "presupposes" the prior disclosure of a world. That is, the ontological structures that permit the experience of a resistance exist prior to any phenomenon that exhibits them. But this thesis is by now completely familiar: existentials are those ontological structures that make possible ontic experiences.

3. Reality and caring.

Although his previous subtitle would have led his readers to believe that a solution to the ontological problem of "reality" was at hand, reflection on the material of that section shows only that the problem was not solved by either Dilthey or Scheler—or by Maine de Biran, who brought the theme to prominence a hundred or so more years earlier, when philosophers were being referred to by Napoleon as inimical to his imperial designs. Heidegger reminds us, of course, that ontological problems do not have ontic solutions, since it is precisely the ontic experiences of our living that pose the ontological problems. Backtracking one step into the text, however, gives us a clue to Heidegger's strategy.

He had claimed in considering the epistemological problem of reality that there is none: a world is given to us as disclosive beings, so no "proof" need be given for the existence of such a world. And resistance, although it is a phenomenon of life, presupposes the same sort of prior disclosure of a world. In both cases the phenomenon of care is adduced as the ground for the ontological claims made. Hence, if there is truly an ontological problem of reality, its solution should be found in a reconsideration of the phenomena of human caring. That hypothesis is borne out in section 43(c), entitled "Reality and Care."

The methodological gambit here is to read the answer to the ontological problem of reality off the phenomenological description of the care-structure explained in my chapter 5. For example, if *reality* refers to that being which is external to human being, it can encompass only the presence of natural objects, the serviceability of tools, or the existence of other subjects. But the things of nature, indeed nature itself, considered as the laws binding the appearances to consciousness of the things of nature, possess ontological significance only on the basis of the phenomenal disclosure of a human being's being-in-the-world, that unified context of significance that is given to circumspection as a totality of involvements in which we exist with others. The worldliness of a human world, considered as a phenomenon, is possible, further, only on the basis of the self-disclosure of a being that understands its involvement.

For this reason, says Heidegger, there is something like a real world only because human beings exist—as projections upon potentialities for being, from a world in which they are abandoned and as being alongside the entities of their concern or solicitude. Only a human being exists in this way. Entities are; they do not exist. Being in general is not, nor does it exist. Borrowing a rhetorical trope from German grammar, Heidegger insists: Being gives (*Es, Sein, gibt*).[9] What? The entities that are, to humans who exist. Consider the matter for a moment. If there were no human beings, one could not claim that reality was either dependent upon or independent of consciousness, either ideal or real. For this reason, if there were no consciousness (or, more properly, no human being as possessing a preontological comprehension of being), nothing would *be* in-itself, as independent of consciousness.

If there were no human reality, it would be impossible to say that entities were or that they were not. There would be no one to know the difference and no one to utter the statement. Such is the "transcendental idealism" established by the Heideggerian existential analytic.

Under the counterhypothesis, however, that is, assuming the existence of human beings with an inherent understanding of being, we cannot say that entities (things, tools, or other humans) depend for their existence upon some consciousness; only that their reality (independent existence) does. The reality of natural objects depends upon the ontological self-disclosure of human beings but not the real objects that are co-disclosed in our world. But this says only that an understanding of being is necessary for entities to become accessible to human contemplation through the circumspection of a world of involvements in which the entities are given to our concernful, solicitous dealings.

Thus, the truth of idealism is not the ontic idealism of Berkeley and Hume that defines an object as a congeries of sensible ideas or impressions; it is, rather, a transcendental idealism that asserts the dependence of "reality" upon the only understanding capable of grasping it—human disclosedness.

Heidegger's discussion of the traditional notion of "truth" gives further sense to the distinction he draws between "the reality of the real" and "the truth of being." As one might already have suspected, the difference is ontological. *The real* is an abbreviated reference to the innerworldly objects of human concern; *reality*, to "their appearance" or presence to us. *Being* is the transcendental notion it was Heidegger's purpose to expound upon the basis of his preparatory existential analysis; and its truth is its unveiling.

The question had been posed in the beginning as directed toward entities (the real), concerning their being (reality), so as to grasp the meaning of that being (being present to a being that understands being). The only difference between the initial posing of the problem and the current context is the deliberate separation of the ontic from the ontological dimension of the original "problem." Before, our comprehension was only preontological; now, it has an ontological foundation. Moreover, until now, the "truth" of human speech has been taken as an ontologically unanalyzed term. We must now proceed to the analysis, which Heidegger gives in section 44 of his text.

The movement in thought is to start with a criticism of the classical notion of truth, arriving at the "primordial phenomenon of truth" as expounded through recent phenomenology; from there, to show how the ordinary sense of truth derives from that; and, in the third place, to discuss why "truth" must be presupposed against the claims of skepticism.

1. The classical notion.

The question of truth, according to Heidegger, has been tied up with the study of metaphysics since the time of the pre-Socratic philosophers. Parmenides, he says, was the first philosopher to discover the Being of entities as a theoretical problem and the first to identify Being with a "perceptive understanding" of the Being of entities. Heidegger's own idealistic interpretation of this notion was given in the previous sections:

> [N]ur wenn Seinsverständnis *ist,* wird Seiendes als Seiendes zugänglich; nur wenn Seiendes ist von der Seinsart des Daseins, ist Seinsverständnis als Seiendes möglich.[10]

> [O]nly if an understanding of Being *is* are entities as entities accessible to us; only if an entity has the nature of a human being does the understanding of Being become possible as an entity.

The two theses of Heidegger—that the understanding of Being comes to be only in the disclosedness of human beings, and that through this understanding human beings may gain access to the beings of the entities within their worlds, either as presence or as serviceability—are expressed in the varying translations of the fifth Parmenidean fragment[11] recorded by Diels: "Thought and being are the same thing"; or, "It is the same thing that can be thought and can be."[12] And, of course, it was Aristotle's metaphysics that applied philosophy as the science of truth to the study of being qua being, or of entities insofar as they come to exist. Both these ancient philosophers, says Heidegger, were merely following "the necessity of what shows itself" in a cautious inquiry.

What shows itself—as it is in-itself from itself, of course—is a phenomenon. So the current inquiry is made to show how the classical notion of truth came to diverge from its phenomenological foundation in order to be reassociated with it in the co-disclosedness of a human understanding and its proper objects. This first step, then, is toward a recovery of the phenomenological notion of truth.

Traditionally it has been claimed that only sentences are true; that the essence of the truth of statements is their agreement with matters of fact; and that it was Aristotle's development of logic that introduced the prior two theses into the Western philosophical tradition. His statement, in *De Interpretatione*,[13] that ideas are occurrences within the soul that correspond to the things of nature, may be given a purely phenomenological interpretation, or as our Western history has determined, a purely linguistic interpretation. According to the nineteenth-century German idealistic logicians, the locus of truth was in the mind of the person making a judgment when that "judgment" was in accordance with the facts.

But how can our ideas or their recording in statements actually correspond to the facts of reality? The relation is rendered in various ways: as agreement, as correspondence, or as broadly as merely "jibing with"; from *übereinstimmen* to *stimmen*. Whichever, the respect in comparison to which the agreement is asserted may vary from pure quantity, as in arithmetical "judgments" such as "$6 = 16 - 10$," to some other unspecified respect. But there is no quantitative basis for the comparison of our ideas and reality. Is the relation then only one of similarity instead of equality? If so, what similarity is there between an idea as a conscious event and a reality that the idea records in perception?

As if to avoid the embarrassment of not being able to stipulate the basis of comparison between an idea and the reality it correctly records, the notion of a "subsistent truth" was invented to insure that once a truth had been established, its statement would always be true, and for everyone. In this way the establishment of a truth fixed a norm for all future judgment. But the ontology for the subsistence of a truth has never been made clear and has only become more obscure still by the employment in theological concerns of the notion of "eternal truths," those presumably fixed in us by our nature as thinking beings, as that nature has been determined by our Creator. In this latter instance religious faith seems to constitute the only ground for the belief.

To avoid the possible errors stemming from an ungrounded notion of truth, Heidegger appeals to the demonstration and confirmation of the truth of a simple quotidian statement. When I say, for example, that the picture on the wall is hanging askew, what transpires in the experience of an interlocutor? The sentence is not a mere representation of a putative fact; uttering it communicates a mode of my own disclosedness, my own perception of a real state of affairs as an event within my world. Calling attention to the aspect of the object—to the how of its hanging—allows another person to confirm or disconfirm the statement in his or her own experience. What is the ontology of this situation?

To answer this question, Heidegger reaches back into the fore-having he has been modifying for us all along. Making an assertion is a way of our own being-toward what is put forth in the assertion. The statement indicates or records our perception of the object hanging crooked on the wall. Our knowing, still a founded way of being-in-a-world, remains related solely to the entity and the way it has appeared to us. The being-uncovered that is revealed in the statement is that very thing, the painting out of kilter. And as such, it is related to a being that uncovers—the understanding of a human being that is expressed in the assertion—my perception of the fact.

In summary, then, for any assertion to be true, two things must be co-disclosed: the being-disclosing of the act of assertion and the being-disclosed in the statement asserted. The primary sense of the relation involved in the measuring of a truth is the "uncoveredness" of the object pointed out in assertion. Ontologically, truth is this uncoveredness; a veritable phenomenon always shows the emperor without his clothes.

2. The primordiality of the phenomenon of truth, and the derived character of the traditional, linguistic notion.

In the foregoing "phenomenological" analysis of the truth relation, two correlative notions of truth have surfaced. The first is the being-uncovering of human disclosedness, which is primordial, and the second, the being-uncovered of the entities of a human being's world, which is equally primordial with the first, since they are co-disclosed, but which constitutes the source of the derivative sense of truth. These two aspects of ontological truth are related to the human care-structure as follows.

The uncoveredness of the entities within a world depends upon the disclosedness—its opening into a region—of the human subject. Disclosedness was interpreted as feeling, understanding, and discourse, directed toward the world, our being in it, and our own selfhood. But since caring spreads the human existent into three dimensions—being already in a world when the question of its existence arises, being ahead of itself in a projection upon a potentiality for being what it is to become, and existing alongside the entities of its world—the "truth" of the self lies hidden in the fall toward identification with its innerworldly objects.

Countless are the numbers of people who identify themselves by what they own, or who define themselves, in bad faith, by reference to their purely physical natures. Hence, if a human being is initially in the truth, in that truth ontologically determined by its disclosedness, then in its falling, it can lose itself in the objects of its world and allow the objects it discloses to surface as the newer standard of truth. Ordinarily, of course, it is the facts that serve as the measure of the truth of statements. The fall into inauthenticity is thus a fall from being in the truth to being in the untruth, two possible ontical situations of existent subjects.

The process may be summarized in the following way. A human being's way of being in a world is to disclose that world to itself. As abandoned in a world from the beginning, it is already thrown into a world, alongside a definite range of possibilities. As existing, however, it projects itself upon certain of its potentialities for being; what it is, it has yet to be. Consequently, it can understand itself either in terms of the world and other humans or as motivating itself toward being (responsible for) itself. Existential falling indicates the choice of inauthenticity, or behaving in such a way as being other than oneself.

In the fallen state, a human being views its personal project as it has been tranquilized into the public world, feeling as everyone feels, understanding as everyone understands, mouthing the same platitudes everyone has already spoken. Through this public interpretation of our being-in and of the world we all share because no one of us has chosen it, our human being finds itself in the untruth; objects as they are, are hidden from our view; the "truth" has been covered up.

To regain the truth, it must be wrested anew. Things must be uncovered as they are. Such is the source for Heidegger's interpretation of the Greek *alētheia*, as *a-lētheia*. The alpha is privative: things are true when their being has been dis-covered, when we allow them to show themselves as they are.

Truth, in this scheme, is an ontological notion. Most primordially, it is a human being's disclosedness, to which belongs the un-coveredness of entities. In its everyday acts of caring for itself, for others, and for the objects of a shared world, a human being is both in the truth and in the untruth.

So much for the primordiality of the ontological notion of truth as phenomenologically determined. The derived nature of the traditional linguistic notion likewise may be "read off" Heidegger's previous elaboration of the forestructure of the human understanding. Consider. If I assert that the picture on the wall is hanging askew, my statement exhibits the "apophantical 'as' " that reveals the property of the foresighted thing; and this "as-structure" of my assertion is the projection of the hermeneutical "as" of an interpretation, reflecting the positioning of the painting within the totality of my involvements I had experienced as "significance," the affective counterpart of my being in that world. The assertion is about something, the entity—the picture—in its quality—as being oriented toward the framing background of the wall.

What the statement is about is the object as uncovered to my prior disclosive perception. The act of asserting changes the nature of the purely human world in that the statement itself is an entity whose being is its serviceability, existing for the purpose of pointing out the properties of things—either serviceable tools or merely observable things. This act reveals my own being-toward these entities and indicates the same possibility of being for others. Because the statement is couched in ordinary language, the specificity of the disclosure, that is, of my being-toward those entities as uncovered in the assertion, may be covered over; only the object and its properties remain in the center of an interlocutor's attention. Still, the assertion itself has the being of utility and retains it in the act of communication. Existing in ready-to-hand fashion and related to the entities they uncover, assertions contain a relatedness of being between two distinct entities: the assertion as ready-to-hand and the objects it brings to light.

This relation between the assertion and its object is in an act of reflection an object of pure observation and hence present to the observing consciousness. The comparison that would establish the relationship of agreement between statement and its object is now possible; both are objects present in the world. And such, Heidegger presumes, is the phenomenological ground for the Aristotelian, or classical, notion of truth as the agreement between our ideas and the world of our experiences.

Within the tradition, however, there has been a confusion of the ontic and the ontological features of acts of assertion. Since statements are the records of acts of assertion, their objectness has taken precedence over the being-uncovering that is co-disclosed with every being-uncovered. Where primordially the *logos* is an assertion about something that gets uncovered in the asserting, the phenomenon of *apophansis* has been treated as an objective relation between two purely "objective" phenomena, that is, between entities existing as present-at-hand within a common world. In this way, the primordial phenomenon of truth, which is an existential, like the worldliness of that world, its significance, and human disclosedness itself, gets covered over; and those human beings who are victims of the ontological reversal between the existential and the categorial interpretation of the "truth" are themselves in the untruth, since their attitude reveals their own lostness within the "objective" world.

The linguistic tradition stemming from the hermeneutics of Aristotle has simply falsified (i.e., covered over) the primordial phenomenon of truth as it is open to existential analysis. Statements are interpreted as themselves objective affairs that either cover over or uncover other states of objective affairs: a true statement is one that states a fact, and a false statement misrepresents a fact. But this derivation of the notion of an objective truth reverses the ontological order of things. It is simply not true that positive, ontic assertions or statements are the primary locus of truth's happening; primordially, it is the truth of human disclosedness, that is, being-disclosing or understanding, that is the ontological locus of assertion. There can be a categorial interpretation of truth only because truth is an existential structure of a human being's self-projection into a world.

3. *The* being *of truth and why it must be presupposed.*

Nothing spooky is being claimed here. We must read the expression "the being of truth" as meaning the uncoveredness of objects in a human world. The purpose of all phenomenological investigation is to allow the objects of one's world to show themselves as they are: to permit the truth to happen. In no one's world is truth guaranteed as a matter of right.

Following the analysis of "primordial" truth and its modification into the truth of sentences as given above, Heidegger states that there is, and can be, truth only insofar as human beings exist—only insofar as their conduct uncovers the entities of their worlds. But this too is a simple tautology: without disclosedness, there is no truth, nothing disclosed. Before their discovery, "things" were not true, because strictly speaking things are never true—or false, for that matter. This does not mean that before their discovery entities did not exist. The laws that became true in Newton's discovery of them existed prior to that discovery, but since prior to his recording of them they were not disclosed to any human being, they were not true. And when there are no longer any human beings to be aware of their existence, they will no longer be true. An "eternal verity" presumes upon a past and forecloses on the possibilities of the future.

As an uncovering, truth belongs to the being of human beings; it is a function of the care-structure and not a purely subjective whim of a being lost in an objective world. Primordial truth is not relative to the discretion or indiscretion of living beings, however authentic or inauthentic they may be. Indeed, if knowing is a founded way of being in a world, then the uncoveredness of an object is co-disclosed with the uncovering acts of human beings.

For this reason, the being of truth must be presupposed, and epistemological skepticism is refuted. Consider. "To presuppose something" is to understand, or interpret, it as the ground for the being of something else. We must presuppose the existence of truth as uncovering if there are objects whose existence is uncovered in an analysis or scientific investigation. All such investigations reveal truth itself as that for the sake of which the human being exists, since it exists only as open to the world. But it must be remembered that in every ontic act of caring, the being of the human being is at issue; and so the most basic act of "uncovering" the conditions of any truth whatsoever is one of phenomenological ontology. The truth that is presupposed in any ontic inquiry, therefore, is not the truth of the entities inquired into, whether sentences or the facts of nature, but the truth of the inquiring human being.

In sum, we must presuppose the truth of our own being as revealers of the truth because that truth has already been established by a society of "knowing" beings existing in their worlds, only some of whom have been scientists or philosophers. Immanuel Kant, we recall, attempted to defeat the skepticism of David Hume, for whom any matter of fact could be doubted. We need not, like Kant, posit the existence of an ideal subject, or Transcendental Ego, whose purely subjective faculties of sensibility, understanding, and reason establish the limits of our power to know. That notion is a fanciful idealization, since there can be no consciousness in general, but only individual conscious acts.

Heidegger's investigation, like Kant's, is transcendental, making appeal to a priori structures that must be "presupposed" as the ground for the possibility of actual events; but in Heidegger's case, these structures are not limited to acts of knowing. If anything at all gets judged in a human world, truth is presupposed; and even if no judgment is made, a human being in its disclosedness presupposes its own—ontological—truth. This proposition cannot be refuted, since any evidence brought forth to defeat it would presuppose it; nor can the being of truth be demonstrated in mathematical fashion as the consequence of propositions necessarily true. The evidence for its truth is the factical (*faktisch*) existence of a human being, the ontical determinants of which "presuppose" the ontological structures that make such existents possible.

The truth of human being establishes the being of truth.

TAKING A POSITION on the two recurring problems of philosophy—the nature of reality and the essence of truth—does not settle the inquiry initiated in *Being and Time*. The question of the meaning of Being in general is as yet unanswered, although the preliminary analysis of being-in-the-world has yielded a description of human being as caring and various ways in which a person may be "in" its world. Such a being is distinct from the tools it organizes into an instrumental complex, as well as from the objects present to its inspection—those objects that have traditionally constituted the reality of the real world.

A method of understanding has been elucidated, by which a primordial and a derived notion of truth have been explicated. What remains to be done? First of all, the interpretation of the meaning of human being, of caring, in terms of the temporality upon which it is projected; and, next, the meaning of Being in general.

To pursue the prior of these aims the question is posed: What is a human being, considered as a whole? Until now, of course, we were concerned with the everyday existence of human being considered in its averageness. Answering the question requires an adjustment in the forestructure of our understanding—which is no longer merely preontological but fortified by the preparatory fundamental analysis of human being.

Two further adjustments will be required, as different aspects of human existence are sighted out of the forehaving for ontological interpretation. After the whole, the unity; and after the unity, the temporal development of a human being becomes the object of our analysis.

So, following an excursion into the perennial problems of philosophy, Heidegger returns to his quest for an understanding of our human being (*Dasein*).

PART II

7

Death, Dying; Conscience, Guilt

THE SCOPE OF THIS CHAPTER IS SECTIONS 45 through 60 of Heidegger's text.

Section 45 explains the necessity of readjusting the explanatory forestructure in order to make up for the limitations of the preliminary analysis contained in division 1. Having begun that analysis on the basis of a preontological understanding of being possessed by any living human being as the general context of interpretation (the forehaving), and isolating the idea of human existence already possessed, being-in-the-world, as the element to be interpreted (the foresight), Heidegger has explained human being in terms of its everyday care-structure (the foreconception).

The limitations of the inquiry stem in part from the average and everyday character of the phenomena interpreted—worldhood, selfhood, and being-in—and in part from the unfinished nature of the total analysis, which is to be achieved in division 2 of the text. Lacking, therefore, are answers to the questions of how a human being can be a whole; how it may achieve a self that is its own; and how temporality constitutes the meaning of its being an authentic whole. How can all these notions be "brought into the new forehaving," which the preliminary analysis of division 1 has prepared for us?

151

I shall discuss Heidegger's answers to these questions in a four-part analysis of my own: (1) the methodological readjustment; (2) death and dying as a living projection; (3) responsibility as grounding conscience and guilt; and (4) anticipatory resoluteness as the new characterization of a human being's mode of being in its world.

1. The methodological readjustment.

The context of a hermeneutical explanation varies with the changes produced by each new act of phenomenological grounding. The end, or purpose, of division 1 was to change the implicit knowledge we all possess of our own being into an explicit ontological interpretation of that being. But since this was done only provisionally, as preparing a further interpretation of the meaning of that being (temporality), a new projection toward that meaning must be made by "sighting out" from the treasure of information we already possess those elements whose phenomenological analysis will complete the original design.

The preliminary analysis, for example, ends with the description of human being as caring. Even if caring reveals itself in a totalizing structure, exhibiting human being ahead of itself, always in, and as alongside the entities of its world, the question arises, concerning the total human being, how care is definitive for each one's own peculiar totality of being. What in a specific situation makes a whole of a person bearing a proper name? The preliminary analysis makes no reference to being a whole and leaves the notion of being one's own self a mere alternative to the fallen nature of an inauthentic personality, whose forfeiture in a present moment is precisely its distance from a "proper" selfhood, one it might call its own. At this point in the demonstration, then, neither the wholeness nor the authenticity of a human being has been brought into the forehaving of our hermeneutical situation. Two more cuts into the context of our founded knowledge must be made to fulfill the lack in our existential-ontological account of human being.

Common reflection upon a human life presents living as a process from birth through growth and maturity to maximal force, and from there through decline into death. If this ontic description is accurate, the whole of a human existence will not have been brought into the forehaving until death receives its existential interpretation. Likewise, if authenticity and inauthenticity are merely alternative potential ways of living a life, and if, as living, a human being is already in its

world as a projection toward the one or the other of these potentialities for being, there must be found a way of giving evidence for—
of attesting to—its proper selfhood.

Conscience is the clue here, as Heidegger plays on the ambiguity
of the German *Gewissen* as noun (conscience) and as adjective (certain).[1] For the moment it suffices to stipulate the interpretation, since
the full ontological account of the phenomenon is to follow later.

Conscience gives us to know for a certainty who we are, even if it
is liable to misinterpretation as the voice of a foreign god. For his
appeal to conscience, we recall, Socrates was brought to trial for
perverting the youth; and members of the Society of Jesus have always
known that whoever controls the conscience of a person controls
that person's acts. Moral casuistry is but another ontic phenomenon
of the human conscience as was Socrates' decision to drink the
hemlock.

Who can judge the rightness of our conduct? If not ourselves, then
another; and if another, and if that decision binds our behavior, we
never leave the public world of everyman. How then can we give
testimony to our own being certain of the rightness of our acts? The
existential analysis of conscience should provide the answer. It is
given below.

Finally, if we can experience our own deaths in anticipation—
Socrates, we remember, chose his by refusing to allow himself to be
bribed out of prison—and if we can be resolute in our drives to self-
determination, assuming the responsibility for our own acts, our
being-in-the-world will still be caring, but caring now characterized
by a newer, existential foundation—by our own anticipatory resoluteness (*vorlaufende Entschlossenheit*). Such will be the new "how"
of our being-in-the-world; and it shall later be given its temporal
interpretation.

As for the foreconception of the interpretation to come, we already
possess as a function of our average way of being in a world a habit
of reckoning with time—experience, for example, of time felt as
waxings and wanings of an interest or of a growth. As a species, we
already possessed notions of the passage of time prior to having
constructed clocks for measuring it. And, lastly, our scientific view
of the material used contains a notion of time as a dimension of the
reality of the material world. Our foreconception is not lacking, only
its grounding is, in the structures of human temporality. But that is
a subject of still later chapters.

Section 45, which contains this outline of a program, is inserted within the text, not as a chapter, but as introducing the methodological problem to be solved in the whole of division 2. Other "readjustments of the forestructure" will be introduced as they are needed, but that material is developed as an integral part of a particular chapter of the text dedicated to the solving of an outstanding problem in fundamental ontology. Of those, more later.

2. *Death and dying, or on being a whole.*

The initial difficulty for considering the wholeness of a human being is the apparent impossibility of ever gaining the necessary point of view. The foresighted event cannot be brought into a given context of explanation (the forehaving), since, as long as it is alive, a human being projects itself forward; in terms of the care-structure, it always exists ahead of itself. As long as it is, therefore, it is concerned with its future, which is not yet. Yet, it is this very self-projection into the future that allows the human being to comport itself toward its various potentialities of being: in despair, it is hopeless; in cynical disdain, without illusions; and in resignation to its multiple indebtedness, looking forward to having settled its accounts. The last recorded thought of the Platonic Socrates was the remembrance of a debt he owed to Asclepius; the hemlock was already progressing headward when Socrates asked that it be paid, even though he would no longer be there to know that it had been paid. To be hopeless, to be without illusions, to look forward to the payment of one's debts are ways of behaving with respect to the future, which is always out there, and never here, now.

Even though "tomorrow never comes," as the old English adage has it, if we can conceive of its having arrived, the self-projecting human could no longer exist. Making a present of the future is the death—the end—of the living human being. This is no mere play on words: a human being is its "there" in the world; should it come to the end, that would make it a whole, it would no longer be there (*nicht-mehr-Dasein*), no longer be itself. Such is the logical force that makes it seem impossible to encapsulate our own living essence. If that is to be done at all, it must be done by someone else, when we ourselves are dead.

Hence, the limitation on the comprehension of the whole of a human being is real, and it is a function of human existentiality. Certainly, it does not reflect some arcane imperfection of our cognitive powers; and it is not owing to a simple confusion of death as an ontical event, or biological phenomenon, with the existential structure we are seeking to describe as a phenomenon. As a result, the hermeneutical investigation must be repeated, with a new specific intent (foresight) to be brought into the general context of explanation provided in the preparatory analysis of human being. So ends section 46.

Section 47 takes up the gambit. Our "no-longer-being-there," that moment in our life when we no longer have anywhere to go and no time to go there, could, in a fashion, be experienced by another person; and so presumably could we, as other to the other, experience that person's no-longer-being-there. Can a substitution of the knower for the known be made? Analysis will show why the displacement of subjects and objects, whether undertaken by virtue of the dialectic of the other, the theory of empathy, or any other tactical procedure, is a vain attempt.

For, the end of any human being, be it subject or object, is the beginning of its merely being there, that is, merely present to someone else's observation. The formerly living human organism is, at its end, a mere physical body—but, alas, not only that. It is indeed a dead thing that was alive. We use the word *deceased,* in German *Verstorbene,* to distinguish dead persons from dead animals, who, in the end, are merely dead (*Gestorbene*).

The deceased person remains an object of concern, to be given a "proper" funeral—presumably according to his or her last wishes, and some kind of memorial, if only to grant a last wish that the person be allowed to pass on into oblivion. Grief now is a continuation of a past love; satisfaction now, of a past hate; indifference now, of a past lack of concern. In all such examples, we, the living, can still be with the other. But the authentic-being-come-to-an-end we are seeking to comprehend is not experienced in these ways.

The death of the dead person is not the same as his dying. And just as care must be understood as caring, so the living of our cares must be understood as dying. In asking the ontological question of the death of others, we are inquiring about their dying, not what kind of being-with the living may experience with the dead.

Jules Romains, in his *La Mort de quelqu'un,* wrote a novel about a nobody who became somebody merely by dying. But all the changes in that transubstantiation took place in the ways in which that unknown personality was recognized by other persons. Before his death, he wasn't given the time of day. After it, the passage of his cortege stopped traffic; the pious prayed; and even the impious nervously doffed their hats.

The story is moving, and if it engrosses us all the more in that it continually reminds us that we too may stop the traffic without intending to do so, like any other *memento mori,* it can only serve to remind us that dying is both an individual and a social phenomenon, that being dead is a necessary but not a sufficient condition for being deceased, and that, in the end, it matters little what the individual has done in his life, what his death will signify to others is up to them. No one can die by proxy: because one's life is one's own. Death, like human being itself, is always mine ("Dasein ist je meines"); and it too must be given an existential analysis.

So ends the problem of phenomenological access to the wholeness of a human being, and with it, section 47 of the text.

Besides the problem of access, Heidegger's existential analysis of dying contains three more general areas of discussion: no-longer-being-there as being-toward-the-end (secs. 48 and 49; 50–52); and my own death (sec. 53). I consider them in their order.

What follows from the fact that the end of a human being is always outstanding, that is, always in the future with respect to the moment when the question of its significance arises? From Heidegger's statement of the problem of access,[2] three conclusions may be drawn: human existence always includes an outstanding "not-yet," which is still one of its possibilities of being; that the coming to its end, once achieved, announces a change in the nature of human existence—from being-there in its world to its no longer being-there (*Nichtmehrdasein*); and, finally, that the process of coming to an end, or dying, cannot be relegated to someone else's proxy. In deaths, as in tastes, each has his own.

How to conceive the always outstanding end of the living being? Compare everyday examples:

1. Some debts are outstanding. That is, something is still owed. Ontologically conceived, an outstanding debt is something of serviceable value—money, for example—that is lacking, not yet serviceable; its being is missing, and hence, still outstanding. Not so, our deaths.
2. Some phases of the waxing moon are outstanding; prior to the full moon, the last quarter is outstanding. The "missing" part of

the waxing moon is a phenomenon of being present to observation. Not so, our dying.

3. Unripe fruit ripens; until it does, its ripeness is outstanding. Ripeness is a condition of the fruit, the result of a process undergone by it in relationship to an environment. To understand the process of ripening, it must be borne in mind that the fruit itself undergoes a change in condition, that is, in its mode of being. Closer to our dying; but ripeness is the ideal condition of the fruit that makes it fit for consumption. A human being achieves its ideal condition before its end, and after that declines steadily into its end.

So rather than the end that is still outstanding, let us concern ourselves with the process of coming to an end, in short, with ending. Again, compare:

4. Ending may be merely stopping, as a road stops or as the rain stops. When the rain stops, it is no longer present and observable. When a road stops, it is no longer present in its entirety, either as finished (made, and therefore useful) or unfinished (to be finished and hence made useful). But our deaths, as endings, are neither observable phenomena nor useful to anyone but our enemies.

5. Endings may be disappearings, as the rain or a loaf of bread disappears in its consumption. But when the rain disappears, it is no longer seen; the bread is used up, or eaten. Once again, our dying is neither a phenomenon of observation nor of practical utility.

How then does a human being relate to its outstanding end? First of all, by living it. A human being is a projection toward its end. Death is one of its possibilities—the last, to be sure, but that can not deter our search for its meaning. In sum, death is not a mere condition of our being, a *Zu-Ende-sein* (a being at its end), but dying is the same process as our living, a *Sein-zum-Ende* (a being-toward-the-end). But this is to say only that in living out the conditions of our life, we project ourselves toward death—the living end of it all. So ends section 48.

Section 49 contrasts this preliminary conclusion with "other" interpretations of the phenomenon of death. Our being-toward-the-end establishes two things: first, it establishes what death is not (a phenomenon of presence or of serviceability), but it is not for this reason a purely ontical phenomenon that might be treated either by one of the positive sciences, or by metaphor, in comparison to natural events. If death is a phenomenon of life, and if it is to be treated ontologically, then, in the second place, it must be discussed as a phenomenon of a human being's being-in-the-world. That discussion will come later; the rest of this section eliminates a number of ontical explanations of the phenomenon.

First, the biological. Whether discussed in connection with expected longevity, propagation, and growth, or with mortality rates and medical prognoses, or with actuarial tables and the risks of insurance, death is defined in terms of life. That a human being should die is considered a fact that is antecedent to any ontology of life (since in the pursuit of the ontical science, an ontology is derived from observed phenomena) yet, curiously, at the same time follows upon the characterization of a human being's basic state, since death is only one of the phenomena of life ontically considered.

Between the fully human condition of dying (*sterben*) and the purely animal condition of perishing (*verenden*) there is an intermediate condition, of dying inauthentically, that is, of coming into the state of demise (*ableben*) or merely living out the round of our days. The difference between authentically dying or inauthentically living out one's appointed number of days is, of course, an ontological difference associated with the ultimate possibility of acting in such a way as to be oneself or in accordance with the self of the public world; and neither mode of being has anything to do with dumb, animal perishing. Dying is personal, and as ontologically determined, has nothing to do with anything reported on a statistical table.

Yet, it is an experience and could for that matter be treated psychologically. But psychologists have been more interested in describing experiences of death typologically; and to do this with any degree of clarity, there must first be a foundational elucidation of the notion of death, such as that herein being prepared.

Theodicy, for its part, has also taken a stand on death: a necessary evil for the entrance into another world wherein to enjoy one's eternal reward for having lived the good life. But theodicy, with its emphasis on good, evil, death, and reward or punishment, concerns itself with speculation about a world beyond the world in which a human being must live and die. Heideggerian ontology remains this-worldly.

Lastly, in theology, there is even an implicit "metaphysics of death." According to Scripture, a man must die because of original

sin. Death itself is a punishment. But if death gives a clue to interpreting the "meaning of life," whether as a natural or supernaturally
ordained evil, and as a consequence is something that is suffered, a
prior understanding of a human being's being would be required for
us to understand the theological claims being made. How does this
part illumine the whole?

For these reasons, neither biology, psychology, theodicy, nor theology has anything important to say about the purely human phenomenon of dying. But then, what does? Only a method of analysis
that has for its object the elucidation of the meaning of being. Death
is an ontological phenomenon.[3]

The existential analysis Heidegger is to use has so far indicated an
order for inquiring into death: the superordinate position of an
existential-ontological analysis over any purely ontical account; and
a (so far) empty formula: living and dying are the same phenomenon,
since living is a projection into the future, and death is the always
still outstanding end of living. As an ontological structure, dying is
living our being-toward-its-end.

The gravamen of Heidegger's existential-ontological interpretation of death is a list of characteristics attributable to the "last
possibility of being" to which a human being may relate itself. Recalling the care-structure, with its projection into the future from a
place already in and alongside the entities of its world, death is a
human being's ever own not-yet. Death is therefore something impending, never as yet an actual fact; nor, since it is only a possibility,
are we ever seriously approaching it as a matter of fact (sec. 50).

How can events be impending? A storm, the remodeling of a house,
the arrival of a friend may all be impending as matters of fact. How
is it with their being? The storm: potentially present; the remodeling:
potentially serviceable; the friend's homecoming: a future mode of
our being-with. None of these relates the human being to its own
possibilities.

Try other facts of existence: a journey to be made, an argument
with bothersome neighbors, letting the occasion for a decision slide
by. Better, since the impending activity would relate the human being
to a state of its own constitution but still not specific enough to
capture the essence of that last, ownmost potentiality of our being.
Each of these allows other activities beyond it.

Death does not. What, then, characterizes it? The listing begins in
earnest: first, it is one's ownmost possibility—belonging to oneself

and to no other (since it cannot be performed by proxy)—of no longer being able to be-there; second, as one's ownmost, it is absolutely unrelational (*unbezüglich*), that is, totally isolating of the human being from the entities of its world; and, third, it is ever-outstanding, that is, not overtakable (*unüberholbar*), since it is always only a possibility and never a fact.

The measure of one's possessing such a distinctive possibility is exhibited in the facticity of the human condition. Thrown into a world in which it must die, the human being's state of mind is anxiety. What before was called "that in face of which" humans are anxious, their being-in-the-world as abandoned, within the nonrelational context of a personal death, creates a state of mind in which they can be anxious only about their own potentiality for no longer being. Such is the structure of anxiety that is already disclosive of our being stretched between a factual past and an ultimate, but only possible, future.

In the everyday world, of course, this feeling of anxiety is attenuated by the state of falling. The human being hangs on to the entities of its world; and everyday living is a flight in the face of death. The dead are the dearly departed, the loved ones,[4] whose present condition is to be institutionalized away from our everyday concerns lest the admission of the death of someone else remind us of our own. No matter what we do to flee the finiteness of our existence, however, no matter how many institutions we may create to hide the bruteness of the fact, we are haunted by the death that is grounded in the care-structure of our very own being. To pretend ignorance of the condition is an expression of our inauthenticity, an escape from the disquieting feeling of uncanniness, which lets us once more feel at home in the world of the present.

What is the result of such an appeal to ignorance? The result reveals itself in the way in which a human being's disclosedness becomes colored by its fixation with the elements of its world. Trace out the process. First, the idle talk about death: in our public interpretation of the phenomenon, it's a mishap, a tragedy, an event of interest to someone or another, no one knows whom. For every death, someone or other has died. The event is real (not a possibility) and occurs in the world. Every day people die (*man stirbt*)—but never ourselves. Obituaries are for the curious, establishing the inauthentic state of mind.

Death in the everyday world is a real event, always happening to another; as such, it is an indefinite something about to happen, but not yet to the person contemplating the event. In this scheme of things, people die, one dies; but no one contemplating the mere possibility ever really does. The understanding of the phenomenon is therefore ambiguous. Personal dying gets perverted into a public occurrence, and one's ownmost potentiality for no longer being there gets passed off as a matter of fact that simply has not yet occurred.

Falling, we recall, is the state of our present relatedness to the entities of our worlds. It tempts us from the truth, and persuades us to persuade others that their cancers are not terminal. In this state, no one is sick unto death; one recovers. It is also tranquilizing, at least to ourselves, if not to the other who knows that he will die in spite of our efforts to convince him he will not. To avoid our own anxiety, which is never comfortable, we rob the other of his right to be himself.

But the ploy fails for both of us: anxiety is merely changed into fear, which can be avoided only by an attitude of complete and total indifference, such as that expressed by both commanders in the siege of Irun, during the Spanish Civil War. Asked to surrender and to avoid useless bloodshed, the captain of the republican militia replied to the nationalist commander in an act of sublime indifference to the impending fact of his own death, "Viva la muerte! [Long live death!]" And not to be outdone by his fraternal enemy, the commander replied in kind, "Viva la muerte!"[5] The sublimity of the act, which is measured in the oxymoron of the expression, reveals the ultimate alienation of a self from its potentialities of being-no-longer as the heroic self, which is merely indifferent to any fact, including its own passing, which would be of no importance to anyone concerned. The battle was long, and bloody, but the city fell.

Beginning with the tempting tranquilization and ending with the total alienation of a self from its ownmost potentiality of being, the state of our falling allows us to evade the issue of our own deaths. Constantly fleeing in the face of death,[6] we continue to hide behind the consoling voice of the other in us: "The Lord giveth and the Lord taketh away," as if that thought could mitigate our grief. But since our understanding of the possibility of death is covered over in such "bromides" as if death were as simple as an attack of indigestion, the ultimate truth of the existentiality of our deaths is concealed. In our fallen state, we are in the untruth, and only the other dies; and about him or her, no one really cares.

Yet death, as the end of our being-there, is always an issue. If it may be forgotten, covered over, or disguised, it shall be brought forth again with the question of our being, within any ontology that understands itself. Indifference, whether pure ignorance or sublime heroism, may appear untroubled; the trouble begins only when we reflect on the conditions of our existence. Everyday conditions of living may teach us there is nothing to fear in death; but they only mask over the anxiety we cannot flee forever. As a disclosive being, in truth as well as in the untruth, one knows that one must die (sec. 51). And in dying "one" becomes someone.

Our everyday being-toward-the-end, displayed as above, exhibits two more characteristics: the certainty of the end, and its indefiniteness. They result from the analysis of section 52. The argument is simple.

It begins with the statement that everydayness merely conceals the truth. In spite of the idle talk with which we conspire to remain in the untruth, death is certain. Not just "one" but everyone dies; and not only this: in our ontological reflection, we cannot escape the conviction that everyone includes ourselves. How so?

The meanings of which we can become aware follow those of primordial "truth" discussed in the previous chapter. When a being is disclosed, there is a being-disclosing. All the facts disclosed in a world are accompanied by a feeling of conviction or certainty that the facts are just as they are revealed. This being-certain (*Gewisssein*) that is human conviction is also an event in the life of the self-projecting entity. It too is a state of our being, and cannot be denied without falling into the untruth of inauthenticity. This happens, of course, when "truth" is interpreted as an arbitrary fiction, a mere "view about something" one might entertain rather than a conviction one cannot avoid entertaining.

One says, for example, that death is certain, since all living creatures die. But a fact cannot be certain, at best it can only be probable: its prediction is never unconditionally true. Any air of superiority we might exhibit concerning the certainty of facts merely betrays a manner of being concerned with the entities revealed in an inquiry. We say, for example, that as a matter of fact, we all must die, thereby misplacing the certainty of our state of mind, which reflects our self-projection toward a future potentiality of no longer being, to an ontic fact that will occur within our worlds.

We may still feel superior to the fact of our own deaths, since they are always in the future, and, as such, indefinite. One dies, true; but not quite yet. For this reason, there is always hope, which tranquilizes the anxious spirit. But the not-yet of our actual death does not take away the certainty of our possible death, which never, qua possible, ever occurs at all. As an actual event, it is possible at any moment at all. Everyone is old enough to die.

Still the perpetual futurity of our deaths, as pure possibilities, tends to mask this last characteristic of our authentic death, its indefiniteness. Since such matters are of facts, of how and when it is to occur we can have no certain knowledge. The only thing about which we can be certain is that it cannot be avoided: "Death is, as the end of human being, in the very being-toward-the-end of all human beings. [*Der Tod ist als Ende des Daseins im Sein dieses Seienden zu seinem Ende.*]"[7]

In sum, the characteristics of an authentic death are as follows: as a potentiality of being that is one's *ownmost*, death is nonrelational, unovertakeable, certain, and indefinite. The factical not-yet of our ontologically certain death expresses the existence of our care-structure, its projection toward a future. In death as being-toward-our-own-uttermost-possibility the totality of our being is conceivable. We understand this totality in anxiety which is a flight from the disclosure of the ordinary events in our worlds. But this flight is itself a disclosure which our everyday lostness in the world conceals. As Sartre will put it later, we cannot successfully flee our fleeing, no more than Descartes could doubt he was doubting.[8]

The problem then becomes one of showing how this concealment may be overcome. Section 53 proposes an answer to this predominantly ontological question.

The previous analysis has yielded a concept of death considered as an existential structure of human beings. The difficulty of understanding the concept stems from the inauthenticity of our everyday existence, in which we act as if we were not ourselves. Anxiety is upsetting; escape into the public world of everyone relieves the anxiety. We evade the issue, cover it up or over, invent countless ambiguous interpretations of the phenomenon of our deaths considered as a fact. All this must be avoided if we are to remain true to the disclosiveness of our interpretive method. Heidegger returns to the meanings already contained in ordinary German for the discovery of a clue to continue his analysis. How can one relate oneself to a possibility?

Ordinary German suggests a number of ways. First as "being out for" something (*aus-sein auf*), as an athlete is out for the team. But the complement of being-out-for-something is always something actual—either known for its presence as having been attained, controlled, set up as foreseen; or serviceable, something produced, gotten ready, adjusted for working. The actualization of a human being's ultimate end would be suicide, however, if one were merely out for it; and if actualized in any other way, it would not permit the observation of the fact or the appreciation of its utility.

Next, one might dwell on, or brood over, a future possibility (*sich aufhalten bei*). The monk brooding over his own death with the help of the skull of another maintains the possibility of the event of his own death but weakens it into a future state that is still distant. Dwelling on a possibility, brooding over it, is a present concern for a future possibility that will be actualized. In that concern, the predominant feature of the worrisome attitude is how that possibility is to strike home. Authenticity, however, demands that we understand, cultivate, and put up with death as purely possible.

So, try expectation (*erwarten*). To expect something is to consider whether, when, and how it is to be a fact of our lives. Once again, possibility is rejected for a future actuality.

There remains anticipation (*vorlaufen in*). Anticipating a possibility comes closer to maintaining the pure possibility of an event as opposed to its future actuality. Understanding that something is possible is one way of anticipating that possibility. The more we understand of the possibility of an event—even the closer we approach its actuality—the farther we are from the actualization of the event. In death what is understood? The possibility of the future impossibility of comporting oneself in anyway whatsoever, indeed of existing at all.

Death is therefore the possibility of the measureless impossibility of a human existence. It is lived as a projection. In order to conceive itself ontologically, a human being is revealed disclosing and disclosed, as an anticipated end. That the end be its own is the measure of its authentic existence.

Section 53 ends with a description of this existential projection. Death as the end toward which we are projected is:

1. our ownmost possibility, that separates us from the tranquilized temptation of the public world;

2. nonrelative, in that it individualizes the human being, isolating it from innerworldly concerns of any kind;
3. unovertakable, remaining a possibility about which we are anxious rather than a feared actuality;
4. certain, as disclosed by the human being projecting, or anticipating the possibility; holding death for a certainty makes authenticity possible; and
5. indefinite, as to time, place, and manner. (As anticipated, the possibility of our death leaves us open to a constant threat of nonbeing, which we understand in anxiety.)

The list is now complete. What conclusions may be drawn? Two. First, an authentic anticipation of the possibility of no longer being in the world reveals our everyday lostness in the structures of the public world, in which anxiety is reduced to fear. Anticipating the end opens the possibility of being a whole self. Such would be the life of impassioned "freedom toward death," at once factical, certain, and anxious.

Second, even though our anxiety in the face of the possibility of our death grounds an understanding that had heretofore only lacked the proper phenomenological interpretation to qualify as an ontological explanation, our own interpretation has fleshed out the idea of an "authentic existence." We now understand authenticity as a possibility.

Is authenticity, being oneself in the face of one's death, a fantastical demand? Can a human being actually face up to its freedom toward death by an act of personal choice? What ontical conditions would be necessary for us to be able to attest in fact to our being a whole and individual personality? These questions are answered in the next chapter of the text (2, 2).

3. *Conscience, guilt, and responsibility.*

Whoever says *Dasein* says *Sein*; whoever says *Gewissen* says *gewiß* and *wissen*. What is the connection between the phenomena of conscience and the disclosiveness of our being-in a world that is certain because, ontologically considered, we are a manner of being-in-the-world? They are one and the same, but unless we are to let the charge of "word-mysticism"[9] stand against our author, his complete analysis of the phenomena must be derived as an application of his hermeneutical method. If some of the evidence comes to us through the tradition as codified in ordinary language, that may be a fact of our social histories; interpreting such a fact still necessitates the ontic-ontological reversal. If we feel guilty, for example, we have a conscience, and have made a conscious or unconscious judgment on the value of a past act. Factual, all this. How stands it with Being?

In his prior description of the human self, Heidegger declared that in the world of the everyday a human being acts, first and foremost, as everyone else acts. In the world of quotidian circumstance, we are, precisely, not ourselves, nor yet another. Always acting as one is supposed to act, one loses oneself in the public world shared by all. That sort of world was described as tempting, tranquilizing, and totally self-alienating; and being in such a world is a way of being in the untruth. But since being-in is one of the constitutive structures of human existentiality, as the being-disclosing for all the beings disclosed within the world, being-in-the-truth is another human potentiality.

The recovery from being lost in the public world begins with the uncanniness felt in the downward plunge of our fall; as an affective state it announces the possibility of a change, of our modifying the ontic circumstances of our lives in such a way as to reflect what we in ourselves truly are. Through the pangs of conscience felt as calling us, as from being lost in the they-world, back to ourselves as projecting our own ends, including our deaths, the veritable end of it all, there must be a decision to recover one's personal choice of a self. Whenever a human being decides to make this choice, it reclaims a potentiality for being that is its own. Whether we call this state "being-in-the-truth" or "authenticity" or, simply, "being one's own person," nothing else has ever been intended.

Responding to the feeling of uncanniness as a call to being oneself constitutes the horizon for Heidegger's interpretation of conscience. The internal but inaudible voice of conscience has always disclosed something to those who are willing to hear; but this is an ontic phenomenon concerning which the facts have always been disputed. Ours is not the intention to classify a set of human responses to known conditions of social stimulation. Nor shall we be bound by the traditional theological interpretation of the phenomenon, according to which conscience is the voice of God informing us what is right and wrong. The very dispute over the interpretation of the facts of conscience indicates that the primordiality of the phenomenon has been missed.

The problem, of course, is to isolate and describe conscience as an existential, that is, a universal structure of a human being's being-in-the-world. From the modified forehaving of our understanding, we select being-in, the disclosedness of human being. As giving us something to understand, conscience constitutes a mode of discourse; it is experienced as a call (*ein Ruf*). But it is not yet clear from what to what. This same call is an appeal (*Anruf*) and a summons (*Aufruf*).

The appeal and the summons help us reduce, somewhat, the unclarity of the nature of the call. The appeal is to the self lost in a public world; the summons, to be its own self by assuming the responsibility for its acts as its own.

Finally, the appeal and the summons call for a response, a "hearing" of the voice that makes no sound, to which we attest by wanting to have a conscience—to get out of the uncanniness that is the source of the call in the initial instance. In the face of all the obstacles to such a choice set up in the public world, in which rightness and wrongness are merely conventional, hearing the call to conscience is choosing to be oneself. This new state of being in the world is called resoluteness (*Entschlossenheit*).

Although Heidegger divides his discussion of the question into six parts, each developed as a single section of the text, I have reorganized my reading of these sections into three parts: the existential-ontological foundation of the phenomenon of conscience (sec. 55); the call of conscience (secs. 56–58); and what is disclosed in conscience (secs. 59 and 60).

The horizon for his existential-ontological interpretation has already been projected. Since conscience discloses something, it belongs to the way in which a human being lives its "there," being open to a world. As always, world and self are co-disclosed; and in its care-structure, a human being finds itself abandoned to a range of definite choices—overall, to act in accordance with its own true self or with the dictates of the impersonal subject of experiences in the public world. In situation, a human being may listen to what everyone says, believe what everyone believes, and act as everyone acts, and so "hear away from" itself; or it may reverse the procedure and choose to assume the responsibility for its own discourse, its own beliefs, its own acts. Whenever this listening away from itself which is a hearkening to the other is broken into, conscience has made its call.

Calling, of course, is a mode of discourse, and gives us something to understand. The call of conscience is an abrupt arousal, calling us away from where we are, whether it be out of a boring party, a love-affair gone sour, or any other situation in which the uncanniness strikes home. The call spans the entire "region" of human spatiality: from afar, where one would be if one had no reason to hear the call, to afar, into the depths of the tranquilizing, tempting, self-alienating world that can never be our own. And it reaches only that person who wants to be brought back unto his or her true self.

Two things, then, are necessary for Heidegger's advanced explanation of the phenomena of conscience: an understanding of human disclosedness as a manner of being-in-the-world, and an equally well-founded understanding of the care-structure of human being. They indicate the horizon within which the interpretation is to be made. There shall be no comparison with any kind of call that might be heard as the registering of sound—which would be "scientific" and therefore only ontical; nor shall any appeal be made to a special kind of faculty—the moral, for example, whether grounded in understanding, will, or feeling. Such appeals would be inadequate since they lack the foundational analysis Heidegger is about to give (sec. 55).

We move, then, to the three sections of the text dedicated to an interpretation of the call of conscience: the mode of discourse of conscience, the phenomenal character of the call, and understanding the appeal of conscience.

Since conscience is a mode of discourse, giving us something to understand, it contains something that is talked about. Tracing the source and the direction of the call will help us understand what that is.

For example, in the call an appeal is made, to the human being as it is in its world. This answer is certain, but remains indefinite. Human being is always already understood, if only preontologically, by the way in which we live out the conditions of our existence: but on the average, and in the world of our everyday concerns, we are more concerned with the entities within our worlds than we are with understanding "how it stands with" our being. Such is the lostness of the purely public world. In consequence, the call of conscience, if it is to be heard as an appeal, must reach the human being lost in such a world.

To what is the lost self called? The summons is to one's own true self in a world beyond the world of the everyday, one in which the person acting is responsible for all his acts. The call initiates from this summoning self, and to be heard, must pass over the entire range of the lost self's world, all its entities, and all other persons. Indeed, the public world must be pushed into insignificance for the personal world to have any significance. Should the call succeed, should one choose oneself, one would have been summoned to—being-in-the-world that is one's own.

What, then, is said? Strictly speaking, nothing at all. Nothing gets called to the self. Conscience operates only internally, to lapse into an older form of expression; it calls us humans forth into our own-most possibilities of being but does not tell us what these are. The summons merely makes clear that there is an alternative to being lost in a public world and calls us to fulfill our own potentiality for being a self.

The mode of this discourse? Silence. The conscientious person is forced into reticence by the enormity of its project. No one can inform anyone what one ought to be—or to do. The responsibility fills us with anguish.

Still, there are various ways of interpreting the call, depending upon the susceptibilities of our understanding of our own being. The call is from a certain direction and to a certain direction; but only these directions are given, albeit with the sureness of one's being. Unfortunately, however, there are those who mistake self-righteousness for righteousness; and so interpret the call of conscience as if it stemmed from the public self, one that has been merely drawn off into a soliloquy "in which causes get pleaded." What better description could be given of Hamlet's tragic fault!

In sum, the call of conscience is to the public self in its lack of selfness; what one is summoned to is to be more human, to fulfill one's own potentialities for being a self; and so, within the call of conscience, a human being is asked to assume the responsibility for its own possibilities.

So much for conscience as a mode of discourse (sec. 56).

To describe the phenomenal character of conscience's call, i.e., how it makes its appearance, Heidegger chooses to probe deeper into who calls and who responds to the call. Since what one is called to in the concrete remains empty, the authentic self remains indefinite. Although in responding to the call, the inauthentic self has been reached, the caller remains aloof; after all, I am called to do something as a possible future of my present self. Yet all this emptiness, indefiniteness, and aloofness is not nothing but rather a positive feature of the phenomenon of conscience.

The caller is wholly absorbed in the summoning and is heard only as such. This means that in conscience a human being calls to itself. But not under the same aspects of its being. The self that is appealed to is the everyday self, lost in the objects of its world; that to which this lost self is summoned is its ownmost potentiality for being—or no longer being—in the world. The calling is a present projection into a world; and already abandoned to some existent world, I myself play the roles of caller and called, and no third agency, such as God, or society, or superego over which I can have no conscious control, is necessary for the phenomenon to be exhibited.

To understand the phenomenon we need only recall the structures of human existentiality. My factical existence as fallen is to be engrossed with the objects of my world; but I have been thrown into this world by a past over which I have no further control, and I have to be what I am to be, that is, what I am and can be. That is the care-structure of my being-in-the-world.

The why of any given factical situation may be hidden from me but not the fact of my being thrown into the world, which is given in all my affective states. My thrownness into the world is revealed to me along with the significance of my worlding world, and it continues to be revealed to me by my changing states of mind. If I choose the tranquility of the public world, I flee from myself and the anxiety that being a self entails. But I cannot flee the fleeing. If I face up to the nothingness of the public world, I am brought back to my anxiety.

Why should my anxious human being not be that which calls me out of the conventionality of the public world? As being the person it is, and worldly at that, it is still indefinable, that is, indefinite and aloof. But at the same time, it is primordial thrown being-in-the-world disclosed to itself as uncanniness. Since this self is unfamiliar to the everyday, public self, its call will always seem like an alien voice.

As it is, however, the call cannot be grasped by the inauthentic modes of disclosedness; curiosity scatters one's attention, and idle chatter, which would pass along the information, merely formulates the ambiguities of the ontic situation. For this reason, the only mode for receiving the call is reticence. In conscience, one is called from the chatty world where causes are pleaded into the reticence of the self.

Buy why should the message be unmistakable? Because of the care-structure: in its world, a human being is forsaken and abandoned to itself. Whatever the depth of the self-alienation felt by constant exposure to quotidian concerns, uncanniness pursues the human being that is alive to its possibilities. This uncanniness, a form of human self-disclosiveness, is a persistent threat to the domination of the public world, in which it has forgotten itself.

The original emptiness of the formula by which conscience had been described as a call from self to self has now been removed. What is manifest in conscience is the call of care. Consider: the caller is the human being, who in its thrownness (as already in a world) is anxious about its potentiality for Being. The called is the human being, summoned to its ownmost potentiality for Being (as ahead of itself). Since in the present it is falling into the publicity of the they-world, it hears the call as being alongside the entities of that world. In responding to the call in the feeling of uncanniness, it allows itself to be summoned out of its falling. Hence, there can be a phenomenon of conscience because a human being's being is caring.

For this reason, again, it is not necessary to resort to powers or agencies beyond simple human existentiality to explain the phenomenon of conscience. What would one gain for a so-called objective explanation by divine infusion, by a universal voice of humanity, or by the pressures of our social worlds? Each of these fails in its own way. God's voice may be "objective," but appealing to it evades the question of how that voice reaches us. There may be a universal voice attributable to all human beings; but if so, it would still be an "it" and a nobody. And any appeal to public pressures reinstates the primacy of the public world. In every case, the call of conscience and the response to it, is my own. "Dasein ist (immer) je meines!" But that does not mean that conscience is merely subjective, either. A self and a world are co-disclosed, whether they be authentic or inauthentic, whether I am tranquilized into insensitivity or anxiously facing the uncanniness of having chosen the wrong world.

Why then does the everyday call to be oneself get interpreted as warning or reproving? Another way of being in the untruth. The public wisdom has difficulty conceiving how a lucid self need warn or reprove its own actions and so supposes that some objective agency determines the feelings of guilt, as if all these were occasioned by some act of disobedience. Factical guilt is an ontic phenomenon, not an ontological structure of human being. Ontologically considered, our feelings of guilt have no significance at all. We must look beyond feelings of guilt to the existential structures that make them possible.

The reason: the attestation of our willing to have a conscience comes from a response to the call. The only feelings involved in this ontological interpretation are those of initial comfort in the publicity of the conventional world and the uncanniness of our personal anxiety. Both these feelings are modes of a human being's self-disclosure. If the human response to being called to oneself is heard or misheard, the interpretation of the phenomenon must come from the analysis of human being itself. For a full explanation of the call of conscience it will be necessary to hone in on the ways in which it is possible to respond to the call.

Since for the most part conscientiousness is troubling, and to have a conscience is to be disturbed about our factical guilt, it is necessary to investigate the ontological foundations that allow us to "hear" the call of conscience in this univocal fashion. What, indeed, is the relationship between our factical feelings of guilt and our being as abandoned in the world? The answer to this question is formulated in section 58.

The question, however, is announced as the relationship between the appeal of conscience and "*Schuld.*" I place the word in scare-quotes, because without them it is not clear, even to the German reader, what is intended by the ordinary concept employed. *The Cassell's New German and English Dictionary* gives us a clue. We read: "*Schuld*": debt; obligation; fault or blame; offense; sin; crime; guilt or indebtedness.[10] Nothing in this cluster of associated terms indicates that a moral or legal guilt is the primary intention of the term.

And the corresponding adjective, *schuldig,* is no clearer: due, owing, indebted; guilty, culpable, in fault; obliged; bound. Although the term occurs in the title of section 58 without the scare-quotes, for the next four pages of the analysis Heidegger uses them, presumably to call attention to the difference between a factical debt, fault, or crime, which as a fact would be given ontological sense only if a more universal, ontological significance could be found for the term.

In my own interpretation, contrary to that of Macquarrie and Robinson,[11] that ontological significance is "responsibility" for the noun, and "responsible" for the adjective. Macquarrie and Robinson retain the scare-quotes around "*Schuld,*" but translate it consistently as "Guilty"! In doing so, they have unwittingly given to English readers of the translated text ammunition for a bad-faith interpretation of existential responsibility as primordial moral transgression.

One interpreter even refers to Heidegger's earlier religious training (external evidence) and to his earlier explicated doctrine of *Verfallenheit* as the equivalent of the religious doctrine of original sin, as grounds for classifying our author as basically theologically oriented.[12]

A closer examination of the text will show that Heidegger is indeed concerned with differentiating religious, moral, and legal guilt as resulting from a factual decision or factual act and the existential constitution of the human being who makes the decision to act, and who might therefore be judged as guilty or innocent. We all may be sinners, as the preachers of this world claim, but that is not an ontological affair. Let us therefore return to the text, to see how things stand with our being.

The problem is generated by the reticence by which a sensitive human being responds to the call of conscience. Feeling guilty, of course, is one possibility; but it is purely factical. We are still interested in how this factical feeling is possible, knowing full well that it exists. Hence, we are not interested in what gets called in and to each particular human being in his or her situation, but rather in what belongs to being called to one's existential possibility, given the factical circumstances in which the call, as appeal, is interpreted.

For the authentic understanding, the appeal is to the factically situated self in its falling; but the summons is "forward" to that self's ownmost potentiality for being. The discrepancy between the self to which the appeal is made and that to which it is summoned is registered as uncanniness, a present moment of conscious experience tracing a region of strictly personal concern. "Conscience" as a psychological phenomenon is the awareness of being called forth, from our lostness in the public world, where we would be comfortable but for the onset of the uncanniness.

The "vulgar" interpretations of conscience as "moral," and therefore as "good" or "bad," indicates that the call of conscience is interpreted as warning or reproving. A bad conscience is troublesome, and a good conscience is, paradoxically, one which is aware of no guilt. But the "goodness" or "badness" and therefore the guilt or the innocence of a conscience cannot be the starting point of our investigation, since what is sought in such an investigation is a phenomenon of the public world, in which guilt is determinable by some standard independent of the acting subject—custom, for example. Existential responsibility is presumably internal to the constitution of the human being and not something external imposed upon it. So, a reconceptualization is needed.

Heidegger takes on the project by once again probing the collective unconscious of the German people by examining the ordinary meanings of being (factically) guilty, *Schuldigsein*. Not surprisingly, the first attempts have more to do with indebtedness than with fault or crime. After all, if I ask a German merchant, "Wieviel bin ich Ihnen schuldig?" he knows I asked how much I owe him, and he cites the appropriate amount. Indeed, this example occurs first in the list, as follows.

The expression is *Schulden haben,* to have a debt or to owe something to someone—a phenomenon, clearly, of our being-with others, in which we have incurred a debt by borrowing, depriving, buying, or stealing something belonging to the other. The burden here, however, is with something about which we can become concerned as an item of our world, not something which stems from our innermost being.

So, try *schuld sein an,* being responsible for something, as the cause of what has happened to oneself or to another. But one can be responsible for something without owing anything to anyone; and one can owe something to another without being responsible for the debt, since it may be incurred in one's name by another. As a result of these two meanings, we understand that owing and being responsible are not the same phenomenon, although assuredly related.

The next term, *sich schuldig machen* (making oneself responsible for a debt owing to others) takes away the attribution of indebtedness by proxy permitted by the former and still succeeds in capturing the way in which we exist and have moral relations with others in the public world: we make ourselves responsible to the judgment of others by breaking a law or violating a custom and in this way come to owe something to those others.

My responsibility to the other, however, is not merely occasioned by my having broken a law, custom, or agreement, so much as having caused damage to the other by having done so. If I am guilty, therefore, in my relations with others, it is for having been the cause of a lack in the being of those others. In this sense, and in this sense alone, can factical guilt aid our understanding of our universal responsibility. When we harm others, we make ourselves guilty for some kind of lack in their being.

Coming to terms with our factical guilt, therefore, is not a matter of reckoning debts or of prescribing actions in terms of any moral law or universal "ought." The lack or deficiency that gets interpreted in such calculations is something that should be present in the world, but is factually missing. What remains to be done is to find an ontological equivalent to this sense of there being something missing in the world because of my experience of that world.

Heidegger refers to this "missing" or "absent" something as a "not" ("ein Nicht"), a "nullity" ("eine Nichtigkeit"), even a "not-ness" ("eine Nichtheit"), as he creates a term to express a condition of privation as an essential component of our existential constitution. Grounding such a notion is performed by a re-reading of the care-structure. Being-responsible means being the basis for a being which is defined as a "not."

Consider, first, thrownness. A human being is always already in a world and projected to its potentialities for being. Its basis for being what itself is has no basis; it must be accepted as it is given. Thrown-ness, as the baseless basis for a human being's projection into a future, therefore exhibits a *not*.

Next, existence: that possibility of being toward which I project myself does not yet exist; a pure possibility and not an actuality, which allows my freedom of choice. Here, too, a *not*.

Lastly, in falling or facticity, in the contingency of the present moment, I experience my own *in*authenticity, another *not*, that creates the *uncanniness*, still another, as the feeling of *not* being at home in the world of conventional existence.

Since this is what a human being is, in its ontological constitution, we cannot say that our "existential nullity" is an absolute privation; it is, rather, a positive basis for our being the way we are. It is this ontological structure, our being as a factically thrown projection, that makes us responsible for "the not" we are. A person is not a thing.

When we are called to be ourselves, we are called to assume the responsibility for our actions. A human being, in its very constitution, is responsible for what it is, and for this reason may incur factical debts and become guilty of various crimes of omission or commission. What we flee in seeking the temptations of the public world is our own awareness of being responsible for being ourselves.

In sum, then, the call of conscience is reaffirmed as the call of care. The appeal of conscience is to the public self from that ownmost potentiality of being which is our true self, spanning the region of our existential projection. The motion is both back and forth. We are called forth to that which we are not yet and back to the thrown facticity, which as contingent has no foundation.

The ontological definition is worth quoting:

> Der vorrufende Rückruf des Gewissens gibt dem Dasein zu verstehen, daß es—nichtiger Grund seines nichtigen Entwurfs in der Möglichkeit seines Seins stehend—aus der Verlorenheit in das Man sich zu ihm selbst zurückholen soll, das heißt *schuldig ist.*

> The calling back of conscience that calls us forth gives the human being to understand that it itself—as the null basis of its own null projection standing in the possibility of its being— is to bring itself back unto itself out of its lostness in the public world, i.e., gives it to understand that it is responsible.[13]

Thus, the ontological condition for any factical guilt that may result from failing to fulfill an indebtedness always exists before our consciousness of such guilt. Since a human being exists understandingly in its world, it understands through the call of its conscience that it is responsible for the manner in which it exists in that world.

But given the two overall possibilities for a human being to be, that is, its own self or determined by another, it may let itself be called forth, opening itself to receive the call; or, on the other hand, to reject it in favor of the tranquilized self-alienation of the public world. Its feeling of uncanniness in that world announces that it is free to choose itself; but to respond in the proper manner, it must make its own choice. Its choice of authenticity is to want to have a conscience, to accept the responsibility to which its conscience calls.

As practicing moralists have always told us, we cannot be guilty for any action for which we cannot be held responsible. Being-responsible (*Schuldigsein*) is an ontological precondition for being guilty. To choose to have a conscience, in the ordinary sense of the term, is to free ourselves for assuming the responsibility for our own being. Once it has chosen responsibility, the human being allows itself to take action; and so is answerable for the consequences of that action, be they merely psychological, moral, or legal.

What one is summoned to, therefore, in response to the call of conscience, is the positive determination of one's own being. The call is not merely critical nor does it give any more specific information about what, precisely, must be done in a particular factical situation. Wanting to have a conscience does not tell us what or what not to do; it only increases our personal anxiety about whether we have done or are about to do the right thing.

So much for the phenomenon of conscience. It remains to be seen how this phenomenon has been treated in the everyday manner in contrast to the existential-ontological account of the conscientious human being given above, and completed below.

Section 59 contrasts the existential and the everyday accounts of the phenomenon of conscience.

Heidegger arranges the evidence into a set of four criticisms one might bring to his account from a traditional point of view. He begins with the observation that his interpretation fails to explain the difference between a "good" and a "bad" conscience, between that which warns us of some evil to come and that which reproves us for having committed an evil in the past. The everyday "reproving" conscience points to a past action and does not necessarily call us forward to anything at all. True, the reproving factical conscience points toward a past forbidden act; but this does not preclude our being called forth to a time in which our debt will have been paid, by a change in behavior; this is what happens, for example, in the case of the rehabilitation of a criminal. Feeling guilty about a past act may motivate us to change our behavior, that is, a factical indebtedness could be the occasion for our making a decision to modify our conduct to "reform" ourselves. The call occurs, and it does call back, not just to the past act, but to the thrown existence that had committed that act.

What, then, about the so-called good conscience? It is pharisaic. Only the good person could say "I am good," and that person won't, for fear of committing the sin of self-righteousness. Since this is the case, and it is generally recognized as such, having a good conscience has come to be interpreted as not having a bad conscience, or of forgetting that one has a conscience at all. We can, of course, choose not to have a conscience in our inauthenticity, but then there is nothing to be good or bad.

Moreover, if the good conscience warns us to avoid a future evil act, it seems to be at least consistent with the forward character of the existential conscientious summons. But this seeming, says Heidegger, is illusory. To heed such a warning would be to forego what we have already willed, but we would be able to do so only if the authentic call had already been heard.

Next, the charge is that experience has no acquaintance with our (ontological) being-guilty. True, but there is a difference between being factically guilty and being ontologically self-responsible. A human being exhibits a care-structure according to which it is falling into a public world; in this present falling, it tends to cover over the truth. Moreover, experience is of facts, of deeds willed or performed. Factical guilt is therefore a matter of ontological presence; it is an innerworldly event, rather than of the ontological constitution of the person. And if experience claims that conscience serves as the arbiter and admonisher of justice, there must be some kind of "metaphysics of morals" that would explain how conscience serves as witness and judge in this court of the moral law.

Thirdly, the Heideggerian account overlooks the fact that conscience always emits its call in relationship to some specific deed, actualized or willed. This is often the case, says Heidegger, but the full range of the phenomenon of conscience may not be disclosed in a particular instance. The facts for an empirical interpretation of conscience, which should be present if we are to be able to make the interpretation, are not always completely available for a decision to be made on the basis of a ready reckoning, such as those made in household inventories.

Lastly, it could be stated that the existential account misses the essentially "critical" character of conscience. To an extent, of course, this is true, since nothing definite is said by conscience. But it is a mistake to expect a positive statement about what must be done, since there can be no assurance that something useful will eventuate from reckoning with any future possibilities. The future as not yet present will always remain indefinite. To expect otherwise is to confuse morals with economics; a business procedure calculating profits is no substitute for our choosing to have a conscience, although in many cases an economist may attempt to convince us otherwise.

But if conscience does not give us an unerring aid for determining what we must do, it doesn't give any negative criticism either. In the call of conscience we are called to nothing that is external to ourselves, nothing with which we could concern ourselves in the world. The phenomenon concerns our personal manner of existence only. But since it eventuates in our choosing to have or not to have a conscience, it can only motivate some action that is left for our free election to decide. For this same reason, we shall never have enough evidence to convince ourselves, much less others, that our "conscience is clear."

How then is our existentiality disclosed in the phenomenon of conscience? The answer is proposed in section 60.

Since conscience gives us something to understand, and understanding is one of the equiprimordial structures of human disclosedness, along with feeling and discourse, it may be profitable to review these structures of our being-in our worlds. To understand something is to project it, within a general context of interpretation, upon a specific forehaving. Our preontological comprehension of our own being was the ultimate horizon of our first ontological projections, and that has been modified by our being a whole and, now, our being an authentic personality. Conscience calls us forward to project ourselves upon our ownmost factical possibility; it does not tell us what such possibilities may be, outside of the last, which is the possibility to no longer be in the world. The call indicates how to make death our own.

The clue to this interpretation is in the mood. Conscience arises in our feeling of the uncanniness of the public world and calls us to the acceptance of our anxiety as our own, even down to our being-toward-death as constantly anticipated.

But as a mode of discourse, conscience occurs in reticence, in which we face steadfastly the ever-present possibility of factical guilt—of failing to achieve our innermost drive to be ourselves. This court is always in session. The chattiness of the public world calls us to the soundlessness of our innermost uncanniness, from the stillness of the self lost in the public world to one which shall never be able to vaunt its success or its failures in audible discourse.

In sum, conscience as the call of care is the reticent self-projection upon one's ownmost being-responsible, in which we hold ourselves open to anxiety. This condition of our being is resoluteness (*Entschlossenheit*). It is the primordial truth of our existence (being-revealing-revealed), an existential structure of our being. Indeed, it is that existential that allows us to determine what it is to be our own person.

For this reason, the resoluteness by which we accept the call to assume responsibility for our own anxiety is the fullest characterization of our being-in-the-world given so far. When in resoluteness the self becomes freed for its own self-determination, it is capable of choosing that ultimate for-the-sake-of-which any given action is undertaken. Resoluteness is the principle by which a world becomes closed; it is how a context of involvements becomes our own.

Two consequences of some importance follow from this description. The first is a reminder that resoluteness is a manner of acting; it is always relative to some human being's decision, at a particular time, to assume the responsibility of its own being. But since nothing in the factical situation indicates what must be resolved, that is left to the freedom of the individual acting. What actually occurs in every practical situation is a concurrence between the physical limitations on a set of possibilities and the acting person's ingenuity to use them in his or her disclosive projection.

But this had already been said when Heidegger described the self and world as being co-disclosed, the two equiprimordial moments of ontological truth. We know in general the conditions under which a choice for resolute self-determination must be made; we must pursue our own being in a manner of concernful solicitude for others. But this is always threatened by our falling into a public world. Resoluteness is letting oneself be summoned out of lostness in the world of everyman and everywoman.

Second, the resoluteness of our decision to be ourselves illuminates the ordinary concept of *situations*. Factically, a situation is a purely spatial concept. But the psychological and the sociological acceptations of the term become clear when we realize that a situation, as a locus of possibilities for action, does not exist before an action. It is only a resolute decision to act in one way or another that makes clear what the situation is.

Ontologically considered, a situation is the "region" determined by the individual self-projection into a future from a "place" in the world in which the acting human being always finds itself already thrown. In a word, a "situation" is the counterelement, as a figure is the counterelement to a ground, and vice-versa, to a personal identity (sec. 60).

And although Heidegger does not mention it, since the phenomenon had not yet occurred, this description of the relationship between a living person and its situation has since become the ground for a newer ethical system called "situational ethics."[14] But that is something that need not be defended here.

4. *Human being and anticipatory resoluteness.*

At the end of division 2, chapter 2, Heidegger has arrived at a new characterization for the being of human being. Preontologically understood, because it is felt, as being-in-a-world, human being has advanced from caring to "anticipatory resoluteness," or "resolute anticipation" of one's ownmost, ultimate potentiality for being. Should we be tempted here to graph the vectors described by the "call of conscience," of course, the diagram would be the same as our last figure,[15] with only a slight change in the designation of the "directions." In the future, represented by the projectional aspect of life, we now find the authentic self—that which I am not yet but will be if I respond to its call; in the past, the thrown self I am attempting to overcome or to reinforce; in the present, my fallen self occupied with the things of my world but disturbed by the uncanniness of it all.

This should be apparent from Heidegger's interpretation of the phenomenon of conscience in terms of the care-structure of our human being. The only difference between the former "caring" as a description of that being and the current "anticipatory resoluteness" is its further determination as a manner of being in its world. At least one interpreter of Heidegger has mentioned that the description of human being herein given—as freedom for self-determination and hence for creativity as a way of life—is one of the reasons his existential ontology should be taken seriously.[16]

Whether we adopt the moral point of view or the aesthetic as our point of departure, our view of human nature must permit the belief that what a human being does makes a difference in who he or she is. In a word, human beings not only can but should be held responsible for their acts and should be allowed the range of freedom to discover just which acts, precisely, are their own.

I finish this comment on anticipatory resoluteness with a flourish that imposes itself on any sensitive reader's mind. Previously, Heidegger had discovered in a myth of Hyginus, entitled *Cura*, a preontological "self-interpretation" of human being as caring. That he should avoid a similar reference to the Socrates of Plato's *Euthyphro, Apology, Crito,* and *Phaedo* is almost incomprehensible. In these dialogues, which are as much fable as the myth of Hyginus, Socrates is presented as a person who lived a life of anticipatory resoluteness—that is, who faced the ultimate potentiality of being—which is to no longer be there—with justice and self-acquiescence, because not to do so would be to have made a choice that was not his own. The whole of the matter is put by Socrates to Crito, his rich friend who offers to bribe Socrates' way out of jail: All my life I have preached justice. You ask me to commit an act of injustice in order to live a few more paltry years. How can I think one thing is right and do another?

And, in the *Phaedo*, his last recorded words were to remember a debt, which he asked to be paid.

If not compelling, it is tempting to revisit the last Socratic dialogues of Plato armed with the Heideggerian analytic of human existence. Not only is anticipatory resoluteness an adequate description of human wholeness and integrity, it also fares well as a description of what is the best and most noble achievement of the human spirit. Plato revered Socrates in this way and quite obviously viewed the latter's self-sacrifice as an act of resolute anticipation of the end. If Socrates had listened to Crito, he would have been just another Sophist, a lawyer whose limping case for justice failed to save his own life in court, but who succeeded in copping a postcurial plea to avoid the consequences of that act. Such a person could not have founded the study of ethics. Indeed, one of the reasons cultural historians have created an epoch of "pre-Socratic philosophy," which Heidegger loved so much he was willing to undertake the destruction of the history of ontology to regain its insights, was the fact that Socrates had lived an authentic existence.

8

From Death and Conscience to Temporality and Time

THE PASSAGE—FROM DEATH AND CON-science to temporality and time as ontological structures of human being—is both methodological and methodical. It is methodological, in that Heidegger finds it opportune, in division 2, chapter 3, of his text, to summarize how his analytic has reached this point in the interpretation of the meaning of Being; to remind us that all onto-logical interpretations are circular and that coming to know some-thing of its world or of its self is a way for a human being to be in the world; and to project a mode of further inquiry, which will bring him closer to his goal of linking the notions of being and time. It is methodical since each of the moves either summarized or projected is an application of his hermeneutical methodology.

The casual reader of the text may heave a sigh of relief during the summary, if for some reason the methodical nature of Heidegger's prior moves has gone unnoticed—as they will, if one is solely inter-ested in results. The cultivated reader, on the other hand, will view the summary as the gathering of forces for a further charge into the breach. He or she knows that the forehaving of an interpretation is in continual revision as newer descriptions are found for the phe-nomena being interpreted.

The original foresighted element was human being (*Dasein*); it was interpreted, in the preparatory analytic, as existing in a world. The existentiality of this existence was analyzed into worldhood, selfhood, and being-in. By its disclosedness—its manner of being-in, through its feelings, understanding and discourse—a human being comes to know itself explicitly as caring, always ahead of itself in a projection toward its possibilities, abandoned in a world, and alongside the entities within that world.

But the hermeneutical situation of the preparatory analysis was established by electing the average condition of the human being, that is, how it exists, first and foremost, in the world of its everyday concerns. It gave no point of view on how the human being could be a whole, nor an authentic person. So, still guided by the idea of existence (as befitting only a human being), Heidegger sought to isolate those structures of existentiality that would permit a human being to be conceived as a whole and at the same time as being its own person. As a result, the phenomenon of death was given its existential interpretation—as the last possibility of its being; and of conscience, as the choice to assume the responsibility for its own being, even in the face of the various degrees of nullity that choice entails. All this is explained by reference to the original care-structure.

A human being may experience its death as a possibility in anticipation; and it may become its own person by wanting to have a conscience, that is, by responding to the summons that calls it out of its lostness in the world of the everyday. Making such a decision is an act of resoluteness. Can the wholeness and the unity of a human existence be brought into a significant relationship? How could a human being attest to its anticipatory resoluteness or to its resolute anticipation as a single phenomenon?

Such a description is the object of division 2, chapter 3, where Heidegger selects resoluteness as his theme and asks whether, within a given ontic situation, resoluteness points toward its own last potentiality for being. We need only remember that we are not dealing with an entity whose being is to be present in the world but rather an existent projection into it. As an existent, the human being is always projected upon its own possibilities; that much was established in the care-structure. What must be done in this instance is to project the existential structures of human caring onto the actual possibilities of the given ontic situation and, as he says, think the situation through to its end.

In this way, there would be no simple addition of resoluteness to anticipation but a radical thinking-through of their relatedness. Just as, earlier, death was interpreted through care as the critical fore-having, so now resoluteness will be interpreted through death as that ultimate possibility toward which a human being may project itself. And once this interpretation has been made, it will become possible to view in advance the basic constitution of an ontically situated human being. Neither substance, nor independent subject, the living human being determines itself to be what it is, as it resolutely projects itself toward its end.

The how of that projection is yet to be made clear. The previous existential analysis permits us to "view in advance" the situation of a given, living human being. Plato's description of the death of Socrates gave us a literary description of the phenomenon, but it must still be shown how such an ontical possibility can be authentically one's own.

Death and conscience illuminate the structure of care. They give it a wholeness and an integrity that it lacked in the preliminary analysis. Moreover, the ontological meaning of care must be arrived at methodically—not just as the temporal foreconception it was announced to be in the prior analysis. If the meaning of human caring is to be shown to be temporality, thinking through the existential constitution of anticipatory resoluteness must show how temporality gets experienced in a primordial way. How a human being experiences its temporality should show it as developing through time, as, indeed, it temporalizes itself (*sich zeitigt*) into a personal history. When we shall have reached this stage of our analysis, not only the wholeness and the integrity of the human being but also its temporal development will have been described. And, at that time, it will be possible to repeat the analysis of human being in terms of its everydayness, its historicity, and its being within time of the natural world.

Such is the summary and projection of section 61. The end of the analysis is now in sight.

That the analysis should end with a description of a human being's situation within the time of the real world should no longer dismay us. That is where Heidegger found his *Dasein* to begin with, and returning there after the analysis demonstrates that the hermeneutical explanation of a phenomenon is indeed circular.

SO, WE BEGIN with anticipatory resoluteness—the resolute choice of being responsible for ourselves even unto death—and ask how such a choice is possible in a given living situation. In order to explain existential structures, we must relate them to the actual possibilities of an ontic situation in which a human being finds itself involved. As in every case heretofore, the existence of the ontological structure must be attested to in the concrete. Heidegger puts the question in related ways. First, does resoluteness as the possibility of our integrity lead us to the conception of an authentic being-toward-death? Or, second, can resoluteness, which is itself attested to as an ontic possibility for a given human being by its choice of conscience, be modalized through its being-toward-death, that is, its anticipation of an ultimate possibility beyond which there will be nothing? Let us consider his answers to these questions.

By definition, resoluteness is a projection upon one's ownmost being-responsible for whatever it is to become. As such, it is understood by the disclosedness of the conscientious individual who lives constantly as projected toward an end. The "constancy" of the self so projected cannot stem from the metaphysical properties of a categorial substance nor of a self that, according to Kant, accompanies our every thought as the form of its synthesis. To be resolute is to be constant in one's self-determination—always, until the very end.

But the prior analysis of being-at-an-end has shown that such a being would be merely present in the world (of nature), and moreover, as dead; so the projective being, self-directed toward its end, remains alive only on the condition of continually anticipating that end (as a condition of its wholeness), and understanding the process as it occurs. This understanding, of course, is motivated by the anxiety that breaks in upon the uncanniness of not being at home within the everyday world.

The same resoluteness that allows us to have a conscience by willing to have one forces us to face up to the finiteness of our human condition. To be resolute it is not sufficient merely to want a conscience; that fact must be attested by the assumption of the responsibility of our condition; and since that condition will terminate with our deaths, being resolute likewise implies the necessity of assuming the responsibility for our very being-toward-the-end, which is death ontologically considered. It is dying, but it is also living, since, given the finiteness of our condition, the two processes are one.

Considered in this light, resoluteness as a way of life harbors an authentic being-unto-death as the one possible ontic modality open to it in the achievement of its own being, which is to be responsible for itself. Since resoluteness is attested to by every action in which a human being allows itself to be responsible for its acts, and it is with the knowledge of our own being-responsible that we act, to be resolute or not within a given lived situation is an ontic possibility for the person finding itself in that situation. For this reason, every acting person may experience ontic guilt, either consciously or unconsciously, authentically (i.e., having willed the indebtedness) or inauthentically (not having done so). In assuming its ontic indebtedness, the human being assumes responsibility for its acts. And, with respect to its own death, assuming responsibility for that "indebtedness" means taking upon oneself the burden of deciding how to die—authentically, in anguish, or inauthentically, in fear.

We must therefore be led to understand what our resoluteness shows us, that in the end the call to conscience discloses our existentiality, along with our facticity and our fallen condition. And it was in analyzing this "care-structure" that being ontologically responsible was said to disclose a three-dimensional "nullity" within our basic constitution: as thrown, a ground*less* basis for being in the world; as existent, projected to our end, the last possibility of utter *im*possibility; and as fallen, lost in an *in*authentic world for which no one is responsible.

Heidegger's next move is to show that death complements conscience, since each forms an equiprimordial structure of human being considered ontologically as caring. First, the claim; then its demonstration.

The claim seems simple. It is only in choosing responsibility for its own acts until the very end that a human being can be both authentic and whole. But since ontological death is a possibility of no longer being, it must be anticipated as that final condition if it is to be "experienced" at all. Not to face one's finiteness resolutely is to be irresolute and inauthentic. To stress this fact Heidegger says,

Die vorlaufende Entschlossenheit versteht erst das Schuldigseinkönnen *eigentlich und ganz,* das heißt, *ursprünglich.*

Only anticipatory resoluteness understands our being able to be responsible both authentically and wholly, i.e., primordially.[1]

And, *primordially* here should be read as meaning "in our very being."

To demonstrate this "founded" mode of our being, relating its wholeness to its integrity, Heidegger retraces the ontological determinations of death as they may now be related to human self-responsibility. Recall, death was described as a possibility: one's ownmost, totally isolating (nonrelational), unovertakable, certain, yet indefinite. Each of these bears a relation to our resolute choice of a self.

1. *Our ownmost possibility.* The call of conscience from authentic to inauthentic self reveals our lostness in the everyday world and calls us back to being our own person. Uncanniness and anxiety are the corresponding affective states accompanying the silent discourse.

2. *Totally isolating.* The call reaches from "afar"—the authentic self—to "afar"—the lost self—passing over all worldly considerations; and there is, hence, nothing to which this end may be related, within the silent deliberations of conscience.

3. *Unovertakable.* Ontological responsibility exists before and after every factical indebtedness, before its having been contracted and after its having been paid off. The priority of the ontological structure is merely covered over in our everyday dealings and commerce until it has been made possible through our understanding that death is the last of our possibilities. Until then, each act of incurring or settling an indebtedness can be considered a mere ontic fact, and hence overtakable in natural time; but our basic being-responsible cannot be eradicated by any factual data.

4. *Certain.* Being certain accompanies every act of revealing an entity within our worlds; it is a state of mind accompanying our being-revealing. Moreover, resoluteness creates the factical situation in which a human being incurs an indebtedness: without responsibility, there is no indebtedness and no guilt! So, in all those situations in which a factical debt has been incurred, the agent holds himself as free and responsible for his act. But if he can hold himself as free, he can also hold himself back. Authentic resoluteness demands a constant resolve to repeat being one's self, which can be taken back, finally, only by death. As long as there is such a resolve, one holds one's freedom as true; and that is the condition of certainty. But a resolve may be changed. If so, our being is not constant, and we fall once more into inauthenticity: we allow others to pay our debts, or we attribute our own faults to them.

5. *Indefinite.* Whatever definiteness might exist in the experience of death comes from the contingencies of a current factical situation, created by a prior resolute or irresolute decision. We may fear our

actual death, or be anxious before the possibility of our no longer being-there. In the truth, a human being holds as true the certainty of its death. In the untruth, the constancy of this resolve has been broken. But even then, in the irresoluteness of inauthenticity, one can hold as true, that is, be certain of, this possibility of being.

Whether authentic or inauthentic, here "resolute" or "irresolute," the difference can only be judged by relation to the current situation. And, as such, the object of the resolve must remain indefinite. The precise moment, not to mention manner, of one's death, the moment when one's authentic possibility is that marking the utter impossibility of further existing, and the manner of this transition, cannot be known for certain. The indefiniteness of our deaths feeds our anxiety; but this anxiety, which we are, is resolutely reaffirmed by our response to the call of conscience.

In sum, then, each of these prior-developed characteristics of a human death, when considered in relationship to a resolve to be oneself, shows how resoluteness comes to modalize our basic being-unto-death. Not only is the potentiality for being a whole (that is, our dying) authentic, it is also made to fit our ontic situation by our response to a concrete call of conscience. Anticipating one's death, therefore, is not a mere conceptualization of the end of a life, but rather an authentic way of resolving to be responsible for oneself under actual living conditions.

We no longer have two phenomena—death and conscience, attested to ontically by anticipation and resolve respectively—but one: our being in the world as anticipatory resoluteness. The unity of the two phenomena is demonstrated in a question and an answer. How can one experience one's potentiality for being a whole? Answer: by resolutely choosing it. But only the interested individual is capable of giving that answer, since only an individual chooses to be or not to be itself.

Our inquiry, which began with the ontic priority of human being only to search for those ontological structures implicit within every ontical action, has now returned from a description of human existentiality (the ontological) to a localized and temporalized individual person whose actions in a current situation (the ontical) are necessary to "complete" the demonstration. That is, the phenomenon of an authentic being-a-whole has been described; but only a living individual may exhibit it in his or her conduct.

This return to an ontic dimension of an ontological "demonstration," of course, is no accident. For Heidegger, it is required by the nature of an interpretive understanding, as is by now clear from the hermeneutical circle we have been traveling. But, lest a reader have missed his last explanation of the circle and been so imperceptive as not to have seen it in his work thus far, Heidegger spends an entire section of this chapter rehearsing the hermeneutical methodology of his existential analytic, readjusting the forehaving for a further interpretation of the meaning of being of care.

The section is 63. I shall be brief in my summary.

Our ultimate aim has been to explain the meaning of the being of care. We began with the knowledge a human being has of itself as a being existing in a world. Although the knowledge with which we began was only implicit, in that we are that being, this purely ontic foundation of our inquiry was an absolute necessity. Without it, our ontological investigation would have been ungrounded. Since, ontically, a human being knows itself as a projection toward possibilities, it was our purpose in the ontological interpretation of this projection merely to describe the structures of existentiality—called "existentials"—which make such behavior possible. The number of such existentials has now become enormous—from the mineness with which we began, through averageness and everydayness, up to and including the anticipatory resoluteness most recently discussed.

But the preparatory analysis began with the everyday characteristics of human being, in their averageness. As a result, the self that gets expressed in the everyday activities of this being is not one's own. It is inauthentic—a condition that is nevertheless a genuine possibility of human existence. If caring is the being exemplified in human existence and our everyday manner of living such an existence is inauthentic, our authentic being gets covered up in the day-to-day choices we are forced to make to adjust to a conventional world and hence is ignored by the preliminary ontological analysis.

What is needed, therefore, is a method to force the uncovering of our authentic being. Our ontology must reverse the initial process and move from a description of the existentials going to make up human existentiality to a description of authentic being as one of the possibilities inherent within our ontic situations. How?

Consider. Interpretation, as a way of knowing, belongs to a human being's disclosiveness. By making an interpretation the inquiring human being projects a significance. At the beginning of our analysis we chose the idea of existence—human self-projection—as the theme to be interpreted. That self-projection discloses a world and human concern as correlative phenomena. When the question was asked, at the beginning of the second part of Heidegger's treatise, what it meant to be a whole and authentic, and then an authentic whole, the method was still hermeneutical. Being an authentic whole was based upon an actual lived situation, as one of its possibilities. Such possibilities are made possible by ontological structures, such as worldhood, selfhood, being-in, but these latter do not distinguish the authentic from the inauthentic possibilities open to human choice.

Anticipatory resoluteness, as a way for a human being to be an authentic whole, was given meaning by being projected "backward," so to speak, upon the care structure of the preliminary analysis. Have we gone as far as we can? Hardly. In a hermeneutical analysis an entity gets interpreted in terms of the being that is its own, and this being is given a structural analysis. The meaning of that being, if we are to be able to describe it, is that upon which the structures of the being of the entity—the existentials—are projected, where the further projection is still to be guided by the original foresighted idea of existence. The entity, of course, is a human being; its being is caring; and the anticipated meaning of that being is temporality. All these steps are in some sense already presupposed by the idea of existence that was our preontological comprehension of our own being.

The results of our analysis have been threefold: first, the differentiation of human being from the being of things (their presence or reality) and of tools (their serviceability); second, the description of the formal structure of human beings as care: being projected into its world, already abandoned there, and, on the average, lost among the objects of that world; and third, the reconsideration of the initial notion of a human being as being in a world, ending with the same notion, now ontologically clarified. The circle is therefore apparent.

But there are two kinds of explanatory circles. The first, the so-called vicious circle, consists in assuming what one would like to prove. Both formal logic and common sense reject such a procedure. And correctly so, if what one presupposes to begin an argument is precisely what one concludes. The hermeneutical method ends with the same idea with which it began, but does not leave it in the same state. The care structure is implicit in our ontic concerns and is only made explicit by the ontological interpretation.

To understand the difference between a logically vicious circle and the hermeneutical circle of explanation we must remember that understanding is a way for a human being to be; and that our being exhibits a structure that is itself circular: a projection toward a future possibility, but as authentic, resolutely repeating that act which is most our own. Care is circular, the call of conscience is circular; and in projecting an explanation of these phenomena, in terms of the existentials already isolated, our understanding is likewise circular. Albeit enriched by the journey, we have only returned to where we were at the beginning of our inquiry.

Since understanding is not a pure product of our thinking, of a substantial self, or of a world that merely impresses itself upon us, it is something else; so why may it not be a manner of our being in the world through which our basic ontic concerns are carefully interpreted? If that is right, our understanding is interpretive, that is, projective; and to proceed beyond the point we have reached up until this methodological digression we must keep the care-structure in mind as the fruit of a past analysis, and as the basis for the one to come. That will be a further projection—from our being as an understanding to a fuller (ontological) understanding of the meaning of that being.

How can an authentic self, as a special way of caring, be ontologically understood? Up to now, we have only shown that it is one living possibility for every human being. That was the backward look. To interpret it further, we must project it upon still another structure, the one which, presumably, makes it possible for us to be an authentic whole. We have known from the beginning that this structure is temporality, but that idea is still uninterpreted.

HOW IS THE care-structure to be projected upon temporality in order to determine its meaning? Following the methodology sketched out above, we must answer "carefully," that is, our understanding and its projections are themselves ways of caring for ourselves in a world. What gets in the way of the simple comprehension of this matter is the fact that the preparatory analysis of being-in-the-world arrived at a care-structure whose unity and authenticity posed an additional problem for ontological elucidation. Again, Heidegger reviews his past results.

Existence, as a structure of human being, interprets that being as ahead of itself, as a not-yet, which necessitates the concept of our being-toward-the-end. This was procured in the analysis of death. Then, how this whole can be one's own posed a problem, and the call of conscience gave the answer to that. That we can achieve an authentic wholeness of our own is attested to by the ontic possibility of resolutely anticipating our own no longer being in the world. Anticipatory resoluteness is therefore the necessary condition for a human being's actually choosing the possibility of being a true self.

But even here a new problem announces itself. How can the care-structure, constituted by existentiality, thrownness, and falling, even summarized as anticipatory resoluteness, be described as organizing or articulating our experience? What gets in the way of our finding a quick answer to this question is not itself a simple phenomenon. First, there is common sense, which considers the unity of the self as if it were something that might be taken for granted. A self, from this point of view, is an entity that is both subject and object of experiences, known primarily by its reflexivity. In discourse, the self is named by each "I" that proclaims itself a speaker. Who am I? The speaking person, the one whose thoughts are expressed by the words it enunciates.

Descartes interpreted this entity as a simple substance, which is always the subject and never the predicate of an attribution. But already in the critical philosophy of Immanuel Kant, the simplicity, the substantiality, and the personality of the speaking self were called into question in the "Paralogisms of Rational Psychology."[2] The reason: Descartes' explanation of selfhood does not gibe with the phenomenal experience of being a self.

Well, does Kant himself fare any better? A little, but he too leaves ontological questions unanswered. For Kant, who replaced Descartes' Latin *cogito* with the German *ich denke*, selected this expression for the express purpose of showing just how Descartes failed to capitalize on what was given in the cogito argument. The speaking "I" is not a substance and therefore not a perduring entity; indeed, it is no real entity or thing at all; it is a form.

For Kant, the self is consciousness, considered as the form that accompanies all conscious representation. To say "I think" is always to say "I think something." What I think is a representation to myself of "intuitions"—synthesized manifolds of sensuous impressions—that are eventually interpreted through concepts deriving their meaning from the categories of the understanding. In thinking, the subject binds together the properties of things in an intuition and interprets them through concepts. And so the "I think" in its concreteness names the "logical subject" of knowing.

As the form that accompanies all representations, the self as subject underlies all thinking; and as the "transcendental unity of our apperception" it is the necessary condition for there being any knowledge at all. Instead, therefore, of being presupposed as the substance for our attribute of thinking, as with Descartes, in Kant, the self is presupposed—our knowledge of it is still a priori—as the formal condition for the possibility of the knowledge we actually possess.

Is there a difference? Yes. Heidegger claims that Kant's explanation is much closer to the intuitive content of the common-sense understanding of "I-saying." It does not assume the categorial determination of the self as a substance and so sticks closer to the "data" of common sense. Still, in sticking to the subject, rather than retreating to a substance, Kant was unaware that his ontological understanding of the self was inadequate. Showing how will give us the clue for our own ontological interpretation.

Arguing by transcendental deduction to the existence of a pure self, Kant assumed that the pure subject of knowing was characterizable as a self; but what that concept covered was not selfhood (*Selbstheit des Ich qua Selbst*) but rather the self-sameness and constancy (*Selbigkeit und Beständigkeit*) of something that was always present in an act of thought, even though only as a form, and so still as something real. Kant's analysis in the end failed because it treated Descartes' *res cogitans* as a real, rather than as an "existent," entity. As if to drive the silver spike through the heart of the vampire, Heidegger adds: besides, Kant never did explain just how the transcendental unity of apperception accompanies our every act of thought. Since the thoughts themselves were considered purely "empirical," and therefore not the subject of the critical analysis, one would indeed be hard put to explain any phenomenal connection between the thinker and his thoughts.

But if the objects of a phenomenal thinker's thoughts are those he finds in the world, then it is the concept of the world—the withinspaceness and withintimeness of these objects—that eluded Kant. When the ordinary person says, "I think such and such," he refers not only to what he thinks, but to himself as the very person thinking, to himself as being in the world and as therefore having something to say. Therefore, "I-saying" expresses a human being as being-in-the-world ("*Im Ich-sagen spricht sich das Dasein als In-der-Welt-sein aus*").[3]

Our prior existential analysis of this phenomenon, however, yielded an inauthentic self, lost in the objects of its world. Having identified itself with the objects of its concern, the inauthentic self covers over its lostness by always saying "I", "I" when it is the least constant, steady, and persistent, that is, when it is most influenced by others. Those properties of an ontologically elucidated self, after all, are the result of a human being whose care structure has been exemplified in anticipatory resoluteness; and the testimony to its constancy, steadiness, and self-persistence is a reticent response to the call of conscience. The true self knows itself best in facing its anxiety and not in speaking at all.

In sum, the care-structure of our preliminary analysis is not founded in a self whose existence as substance or pure subject can be taken for granted. Existentiality, which is partially constitutive of care, provides a basis for the self-constancy exhibited in anticipatory resoluteness; but the same care-structure yields the everyday being of the human animal as falling, and so provides an equal basis for human inconstancy. In a word, the care-structure includes our self-hood as a constituent structure that may be experienced authentically or inauthentically. And that phenomenon needs to be given temporal interpretation (sec. 64).

That interpretation begins, in section 65, with a review of the hermeneutical account of "meaning." From our consideration of understanding as a function of a human being's disclosedness, "meaning" (*Sinn*) is that wherein the understandability of something is maintained. If things or entities are to be understood, then they must be given an interpretation by which their meaning is held fast. For this reason, the meaning itself is the "upon which of a primary projection," that is, the context according to which the interpretation is made. Most basically, for a hermeneutical analysis, the context of interpretation is established by the forehaving of the situation. Every projection beyond what we already understand, undertaken in the light of a foresighted idea—such as that of existence, in the present instance—is an anticipation of a meaning that is brought back into the forehaving of the interpretive structure. To understand an entity ontologically, the projection is toward the being of that entity, which allows the conception of that entity as the thing it is, and under the conditions of its possibility to be that very thing.

Since we began our ontological investigation with the human being as an entity, we selected as our first approach to its ontological meaning its being as an existent; and existence was given further interpretation in terms of the structure of caring. A similar process must be followed for the ontological interpretation of nonhuman entities, such as things or tools. The real thing has as its being its perceivability; the tool, its usefulness. Whence, if the structures of care, presence, and usefulness are to have meaning, they must be projected upon something more primordial, for example, temporality, perception, and a totality of involvements in which the serviceability of a tool has been phenomenally revealed. The primordiality of this ontological projection is grounded in human being as being-in-the-world, the concept with which we began. The process of determining the meaning of the being of an entity is therefore still circular.

The projection about to be undertaken will display this same pattern. Our previous analysis has brought us to the stage wherein the human being has been interpreted as care: an abandoned, self-projected existent, residing alongside the entities of its concern. And this care structure has since been reinterpreted as anticipatory resoluteness, a single attitude that allows the human being to be a whole and to be one's own self. The current projection is toward those structures of possibility that allow anticipatory resoluteness to be expressed in an average, ontic situation.

The argument runs as follows. In answering the call of conscience, the human being allows itself to come toward itself, to experience its *zu-Kunft*. That toward which it comes, of course, is its authentic self, and not some unactualized future moment of its actual existence (*Zukunft*). As primordially futural, the self is *now* coming toward what it authentically is.

Assuming the responsibility for its actions in a lived situation, the human being takes over its thrownness by accepting the responsibility for it, thereby becoming the "null basis of its own nullity." My present is therefore lived as a coming back to where I have been—abandoned into the world. Since, in my primordial being-responsible, I am as having been, my present spans both my future and my past; and so, in the moments of my authenticity, I may come "toward myself futurally" in "coming back" to the point of my present projection. If this were not possible, there would be no "constancy" for an existent being, and no one could ever be authentic. Being caught in this circle—projected into the future only to come back to what I am now as having been just that—is what Sartre had described as the circuit of ipseity.[4] For us, this circle is no different, of course, than the circle of our hermeneutical understanding, if we remember that understanding is a way for us to be in the world.

Anticipatory resoluteness in this way discloses the current situation of the human being's basic disclosedness—its "there," in the regioning of the world that is revealed to it through its circumspective concern for the totality of its involvements. Existing alongside the entities that serve as its tools, the human being makes these entities present to itself; and as observed in an attitude of inspection, the being of such entities is their presence.

Thus, the being of a human being, its care-structure, is constituted through temporality, the most primordial interpretation of that being yet arrived at, since it is temporality that makes anticipatory resoluteness possible.

We may be able better to envisage the internal structures of human temporality by recalling our diagram of the care-structure. I shall repeat the drawing and indicate the change in nominal reference to the constituent structures (see figure 7). The central vector is the

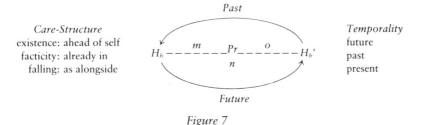

Figure 7

projection of a future self, that toward which we are called by conscience, in the present. Within the care-structure, it is existence that projects a future. The two arcs represent the circle of ipseity, the coming toward itself and the returning to what I am as having been it, reflecting the future and the past respectively. In an inauthentic self-projection, of course, the present would be represented as falling, allowing oneself to be determined uniquely by the entities of one's world, the *m*, *n*, and *o* of the design. H_b and H_b' here refer to human being.

If there still is some difficulty in reading the diagram, the reason may be the confusion between inauthentic temporality (the time of the world) and the authentic (the primordial meaning of human being). In authentic "temporality" the care structure is given the interpretation of a real (i.e., merely present) thing: the future gets identified with *being ahead of itself;* the past, with our *being already in;* and the present, with our *being alongside the entities of our worlds.* As instants of the time of the real world, the future is not yet; the past, no longer; the present, now. If that were the case for our human being, we would be entities running a course in time, and present to the observation of ourselves and others.

For this reason, the "before," the "already," and the "now" must be given their primordial interpretation. "Existing before itself" means that the human being projects a future that make it possible to exist in such a way that its very potentiality for being one way or the other is an issue for it. "Already existing" means that a human being is now as it has been, not merely reliving its past, but assuming the groundlessness of its facticity. The "now" is to exist alongside the entities of one's world; in our fallen condition, allowing ourselves to be determined by those entities. Making those entities present (*gegenwärtigen*), in the sense of merely observing them, is the basis for our falling; it is no longer we who are the ultimate "for the sake of which" assignments of value are made. Indeed, in such a state our possessions may take precedence over ourselves.

As a consequence of this description of primordial temporality, we can easily understand that the three "dimensions" of our lived time are ek-static, that is, ways in which a human being stands out from itself. That too is readable in the preceding figure; as is the finiteness that was uncovered in the phenomenon of death. The infinity of scientific time, like that of its space, is a derivative concept necessitating a modification in the way a human being concerns itself with the entities of its world. At the present time, that derivation is a problem that Heidegger postpones considering.

For the moment, it suffices to remember that primordial future, past, and present are equiprimordial moments of a human being's basic temporality.

HEIDEGGER'S SUMMARY of the properties of "primordial" time is a convenient place to begin the commentary of section 66, although it actually occurs as the next to the last paragraph of the previous section. So far he has listed the following phenomena:

1. Time is primordial, insofar as it is, as the temporalizing of temporality, that is, as articulating the developing process by which

a human entity becomes what it is in projecting its situation. It makes possible the actual, ontical situation of a care-structure.

2. Temporality is essentially ek-static, including in an equiprimordial manner the three dimensions of practical time reckoning.
3. Temporality temporalizes itself primarily from the future, since the future's conception is privileged by the nature of existence: the ahead-of-itself is given in every present projection.
4. Primordial time is finite.

In section 66, "The Temporality of Human Being as Necessitating a Still More Primordial Repetition of the Existential Analysis," Heidegger stipulates the reasons why his investigation must continue. Still another projection to come, then.

The central problem is created by the fact that a human being is equiprimordially in the truth and in the untruth, either disclosing its true nature or succeeding in covering it up. This too is grounded in existence: as existent, a human being can be either authentic or inauthentic. But for the most part and on the average, a human being's existence is inauthentic, during the course of which it conceives of itself in terms of the time of its world. How can the fall from authenticity to inauthenticity or the rise from inauthenticity to authenticity be interpreted in terms of temporality? To answer this question one must conceive of the everyday temporality of the inauthentic human being.

Moreover, if our anticipatory resoluteness guarantees the constancy of the authentic self, and if our true selves are not conceivable as a substance or as a pure subject of knowing, then a fuller description must be given of the way original temporality gives an articulated structure to the authentic self's existence. To the non-self-constancy of the everyday subject of experiences we must be able to oppose the self-constancy of the self called into existence by anticipatory resoluteness.

For the concrete situation the "temporalizing structure of temporality" (*die Zeitigungsstruktur der Zeitlichkeit*) is the historicity (*die Geschichtlichkeit*) of the human being. In inquiring after a human being's historicity, we are not seeking to explain how within the ontic situation a human being or institution is a world-historical phenomenon; such an inquiry is purely ontic. What grounds the possibility for a historical treatment of human events is not the course of these events themselves but the human historicity that makes possible such historical understanding of the events.

For a more complete account of human temporality, therefore, two more problems must be addressed: the everyday temporality of the inauthentic self, and the human historicity that makes it possible for an authentic self or society to live a history of its own.

And the last problem to be considered is how primordial temporality gets modified into the ordinary, scientific notion of time as a dimension of the real world.

The following is a sketch of the way the scientific notion of time derives from primordial temporality which, in our interpretation, grounds the care-structure of human being. Beginning with the repetition of the ontological priority of the human being, for whom its being is always an issue, the following descriptions have been devised:

1.   A human being uses its existence for its own sake.
1.1 Its concerns in the world are, first and foremost, circumspectively determined.
1.2 In using itself for itself, the human being uses itself up.

2.   In using itself up, a human being uses itself, i.e., its "time."

3.   Circumspective concern therefore reckons with time.
3.1 Time reckoning constitutes the manner in which a human being lives in its world.
3.2 As a result, the totality of involvements and the tools and things of its world are encountered "in time."

4.   The "temporal" attributes of worldly entities are conceived as their being within time.
4.1 Withintimeness becomes the ground for the traditional conception of time.
4.2 But "time" gets hypostatized in the process; it too is interpreted as a real determinant of nature.

5.   If we are to unhypostatize within-timeness, it must be seen as reflecting the essential temporality described above.

6.   The time of the world, then, is a concept that derives from the ontology of the human being and cannot be used as an explanation of the being of a human existent or any of its institutions.

The remaining chapters of the published portion of *Being and Time* are concerned to supply the lacking ontological elucidation of the "temporal" references in the foregoing sketch. Practically, the remaining problems are three: the ontological clarification of everyday temporality; human historicity and the possibility of historical studies; and lastly, the full derivation of the scientific notion of time from the ontological understanding of human temporality. In short, everyday temporality, historicality, and time.

But that is another projection, for another time. For the moment one need only note that the transition from death and conscience to the projected study of temporality and time is itself now history.

9

Temporality and Everydayness

FROM THE BEGINNING OF HIS TREATISE HEI-
degger has been using the expression "*zunächst und zumeist*" to refer
to the state of human being as it exists under average conditions
during most of the "time" available to it. Averageness is the ontic
condition of a human being, as it exists everyday. First introduced
as existentials, that is, as structures of the being that exists, averageness (*Durchshnittlichkeit*) and everydayness (*Alltäglichkeit*) were depicted as those structures which permit the human being to lose itself
in a public world, acting conventionally as the impersonal self everyone must assume to adapt to such a world. But since the treatise has
now progressed to a description of human being as caring, still
projected into a world, sometimes of its own making, but mostly
not, and of the meaning of that being as temporality, which temporalizes itself into the experience by which a human individual expresses
itself in caring for its world, the time has come for an ontological
elucidation of this common German expression.

Both *zunächst* and *zumeist* are adverbial expressions and hence
adequate for describing or modifying an action. The difficulty in
translating the terms begins with *zunächst*, which is both an adverb
of place and of time: of place, it indicates an immediately contiguous
position; of time, something like "first," "foremost," or "right off."

For the conjunction of the two terms Macquarrie and Robinson opted for something that doesn't sound very English: "proximally and for the most part." "For the most part" catches the meaning of *zumeist,* but the "proximally," which may indicate a proximate spatial or temporal position, hardly catches the sense of *zunächst* as indicating the starting phases of an activity (the firstness) and the importance of that activity, which is indicated by the translation "above all."

From the beginning, I have opted for an inadequate "first and foremost," which has at least the virtue of being current English as *zunächst und zumeist* is current German. My translation, of course, lets the "for the most part" or "above all" go untranslated. Nothing was lost thereby, however, since the German expression was never used in a technical, ontological sense. Rather Heidegger continued to use it in the ontic sense he first gave the expression, merely to begin his inquiry. The aim of this chapter, a commentary on Heidegger's chapter 4, division 2, is to provide a formal ontological sense for the term.

Heidegger has consistently employed the expression as a description of the way in which the impersonal self relates itself to the everyday world. How is a human being in its world? Well, "above all and as a general rule," caring for the objects it finds either within the totality of its involvements or merely present to its powers of observation. The first of these modes of concern is circumspective, and the second inspective. After the temporal interpretation of caring, however, we must ask how the totality of the temporalizing care-structure gets articulated into the whole we know it to be (from our being-unto-the-end) and as authentic (by our response to the call of conscience). So, to get the ball rolling once more, Heidegger readjusts the forestructure of explanation once again.

Caring is the ontological determination of a human being's being-in-the-world. That concept was elucidated through the analysis of the phenomenon of *world,* experienced as *significance.* Significance was determined by the totality of involvements of the individual, which assigns itself as that for the sake of which all other assignments are made in the system of means and ends that defines the serviceability of an instrumental complex. The end for which any activity in the world is performed is the person who projects ends, who assigns the values that lead to significance.

This projection, moreover, is the human being's openness to its

world, its being-there, in the world. As open to its world, and in the
clearing of its self-projection, the human being understands itself as
projected upon its possibilities of being. And along with this understanding there is a coterminous affective state (*Befindlichkeit*) that
corresponds to a person's finding itself attuned to its world as thrown
and itself as abandoned there. Understanding and feeling ultimately
give the person something to say. Discourse is therefore the last of
the "equiprimordial" structures of the human being's disclosedness.
The difficulty begins to mount when we recall that human being
exists above all and as a general rule (*zunächst und zumeist*) in a
fallen condition in which its understanding of itself is given through
the objects of its concern. That is its world of the everyday.

Therefore, if we should like to show how human temporality
temporalizes itself in an everyday manner, we may use the three
modes of human disclosedness—understanding, feeling, and discourse—along with fallenness from the care-structure, as the basis
for the interpretation. Beginning, then, where we are "first, foremost,
and on the whole," that is, concerned with the entities of our circumspection, we may explain how this circumspection may be modified,
temporally, into an attitude of theoretical knowledge of the real
world; how the spatiality of human regioning gets temporalized; and
lastly, on the basis of the foregoing, what that technical sense of
zunächst und zumeist is when we move from an ontical account
accepted until now to the full temporal understanding of a human
being's everydayness (sec. 67).

I shall follow Heidegger's division of the problem of everydayness
into three sections—the temporality of human disclosedness; the
temporality of being-in-the-world and the transcendence of the real
world; and the temporality of spatiality. In conclusion, both our
chapters end with an account of the "temporal meaning" of human
everydayness.

1. *The temporality of disclosedness* (sec. 68).

Disclosedness is the way a human being holds itself open to its
world, either in seeking to understand it, to describe it, or merely to
experience its significance according to the manner in which it finds
itself there. Rather than the usual double interpretation of being-in-
the-world as exhibiting a specific care-structure and an openness to
its world that specifies how that caring is experienced, both authentically and inauthentically, Heidegger here abridges his previous explanation of our being-in to an understanding that is projected on

the basis of an attunement to the world in which we find ourselves abandoned; and, conversely, to an affective state in which we merely find ourselves, but which is interpreted via the understanding. Thus, every understanding has its attunement, and every tone of that attunement gets interpreted on the basis of the context in which it occurs.

But on the average, the attuned understanding is falling (an importation from the care-structure), and this everyday understanding gets expressed in discourse, following the patterns of the as-structure of interpretation, the as-structure of apophansis, and the sentence structures of an ordinary language. The task here is to trace how human temporality is temporalized in these various structures of human experience.

Since the future is the privileged *ekstasis* of human temporality, Heidegger begins with the projections of the understanding. To it corresponds the *existence* of the care-structure. Under this aspect, a human being is self-projecting toward a possibility of its being that it is yet to be but which still constitutes "that for the sake of which it exists." Its knowing what it can possibly be is established by holding itself open for that very possibility. With respect to the anticipatory resoluteness by which the human being continually holds itself open toward that possibility beyond which there is none, this knowledge is guaranteed by the individual's response to the call of conscience.

In responding to that call, the human being is brought back to itself (*auf-sich-zukommen*), as having been lost in the world of the everyday, but now as having felt the uncanniness of living in such a world, and facing the anxiety of projecting one's way out of it. The mode of relating oneself authentically to the future is anticipation, and the call of conscience relates the self only to the self. But that goes only with the resolute facing up to the anxiety we feel as having to assume full responsibility for what we are. It is always a lived possibility of the human being, but it is rarely achieved.

As a general rule, a human being is above all irresolute; and when it is, its temporality is temporalized out of an inauthentic future: it merely awaits itself, as if its caring for the world had intercalated a loop between what it was and what it is to become, and it had only to appropriate care for the things of its world in order to be a self. For this reason, ontological understanding interprets the authentic possibility of being responsible for oneself as a condition that is won through a modification of the routinely inauthentic future.

Consider the terms our author has to play with: *gewärtig, gewär-*

tigen, erwarten, warten auf, and, as before, *vorlaufen in.* The verb
"to await" (*gewärtigen*) is built on the root of the adjective, *gewärtig,*
which is as ambiguous in German as it is in English. The translations
of the adjective carry the clue of the change from an inauthentic to
an authentic future, as awaiting, expectant, attentive, standing by
for. *To be attentive to something* and *to stand by for it* both carry
the double sense intended: doing something now on behalf of a future
moment when the attentiveness becomes attention, the waiting for
becomes a waiting on, or caring.

The inauthentic future is projected in the action indicated by
gewärtigen, to expect, to await, to hold oneself ready for, to lay
oneself open to. If the object of all these verbs is the self, that self is
inauthentic since the waiting gets dissipated in caring for the things
of the world. Remember Beckett's Didi and Gogo?[1] Their tragedy
was to have been lost totally in an inauthentic future, merely waiting
for Godot, and it makes no difference who or what Godot might
have been; waiting for something to wait for something else is no
future one can live with.

What differentiates the inauthentic from the authentic future, then,
is the entity that one holds oneself in readiness for: either one's
ownmost, nonrelational, and final possibility or the self that, qua
impersonal, is everyone's, that defines itself by the objects that surround it, and that always succeeds in repressing its finitude. For the
inauthentic, impersonal self, the world always gets in the way; such
a self can only keep awaiting the results of its attending to the objects
of its world.

But this holding oneself ready for a future event is eminently
modifiable. One way to do this is to expect, to look forward to, but
actively (*erwarten*), that is, to become attentive to the necessity felt
in the uncanniness of the everyday world. This kind of expectation,
Heidegger tells us, is a mode of projecting a future based on our
holding ourselves open to such a possibility (*gewärtigen*) that is
temporalized as an anticipation (*Vorlaufen*). On the downward side
of the incline, however, our holding ourselves ready for a future gets
siphoned off into a passive waiting (*warten auf*), even for those
objects to which we habitually attend. Our caring for "that for the
sake of which" we care at all is something that gets indefinitely
postponed, however active we may become in our service to the
things or persons around us.

Yet we must remember that the future is but one *ek-stasis* of a totalized temporalizing structure and that therefore every future has its past and its present as an "equiprimordial" dimension of its temporalizing. When the future is authentic, the present (*die Gegenwart*) is that moment of vision made famous by Kierkegaard's description of an ontic "now" as the present moment of decision to accept the "absurdity" that the Eternal had made itself temporal in the person of Jesus Christ.[2] Kierkegaard's use of the expression is therefore bound to time as the withintimeness of actual events.

What does one do in the moment of vision? Our resoluteness in the projection of ourselves toward the future takes place in such a moment, and so the same resoluteness defines the current situation in which the self is called out of its distractive waiting on the objects of its world to a repetition of what it had previously been determined to be. Such, we recall, was the steadfastness of the true self.

The "moment" of the expression "moment of vision" is the ekstatic presence of the true self as a pure possibility understood as a possibility that must be repeated to be my own; as such, it is one structure related to the other component structures of my temporalizing being. But all three temporal *ekstases* are momentous in this way. So the complement in the expression, "of vision," distinguishes the present from the past and the future by the blinking of the eye (*Augen-blick*), by which a lived possibility gets lit up as my own.

Inauthentically, the present is a waiting that gets directed to the objects of the world, a *Gegen-wart*, so the activity that allows such a waiting to take place is properly called a *Gegenwärtigen*, a basic concern that is either circumspective or inspective, but which always makes the objects of those concerns present to us. And in the fallen condition of our care-structure, these are the only objects that we know. For this reason, our present inauthentic self concerns itself with "making present" the objects of the everyday world.

To me it seems clear that Macquarrie and Robinson's rendering of *gegenwärtigen* as "making present" is far superior to Hofstadter's pretentiously Latinate "enpresenting."[3] Although, on the face of it, it seems clear enough that one makes an object present to oneself by attending to it, it escapes me what *enpresenting* might bring to even the most sympathetic reader's intuition.

Whereas the authentic future was conceived through the "coming toward one's self" of a projection, the authentic past may be conceived as coming back to (*zurückkommen*) one's self as attested to by our resolute decision to have a conscience. The circuit of ipseity spans an authentic future and an authentic past; as we recall, the call comes from afar to afar, from the anticipated possibility I currently hold myself ready for, back to that thrown entity I am as having been (*mein Gewesen-sein*). To complete the resoluteness of my act and to fulfill the steadfastness of my self, conscience calls me to a repetition of that condition of my having-been.

Curiously, Heidegger fails to note an indebtedness to Kierkegaard for the importance of repetition as an existential structure in a developing self.[4] The description occurs only one page away from that of the moment of vision, in which such a debt is acknowledged in a footnote.[5] No doubt Heidegger's disdain for merely ontic treatments of the issue explains his forgetfulness.

Forgetfulness, indeed, is the attitude of the human being whose temporality temporalizes itself in an inauthentic past. What gets forgotten in an inauthentic past is the self one has been, because, precisely, it has been lost within the objects of the everyday world. If such a past self is perchance remembered, the reason would only be that it had been previously forgotten. What gets remembered in overcoming our past forgetfulness is the lostness of ourself in that forgotten past. In this way, remembering the past selves we have been is as inauthentic as forgetting ourselves—which we should never do, at least not in public.

The second mode of disclosedness treated by Heidegger is our affectivity, and it seems no accident that it should be associated with the temporal dimension of the past. After all, his discussion of the tripartite temporal structure of the authentic and inauthentic understanding has just ended with an account of an inauthentic understanding of our past. So the question naturally arises as to the affective state that accompanies that understanding. And we have already been previously informed that thrownness is the dimension of the care-structure that correlates with our sense of being already in a world when our understanding projects an interpretation of our being there.

Nothing more has ever been intended by the expression *thrownness* than the fact that a human being "finds itself" (*sich befinden*) or feels itself in the grips of an affective state or mood. The mood (*Stimmung*) is that by which a human being is attuned (*gestimmt*) to being in its world. This mood brings the human being face to face with its abandonment in the world, whether authentically revealing it or inauthentically covering it up. The temporalizing structure of having found oneself in this or that attunement to the world is the past in its present form of having been (*Gewesenheit*).

Here, as always, purely ontic discussions of moods, as passing conscious phenomena which merely color our experience of inner-worldly objects, call attention to something with which we are very familiar but which cannot be understood until the ontological inter-pretation of such phenomena gets worked out; and this, with specific reference to the manner in which temporality temporalizes itself in the disclosive attitude in question.

As they are temporalized, moods bring us back to (*zurückbringen auf*) our having already been in the world. As an example, consider the temporality of fear. On its face, the example seems counterintui-tive; for, on the whole, fear occasioned by a threatening object seems to be of a future evil. But that only tells a part of the story; the fear is also about something, precisely about oneself as being in the world wherein the threatening object has been revealed as present. The fact that the fearing individual must await or do something to avoid the threat only bespeaks the inauthenticity of the state of mind, which is linked to the actual events of the world. Such a future exists only in time; it is not created by one's being summoned forth to a pure possibility.

To the coming toward oneself of an authentic future there corre-sponds, by the circuit of ipseity, a coming back to oneself as aban-doned in the world. What the inauthentic self is brought back to, out of its inauthentic future, is itself as threatened with evil, and as merely biding its time, another object along with the things of its environ-ment. Fearing is in this way a forgetting of one's true self, not just an expectation of evil.

Hope as the expectation of a future good has the same temporal patterning as fear. If we abstract from the object of our expectation, there remains only the feeling and what that feeling is about—our own condition. To hope for something may be almost magical in its effect; but if it succeeds in changing our attitude of doubt or despair, it can do so only as long as the feeling of hope brings along with it a reference to the self that has experienced these other feelings. Hope, like fear itself, temporalizes itself inauthentically. Both are expecta-tions based upon a making-present of a self that has forgotten its authentic condition.

Anxiety, on the other hand, is authentic. Here that before which and that about which we are anxious are the same thing, our being-in-the-world, as projected ahead of itself and as abandoned in the world of our concerns. Once the feeling of uncanniness overtakes the lost self, its anxiety brings it back to its thrownness. And once the call of conscience relates these two aspects of the authentic self, the environing world loses its significance; the feeling comes from nothing other than the self in the world.

Feeling anxiety therefore is not a phenomenon of expecting or laying ourselves open to a future event that will take place in the world. Our anxiety reveals the irrelevance and the insignificance of the natural world along with the "nullity" (*Nichtigkeit*) of the objects of our concern located therein.

The feeling of anxiety brings the self back to its naked uncanny thrownness. And along with this authentic past, which has been neither forgotten nor merely remembered, one is presented with a choice that may be repeated; in being called to assume responsibility for itself, for its own abandonment in the world, its thrownness becomes a possibility for repetition. In the process is revealed an authentic possibility of being oneself.

Projecting this possibility is the futural dimension of the past revealed in anxiety; and holding oneself ready to respond with the resolve to become what only it may become is the felt tension of the decisive moment. At this moment, Heidegger says, *the present of the anxiety holds us ready for the resolve, for the moment of vision in which it itself and nothing but itself can be,* since its world has sunk into insignificance. In anxiety, the moment of vision is held, as it were, at the ready: "Ihre Gegenwart hält den Augenblick, als welcher sie selbst und nur sie möglich ist, auf dem Sprung."[6] Living an authentic past makes possible the projection of an authentic future.

The differences between fear and anxiety stem from the differences between inauthentic and authentic selves. Fear assails us from without; anxiety gnaws at us from within. Fear is a result of our being irresolute, while anxiety is possible only for the resolute self. Fear overwhelms the self; anxiety liberates it from possibilities that mean nothing. And although both affective states are grounded in our having-been, fear forgets its past and roots us in a lost present, while anxiety calls us out of this being lost among the objects of our worlds by projecting the resolute repetition of our own self-responsibility.

Other feelings, such as indifference and equanimity, have temporal structures similar to fear and anxiety and illustrate how an inauthentic and an authentic self are brought back to that being it is as having been that very self. Forgetting, remembering, or repeating are all ways of living a past.

Falling is the condition of the present self that has forgotten its past in waiting for that future event that will determine its being. And although a fallen present may be discussed in terms of understanding, discourse, and affectivity, Heidegger again goes for the easy transition. Having finished his discussion of affectivity as the mode of disclosedness that reveals a past that is lived either authentically or inauthentically, he continues with an account of curiosity, the inauthentic state of mind par excellence. And he will leave the consideration of ambiguity and idle chatter, as inauthentic understanding and discourse respectively, up to the reader's imagination.

The potentiality for being that gets expressed in everyday curiosity "sees," that is, grasps things by their external and superficial aspects, through which they are in this way encountered. "Seeing" the objects of one's concern makes them present, so curiosity is grounded in the present. But curious seeing is not for the purpose of understanding and so forms no part of the deliberative process. Rather, such seeing is merely for the purpose of seeing or of having seen.

Yet curiosity (*Neugier*) turns into a craving (*Gier*) for the new (*nach dem Neuen*), a direction indicating its futural dimension, by which it is driven toward the not-yet-seen. The passing of the curious gaze from thing to thing does not allow it to hold onto the object thus made present but forces it to leap away from the seen objects in search for other objects to be seen in the actual world. Its inauthenticity stems from a shift in its manner of awaiting, or holding itself open to the future, from fully anticipating the possibility of determining itself to merely waiting for the actuality of the thing that determines it by fulfilling its craving. Rather than tarrying alongside the objects made present in an effort to understand them, curiosity continually leaps away (*entspringen*) from one object to search for another.

That kind of present and that kind of future Heidegger calls a peculiar modification of normal expectancy. Never tarrying alongside the objects of its vision, the curious person leaps away from one object in anticipation of an other; but this anticipation is a form of opening itself to a future (*ein Gewärtigen*) that leaps after the present. Thus, the expectancy of a future is not held onto by the fixation of an ontological possibility (which would be authentic), nor even by a single visual object that would fulfill its drive at a specific actual moment. Leaping after the present is a futural mode of being brought back to the present, where something else is to be seen.

Such a mode of being in the world is distraction, which belies the human condition by never dwelling anywhere. Not only does it lose itself, but it loses its world as well, because curiosity has cut itself off from a past. It allows itself to be distracted and tranquilized by the attractions of immediately visible objects. All the structures of the fallen world—the temptation, tranquilization, alienation, and self-entanglement—tend to reinforce the present attitude of leaping away. Even should one be able to conceive of the possibility of having seen everything, the curious person would invent something new to be seen.

But the temporality of a human being is finite. It has an end beyond which there is absolutely nothing more to be seen. Even though the curious person is inauthentically fleeing its end, that it should exist toward its own proper end is part of its thrown condition. That is, its existential projection always has the two points of reference. That the present should continually seek to leap away is motivated by an effort to escape its thrown past, and the fact that this motivation is closed off from its awareness in leaping away only indicates the facticity of the inauthentic self that continually forgets its past.

And the only solution for finding oneself lost in such a world is the onset of the uncanniness that may prompt the resolute decision to be a complete and integral self, that is, in a moment of vision uniting an authentic past held on to as repeatable and the authentic future by which one's own proper end is anticipated. So curiosity too is illuminated through a forgotten past.

Articulating the unity of the three constituents of human disclosedness—here, understanding, feeling, and falling—is the task of discourse. For this reason, Heidegger says, discourse does not have a primary temporal ekstasis. Still, within the factual world of the everyday, discourse expresses itself for the most part through speech; and speech addresses itself, first and foremost, to the things revealed within the world. For this reason, the present, as making present, seems ideally suited to discourse. Not only does our describing them make things apparent to us, but in speaking with others about the things of a common world we may make them apparent to these others as well.

To be avoided here is the easy association of the tenses of verbs as referring to a time within the real world when an action has taken place, as well as the commonplace that speaking itself takes place in a moment of psychical time. Such events are ontical. We are concerned with the temporality of discourse itself, as an existential, or ontological, structure determinant of a human being's being-in-the-world.

Since discourse reveals the entities of a world, its temporality must be gauged on the relationship between human being, as disclosing a world, and other entities, as disclosed within that world; in a word, we must understand how a human being may be in the truth and in the untruth. To an extent, we have done just that. In the truth a human being is projected to an authentic future, related to an authentic past and present, as explained above; but in the untruth, it projects itself toward an inauthentic future, related to the same sort of past and present.

Our own ontological discourse (Heidegger's text, for example) has attempted to make clear how a human being can be in the truth and in the untruth, how the irresolute being may be brought back to resoluteness, and how the temporal structures of human being are exhibited in all these behaviors. We have intimated that the source for all "significations" is the interpretive activity of making present a relational component of the context of involvements that determines ontological significance, and at the same time how a proper analysis of the meaning of human being may suggest the significance of the verb *to be* as something other than a link between the subject and predicate of a sentence. All this has already been done.

What we must do now is to remember that although each form of human disclosedness is temporalized through a specific ekstatic dimension of temporality, all three of these dimensions exhibit human temporality as a whole. For example, understanding is structured through the future, both authentically and inauthentically, and both these futures have a specific kind of past and present. And the same is true for affectivity and discourse. In sum, temporality temporalizes the care-structure: the existence, facticity, and falling of human beings.

To close this section, I append the following table as summarizing the relationships between caring (human being) and temporality (the meaning of human being):

TABLE 1

HOW TEMPORALITY TEMPORALIZES ITSELF

The Temporality of Human Being			
Being-in-the-world : Modes of Caring			
Existential structures : Existentiell possibilities			

Care-structure : Disclosedness :	Temporal Ekstasis		
	Authentic	:	Inauthentic

Existence	: Understanding :	Future		
		Anticipating	:	Waiting for
Facticity	: Feeling :	Past		
		Repeating	:	Remembering
Falling	: Discourse :	Present		(forgetting)
		Moment of		
		Vision	:	Making-present

2. The temporality of being-in-the-world and the transcendence of the world (sec. 69).

Having entered the third phase of his existential analytic since leaving its preliminary stages, Heidegger has made good on his boast to display the temporal meaning of human beings, both in terms of the temporality of the care-structure and that of disclosedness, by eliciting the ekstatic unity of the temporality that temporalizes itself in the behavior of those beings who exist in the world. But the job still remains only half done. We now have some idea of human temporality but little of the temporality of the human world and none at all of the time of the real world. The task to be fulfilled in this section is to supply these further descriptions of a human being's manner of caring for the objects of its world.

The demonstration is given in three parts: the temporality of circumspective concern; the temporal meaning of the modification of circumspective concern to scientific theorizing; and the temporal status of the world's transcendence. I consider each of these in the indicated order.

Why begin with circumspective concern? Because that concept has been all but lost since the demonstration of the phenomenon of worldhood. It had been replaced by the correlative notion of being-in as disclosedness, as well as by the character of the self (authentic and inauthentic) that discloses the entities of a world. However, by "existing" its being-there, a human being has been described as opening a world, clearing a way toward significance, and illuminating the entities that may henceforth be "seen," whether in mere curiosity, in the circumspection of its concerns, or in the deliberate inspection of those entities that have been freed by an act of deliberation. But the temporal interpretation of all this is still lacking.

If temporality is truly the meaning of being-in-the-world, then the ekstatic unity of its temporalizing in human affairs should make possible the phenomenon of worldhood, the circumspective concern by which a world announces itself, and, ultimately, a humanistic meaning for the scientific concept of the time of the real world. By now no one will be surprised by the fact that this investigation actually brings us back to that first approximation of human being as being-in-the-world. Heidegger's method of interpretation is still circular, and, as always before, the concept is not the same after as before the interpretation.

Understanding the temporality of the everyday depends upon our ability to give a temporal interpretation for the way in which human beings are in their worlds—*zunächst und zumeist,* that is, above all and as a general rule. First, foremost, and for the most part, a human being finds itself in an environment, taking care of those things it finds useful for its survival. Indeed, the being of such things has been described as their handiness, as opposed to the mere presence of the objects of nature.

But nothing can be handy in the absolute; a tool is useful for something. That the thing ready to hand should be a tool indicates an involvement of the human being *with* it, and *in* a system of involvements, closed in the final instance only by its own being as that for the sake of which the assignments of values have been made— its own well-being, for example—in determining the total context of its involvements.

Every work situation involves retaining or recalling one's having already been thrown into a system of involvements that had been established by circumspective concern, and is experienced as a present being-alongside those entities one can use as tools in performing a job. And the purpose of the working activity is to make present those objects we anticipate as the end of the activity. Roughly seen, in this way, the context of involvements exhibits the ekstatic temporal unity of human being as care.

But a finer analysis is possible. Once a work situation is clearly recognized as such, there are grounds for recalling a previous manner of being in which the very act of circumspection establishes the connections between those items of equipment that are related within the context of involvement. This more primordial kind of being-in is still our being-in-the-world but one that lets things be involved. Letting things be involved in a system of assignments is therefore an existential structure of our mode of caring for tools. Since I have already shown how the unity of the care-structure is made possible by the ekstatic unity of temporality, it is easy to comprehend how my previous account of the work situation exhibits the same kind of unity. That much can be read from Table 1.

Had the topic of circumspective concern been the subject of analysis, I might have indicated the temporal interpretation of the phenomenon merely by adding one more column. But still another technique is open to me. I shall first exhibit the structure of letting things be involved and then project it upon the same diagram used to illustrate the care-structure.

Obviously, in letting things be involved we are already involved *with* something, *in* a certain context. That within which we let the tool be involved is a "toward which," that is, a purpose beyond itself, with respect to which the tool may be used or actually be in use. But that "toward which" must be awaited; it is futural. And unless our experience is hopelessly disconnected, the waiting on the achievement of a purpose is linked in the working itself as retaining the item of equipment used as the tool.

Naturally, the actual goals or the intended finished product of the work are not to be mistaken for the ontologically determined structure we are describing; but they do exhibit that structure in the same way fearing exhibits the structure of inauthentic affectivity. Nor does the actual retaining of the tool as a thematized item of awareness constitute a part of the structure of letting-things-be-involved. Rather than being an actual object of perception, the tool as item of the instrumental complex is a point of reference: a "toward this" that gets retained. The totalizing ekstatic structure of human temporality has already made it possible for the caring human being to "lose itself" in concern for its tools by the circumspection of its environment. There we have noted a "toward which" an involvement has been made and which must be awaited in the actual context of work, and a "toward this" of the item of equipment that must be retained. Unfortunately, however, the past that is retained is always inauthentic; the self gets lost in the system of its own involvements. In returning to the entity that is handy for it, the self is forgotten. Two thirds of our diagram is now complete.

The missing third is the making-present that awaits and retains. It is established by the familiar use of the tool. Being already familiar with whatever is handy for the achievement of one's purposes is an apt description of knowing one's way about. In using this familiarity with a system of involvements we do something with the items of the equipment; they fall into that rough and ready description of being known through their inconspicuousness, unobtrusiveness, and pliancy. When they are not known in this way, in their use, they become unhandy. But that is a further topic; at present it suffices to summarize this account of temporality of a system of involvements. This can be done in a glance at figure 8.

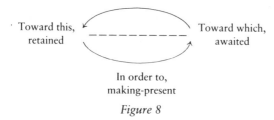

Toward this, retained — Toward which, awaited

In order to, making-present

Figure 8

A tool may fail in a number of ways, but these too illustrate a peculiar kind of temporality. First of all, it may be damaged and fail to function; and when it does, it becomes conspicuous. Consider the temporal relations here: the awaiting-retaining that makes present gets held up, and the revolving order of the future and the past gets separated into distinct items available to independent encounters with separable determinations. The making-present then diverts itself into a looking over the situation to find out what went wrong; I begin to inspect my tools that are no longer pliant and have become conspicuous and obtrusive. But for this to happen, note, the more primordial situation is the one in which my tools function, and I go on happily about my business of achieving my ends.

Heidegger notes four more ways in which the original context of involvements that is lit up by our circumspective concern may be disordered.

First, by finding something missing, that is, by making something "unpresent" that has either always been at one's disposal and is not retained as such, or has been expected, but not produced. The ekstatic unity of temporality is complete but maladjusted to our ends.

Second, we may be surprised by producing something we did not intend. If so, we were not awaiting it; but the surprising thing is made present because it has a relation to something else, which we did await, still retaining the instrumental character of the tool used to produce the surprising result.

Third, there is the case of the insurmountable difficulty. Here the wise human being resigns itself, which is still a way of letting things be involved: resignation is to the disturbing item. Although it is not retained as functioning, our resigned awaiting makes present the difficulty that cannot be overcome, and so retains the obtrusiveness of the difficulty.

Lastly, there is the case of an unsuitable but still available tool. Our hammer may be too heavy to drive a brad, if precisely adequate for driving a spike. In such a case we do not reckon with the unsuitable tool, and not reckoning with something that is nonetheless available is one way of concerning ourselves with what cannot be clung to, in an active retention. The unsuitable tool is not forgotten, it gets retained as unsuitable. This retention is another form of deliberation, which is to be explained later.

The point to be registered here is that within a totality of involvements as made visible by our instrumental complex, the concern of circumspection is totalized in the same way the ekstatic unity of temporality is totalized: in all our concernful dealings with an equipmental complex, our action is a making-present that awaits and retains. What is made present is either the world of the acting human, in the case of inconspicuous familiarity that allows us to exist in that "world," or a single item of equipment that may misfire in a number of ways but still illustrates the totality of the ekstatic structure of human temporality.

The modification of circumspective concern into deliberation and the modification of deliberation into scientific thematizing of the objects of the natural world are likewise conceivable on the basis of how human temporality comes to be temporalized in these activities. Following out this temporalizing process permits Heidegger to sketch out "an existential conception of (natural) science."[7]

The first step in his program is to state the most obvious of the errors to be avoided. For example, philosophers of science must desist in their attempts to describe science in the same way scientists describe natural phenomena. Making a scientific investigation is still a way for a human being to be in a world. Moreover, the assumption that the changeover from circumspective concern to deliberative inspection is sufficient to describe "science" as a purely theoretical concern, divorced from practice, must be given up.

Just as all praxis has its theory in the ontology we are expounding, so every theory has its peculiar kind of praxis: reading gauges is a practice dictated by theoretical correlations; without a microscope or a telescope, certain kinds of observations cannot be made; without archaeological diggings, no remains of lost civilizations; and even for the most abstract kind of mathematical calculations, without writing instruments and a suitable surface, or (in today's circumstances) without a suitable computer, they might never be made, or be made too slowly to be effective. Indeed, all these observations are mere comments on the necessity of a prior awareness of knowing one's way about a world of circumspective concern. So we shall begin with it.

Circumspective concern establishes the worldhood of human significance, as this is made clear by the system of involvements structured into an instrumental complex as actually used for the sake of our continuing existence. Using any handy tool successfully brings the whole complex of our involvement closer to us. But prior to any use, the concern we call "circumspective" has already ordered the items of our equipment by interpreting what has been "sighted" or lit up by our "being-there" alongside those entities.

The bringing closer of something by interpreting it in a circumspective manner is to deliberate, an activity pursued in such a way as to propose conditions on and expect consequences from the way in which we relate to our practical environments. If something is to be produced, we must do this or that. Deliberating, obviously, exhibits the temporality structure: it makes present what has been circumspectively revealed by retaining the context of involvements and awaiting a possible consequence. Even envisaging a merely possible result constitutes a mode of making it present by retaining awareness of the conditions and awaiting it as a consequence.

But we can deliberate over possible consequences only if what we take to be the conditions (the "if" part of the sentence) have already been understood as something, from which the conclusion (the "then" part) will follow. The circularity of the as-structure of interpretation has already been made clear. In every interpretation we project an entity upon its being to interpret its meaning. We anticipate, and we bring the anticipated meaning back to the entity, which we retain, as possessing this or that property.

Consider the circularity of the as-structure as previously explained with respect to the sentence "The hammer is heavy." We interpret: this tool with which I am already familiar as suitable for driving a nail requires a bit of force; it may bend the nail; at any rate, it will be hard to manipulate. That is the interpretation of deliberation on the totality of involvements lit up by our circumspective concern. Here the hammer is made present on the basis of awaiting and retaining the other items of the equipmental complex.

But there is a second interpretation: the hammer has weight; if I let go of it, it will fall; and the like. Here the same item of equipment is interpreted in terms of things possessing mass; the concern is purely physical. Heaviness here is a property—which we have brought to presence by envisaging different sorts of consequences and retaining a different frame of reference, a purely theoretical one. But the interpretive process is still circular, and still exhibits a totalizing temporal unity.

The change in "frame of reference," of course, is very important: in the physical context, the object (the hammer in question) is no longer "placed" in a system of involvements; it is now situated, indifferently as to its placement, within the spatio-temporal ordering of natural events. With respect to the determination of its mass, it occupies a "world-point." So the original placement in the instrumental complex has been modified into a multiplicity of possible positions in the world order of physical relations. The original placement has given away to space wherein objects may be envisaged as being freed from the constraints of the prior circumspective ordering. Envisaged in this way, the world as a complex of extended entities has been brought to the fore. The object whose being was its handiness now exhibits the being of presence to our observation.

Heidegger then enters upon a digression concerning modern mathematical physics, as grounded in the human interpretive understanding. The value of such a science is not its exactness nor even its use of mathematics to summarize, generalize, and predict physical phenomena. The value of mathematical physics is its projection of the concept of nature, of the natural world, into something that is mathematically determinable. By making this projection, modern physicists have made use of the deliberative schema noted above. They presume that within the world of nature something—matter—is constantly present for our observation and treat this "something" as determinable by such quantifiable "properties" as motion, force, location, and time. The method of contemporary physics is also a circular projection and exhibits the temporalizing structures of human temporality.

According to Heidegger, full existential conception of science would include a fuller explanation of the prior state of Being, projected as the basis of significance to be observed; and as a result, suggestions of methods for making observations, forming concepts, differentiating true from false statements within its domain, determining what constitutes proof or grounding, and indicating how its results become binding upon us.

I have followed this digression only to anticipate what Heidegger will be attempting in a later chapter: the full existential conception of the historiological sciences. Here we may conclude his discussion of the temporality of scientific interpretation by showing the temporality of scientifically thematizing specific objects within the natural world.

The aim of scientific thematizing is to free entities within the world in such a way as to let them "throw themselves against" our observational capacities. Here Heidegger plays with the Latin root of *object*, rather than the German *Gegenstand* for the same word. Had he chosen otherwise the result would be the same: for, in freeing the entities of the world for presence, we let them stand over against us.

Thematizing objectifies, but it does so in a specific, temporal patterning. The being which objectifies already exists alongside the entities of the real world, and objectifying is a distinctive kind of making present that awaits the discoveredness of the entity in its presence— our there and over against our perceiving organs. This kind of awaiting retains an original resolve to be-in-the-truth, that is, to fulfill our being as being-revealing. Thus, thematizing is a making present that awaits a being-disclosed and retains a resolve to be as being-disclosing. And in this way, says Heidegger, the attitude of science is derived from concernful being-in-the-world.

Either way: if a human being is to be able to project significance for the items of its equipment, it must first be familiar with the totality of its involvements, that is, its being-in-the-world; and if a human being is to be able to project significance for the objects of the natural world, the concept of that world must be presupposed—as deriving from the knowledge gained from the totality of involvements in a purely human world.

Yet, one further problem remains to be discussed. If a human being is to be able to thematize the objects of the natural world, it must transcend the objects it thematizes. How is the transcendence of the world (its being other than the thematizing subject) to be given a temporal interpretation?

Answering that question is the last task of this section. And, as always, the demonstration begins by recalling the result of a prior analysis. A world, we are reminded, is organized into significance by a human being's self-projection toward its potentialities of being. The care-structure—being ahead of oneself, already in, and existing alongside the entities of one's world—is already understood as exemplifying the tripartite unity of the temporalizing temporality.

Moreover, the analysis of circumspective concern just completed has yielded a description of the human world as organized through a context of involvements that has come to closure through the projection of that last potentiality for being which is no longer to be and which, to be authentic, must be chosen in resoluteness. That for the sake of which a human being exists in its world is its own authentic self. But the projection of that self is through a "toward which," related to a "toward this," defining a present "in order to." The unity of these practical determinants of an action constitutes a "world," revealed in circumspective concern.

Yet, caring, a human being is always already in such a world; that is its facticity, to be thrown over and abandoned to a previously determined existence. The condition is known in affectivity, which gets understood, in the fallen condition of humanity, as being lost among the objects, even those serving as tools, within the context of its involvements. In order to be able to live as it does, projecting itself as the ultimate value for which assignments of value are made, a human being is never without its world. A human being and its world are codisclosed in the primordial revelation of truth, by which a being-revealing necessitates a being-revealed, and vice versa. But at the same time, a human being is never in its world without projecting ends. That toward which it is projected is, ultimately, itself as that for the sake of which it exists.

Existence, facticity, and falling are made possible by the ekstatic unity of temporality as awaiting, retaining, and making-present. And since a human world is made what it is under these same conditions, there is a horizonal schema for interpreting the structure of this "worlding" world. The human being comes toward itself in the future created by its self-projection; its abandonment is experienced in the face of all those facts that had determined what it was; its present is an enduring moment when it acts, in order to fulfill its drive to completion.

Then projecting one upon the other, Heidegger declares that the unity of these three horizonal schemata constitutes the "whereupon" onto which all factically existent human beings, whose being is care, are projected to determine the meaning of that being.

As a result of this explanation, the "world" is conceived as something disclosed equiprimordially with a human being's "being-there." It is for this reason that, in the earlier sections of this commentary, I have usually added the expression "in the world" to qualify "where" humans exist: that "where" is to be strung out between a there, somewhere in the future and a here, where I had already been abandoned in a past. The human world is revealed through circumspective concern in the present.

The real world of nature, however, becomes a theme for us when a context of human involvements gets clogged, and the instruments at one's disposal become rigid, rather than pliant, conspicuous in their failure, rather than inconspicuous in their success. When items of equipment lose their "placement" in a context of involvements, they are no longer tools but mere objects of observation. And the abstraction from placement within the significance of a world allows the conception of nature as a whole, within which events come to pass in time.

But even this real world, then, must be treated as having significance because of the unity of the horizonal schemata of human temporality. Both these worlds are transcendent: the natural world by thematizing theory; the human world by the fact that, in its being-there, the human subject always finds itself already there, and under factical conditions encounters the entities it finds itself alongside.

In sum, when a factical human being understands itself as awaiting, retaining, and making-present the objects of its worlds (both the human and the real), it has conceived the conditions under which it is possible to encounter "objects within a transcendent world."

Does this make the "world" "subjective"? No doubt, since there is no world without a self-projecting human being that might be considered a subject. We had already met this theme in Heidegger's discussion of "worldhood and reality." That prior discussion has now been given its temporal interpretation. But since this "subjective" world has been shown to be temporally transcendent, it is still more objective as a whole than any possible "object."[8]

In saying this, Heidegger means, I think, that since the ontological conditions for the existence of such a subjective world are objective in the sense of being transcendent to an actual subject, and since these same determinations condition the appearance of objects as made-present to experience, but only under the further condition that an original circumspective concern with the entities of a human world has been modified to scientific inspection, this originally "subjective world" is far more objective than any conceivable physical object.

So no one need worry about the subjectivity of our human worlds.

3. *The temporality of spatiality* (sec. 70).

Here Heidegger gives further interpretation of the nature of the world in which humans exist. He attempts to answer the question: How is the spatiality characteristic of a human being temporalized within an everyday situation? And to begin his analysis, he recalls how spatiality was described in his preliminary interpretation and then projects that description into the present discussion of the temporalized care-structure.

Let's begin with the recall. A human being is spatial, not in the sense of taking up space, but rather in the sense of its projecting of a there from a here. As it exists stretched between its here and its there, it creates a region for itself. That region has the same diagram as the future, past, and present *ekstases* of human temporality; so the relationship between human spatiality and its temporality should not be difficult to describe.

All we have to do is to change the emphasis from the region created by a human being's self projection—a hither and thither defining a whither of possible action—to the activity by which the region is created. Call that "regioning." As a process, regioning creates a fluctuating "locus" wherein the human individual, factically existent as falling, makes room for becoming concerned with the objects of its environment. Heidegger calls the "space" of this regioning a "Spielraum."[9]

Having projected its furthermost thither as its own proper end, the acting human being must return to its "place" to play out its destiny. Within this room, which a human being creates for itself, circumspective concern discerns a directionality (established by the assignment of values in a context of involvements) and expresses itself in such a way as to reduce the distance between the objects of its concern and itself (in the actual use of a tool, for example).

But both the directionality established by the placement of items of equipment in an instrumental complex and the reduction of the distance between itself and its tools and the other objects it envisages to produce by using its tools exhibit the structure of an ekstatic temporal horizon. Consider.

Just as, in order to constitute its region, an individual had to await and retain the thither and hither of its action in order to make present the whither of its intended action, so awaiting a particular result and retaining the means for acting make present the necessary direction.

This same pattern has already been found in the "significance" of the context of our involvements: we await the possibility of self-fulfillment while retaining the context of our involvements; but since, on the average, our existence is falling, this awaiting and retaining makes present what is closest to us—those things handiest for the accomplishment of our purposes. Human spatiality is therefore de-distancing as well.

Bringing close the objects that are handy for our action is what makes it possible for us to busy ourselves in a concrete situation. But even here the general patterning of the ekstatic unity of temporality is apparent. In the fallen, factical situation the bringing close is an action emphasizing the present dimension of the temporal totality. Brought close to the present, we await the close, which is to be brought near by our action, and forget the distant, which is still our own being as that for the sake of which an action is projected. We lose ourselves in our own tools. As we articulate a human region by bringing objects closer to us it seems apparent that the first thing observable in our regioning endeavors is something present in the real world. But that is only apparent.

In conclusion, treating a region as an active process of regioning, whereby a human being creates a space for itself, enables us to show how the spatiality of our human being gets temporalized in our everyday concernful dealings with the things of our environment. Although the region is conceivable as independent of its temporalization, when we do consider how spatiality gets temporalized in an ordinary human project, we can be led to understand how deep an impression is made by the temporalizing pattern of the fallen human concern for its tools considered as physical objects. In forgetting the distant and awaiting only the closest objects of our concern, we are led to live in a present where the very being of an object may seem to be its presence.

But this means only that on the whole (*zumeist*) a human being is above all (*zunächst*) inauthentic: it understands itself, in its fallen condition, in terms of the objects of its concern; and, from the way spatiality gets temporalized, as being alongside real things in an objective space.

Section 71 of the text summarizes Heidegger's discussion of temporality and everydayness, evaluates the completeness of his ontological description of how human temporality structures an everyday experience, and projects further tasks to be completed.

Everydayness, we recall, was one of the first existentials used by Heidegger to characterize the ordinary ontic situations of human beings; indeed, it was coupled with the averageness of an ordinary life. In order to characterize everydayness, Heidegger continually used the adverbial expressions *zunächst* and *zumeist* as a single qualifier of human action. For this reason, everydayness is a way for humans to be; adverbs qualify verbs. The existential designates a definite "how" of existing that dominates human experience.

How this domination is to be interpreted is given in what the two adverbs signify. *Zunächst,* meaning something like "above all" or "principally" as unifying the two English senses of "in the beginning" and "most importantly," refers to the manner of daily existing as everyone exists, that is, with other persons in a shared world. *Zumeist,* meaning "for the most part" or "on the whole," designates the way everyman shows himself as a general rule.

The self that gets expressed in this way is inauthentic, that is, governed by the conventions of a public world, and for this reason, finds itself tempted, by the convenience of the arrangement, to further degrees of self-alienation. In living this way, one seeks the comfort of the accustomed. And under these conditions what can be expected tomorrow is the same as was found today and the day before that.

Temporally interpreted, to live the conditions of the everyday is to await the events of tomorrow as if they were the events of yesterday. But the mood by which we know how it is to be awaiting something by retaining what has already been and thus making present the public character of our shared world is a "pallid lack of mood [*eine fahlen Ungestimmtheit*]," a lack of definition that we may suffer in its dullness or try to escape by diverting attention to other things. An authentic moment of vision may master it, but only for that moment; the most resolute of our decisions have a way of falling back into irresoluteness. And it is for this reason that everydayness in the present schema of its temporal horizon is characterized as falling, a condition in which we are lost in the things of our accustomed worlds.

It would be convenient to end the discussion here. But that surely would be false hope. Along with our everyday understanding of our being, we know that our experiences of an accustomed world are drawn along from day to day; and that in spending our time—or temporalizing our temporality—we reckon with time and date the events of our lives. If everydayness is a characteristic way in which temporality gets temporalized in a customary world, these two aspects must be given ontological interpretation for a further understanding of the temporality of the everyday. In the sequel those topics are labeled "historicity" and "withintimeness."

In the meantime, just for the pleasure of it, contemplate the manner in which Shakespeare inverts the negative value of an inauthentic temporality into the positive one created in the purely verbal tensions that raise the reader's consciousness to a veritable state of sublimity:

> Tomorrow, and tomorrow, and tomorrow
> Creeps in this petty pace from day to day,
> To the last syllable of recorded time;
> And all our yesterdays have lighted fools
> The way to dusty death.[10]

Another poetic example of the preontological comprehension of our human being? Why not? Time passes.

10

From Temporality and Historicality to Historicity and History

CHAPTER 5 OF DIVISION 2 OF HEIDEGGER'S text is the next to last of the published treatise. By the time the reader has arrived at this point, he or she has become accustomed to the spiraling twists of the Heideggerian style.[1] That style, after all, is determined by the interpretive methodology used to develop his phenomenological ontology, which, if Heidegger is right, is not an accidental or purely personal characteristic of its author but rather itself an ontological determination of human disclosedness considered as understanding—one way, along with feeling and disclosure, that a human being may give testimony to its being-there in the world. The interpretive understanding is projective, relating an entity to its being and that being to what is already understood prior to the initial projection. Heidegger's style merely reflects the "forestructure of the understanding."

In each swing of the mounting spirals a description is achieved that relates a foresighted entity to a conception deriving from the context of knowledge already possessed—the forehaving of the interpretation—that is thus enriched through the disclosive verbalization. The process of understanding thus exhibits the same structure as caring, as the temporalizing of temporality, and as the regioning of human spatiality. The movement is forward toward the future in a present that either repeats or remembers a past in which one has been abandoned. For this reason Heidegger continually asks the question: Has the foresighted entity been brought back into our interpretive forehaving? If it has, its explanation has been completed; and if not, a new projection must be made. For this reason, too, each new chapter begins with an "adjustment of the forehaving," which looks ever so much like a simple summary of past results and the projection of a new interpretive aim. This phenomenon in reading *Being and Time* is a constant; it may be found at the beginning of the book, in the introduction; at the beginning of each division; of each chapter of both divisions; and of each section of all the chapters in both divisions.

Although this phenomenon has not been missed by readers sensitive to an author's style, it has not always been observed that, in his return to the explicative forehaving of an interpretation, the conceptual context gets increasingly enriched. Heidegger never returns to where he was in the same state as when he left. The preparatory analysis of human being was made for the purpose of enriching the original preontological comprehension we all possess of our own being. With that enrichment he approaches human ipseity, no longer from the point of view of an impersonal self living solely according to the strictures of a public world, but of the caring person who may be both its own authentic self in the constancy of its resolute decision to accept its own finitude and that inconstant, irresolute self that knows no limits because its dominant mood is curiosity, its understanding ambiguous, and its discourse idle chatter.

But even anticipatory resoluteness, once related to the care-structure of human being and projected upon the patterns of temporality that temporalize themselves in the phenomena of being-unto-death and the resolute retention of a past, gives only a partial view of our human reality: its *wholeness* and its *integrity*. At this stage of the ontology there was lacking a clear phenomenological description of the *development* of a self. For that, temporality became the theme, and Heidegger characterized the temporalizing patterns of both the authentic and inauthentic selves before returning to everydayness as constitutive of a human being's ontic insertion into a world. That is the point where the last chapter ended and where the present is to begin.

In a word, we now have a clearer picture of human reality: thrown into its world where it is abandoned to a past and projected toward its own end, a human being exists as that for the sake of which assignments of value are given to the elements of that world. But the prior analysis of this human self-projection upon its own possibilities of being—as authentic—has stressed the anticipatory resoluteness by which one assumes the responsibility for being as one is—that null basis of its own nullity—as a finite temporal process. Although being-unto-death characterizes with sufficient clarity the ontological ground for personal anxiety, it does so with respect to only one end of the projection—that future possibility beyond which there are no more personal possibilities.

As a matter of ontic fact, however, human being is stretched between two "ends," its birth and its death; and no description of the temporalizing process which neglects either end of this stretch can be considered complete. Our births are equally as distant from any current project as our deaths, if we consider the matter as an ontological whole. The difficulty with the ordinary or vulgar under-standing of the life process is that every moment making up such a life is considered a present: a now that was, that is, that will be. And if life is a sequence of nows, past, present, and future, it is constituted by a series of events that are all present to someone's observation, and the older we get the further our births recede and the nearer our deaths approach.

Heidegger brings two objections to this vulgate interpretation of life: first, human being is caring, and caring's being is temporalized temporality; and second, when the temporalizing process is consid-ered as a whole, both ends of the process are understood to exist simultaneously. At the moment of birth we are already dying; and dying, we have already been born. As it cares for its own existence a human being finds itself always in-between: having become what it is and projected toward its own end. Standing in-between, from a temporal perspective, a human being is historical (*geschichtlich*); it develops in and through time, within the time of the world and through the temporalizing of its own temporality.

In this way, the new existential to be described is human histori-cality (*Geschichtlichkeit*). And to produce this new description Hei-degger must explain how personal temporality gets historized, how its historicity comes about. Although the verb is usually translated as "to happen," Heidegger selects *geschehen*, presumably for its cognate value, to characterize the process of a lived human history; and until some kind of ontological explanation is given to the difference between a lived and a written history—between *Geschichte* and *Historie* in Heidegger's terminology (although both terms possess the same inherent ambiguity, the only difference being the Germanic derivation of the one and the Latinate of the other)—the question of what happens in history will remain ambiguous.

Macquarrie and Robinson translate *geschehen* mostly as "to historize," accepting Heidegger's suggestion that the historical happening is a concretization of human historicality in the same way that a temporal happening is a concretization of human temporality. There, the verb was *sich zeitigen,* which was rendered as "to temporalize itself."

Both lived and written history may be authentic or inauthentic, as these two general possibilities are always open to human self-determination. An authentic lived history discloses the constancy of a self in a pattern that must be described; an inauthentic one shows a self dispersed within the events of a public world. That too must be described, not as something present to our observation or our "historical" speculation, but in the manner by which our historicality becomes history. Nothing is obvious here.

If we look at written history as an account of an authentic potentiality for being a whole achieved in self-constancy or lost in successive moments of inconstancy, we must remember that the accounts of written history usually attempt to reconstruct the lived events of an historical being as taking place within time; as ontic, such events are made possible by the ontological structures of both historicality and temporality.

Before dividing the subject of his chapter into its constitutive elements, Heidegger provides the following warning: A human being is not temporal because it stands in history as inauthentically interpreted, but is historical, either authentically or inauthentically interpreted, because its being is temporal. This warning, of course, does nothing but remind the reader that existential structures take precedence over the ontic events in which they lie implicit. They are still known a priori as that which makes possible an actual ontic event. Temporality temporalizes itself into caring; and historicality gets historized into human history as it is lived.

Rather than following Heidegger's division of the subject, I shall propose another: first, the conception of a new interpretive task (secs. 72 and 73); second, the fundamental (ontologial) conception of historicality (sec. 74); third, inauthentic historicality (sec. 75); fourth, written history (sec. 76); and fifth, history as the methodology of the humane sciences (sec. 77). The only change I have effectuated here is to group sections 72 and 73 into a single topic.

Before preceding to my commentary, I may issue a warning of my own. The other, most often unremarked, side of the Heideggerian style of exposition is the growing complexity exhibited in the returns of his "sweeping spirals." Just as the Aristotelian metaphysics furnished the basis for the classical sentence structure of subject and predicate (reflecting substance and attribute), a Heideggerian sentence often expresses the deeper structure of his ontology. Consider the following example, just as a sentence:

> Wenn das Dasein vorlaufend den Tod in sich mächtig werden läßt, versteht es sich, frei für ihn, in der eigenen *Übermacht* seiner endlichen Freiheit, um in dieser, die je nur "ist" im Gewählthaben der Wahl, die *Ohnmacht* der Überlassenheit an es selbst zu übernehmen und für die Zufälle der erschlossenen Situation hellsichtig zu werden.[2]

We notice the play on words connoting power, but within that play the description of fate or destiny that embeds the following Heideggerian existentials: anticipatory resoluteness, caring, temporalizing, and human disclosedness, all as descriptive of the historizing of a personal history. I translate, retaining the complexity:

> If a human being, by anticipating its own death, allows its last possibility [*den Tod in sich*] to become effective in its life, then, in the overwhelming power of its finite freedom, it understands itself as free for death, so that in this freedom, which exists only insofar as it has made this choice, it can take upon itself the (responsibility for) the powerlessness of its abandonment and so, clearly visualize the accidents of its disclosed situation.

Death and responsibility, conscience and freedom, have been projected upon facticity, existence, and falling (here denied by the resoluteness of the decision); that is, upon past, future, and present in a moment of intense vision that is an insight into a personal fate or a national destiny.

The irony to be found in such returns to the forehaving of an

interpretation is not only the reflection of the complexity of ontological structuration in the complexity of Heidegger's sentences, but the
intimation that the last and so far missing chain in Heidegger's
explanation of human existence shall be constructed by a return to
its thrownness, that is, to the effect of the past in the constitution of
a present projection into the future.

All this should become clear in the sequel.

1. *On the way to written history.*

The first step had already been taken in section 72, where Heidegger makes his accustomed adjustment in the forestructure of interpretation. We now know that the previous description of the "wholeness" of a human self was incomplete, even as complemented by his
description of its integrity. And the new task, to conceive of history
as the development of human existence, was sketched out as
grounded in temporality as the meaning of human caring. Temporality as spread, that is, as temporalizing itself into everydayness, in
which it first gets experienced by the thrown individual, constitutes
that individual's historicality; this, in turn, is lived in a series of
happenings, the personal history of that individual.

The new problem in interpretation arises at this stage. The happenings of personal history (*Geschichte*) may be given the vulgar
interpretation of being a series of events whose being is their presence;
or they may be given a fundamental ontological interpretation. According to this latter, moreover, personal histories may be either
authentic or inauthentic, depending upon whether the self that is
developing is constant in its resolve to accept the limitation of its
finiteness—which acceptance in fact liberates it for a meaningful self-
determination of its potentialities for being—or is inconstantly pursuing novelty in a series of ever-renewed nows, that seems, to the
curious imagination, to have no end.

The problem becomes more complicated still when we realize that
writing history is one way of experiencing a personal history. Like
any other science, however, history thematizes its object, which,
according to the above, may be either authentic or inauthentic. That
written history which would disclose the truth concerning human
events will therefore have to be conceived on the basis of an understanding of the being of those events that are primordially historical.
And as the argument continues it should come as no surprise that an
effective written history will concern itself as much with the possi-

bilities of human action as with actual, factical events. That constitutes a problem, which disturbs Heidegger only for a moment. But the source of the disturbance is the everyday predominance of the vulgar view of history; and an explanation of the changeover from the vulgar to the fundamentally ontological interpretation of history—which merely follows the already familiar pattern of ontic-ontological reversal—suffices to remove the disturbance.

The changeover begins in earnest in section 73 of the text.

What, ordinarily, is "objective" history? Think history, and you think the past: an event or a series of events no longer present to our observations; or if present, no longer effective in the same way as in the past. When the object so described is a person who has in the past excelled in some form of endeavor but whose current performance is no longer noteworthy, we call that person a "has-been." Such a person belongs to history—and not to the present. Yet the pastness of the person or the object may be such that, although it is no longer present to our observation, the effects of its having been present are still felt in the living present. For example, a Greek temple is now nothing but a set of ruins; yet the style of life that produced such objects and consecrated them to their religious purposes still has its effects. We can, of course, choose to ignore the culture of the classical ages, but only by becoming less human in the process. For this reason, it is said that one cannot escape history.

But being past in some way or another is only one of the determinants of the historical as ordinarily interpreted. Something experienced or valued in the present may simply have derived from the past. For this reason, we speak of "epoch-making" events, in which a certain kind of future was determined in a past present. It was this sense of the past Ralph Waldo Emerson had in mind when he said that every successful institution is but the shadow of some great man—an idea that was overworked into the "great man" theory of history.

Most generally, history, whether of the past, the present, or anticipating a future, may be conceived, in the third place, as the totality of entities undergoing change in time. In this sense, history defines a "spirit" or culture that is differentiated only from the purely physical events of nature. Using this sense of the term, Germans distinguish the *Geisteswissenschaften* from the *Naturwissenschaften,* the humane from the natural sciences. The distinction is useful as a clue for determining a historical methodology for the humane sciences—and, some would say, it is yet another idea that has been given undue stress in humanistic studies.

The fourth connotation settled upon the historical is that it may be defined by whatever has been handed down, as a tradition, to a society or a living culture.

In effect, then, neither pastness, derivation, cultural determination, nor inheritance of a tradition is sufficient to lay out the province of history. Better, says Heidegger, to synthesize these four ordinary conceptions of a historical event into a summative, but still ontical definition. Then, as an approximation we get something like the following: history is that specific historizing of an existent human being (its coming to be, or happening) that comes to pass in time, so that the "historizing" that is past in our being-with-others and that has been "handed down" to us, and is continuingly effective in our living present, determines the way in which we live.[3]

In each of the previous definitions of the historical a human being is central for the determination of the crucial events. But how human being inheres within these events, how it belongs to them, determines or is determined by them, lacks ontological elucidation. So Heidegger pursues a second attempt, this time by way of example.

Consider a piece of household equipment placed in a museum as a record of a past way of life. Washboards, mustache cups, celluloid collars, iron maidens, and chastity belts come to mind. What is "past" for each of these "historical" objects is the way of life in which it functioned as a tool. Each of these tools had meaning insofar as it was useful for the purposes of some living people. Although its being now is its presence in the museum, its past being was its utility, as measured in a context of involvements. Thus, what is past is the worldhood defined by that context of involvements in which these objects functioned purposively.

But the human being cannot merely "be" its past; its being is its existence, its trajectory toward a future. The past of a human being (*Dasein*) is only its having-been-there (*da-gewesene*) in that world. And, as we all should recall, the human is that for the sake of which a world is structured as it is. That human being whose being was to have been there is thus the primordially historical event; the tools and things it encountered while having-been-there in its world are only secondarily historical.

For this reason, again, from the ontological point of view world-historical events are not determined by being objectified in some thematizing account of history but as having been the entities they were in some human world. Consider again the list of museum pieces noted above. The furthest removed from the present—the iron maiden—is not the most historical entity; insofar as each of these tools no longer functions as part of a living tradition, no reference to the now of today has any particular significance in the determination of its historicality. But it still remains to be shown how human being, which is primordially historical, constitutes the historicality of the world-historical events it has encountered as having-been-there, in that world which no longer exists.

Heidegger gives his answer to this question in section 74.

2. *The fundamental (ontological) conception of historicality.*

The basic constitution of human historicality is given its interpretation when Heidegger resumes the theme of anticipatory resoluteness. Resolutely anticipating one's final possibility establishes two things. First, it establishes the limitation of finiteness, which is not merely a negative condition, but rather a positive one in that it permits the individual human being to determine its own projection into a personal future. Second, it establishes one's wanting to have a conscience, the assumption of the responsibility for its own having been thrown into the world in the past. In the dispersal of the temporal moments of its time within the world, of course, these two "moments," which we recognize as future and past, have an identical determination—a fact that may be read from my final diagram, figure 9.

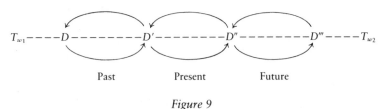

$$T_{w_1}----D--------D'--------D''--------D'''----T_{w_2}$$

Past   Present   Future

Figure 9

Within the time of the world, the future and the past are both moments of actuality, with D representing the beginning of a personal temporality and D''', its actual end. Descriptions of such a stretch of one's being historical, however, are of an inauthentic self that is considered as a world-historical event.

Simultaneously with the representation of an inauthentic self, however, figure 9 shows a temporally stretched out care-structure as the anticipation of an end and a retention of a beginning, in which, during each moment of the stretch, temporality temporalizes itself as a whole: the past is a present anticipating a past future; the past future is a present past, which I may retain while projecting a present future; and the present future is a future past, which, if I remain resolute, I shall retain while anticipating a future future.

The beginning and the end of the temporalizing temporality are still marked by birth and death. And only the time of the world, which is a thematized construct of the structural world, extends beyond these limits. The difference between the resolute and authentic self and the irresolute and inauthentic self is the constancy of the former and the inconstancy of the latter.

Section 74 is devoted to the interpretation of authentic historicality; section 75, of the inauthentic.

We are reminded in section 74 that human being is caring and that caring is expended through a temporal stretch in which an individual projects itself upon its possibilities of being (its existence) from its abandonment in a world (its facticity), while concerning itself with the entities of its world (ordinarily, its falling). What brings the authentic individual out of its present state of falling is conscience, which as call spans the temporal gap between the future possibility I shall become in actuality and the past I was as having been *(da-gewesene)*. Along with every projection into the future, then, there is a corresponding calling back for the assumption of the responsibility *(Schuldigsein)* for one's own abandonment in the world. This, we recall, was explained as taking over one's thrownness, one of the determinants for the freedom of human action, that is, acting in consequence of a self-understanding by which the acting self recognizes that it and it alone constitutes the "null basis of its own nullity."

But this condition, like that of a human finiteness established in an authentic death, is not merely negative. Ontically, of course, it is just that—a refusal to allow oneself to be determined by purely worldly events; but ontologically, the structure of facticity is such that in assuming the responsibility for one's having-been-there, the acting person determines its own self-projection—from both ends. That is, in viewing the situation into which it has been factically thrown and ontologically abandoned as offering a number of possibilities for continued action, a developing self is presented with choices for its election; and if over our births we have no control and of our gender no free election, what we do with the conditions established by our births and the nature of our gender is a matter for which we may be entirely responsible. It all depends upon whether we respond to the call of conscience with resolution, or whether we ignore the call and continue to allow ourselves to be lost in a purely public world.

Although a purely ontological analysis has nothing at all to say about an actual human choice in a given factual situation, since it is concerned with human being only as possible, it is meaningful ontologically to ask about the source of one's ontic, factical choices that a given situation offers to our election.[4] The concreteness of a self-projection toward the future demands that the analyst pay as much attention to the facticity of one's situation as to the closed futurity of an individual's personal end. Whence, to complete his account of the basic constitution of human historicality Heidegger returns to the theme of anticipatory resoluteness, with the promise of paying as much attention to the beginning as to the end of an existence.

As thrown, indeed, a human being is brought back to itself, as a being-in-the-world. There, it may be lost in the hurly-burly of the public world it shares with its neighbors, or it may resolutely assume the responsibility of its having-been-there. Anticipating its end and retaining its past, not by remembering or forgetting, but by repeating the choice of itself, the resolute human being becomes master of its situation in the world. Since it is its situation that determines the possibilities it may elect for the concrete development of its selfhood, in choosing to repeat the action that best represents itself, the acting individual, by returning to itself, hands down to itself that fixed determination that allows its self-constancy throughout the temporalization of its finite temporality: D through D''' of figure 9. It is in this way that it creates for itself a heritage, which it takes over in the constant repetition of itself—or rejects in losing itself within the public world.

The choice of self eliminates all other choices. We must die, so we choose our own finitude; we had to be born, so we must choose to do something about that as well. When we repeat a past choice, thus making it our own, we establish a heritage that is likewise ours to choose. When we do, our historical happening—our *Geschichte*—is authentically fateful.

I am translating *Schicksal* as fate, following Macquarrie and Robinson. They remind us that Heidegger has chosen this term, along with *Geschick* for a communal "destiny," since both these terms bear an affinity to *Geschichte* and *geschehen* already used for the historizing happening of a developing self. Heidegger does play on the reverberating tonalities of the related vocables, but surely the German ear is equally in tune to a similar set of harmonies with the verb *schicken,* to dispatch, order, or send, in one sense; and to come to pass and to be fitting for, in others. However this may be, in the fateful choice of self-repetition the acting human being bestows upon itself a heritage from its past, one that befits its current situation.

To choose oneself, in the current Heideggerian frenzy of verbal association, is to exert a "superior power" that may overcome one's "powerlessness" in being born or of always finding oneself already in a world, thrown there and not being able to avoid making a choice from among the possibilities such a situation offers to human election. If, anticipating our deaths and coming back to our abandonment in a world, we create the conditions for a truly free choice, it is the moment of vision, that authentic present spanning our finite future end and the retained past we repeat with resolution, that allows us to perceive the structures of our personal insertion into history as a living situation uniting the self with the accidental characteristics of the public world.

Although it is sometimes read as meaningless jargon,[5] consistent with the kind of political jargon later used by official Nazi party propagandists, we read "Fate is that powerless superior power which puts itself in readiness for adversities"[6] as a simple statement of the care-structure that temporalizes itself into an authentic lived history. As powerless not to have a past, but choosing its own proper end, an acting individual faces the contingencies of a present. How? The rest of the German sentence makes that perfectly clear: in silence (because of the phenomenon of conscience), ready for anxiety, projecting itself toward its own end, taking up its own responsibility, fulfilling the conditions of a temporalized existence.[7]

Even so, actual situations are lived under the ontological conditions of our being-with others. No problem; under these conditions the cohistorizing repetition of an inherited past choice by some social group exhibits the same temporal structures. But instead of *Schicksal* (fate), Heidegger refers to the establishment of an authentic collective entity—which could be exemplified in the German nation—as a destiny *(Geschick).*

Talk of humanity's fate or of a nation's destiny can be heady stuff and can be indulged in for many purposes. Heidegger's purpose was to complete his fundamental ontology, and he summarizes his ontological claims for human self-constancy in another of those super-loaded sentences, this time italicized for emphasis.[8] I paraphrase: a human being's being is essentially futural, freeing itself for its death by projecting its own end and allowing itself to be thrown back upon its factical "there"; its existence is thus futural, but equiprimordially as thrown back to its having-been it bestows upon itself the possibility it has inherited as its history; in this way, it takes over its thrownness in a moment of vision for its own time. Once again, the totalized structure of human temporality is embedded in a single sentence.

Repetition is the explicit handing down of an inherited possibility, but the original resolute act need not concern itself with the origin of its possibilities, which, as part of the lived situation, are purely factical. In resoluteness, by which we choose to have a conscience, we merely choose self-responsibility; we choose that choice which makes us free from an inauthentic past. As such, the resolute repetition of the choice of self constitutes a reciprocative rejoinder to the possibility of that existence which (already) has-been-there, even as lost in that world.

The moment of vision, which is either the anticipation of a repeated choice or the repetition of an anticipation of the past, lifts the resolute individual out of its lostness in a purely public world. It disavows the "today," which merely follows yesterday and precedes tomorrow. As opposed to ontic world history, ontological historicality is futural and finite, not past and unlimited, as if for every history there were a prehistory that is yet to be written.

When they are authentic, our lived histories, as opposed to our written histories, are structured with equal primordiality by the past and the other two ekstatic dimensions of human temporality: the present and the future. In the resolute choice of a self or of a nation, what gets handed down is a possibility of being, the proposal of an action that anticipates a repetition of its having-been-there now illuminated in a moment of clear vision, whether that inheritance from the past be an individual's fate or a nation's destiny.

It is this feature of authentic historicality, its repetition of a possibility of being that is handed down, that gets emphasized in the common interpretation of history, as a record of the past. What gets forgotten in such accounts is the moment of vision in which the anticipation of a future and the retention of a past are united. All we need do to understand this conjunction is to keep in mind the fact that anticipating and retaining are present acts.

Heidegger skirts the logical problem created by the anticipation of a national future. Surely that is not finite for the same reason that a human being is finite; and if all the entities of a collectivity are finite, the collectivity itself need not be, since they need not all die at the same time. Thus, when he says that in full anticipation of our constant existence through time we resolutely choose our authentic historicality in the act of handing down a future by repeating what we have seen, the finiteness of that future is not established by the death of a nation, but by something else, such as—perhaps—the limitations of time set upon the achievement of realistic national goals, subjugation through conquest, or defeat in a war. But this is a problem that concerns the full ontological conception of our being-with. Ordinarily nations do not die, although empires in due time may be lost.

If we return to the individual existence, we may still envisage a further problem in determining the sense of an authentic personality: the connectedness of the events from birth to death still have not been given an ontological interpretation. In every factical situation there is a constant threat of falling into inconstancy, of allowing everyday public events to intrude upon our own resolute self-determination. What are the structures of inauthentic historicality? Consider. If a human being always exists historically, then even an inauthentic existence must be historical. How does an individual historize itself into inauthenticity?

Presumably, without resoluteness, that is, inconstantly rather than constantly, and without anticipation, allowing itself merely to be dragged along by current events. From this point of view, most written histories are thematizations of inauthentically lived histories; or they are ontologically groundless thematizations of a possible authentically lived history, since for the most part written histories look backward for their explanatory events, leaving out of the account any reference to a possible future, since, ordinarily, historians are not prophets.

Since to answer these remaining questions we must consider those conditions under which a human individual may lose itself in the objects of its world, and these events are likewise historical, if only secondarily so, we must turn to the historizing of world-historical events. And that is found in the next section, 75.

3. *Inauthentic historicality: the world-historical phenomena of history.*

Ordinarily, that is, as a matter of everyday existence, a human being understands itself as it projects itself upon possible ways of being. For the most part, these are determined by the items of its concernful attention. Living a world of significant relationships in which means and ends are arranged for its own purposes, bringing the far close-by and expending its energies in work, the human self takes care of its tools and whatever might be given along with their functioning badly or well. In this sense, it understands its world as a set of affairs, something to be done, while attending to the various incidents and mishaps that may prevent the completion of its work. And at the same time, we exist in this world with others who may need our products or supply us with the materials with which to work. We share a public world in which those in the know concern themselves with what is getting done, or what has been tried and failed. Such is the everyday, workaday world.

Why then cannot the history of the events of this world merely be described as a sequence of conscious experiences? Because, obviously, such a view of world-historicality separates what ontology has forever joined together—the self and its being-in-a-world. World history as a string of conscious events separates the experiences of the events of the world from the subject that "has" them and, once having separated them, reduces them in their being to two sets of presences. In a word, the separation of the subject from the object of history repeats all the unanswered questions of the traditional metaphysics and epistemology it was Heidegger's purpose to "destroy."

Fundamental ontology has presented us with the notion of a self— either constant and authentic or inconstant and inauthentic—that exists as projected into a world. What happens in history according to an appropriate ontologically grounded notion of historicality is the historizing of a human being's being-in-the-world. And as described above, two entities are historized simultaneously: the human being who is primordially historical and its world, which is only secondarily so.

The historizing of a human's world has been called "world history"; its events "world-historical." The equipment used in one's work, the artifacts of a culture, the very natural sites of human events are historical: city and countryside develop together or apart; colonizers and exploited may dispute the same terrain, parcels of which may be "hallowed" by bloody battle or consecrated to the purposes of religion. The objects of one's concern and the fateful projection of a self historize themselves in unison. That much, however, we knew from the beginning, when we discovered human being as being-in-a-world.

From the foregoing, it is apparent that "the world-historical" is an ambiguous concept. It may signify the historizing of the world in its unity with the self-projecting human being; or, more limitedly, the historizing of the entities found in such a world, that is, the tools with which people work or the mere things that may, indeed, help or hinder in the working. What "happens" to such things, how they change, how they are moved, depends upon their manner of being: the serviceability of equipment or the presence of things. Simple changes of place do not encompass the movement of history. Consider the ring, whose being is to signify the unbroken relationship between man and woman; the movement from best man's pocket to groom's hand to bride's finger does not capture that being.

Why should movement constitute an ontological enigma in the conception of history in the first place? Answer: because, as fallen into the present, now separated from a past that was a present, a human being tends to understand itself in terms of a temporalized world, as always already existing in an ongoing temporal stretch, before any attempt to characterize this historical happening. Human beings are historical without benefit of historians, in the same way they may pledge their troth without benefit of clergy.

The world-historical understanding of human being's own historical self-projection stems from its fallen nature. In the world, and identified with its objects, the continual development and changes within these objects are given the traditional interpretation of being: their presence to a subject. For this reason, history seems a process of being strung along in a series of present moments; some coming along, some now here, and some already having disappeared. And, since, traditionally, the question of the meaning of Being in general has been forgotten or taken as something self-evidently apparent, ordinary accounts of the world-historical events have never been ontologically grounded. To write history, one merely delivers oneself over to the experiences.

But what of those experiences? In the fallen state, the existent human being gets dispersed into its immediate projects; it is driven about from one of these to another, carried along as it were on the stream of events. Therefore, should it seek to "pull itself together," it must gather itself together from its state of dispersion and disconnectedness. The problem of the connectedness of world-historical events has no other basis than this. Because in the world of the everyday we start with an inauthentic view of history, it becomes impossible to construct an authentic view.

If, however, the problem is posed in another way, its solution has already been sketched out. If we ask "How does a human being lose itself in its world in such a way that it must subsequently seek to pull itself together again?" then we already possess the answer. In the world of the everyday, we flee in the face of our deaths and so do not become free for our fateful self-delivery. If we are resolute, and do not shrink from anticipating our death, on the other hand, the patterns of a historical and authentic self are such as described in the previous section. The dispersion into inconstancy occurs through distraction, the very attention paid to the "works" in which we engage ourselves from moment to moment.

Whereas, in the authentic historizing of our resolute selves, the constancy of our developing selves spans future and past in a moment of vision, which merely confirms the validity of our heritage, in inauthentic historizing, the present moment is reduced to a cross section of universal time. And our written histories, in consequence, rather than recounting our historizing as the recurrence of the possible, give us a punctiform picture of discretely related actual events.

To correct this state of affairs, in order more effectively to effectuate the actual destruction of the history of ontology itself, we must turn to the task of describing the source of our written histories in human historicality itself. That is the task of section 76.

4. Writing history: a mode of caring. Written history as derivative from human historicality.

The problem is to develop a concept of historical science grounded in primordial human historicality. Like any other science, history is both a way of being in the world that projects an understanding of the conditions under which a world has come to be what it is and an act of disclosiveness by which a human subject lives its openness to that world. As a way of knowing itself and the world in which it finds itself thrown, writing history is, for any self-conscious human being, an attempt to thematize, or to make an object of discourse, the historizing of its own historical nature.

In ordinary terms, writing a history is an activity that finds itself in a double bind. It is undertaken in a present moment but projects disclosing the truth either about its own past or the transmission of that past into the present. All such attempts depend to some extent or another upon the prevailing world view entertained by the historian, but which may "correspond" to the facts or diverge considerably from them. Yet, if the being of the historical investigator is itself historical, any written history presupposes the truth of a primordial historical event. Whence, the double bind.

The solution of this double bind is the ready acceptance of the fact that all historians are themselves historical beings; they are either authentically or inauthentically engaged in the very processes they would try to explain. Although on the face of it this engagement in the world its purpose is to explain would seem to make life more difficult for the self-disclosive being, only a moment's reflection is necessary to understand that the prior insertion of a self into a history is a necessary condition for anyone to disclose what it means to have a history. And whether or not our attempts to disclose the truth of our historicality have been accomplished in any of our historical writings, if we were not ourselves historical beings, we would have nothing to write about in attempting to write a history. Our "double bind" then only means that the idea for a written history must originate in our own historicality. But this had been said at the beginning, when Heidegger chided us to observe that human being is always one's own *(ist je meines)*.

Rather than scanning the various ways in which factual histories have been written—for example, the account of developing events determined by the greatness of certain human participants in history or by the "spirit of the times" or by the "invisible hand" of economic laws—it becomes essential to consider under what conditions any such account could possibly be true. So here once again Heidegger proposes that we neglect all purely ontical accounts of the historizing of human being in order to stipulate what an ontologically grounded historiology might be.

First of all, the region of the thematizing effort must be opened up as a specific area of investigation; in this case, a human being's prescientific disclosure of self and world. Then, as in any understanding at all, this entity—a human being in a world—must be projected, in an effort to determine its meaning, upon the Being specific to its historical temporality. In this way the realm of investigation may be circumscribed. Next, there must be a method of approaching the area, a regularization of the ways for acceding to the indicated phenomena, usually referred to as "a method" for managing the results of our observations, including the elaboration of the conceptual apparatus for making the desired interpretation of the phenomena. Once a "past" has in some way been disclosed, we need only consider the conditions necessary for there to have been such a past.

Human historicality, we have shown above, is grounded in temporality, the meaning of human being. If for the moment we select only the past dimension of the ekstatic-horizontal human temporality as our area of investigation, the ontological grounding of the inquiry is in human being as having-been-there in a world *(Dasein als dagewesenes)*. But along with this "primordially historical entity," there is the secondarily historical set of world-historical events. In either case, historians have something to study.

Their access to these events, the materials of their study, are remains, monuments, records, eyewitness accounts, and the like. But if these constitute evidence for the projected historical account, they do so only because they are themselves world-historical, vestiges still open to observation of a world that no longer exists, but which may be understood as having existed only on the basis of the historian's own present existence.

What the historian does in interpreting his data is to project the ontological conditions of his own historicality upon the world-historical sources he has observed. Without this grounding in the prescientific self-disclosure of human being as primordially historical, there is no way into the past.

But with it, it becomes possible to determine what the object of history really is: in effect, the historizing of those humans as social entities that have been there in the same way the historian himself lives his having-been-there, that is either authentically as resolutely repeating a possibility of being they have freely handed down themselves, or inauthentically as being determined by the events of their world. In either case, however, they are projected upon possibilities of being. Why so? Any present fact is a past possibility.

If the idea seems strange it is because ordinary accounts of history are presumably factual. They answer these questions: What happened? Where? When? Why? Any answers to these questions which merely impose some universally explanatory law upon the phenomena—whether psychological, economical, or sociological—lose their ontological grounding in the specificity of the human world that has-been-there. Ontological historiology must deal with the possible to communicate the connectedness of human events in the same way that the historizing of our temporality communicates the connectedness, the constancy of our being. Recall the structure: thrown being in the world comes back to itself and repeats the possibility of being it hands down to itself.

But if, ontologically considered, the being of a human being is to be what it can be, why has the ordinary conception of history been devoted exclusively to the facts? The question is answered if only we ask another: the facts of what? If the answer to this second question is, of a human existence, then the historical prejudice for facts is unwarranted: human beings exist as thrown into a world and as projecting themselves toward future possibilities. The "facts" of a past existence must be interpreted as part of a historizing self-projection.

And when we do interpret them as such, two further problems of historical methodology are seen to vanish: whether history is an account of a once-and-for-all set of events or of universal laws of sociological change, on the one hand; and whether, on the other, history is "objective" or purely subjective. Both questions reflect the traditional bias for the historical event as an actuality, one among many others following each other in the time of the world. And both present false disjunctions.

From the point of view of authentic historicality, the historical event is neither a once-in-a-while occurrence, nor the natural consequence of a positive law; rather, the historical event is the repetition of a past that anticipates a future. It illustrates an existential structure, which is repeatable in different historical agents, and the very ontical action repeats a past choice of action. Both these repeatable characteristics of the historical event may be mistaken for naturalistic universality.

But neither a prehistoriological human being nor the historian who would study its behavior merely recedes backward into the corridors of history. If they did, it would be impossible for there to be a future for either of them. The selection of the historian's "materials" is determined by what has already been encountered as the factical choice of the historical entity that has-been-there in its world.

For this reason, too, written history is neither subjective—open to any choice of the *Historiker*—nor objective—as having nothing to do with the historian's mode of being. His own being—or rather his understanding of it—is the basis for his projected interpretation of historical events.

Since the central theme of historiology is an existence that has-been-there and such a being historizes itself in a world-historical manner, the proper objects of history may be brought to a present understanding. Thus, instead of merely giving way to some dominant world view of his own intellectual age, which can produce history as a pleasing story, the historian projects an understanding of the world-historical events based upon the authentic—or inauthentic—historicality of the human beings who produced them. And this can be done even if one does no more than edit someone else's sources.

Since his discussion of the differences between the vulgar view of historical writing and his own ontological view brings to mind the possible uses and abuses of history, Heidegger ends this section of the text with a gloss on Nietzsche's text with the same title.[9] In his second set of "thoughts out of season" Nietzsche discerned three approaches to the writing of history: the monumental, the antiquarian, and the critical. Each of these, says Heidegger, corresponds to an emphasis on a different ekstatic moment of temporalizing human temporality.

For example, as futural, the historical event is presented in a resolute disclosure of the possibility of being that has been chosen in a projected action. But from that projected future, the agent comes back to itself as thrown into its world and repeats a choice already made; this repetition opens the human agent up to the "monumental" possibilities of its being.

But as equiprimordially past, the repetition creates a second possibility, that of reverently preserving a prior existence that has-been-there. Histories emphasizing this feature of an authentic act are "antiquarian," preserving in their accounts of world-historical events a form of life that would otherwise be lost to us.

Lastly, written histories may be "critical," emphasizing the present *ekstasis* of human temporality, showing, indeed, how a present moment occurs in the tension between a projected future and a repeated past. Since such a "now" of the present is disclosed in a moment of vision or, inauthentically, as coming along in the time of the world, a critical reading of the historical events must be given. And the proper tool for practicing history in this way is to bring the existential forestructure of the understanding to the task of interpreting historical events as the repetitive disclosure of what has-been-there, the lives of the individuals who have lived such a past.

Since all the humane sciences adopt the task of thematizing human lives and world-historical events, hermeneutics constitutes the proper method of disclosing the "truth" of such objects.[10] And on this grounding of a methodology for writing history Heidegger rests his case.

5. *History as the methodology of the humane sciences.*

The final section of this chapter, 77, attempts to show that the methodology sketched out in the previous section has already been adumbrated in the historiological methodology of Wilhelm Dilthey, especially as criticized by his friend, Count Paul Yorck von Wartenburg.[11]

Dilthey's contributions to the methodological sciences are philosophical in nature. Heidegger presents them under three heads: studies in the theory of the human sciences; actual historical research into the sciences of human beings, their society, or state; and an analytical "psychology" of the "whole-person," which would permit an investigator into the human sciences to practice the same sort of hermeneutical projects as those Heidegger has been calling for. The difficulty with Dilthey's approach to a philosophy of life that unites these three interests—historiological methodology, science of history, and analytical psychology—is that Dilthey failed to heed the ontic-ontological difference.

Having no ground in an existential-ontological account of our human being, Dilthey's hermeneutic, based upon on uncritical view of a human self and hypothesizing a method that is purely analytical, rather than critical, was justified by an appeal to a general theory of knowledge, which, Count Yorck intimates, was constructed haphazardly by a survey of natural scientific investigations. Such a procedure cannot justify a specific methodology for a philosophy of life or for the sciences of living beings.

At this point Heidegger intervenes in the exchange of correspondence between Dilthey and Yorck to indicate that the latter was looking for a scientific methodology for the humane, and therefore historiological, sciences, one that could be developed, as was Heidegger's own, on the historicality of human beings, who are both natural animals and historizing events in a purely human world, and one that would guide the practitioners of history.

For example, a critical historiological methodology will exploit its insight into the difference between the historical and the purely "ocular" view of intuited events exhibited in the mechanistic, picture-drawing, form-prescribing techniques of traditional historians. Its own prescriptions of methodological procedures will stem from the nature of the primordially historical events, the lives of human beings that indeed are ontical but ontical in such a way as to exhibit fundamental ontological structures.

This unity of the ontic and the ontological nature of the human animal has already been described by Heidegger in the previous sections of this chapter. As primordially historical, a human being historizes its historicality; as secondarily historical, world-historical events constitute the records for critically reconstructing the lives of those human beings whose being now is to have-been-there in that world that is to be interpreted as history.

In review, Heidegger stipulates the conditions for developing a critical methodology of history. Historians must be led to recognize three facts: first, that historicality is an ontological question about the being of historical events; second, that how lives are lived ontically is likewise an ontological question, as is the ontical progression of purely world-historical events; and third, that the ontical dimension of entities—how they come to be and pass away—is only one dimension of their being.

For this reason, Heidegger continues to maintain that the sciences of history will not be grounded until one possesses an adequate idea of Being itself. All the existential analytic so far traced out for us has as its only purpose the preparation of that science—a fundamental ontology—that would answer the question of the meaning of Being in general. The pursuit of that question, which is now a quest, goes on.

Because the originally planned text was not completed, we already know that the Holy Grail eluded Heidegger's quest, but that must be explained more fully in what follows. In anticipation of that demonstration, it is perhaps better to interpret Heidegger's account of the interchange between Dilthey and Count Yorck as another example of the "preontological self-interpretation" of the historical sciences. If we do this, as we seem impelled to do, then Dilthey's *Lebensphilosophie* serves the same role in Heidegger's treatise as did Hyginus's fable of Care.

Who cares? Who knows? If philosophers don't, then historians must; for the objects of their concern are indeed beings who have already cared, and about whom we still care.

11

Temporality, Withintimeness, Time

IF, IN THE PREVIOUS PROJECTION, THE PATH
of temporality is traced from historicality and historicity to history,
and in tracing it Heidegger has laid the foundation for an authentic
science of history, his conclusions indicate that he has yet another
projection to make. Backtracking to the beginning of the text will be
useful to expose the sweep of those majestically moving hermeneutical spirals, forward in anticipation of a significance to be established,
and backward once again into the forehaving constituted by those
significances already established. In the preliminary existential analysis of human being the idea of existence was interpreted, from the
standpoint of our average and everyday concerns, in terms of being-
in-the-world. This ontological concept was in turn interpreted as a
totalizing structure of the equiprimordial component structures:
worldhood, ipseity, and being-in, this latter itself the same sort of
totalizing structure composed of the affective tone, understanding,
and discourse that constitute the disclosedness of our being-there,
that is, our openness to the world. All these structures and substructures, like wheels within the wheels ("way up in the middle of the
air," as the old spiritual goes), are ways of being in the world; and
these are assimilated to the structures of care: existence, facticity,
and falling.

But the initial projection was undertaken merely to prepare a more fundamental interpretation of human being, this time projecting the existentials of everyday being-in-the-world that constitute care upon temporality, the anticipated meaning of that being. The foresighted idea was still that of existence but this time projected toward the wholeness and the integrity of human being. Accordingly, we met with death and conscience, those two determinants of an authentic self that permit it to assume its finitude and the responsibility even of its having been thrown over to and abandoned in the world. Together, death and conscience are united as anticipatory resoluteness that allows the analyst to project the structures of caring upon an authentic temporality that is not only finite but also strictly relative to the person experiencing the anxiety of being called out of the state of inauthentic falling.

Then, a quick return to the everyday state of the human being, and the derivation of the ordinary state of persons who no longer anticipate but merely await their futures; no longer retain their pasts but only remember or forget them; no longer enjoy a clear moment of vision that lights up the potentialities of a present situation but merely make it present as something to be observed. In this return to the everyday, we rediscovered the originally given ontically constituted person as projecting a self-understanding, but we were left with the description of a totalizing process which, lacking an interpretation for its beginning, remained incomplete.

So, the point of birth was added to that of an authentic death, to give an interpretation of the developing phases of our human being. For this reason, thrownness was revisited, and human being was interpreted as historicality, which like every other form of human being may be either authentic or inauthentic, personal or impersonal. As historical, human being is spanned through the process of historizing into a fateful personal world or, since human being is likewise always being-with others, into a collective destiny. But as no human history may historize itself without a concomitant historizing of the events occurring within the worlds of caring human beings, so there is no primordially historical human being without its accompanying secondarily historical world-constituting events. Such are the world-historical events that enable written histories to be antiquarian, monumental, and critical accounts to reconstitute the record of our having-been there in the world.

Here too, however, the existential-ontological account of the historizing human world has been left incomplete. We must return once more to the everyday, factical situation in order to give it the historical interpretation it demands.

World history develops as events take place in time; to make apparent how this "ontic-historical" phenomenon constitutes the factical nature of human being, still another—this time, the last—projection must be made. How does the human individual, discoursing upon its being in the world, make clear in its natural or its historiological sciences what factical, or ontic, temporality is? According to the natural sciences, prior events constitute the grounds for our knowledge that allows us to predict future events; in the humane sciences, world-historical events follow the same "time-line."

As before, however, the appeal to an advanced stage of the sophisticated sciences for a grounding of self-knowledge is a mistake. Even before tracing events along a line of time, an acting human being has already illustrated an attitude or relationship to time in that it has already reckoned with a set of personal events; and this knowledge is embedded in our temporal adverbs: *before, after, during*, each indicating a time when something was to be done to get along with our affairs. Here we meet the preontological once again. In its concern for itself or with its affairs, the human being either has the time or lacks it and adjusts its responses to fit the reading of its situation. Such is its preontological time-reckoning.

Moreover, since the existential-ontological account of temporality must include an interpretation of world-time along with that of the developing person or nation, the prior account is not only incomplete; it is also defective, as having been developed in abstraction from the factical situation of human beings. Natural and historical events take place "in time"; this withintimeness of worldly events needs an interpretation. How to proceed?

By beginning from where we are, with the ordinary conception of time as either something useful or present, and showing how this ordinary conception results as a natural process of the "leveling off" of the fully authentic temporality described in a previous "hermeneutical swing." Nowhere, perhaps, is the morally neutral sense of *inauthenticity* more clearly expressed than in this account of the leveling off a primordial, personal temporality into the secondary sense of a public, impersonal nesting of worldly events into a universal time. As before, "public" and "impersonal" are adequate translations for *the inauthentic*.

In tracing out this passage from the primordial to the secondary senses of *temporal,* Heidegger hopes to throw some light upon the traditional, paradoxical interpretation of time as being indissolubly both "subjective" and "objective." When most objective, time is still felt as lasting, or passing, or, in utter boredom, as having come to a stop; and if these "seeming" characteristics of time are elevated into the most basic meaning of the temporal, the passage of time is still objectively measurable, even preontologically, by the ways in which humans, as a species, have always reckoned with "their" time, even before the existence of clocks.

Hegel's account, which attempted to show the essential connection between time and "spirit," is examined to show how the paradoxes may be avoided, and to give a clear, but essentially incorrect, notion of the relationship between human being and time. That connection, we are told, will not be completely understood until the project of a fundamental ontology has been completed, a subject to which I shall return in my next chapter.

In section 78 (chapter 6, division 2), Heidegger divides his subject for that last interpretive swing: (1) temporality and our concern with time (sec. 79); (2) the time of concern and the withintimeness of worldly events (sec. 80); (3) the withintimeness of events and the genesis of the ordinary concept of time (sec. 81); (4) Hegel's model for conceiving the relationship between spirit and time (sec. 82); and (5) the existential-temporal analytic of human being and the question of the meaning of Being in general (sec. 83).

My commentary continues, but section 83 will be saved to serve as the basis for my next chapter.

1. *Temporality and our concern with time* (sec. 79).

The temporality of this section is called "human," presumably to distinguish it from the temporality of world-historical events. But even that distinction does not suffice to eradicate the ambiguity of the term, since human temporality may be authentic and primordial or inauthentic and secondary. When we continue reading beyond the heading, however, it begins to become clear that the section is dedicated to the determination of the attributes of experienced time, based upon the conceptual forehaving of everyday concern. The "everyday" is a clue that inauthentic human temporality is meant by the title.

What is the forehaving of everyday concern? All those concepts already given phenomenological interpretation in the prior sections of the text. For example, the care-structure: being ahead of itself, already in, and as existing alongside the entities of its concern. This threefold care-structure is made possible by the ekstatic-horizonal constitution of temporality: as ahead of itself, awaiting a future; as already in, retaining or forgetting its past; and as being-alongside the entities of its concern, making present, or disclosing those entities, along with its own disclosing activity. "Truth," we recall from chapter 6, was either primordial and being-disclosing or secondary and being-disclosed.

In its self-disclosure, finally, human being is open to its world through its affective tone, its projective understanding, and its discoursing on the truth of its being.

When everydayness is viewed as concernful doing or planning, it exhibits the temporality structure on the very surface of that activity: doing, or planning to do, is an activity that makes present one's own situation as retaining the past and awaiting a future. Everyday concern, then, must reckon with time. The future is a "then, when something may be expected"; the past, a former occasion, when an opportunity may have been missed; the present, a now, when an action must be initiated in consequence.

Careful concern for the entities of one's world is given meaning by the temporality structure that makes it possible. The time-reckoning by which this careful concern is made concrete therefore exhibits the same structure, with each ekstatic dimension implicating the other two. For example, if the "then" of the temporality structure marks a future moment, it is a now that is awaited; if it is that of a former occasion, then it is retained in a consequent action or forgotten in curiosity, ambiguity, or idle talk; and if it marks the present "now," it is made present, either by the use of some tool or by a simple act of observation.

But in reckoning with time in our caring for the entities of our worlds we fall into the time of that world, in which *then, on the former occasion,* and *now* all indicate a point in a "now-time." The "then" is a now, not yet; it is experienced as an act of awaiting that retains or forgets. The "on that former occasion" is a now, no longer present; it is experienced as a retention of the past that makes something present as it awaits. In this sequence of "nows," in the sequence of "now-time," making present takes precedence over the other two dimensions of time. Both awaiting and retaining are activities of a present.

And when the "today" of a now-time takes its place between the "earlier of yesterday" and the "later of tomorrow," the temporality of inauthentic being-in-the-world is datable by reference to the occurrence of events taking place in that world. The future is that moment when I shall do something; the past, when I did or failed to do something; the present, as I am in fact now doing something. Our verbs get tensed in this way, and to such a degree that a simple assertion, such as "It's cold," can be expanded without loss of temporal meaning to read, "It's cold today" or "It's cold, now that the wind has changed."

Why should this be the case? The "now that" is not something that is present along with the entities within the world. Why, then, does world-time allow itself to be dated with reference to the events taking place within it? Heidegger's answer: every act of circumspective concern is likewise a self-projection of the human being, which, first of all, expresses itself in its concern for objects, and, second, interprets and understands itself in reflection as a making-present that awaits and retains. That much lies only slightly below the surface of our being intelligent agents of action.

Let us recapitulate, then. A human being is that self-disclosive entity that lives in the openness of its being-there as a making present that retains and awaits. For this reason, temporality is always interpretable as a structure of human openness to its world. Time figures as the structure of worldly events; as such, it is that which has been interpreted in action and addressed in the now, or current situation.

But time, as that which has been interpreted, has originated in the temporality of the human being that interprets itself as the one who makes present by retaining and awaiting. "Now that such and such is the case, I can. . . ." It is in such moments as these that the objects of one's concern are made present. And it is in this way that the "now," the "then," and the "on that former occasion" give a date to the events in a world. And we have even been told, on the highest of authority, that there is a time for everything under the sun. A time to sow and a time to reap; a time to laugh and a time to weep.

If the time of everyday concern is datable by the activities of one's concern, its second characteristic, as experienced by human subjects, is its being spanned. This characteristic could likewise be read off the placement of a "now" between a past and a future. Simply put, between the now and the then, and between the now and the former occasion, there is a time during which something transpires: we wait until then to see what it might be, or we do something to assure ourselves that it be just what we should like to see. From now until then is measured as a "movement" from a then to a then through a period of time that lasts or gets stretched along. In every day of the year something is running its course.

But since it is always possible for a human being to lapse into inconsequence by allowing its own self-projection into the future to be eclipsed by a concern for the objects that surround it, this spanned character of human temporality may be covered up; the self may forget its past and so lose continuity with its personal and authentic future. That's what happened to Clove in Beckett's *Endgame* as he looked out the window watching for something to take its course.[1] The explanation of this one is easy: in inauthenticity the agent loses the sense of being a personal self as it becomes more and more enthralled by objects. In the process, the temporality of the self—the historizing of an authentic history—is replaced by the temporality of world-historical events. When it does, it loses *its* time for the sake of the time of the world. And as engulfed in world-time, it will usually plead its impotence to initiate a meaningful action by complaining, "I have no time to do anything," when what is meant is that "[T]he world is too much with us / Getting and spending. . . ."

When the agent does take its time, however, its temporality historizes itself into a moment of vision that is held in a future that is in the process of having-been; but the moment of vision illuminates only the present situation of the human being, along with its pregnant possibilities. For this reason, the authentic agent always has its own time for accomplishing the demands of the situation; its resoluteness prevents its losing that time.

In sum, the "spanning" of human temporality is the effect of having its "there" disclosed to itself as grounded in primordial temporality. As such, it is ekstatically stretched along, through a time allotted to its being there. Thrown into the world, it can either take or lose its time, depending upon its choice of action.

Lastly, datable, spanned time is public. We cannot forget, of course, that our being-in-the-world is a being-with others. A time may be our time—as the old song has it, even if Rudy Vallee did not, "My time is your time"—when we say "now" together. The clichés keep coming to mind, "We could make such beautiful music together," if only we said "now" together in such a way that my now and your now have been replaced by an our now.

Even though everyday concern understands itself in terms of the "world" of its concern, it still takes its time; but the time it takes is no longer its own. That time, indeed, is not mine or yours or ours; it's everyone's. The time of everyday concern is therefore public and impersonal; but this is only to say, once more, "inauthentic."

2. The time of concern and the withintimeness of worldly events (sec. 80).

The problem in this section of Heidegger's text is to describe the phenomenal character of public time, with particular emphasis upon its measurability. As in all his adjustments to the forestructure of the understanding, Heidegger indicates the reasons for making them and projects a new avenue of interpretation. Here the reason is, once again, the incompleteness of the previous account of public time.

A review of the forehaving shows that in their concerns human beings disclose different times, all of which are datable and spanned as well as public; and the reason for this is that human temporality temporalizes itself in particular actions, each definable by a specific projection. How does this plurality of specific human times (moments of particular interest, for example) become a single, public time? And what sense may be given to the being of such time, if this question even makes sense at all?

To answer these questions only a slight modification of the forestructure is necessary. We note that human temporality is temporalized into public time through joint concerns with others, that this has already transpired when the question of the being of interacting subjects is posed. It becomes a simple matter, then, to observe that, since a single time is used to direct cooperative activity, time must perforce be public in the sense of being co-disclosed to the cooperating subjects. How is the "flow" of such a public time measured? In short, by using "clocks" for dating public events. I scare-quote the term *clocks* because we are not yet talking about instruments artificially constructed to measure the flow of time. Instead, Heidegger makes the case for interpreting astronomical events as supplying the basis for a "natural clock." What is this phenomenon? And what makes it possible?

Recall that a human being exists, falling and thrown, as a self-projection that anticipates its future while retaining its past. This basic, ekstatic-horizonal temporality is not something that is in itself something quantifiable; it merely temporalizes itself in the actions of a being that reckons with time in a rough-and-ready sense. For there to be a public time that is shared by individuals there must be a shared world; that is, different individuals must encounter a system of assigned values established in a context of involvements and be capable, by inspection, of observing those entities that are found in their shared environment. Corresponding to the self-disclosure of these individuals, there is a universe of world-historical events exhibiting a single phenomenon transpiring within the world time. World events display their character as being within the time of the world.

How does one reckon with such time? Consider once more the historizing of circumspective concern. A human being reckons with world-time by determining the set of involvements to which it commits itself in action. It is always the last term of the action, that for the sake of which the action is performed. Between its being thrown there in a world, from its situation as ontically constituted, and the future potentiality of being it envisages for itself, it must project a state of affairs by adjusting the "in-order-to's," its "toward which's," and its "toward this" to accomplish the action projected. For this reason Heidegger says that the human being awaits its potentialities of being; but in awaiting these, a world of nature—the environment that surrounds this action—is simultaneously disclosed. And the objects of the environment may be made present by a simple act of inspection or actually enter into the totality of involvements already lit up by circumspective concern. Whichever, inspection or circumspection, the activity posits the need for sight, and hence for the preexistent condition of light.

The initial disclosedness of the human being responds to these necessities, clearing a region between the two points of its projection, from where it was initially thrown to where it should like to be, as it lives the separation of the here from the there. That is what allows the authentic moment of vision into its possibilities of being, which it anticipates while resolutely retaining its past. What corresponds to the light of the clearing (*die Lichtung des Da*) and to the authentic moment of vision is an awareness of the actual light of day. The difference between day and night, as observable as the hands of one's body, is an item of the inspected natural world that enters into the totality of one's involvements.

During the night, we can only await the light of day, which permits us to accomplish our projected actions. Then, when the sun comes up we can accomplish our mission—such was the basis for the existence of the "Dawn Patrol." Then, when the sun goes down, we can rest from the labors of the day; and when it reaches directly overhead, only maddogs and Englishmen are abroad. For it to be an indication of a "now" appropriate for some kind of action, the sun is disclosed as ready-to-hand or as being handy for our purposes. And this it is, by virtue both of its light and its warmth.

As serviceably observable in recurring positions relative to our position on earth, the sun makes possible the dating of our "daily events." During each repeated day, the sun's being up, down, or directly overhead marks distinctive places—celebrated in our religious past by the ringing of the Angelus at six, noon, and six, which were arbitrarily selected from all the positions of the natural clock, to mark the beginning, middle, and ending of a day. The Angelus called us to work, to break at midday, and to cease work for that day.

In this way, the natural clock measured the time of our worldly being as thrown into a working situation. Indeed human being may still be said to historize itself day by day and to mark its time by observing the "nows" of an appropriate activity. Once it assumes its thrownness into the world, the events of its life may be dated from that day on, to the end of its days. The publicity of this world-time is guaranteed by our finding ourselves under the "same sky," observing the same sun, which, as a natural clock, is no longer an entity of the natural, astronomical world but an item of equipment for determining the passage of time.

The measurement of the passage of public world-time becomes possible on the basis of a public measure—something serviceable for that purpose, regularly recurring, which has already become accessible to the human beings capable of observing the event (making it present) while awaiting and remembering the after and before. But this is what human beings do in caring. Their temporality makes possible the conditions for discovering clocks.

In summary, any dating of events in terms of an environmentally accessible item of equipment in a purely public way necessitates the prior disclosedness of a world that has been itself made possible by the temporalization of human temporality. And already having engaged in events with concurring or competing others, human beings find such dating of worldly events to be necessary for the ordered sequencing of their lived self-projections. In short, the natural clock as an instrument for dating and measuring public events has already been discovered once a human being understands itself as caring, that is, as projected outward before itself, as already in a situation, and as having fallen into a world, where it exists with others.

Yet, the worldly character of publicly measured time still remains ontologically obscure. What is that time that is publicly measured? Consider once again the structure of an involvement complex. The "in-order-to" of a human action, indicating a stretch from one to-ward which to another to a toward this, a process closed only by that for the sake of which the assignment of such values has been made, may be examined as a continuous arrangement of "now" points in which it is either appropriate to do or forbear doing what-ever the intended action happens to be.

What is right to do or wrong is determined by that for the sake of which the action is to be undertaken. But the temporality that tem-poralizes itself in this way—on behalf of the acting person—gener-ates world-time, not because it is serviceable for anything nor because it is observable as a feature of the environment of nature, but because it is the time of a lived significance and, that is to say, of the acting person's worldhood defined as a context of personal involvements.

Therefore, in addition to being datable, spanned, and public, the time of everyday concern is likewise worldly, as belonging to the structure of a human world. That too is a phenomenon brought forward here from the forehaving of interpretation established in the first division of the text.

For any improvement in our understanding of such worldly time, we must consider the history of clockmaking. Every improvement in the technology of clockmaking has had as its effect the strengthening of public time; so much so, indeed, that the clock in some form or other has become the very symbol of the practical man.[2] The greater the flexibility of the instrument, the more universal has been its application in the measurement of worldly time. When it became possible to "read the time" off the clock, the difference between night and day became negligible in the measurement of daily events. The question "What time is it?" is answered by a reading which has enabled a person to tell what "o'clock" it is. Time and its measure in this way become fused.

Whether we use "the peasant's clock" and look at the length of our shadows or the sundial and read a marked position of a shadow, or a pocket watch that can always be carried with us and whose compressed spring is released to move pointers across its surface, we read the time by looking at the clock as a piece of equipment, a looking based upon the way in which it is appropriate for us to "take our time." The alarm just rang; it's seven o'clock: time to get up. It's noon: time to eat—hungry or not. It's four o'clock: another hour to work. Reading the time in this way permits us to regulate our activities, and constitutes a way of saying "now that." And, now that we have reached this point, we certainly must continue.

The full sense of worldly, concernful time is given in the set of characteristics previously determined; it is datable, stretched along (or spanned), public, and "significant" as indicating the structure of an appropriate context of involvements.

But it is still possible for an acting human being to lose its time in inauthenticity. In inauthentic circumstances, the acting person still lives its temporality by making present, while retaining and awaiting an object of observation. When we date the events of our days by the use of a clock, we must first make the clock present in a unique sort of way: we must observe its pointer. But watching the clock is a certain way to lose one's time.

If we are to date an event, we must go further than this; time must be measured by what gets dated, or fixed in a time sequence: in the reading of the time, the ordered passage from position to new position. For this there must be a standard measure, and this standard must have presence (it must be there to be observed) and actually made present in a stretch of time, which likewise has presence. And if the standard is for everyone's use, it must be unchangeable, and accessible to everyone's observation.

The repetition of the "nows" in a sequence can be read off the clock by anyone who has learned to take his time. And that sort of time is not just a numeral printed on a surface but rather something that has been established as a multiplicity of public nows.

The withintimeness of worldly events is one of the more palpable results of the preceding phenomenological analysis of concernful time. Other results are the association of time and space; the necessity of understanding world-time for developing a science of history; and, lastly, a summary description of world-time, which will allow us to bring it into our forehaving for still further interpretations of "temporal" phenomena. A note on each of these in turn.

As read off a clock, world-time indicates a point in a sequence of points in which human temporality gets temporalized. Each of these "now-points" is a point but primarily not on the face of the clock, which is only a spatial metaphor for the spatiality of the human being, which temporalizes itself as a region—the here, there, and yonder constituting the field of the projected human action. The agent allots itself time for accomplishing the act of spanning the division of the "places" in its concernful region.

And whether the "clock" is in the pocket or on the wrist, it can function only on the ground of the universal presence of a measure: second, minute, hour. Making these recurring now-points present by observing them does not change time into space: we merely date time publicly by measuring it through things spatially present. When we "synchronize" our watches we are looking at different spaces to determine what must be done in the one space of the natural world. When an actual measurement of public time has been obtained, Heidegger tells us, there is only a number and a stretch.

In the second place, it becomes obvious that the more we are concerned with time, the less we have to lose of it, and the more precious it becomes. For this reason, the handier our measure of time, the more useful is our prediction of future events; the proper time-piece will save us time. Not only that, the preceding existential ontological account of historiological time and of chronological time must be completed for an accurate representation of the passage of events in a science of history, wherein time is most obviously of the essence and is "measured" in epochs. Heidegger's own account of the improvements in watchmaking was historically grounded, and that history was itself grounded in his ontological analysis of writing history as a human concern.

Lastly, the conclusion of this discussion of world-time. In human concerns everything has its proper time and can have it because each thing is an event transpiring within the sort of time we have been describing: that is, concernful time is dated, spanned, public, and worldly. For this reason, "world-time" may be defined as the time in which entities within the world are encountered in caring. As such, the time of the world is as transcendent as the world itself, which latter transcendence was shown earlier in Heidegger's discussion of "reality."[3] And this transcendence of world-time, as the temporalizing of human temporality, indicates how it is possible for a human being to be a denizen of the two worlds at once, of the purely human world and of the world of nature itself. Through publicly measured time, a human being's temporality is inserted into the one world of nature.

There remains only more question to this section. Does the preceding analysis make world-time subjective or objective? Again, the disjunction is false. It is neither. It is more "objective" than any object, since it is the condition for the disclosure of any object at all. And it is more subjective than any subject, since it is also the condition for the factical constitution of any subject.

As an ontological precondition for the existence of both subjects and objects, world-time is "earlier" than both, since as temporalized it creates the possibility for anything's being ontically earlier than anything else. If we ask, then, what constitutes its being, we approach the limits of sense-making, concerning the determination of time or any other "signification."

The limit is the boundary of our method. We questioned entities to determine their being, and we projected this being upon temporality to determine its meaning. But time is not a being, nor an entity, and so cannot be questioned in the same way as a human being, a tool, or a thing. The "being" of time is presupposed, in Heidegger's method, as a condition ontologically determined for the being of ontic entities of any sort whatsoever.

To understand this consider that temporality temporalizes a world-time through the working out of human concern, which discovers it as the immanent structure of the actions performed in that concern. World-time thus constitutes the withintimeness of all our tools and all the objects of our environment accessible to our observation. Such innerworldly events may be called "temporal," but only in a derivative sense. Human being is primarily temporal, the objects of its concern only secondarily so. And this distinction parallels that drawn between the truth of being-disclosing and that of being-disclosed.[4]

We may therefore conclude that world-time is datable, spanned, public, and, as structured, belongs to the significance of innerworldly events. Such a time cannot be wished away on a subjective whim nor reified into an object of observation. For the truth of the matter is that everyday concern finds its time as tied to that of the entities with which it is concerned, that is, which it encounters "in the time" of its world. And it is from this notion that the ordinary, or scientific, notion of time has been derived.

Tracing out that derivation is the task of the next section.

3. *Withintimeness and the ordinary conception of time* (sec. 81).

Heidegger begins his derivation of the conception of ordinary scientific time by adjusting once more the forehaving of explanation. If withintimeness is exhibited in both human beings and the items of its equipment, as well as in the objects of the natural world, only the temporality of the human being lays claim to ultimate ontological priority. It too finds itself within the world of its concern, where it exists alongside the natural objects of its environment and uses tools, including clocks, to manage its affairs.

Falling into the world as it identifies itself with the objects of its concern, a human being reckons with time, first of all, in a rough-and-ready manner by adjusting the phases of its actions to suit the "in-order-to" restrictions it imposes upon itself by a choice of potentialities for being (its world-time) and then, more explicitly, by reading the time off the various objects it has found in nature or has constructed for the purpose of indicating the passage of time (the universal now-time) by which to date the events of its history.

In every case, however, human temporality has already been experienced as time in the factical concerns directed to working out its destiny; indeed, time is already explicitly present in a human being's manner of ready-reckoning its position in the world. Using clocks to replace this everyday brand of ready-reckoning is only another step toward the fully explicit and self-conscious use of time. In using a clock to measure the time available for use, the human being still reckons with its own being (its own primordial temporality), whose projection is now regulated according to the time of the clock.

Like all other acts of temporalizing, this reckoning takes place with reference to the total unity of the ekstatic-horizonal expression of temporality. Consider. In reading a clock, one makes present the positions of a pointer or the length of a shadow, and the like. In following the positions that constitute the "nows" of an elapsing time, one counts the repetitions of a standard unit. And, in this way, one reads the time that makes itself present in the changes of position.

To grasp this reading as an expression of the ekstatical-horizonal unity of temporality, we need only recall that the making-present of a position of a pointer is simultaneously a retaining of the previous position, now registered as an "on the former occasion," which is a current making-present of a "now-no-longer." Similarly, it is simultaneously the awaiting of a "then, about to be," a making-present of a "now-not-yet." And the making-present itself is the counting, one way in which the human being relates itself to its projects, regulating the phases of its activity by the time it reads off the clock.

Counted time is, from the existential-ontological point of view Heidegger has developed, a making-present that counts the positions of a traveling pointer; it is a making-present exhibiting the ekstatic unity of retaining and awaiting within the horizon opened up by the earlier and later *("daß sich das Gegenwärtigen in der ekstatischen Einheit mit dem nach dem Früher und Später horizontal offenen Behalten und Gewärtigen zeitigt").*[5] And it is this sense of now-time that is captured in Aristotle's definition,[6] when he says that time is what gets counted in the movement we encounter within the horizon of the earlier and later.

But there are differences between Aristotelian, naturalistic time and the Heideggerian time of the world that gets counted as the successive positions of a traveling pointer. First of all, for Aristotle the source of the concept of time was not a problem, outside of his orientation toward the objects of nature. In his view time was merely a dimension of the natural world and could be taken for granted. The being of the natural world and how we understand it both call for the kind of ontological interpretation Heidegger is attempting.

Moreover, in the post-Aristotelian tradition of metaphysics, the determination of time through the activity of counting continually suggested a connection with circumspective concern, as counting is performed for a specific purpose. Yet this connection has remained uninvestigated. Why? The difficulty of the subject, or the lack of an appropriate methodology?

Whichever, naturalistic time is what gets counted as periodical changes of the positions that mark a series of "nows" succeeding each other. The nows that will be are forthwith no longer; those that have just been are no longer present. And the same now which has been a not-yet-now is the present in which I am reading this passage of time. The world-time sighted in this way is "now-time," in which a human being may get lost in its own equipment, which, in its turn, has a time of its own as being in the world. Being read off clocks, now-time is constantly present to our possible perception of its effects, both on the changing positions of the pointer and in the coming to be and disappearance of the objects in our worlds. And as a flowing stream of nows, it gets separated from the forthwith and the no-longer that constituted the horizonal unity of primordial time.

Primordial time changes for being so considered, because of the fallen condition of the human being lost in the items of its equipment or the objects of its world. Falling into the world, a human being suffers a leveling off of time as the true nature of its primordial temporality gets covered up. Tracing out this process will allow Heidegger to give a description of the characteristics of ordinary, scientific time.

Let us begin with the datability of primordial time. It was revealed by the now considered as a "now, that," that is, a moment appropriate or inappropriate for doing or not doing something. Temporality is datable with reference to the significance of human worldhood, that context of involvements in which it interprets itself as that for the sake of which an action is to be performed. But in now-time described as above, both datability and worldly significance have been lost; they have merely been covered up in the making-present of the series of nows counted to regulate one's concerns with the world.

As a mere succession of points or positions, now-time is made copresent with the items of equipment or the other objects of a human or natural world. The nows merely keep coming along—from the future to the present, and from there "pass away" into the past in the order of our being conscious of the temporal flow. The direction of psychological time, let us never forget, is from the future to the past. Only historical or natural time flows from the past to the future, and this change in direction of the flow of the two times demands an explanation, to be given below. It is one of the results of the leveling off of primordial time.

The results of this leveling off continue.

• Natural time is composed of homogeneous moments; the moments of human time are heterogeneous, depending upon the value placed on the lived content of each moment. Now-time is composed of moments each of which is a "now," already vanishing, as we experience it, from the future into the present and the present to the past. But even as ever-changing, absolute now-time (that which is not relevant to our experience of it) remains a constant. For this reason Plato defined time, in the *Timaeus*,[7] as the *moving* image of the eternal, moving itself according to number.

• Natural time is continuous; the sequence of its nows knows no gaps. The moving horizon of changing positions is constantly available to our observation by some instrument of measurement. For every now marked off in this way there is an already, an earlier now from which the present stems. Measuring time in this way "reverses" the direction of human conscious time. It still moves unidirectionally but from the past to the present; and the derivation of the present from the past gives an understanding of the spanned nature of natural time (over a period of homogeneously spaced moments) that covers up the primodial spanning of human temporality, which, we recall, is achieved in a moment of vision that hands down possibilities of being that are resolutely anticipated.

• Now-time is infinite; every now of its sequence is either a just-now-in-the-past or a forthwith anticipated in the future that is not yet. Since every now of the sequence is of this nature, the series is infinite, having neither beginning nor ending. But this covers up our being-unto-death.

• Now-time is objective. Reduced to a "free-floating" sequence of passing moments, separated from the world-historical events they inform, natural time is *in-itself* constantly present at hand within the changing events of history or nature.

In all four of these characteristics, what has been lost from our primordial time? Only its datability, its significance (as being tied to a personal world), its spanning in an authentic moment of vision, and its localizability with respect to a human being's opened region. In other words, it has only lost all human significance. And, in the infinity of natural time, we have also lost the possibility of an onto-logical explanation of our being-toward-our-end. Our understanding of our own death must be sloughed off into ambiguity and given over to the idle chatter of the marketplace, where one may discuss the "high cost of dying."

Obviously, then, primordial time gets leveled off as human beings fall into inauthenticity. Thrown and falling, their wills become irre-solute, their actions indecisive, and they lose themselves in their equipment or the objects of their worlds. Consider the case of our deaths. As fallen, we tend to flee in the face of our own end; so we tend to avoid the finitude of our existence. And for this reason, perhaps, doctrines of immortality have been concocted as a psycho-logical support for the loss of our authenticity.

But even as falling and fleeing in the face of our deaths, we still exhibit a kind of being that projects itself toward the future, only this one is without end. In the public world of impersonal subjects "one" never dies; one always has more time; and so our inauthen-ticity continues.

• Natural time is universal. As publicly available, it governs the fates and destinies of everyone. Human personality has been lost, even within the hushed halls of those "funeral homes" where we continually hear that life—and time—must go on.

• Now-time is independent of what happens to individuals. This has already been established in the "objectivity" of natural time; it is recalled here as being established by the indifference of the flow of time through the sequence of its nows. As flowing past all events existing within it, time constitutes an "in-itself" independent of any subject existing for itself, as that for the sake of which an action is projected. Once again, the personality of primordially existent human beings finds itself distorted.

• The "flow" of natural time is a fugitive passing. Since the inauthentic, or impersonal, self awaits its future while forgetting its past, as these moments slide further back into history, the full spanned character of primordial temporality is lost and the fugitive passing of the time of the clock reflects one's having lost from sight the authentic end of one's self-projection because of one's flight in the face of death.

Yet, the discourse of the subject lost in the public world is not completely divorced from its grounding in temporalizing temporality. When we say, "Time is passing away," or "There's still some time yet to come," we betray the felt loss of a significant past present or the expectant hope of some more meaningful future. Both these affective states can produce the feeling of uncanniness that may trigger the call to conscience.

• Natural time flows irreversibly in a single direction—from the past into the present; but the psychological time of the worldly individual also flows unidirectionally—only in the opposite direction, from the future into the past. The irreversibility of now-time therefore derives from primordial time. As the free-floating sequence of nows whose only function is to structure the occurrence of events, clock-time is conceivable as "running" in either direction. Why then should scientists conceive of it as irreversible?

Because scientists are interested in the average kind of being, that is, in historical events as happening *in time* as already constituted into a univocal, universally applicable concept. For this reason, they may ignore the ontological foundation that makes it possible for us to understand the derivation of the concept. As a concept of science, its meaning is its use. And the concept of the time of the natural world as now-time continues to cover up the true being of primordial temporality from which it is derived. The more the concept is used in this way, the more the primordial concept gets leveled off.

To test the force of this conclusion, let us suppose that the source of our knowledge concerning time were reversed, and that instead of the sequence, temporality—world-time—now-time, we were to try to reconstitute our knowledge of primordial temporality on the basis of an unfounded notion of clock-time. Such an investigation would be impossible to carry through. First, because now-time has already been oriented as it is by the temporalizing of primordial temporality, and it temporalizes itself only inauthentically as a stretch of passing moments constantly present as read off the clocks in the public world. Such a spanning precludes the possibility of a moment of vision holding in its own tense span the retained past and the anticipated future. And from the standpoint of our awareness of *its* passing, the present moment of natural, psychological time permits only the coming to be of a past. From this same standpoint, the historical past has no future, only a past anterior. The natural, psychological movement of history is into prehistory.

Authentic temporality temporalizes itself from the future, resolutely repeating a past the personal subject hands down to itself; the inauthentic, on the other hand, temporalizes itself as a constantly flowing sequence of nows, each like unto the other, but shorn of their ties to any concrete event, except as marking out a place between such events and so referring to other nows. The moment of vision cannot be reconstructed on such a basis. The authentic future that is both datable and significant is not a pure now merely not yet; it is resolutely anticipated. And the authentic past is not a pure now merely having passed; it is fatefully repeated, and projected into the authentic future.

For these reasons, the present now is not pregnant with the now-not-yet—intervening circumstance may color, even change, any of our predictions of the nature of things to come; and the events of our inauthentically historical pasts have no explainable future. That's why history stops where prophecy begins.

What is to be concluded from all this?

That the concept of clock- or natural-time has indeed been derived from a more primitive or "primordial" kind of knowledge, to be sure.[8] But Heidegger draws another conclusion, one that permits the continued projection of his ontological inquiry. The fact that clock-time may be derived from the primordial temporality of human being indicates that a connection exists between the significance of world-time and the nature of human subjects in their subjectivity, that is, of the soul or "spirit." How is this connection to be interpreted?

Heidegger mentions two precedents in the history of ontology: Aristotle's *Physics* once again, and St. Augustine's *Confessions*. For Aristotle, since time is what is measured in the movement between earlier and later, and only human soul or intellect is equipped for counting, there could be no time without the human intellect.[9] And for Augustine, time always presented itself as a kind of extendedness; of what, he didn't know; yet he speculated that the extendedness of time was not what got counted in our reckoning with events, but the very extension of the soul itself that did the counting.[10] Counting is a way for the soul to project itself, self-knowingly, into the world. Augustine lacked only the phenomenological method for making this self-projection clear. That is why he could pray the Lord to deliver him from the temptation of fornication, but not yet.

Aristotle and Augustine both began with the ordinary, natural sense of time, and both discovered a link with the temporality of human being. Can this connection be more precisely formulated? Hegel tried, and his attempt is the subject of my next section.

4. Hegel's model for conceiving the relationship between time and spirit (sec. 82).

Expounding Heidegger's thoughts on Hegel on time and spirit is sure to appear as an attempt to explain an enigma by a mystery. But that surmise would, I think, do an injustice to both thinkers. So, at the risk of treating Hegel as if he were an enigma surrounded by a mystery, I shall attempt to reconstruct his views as Heidegger has appropriated them in this 82d section of his text.

For Hegel, we are told, history is the Spirit, running its course in time. World history, indeed, is the story of the Spirit that has "fallen" into time. And for this reason the notion of time Hegel has in mind is the now-time of the world within which events come to be and pass away—and with them those conscious entities who witness the passage of these world-historical events. Although time is thus considered as a phenomenon of the natural world and is given what Hegel takes to be a "scientific" interpretation, its definition is proposed in the most abstract sense possible as "the nonsensuous sensuous," that is, the nonsensuous form of all our sensuous experiences.[11] As such it is an intuitable, a priori form, as Kant had said.[12]

The trick for expounding Hegel is to show how this nonsensuous form takes on sensuous content in the experiences of the Spirit. For the Spirit to "fall into the time of the world" it must somehow be akin to the essence of time itself. Therefore this investigation will have two parts: first, Hegel's definition of time, which will explain what belongs to its essence; and second, what belongs to the essence of Spirit (i.e., what it is in its being) so that it may fall into time. Hegel's term for this falling is *fallen*, and not Heidegger's *verfallen*, from which the latter derived his notion of fallenness. The two notions are related but in a very peculiar sense to be made clear below.

Hegel, like Aristotle, develops his notion of time within a clearly understood context. Aristotle was concerned to describe time in the context of nature; and so we find that description in his *Physics*. Hegel considers both space and time as requisite parts of mechanics, the science of the movement of objects. From their varying points of view, then, the context of explanation is the same. Aristotelian physics is for Hegel the philosophy of nature, and "nature" is the Idea as it exists outside itself, whereby *Idea* is meant "a concept in search of fulfillment."

Space and time, within the area of mechanics, are what make the science of nature possible. As intuitive forms, they are "the abstract outside-of-one-another," that is, forms for internal differentiation into elements but which, as abstract, are themselves indifferent to any possible differentiation. In themselves, they are "holders" of possible positions.

To understand this, it is perhaps useful to recall Kant, for whom both space and time were forms of the sensibility, known a priori in every sensuous intuition of "inner" (time) and "outer" (space) experiences; but since all the schemata of the imagination by which these abstracts forms take on their first differentiable determinations are ultimately provided by the figurations of time, the form of the inner sense, time is primordial in our understanding of the metaphysics of nature. So when we speak of the observation of the phenomena of nature, although the forms of both space and time are relevant for the interpretation of our experience,[13] the primacy of time needs clarification.

For Hegel, however, the Idea of nature unfolds dialectically following the pattern of being posited in itself as what it is, then as existing for us who interpret that being. As we interpret space and time, we perceive the dialectical *Zwiespalt* (diremption) of the idea posited in itself into the aspects under which we interpret it. For example, space as an indifferent and undifferentiated form takes on the aspect of being divisible into a multiplicity of points; time is the same, as it is divisible into successive moments, the "nows" of Heidegger's innerworldly time.

Both space and time undergo the dialectical splitting into two: in themselves they are one and undifferentiated; for us, they are that, but differentiated into elements as well. Nature, as formed by the structures of space and time within the area of mechanics, is space as it reveals itself to us in time—as the successive points on the face of a clock, perhaps, inform the trajectory of the traveling pointers. That idea is too simplistic, but it is not irrelevant to the current theme. The question to ask here is: How does nature, as space, reveal itself to us as time? The only possible way to answer this question is to follow the dialectic.

Considered in itself, space is the undifferentiated indifference of nature's existence as the Idea outside itself.[14] In Hegel's absolute idealism, the Idea gets "expressed" outside itself. Heidegger interprets, correctly I think, that the abstract notion of space is from that point of view independent of its division into component points, each of which is external to every other. Within the punctiform structure of the objects described by the natural sciences, however, the points of time are equally as important as the abstract and empty form itself.

It is in this way that space suffers the dialectical division, or splitting into diverse aspects. This splitting generates "negation," the motor of history. Consider. As a form, space is a unit, having no differences; as an aggregate form, it is differentiated into points which, although differentiable from each other, are, in their totality, not different from the "whole" of space. Whatever difference there appears to be is only in the point of view.

For the reflecting philosophers, who take points of view, space is a punctiform totality of organizable possible loci or positions. The point—in its separation from its fellows—is the negative of space, considered as a whole, while still remaining a part of that whole. Readers who have not yet learned to "think contradictions," as Hegel puts it, will find this difficult to follow, so continuing from this point on will require a bit of readerly resoluteness.

When we reconsider the composition of space as it was in itself, then *for us,* according to its aspects, and ultimately as it is in and for itself—that is, when the aspects are rejoined with the initial concept as it is in itself, as these "expressed" aspects are "re-impressed into their source"—the Idea returns to itself, now enriched for our interpretation of it. Perceptive readers will notice the similarity between this dialectical procedure and Heidegger's own hermeneutical method. The newer Idea, in Hegel, synthesizes the thesis and the antithesis of the *Zwiespalt*. The Idea is thus raised to a higher level of expression, with its contradictions canceled yet retained. These three notions taken together, the cancellation, retention, and lifting to a higher level of expression, is the famous *Aufhebung* of the Hegelian dialectic.

Let us return to space. Space, from the point of view of its aspects, is the "outside-one-another" of its constituent points; yet from its initial point of view, it had no differences within it. Abstract space is thus *Punktualität*—in English, "punctiformity," since the cognate "punctuality" has been restricted in our language to a more purely temporal content of application, which in German is reserved for *punktlich*. But the difference between the German and the English is not all that great; for, according to Hegel, the punctiform nature of space "transits" into time. How so? Consider.

The point that negates space as a whole creates possible trajectories in separating itself from the others and so may generate larger forms: lines and surfaces. This negativity of space is what generates the motricity in mechanical nature. In-itself, as Being-outside-of-itself, nature exists for itself as possible determinations of the punctiform totality of space. And, in itself, it is still indifferent to its possible inner determinations. But as posited by us (phenomenological interpreters) as expressed into differentiable points, the Idea has undergone inner transformation. For us, space is time, but only because the original negation of the Idea within its self-expression is itself negated through our synthesis of the inner contradiction. The negation of the negation that raises the originally negated Idea to a higher level is the motor of history, as well as of the development of human consciousness.[15]

The transition of the status of an Idea as existing in itself to existing in and for itself takes place via the resynthesis of its inner contradiction. When the "punctuality" of the points of space posits itself for itself, a point of space differentiates itself from the others; it is *no longer* just what it is in itself but is differentiated from all other points of space and, as such, is *not yet that*—a part of the resynthesized aggregate of spatial differentiations. Herein lies the figure of temporality: the point is *no longer* one thing and *not yet* another.

As originally self-positing, a point is a negation of the whole of space and a negation of the other possible points of space. This is the same negation, but with the difference of the aspects of space expressed. As Heidegger puts it, the isolated, self-positing point "gives itself airs [spreizt sich auf]."[16] But when the idea of space is reclaimed through the negation of this negation, it becomes a "now" in a system or totality of the punctiform structure; in the resynthesized idea of space, the points become now-here's followed by now-there's, and the "now" is that through which each point posits itself as a self-sustaining part of the whole of space. It is this process—the negation of the negation—that is continually exemplified in the Hegelian dialectic, and which began here when we considered nature as that being that exists outside of itself purely and simply as Idea, but which has become the locus for the synthesis of the now-points of time.

For this reason Hegel considers time "the negative unity" (the facts of succession as passage) of Being-outside-of-itself. In a word, the concept of space as it exists in and for itself is synthesized back into its more complex unity in time. And it is for this reason that Kant considered the schemata of the imagination as being determinations of the inner sense.[17]

When, however, we consider time as an idea in itself, a similar set of determinations are dialectically encountered. Time, as synthesizing the differentiations of multiple points, is the form of transitoriness; indeed, it is itself a being which, insofar as it is, is not; and insofar as it is no longer or not yet, is. We intuit it, in our experiences of natural events, as becoming, in which an original set of differences were only momentary, each of which immediately becomes the other. Time, as the form of passage, has as its component aspects a set of moments each of which is external to the other, while itself remaining external to that externality.[18] Becoming for this reason is the arising and passing away of determinate positions in space. The being of time, which is the form of this becoming, gets expressed in the sequence of "now's" each of which is both a no-longer and a not-yet.

For Hegel, then, time is now-time—that concept by which "time" is ordinarily understood. But because this is true, the fully authentic temporality that temporalizes itself into the time of the world gets covered up and leveled off. Hegel, after all, began his analysis of space and time as determining the idea of nature, the Idea as it exists outside of itself. In nature, however, there is no stable difference between one now and another; the past, present, and the future are all the same. And as has been shown above, the idea of the ontologically prior, primordial temporality, cannot be reconstructed on the basis of now- or clock-time.

The dialectical methodology of Hegel misses the essential and wavers between two views of time: between the "intuited becoming" in the temporal flow of natural being (i.e., the being of nature) and the "abstraction of consumption," which is our experience of filling the moments of time to "consume" what time we may ourselves possess. The dialectical method can give us no explanation for the latter view, which is, however, founded in Heidegger's existential-ontological view of human temporality as the meaning of human being itself.

To review the foregoing, we repeat the question: "How does the Spirit fall into time, which is conceived as the negation of a negation?" And we can answer this question by explaining the concept of Spirit. Here sources change, with the principal text now being the *Phenomenology of the Spirit,* and we enter into the second phase of Heidegger's treatment of Hegel.

He continues his case in the role of textual hermeneut.

Spirit is the concept *(der Begriff)* or notion—the very form of the thought that thinks itself, conceiving of itself as understanding what is not itself. Hegel's phenomenology traces the development of human experience from the bare awareness of something other than itself—merely pointing, or intending it in sensuous consciousness—to self-consciousness, to reason, and ultimately to the level of the Absolute Idea, that stage of the spirit's development in which the notion no longer has anything to know but itself.

Let's consider how the Spirit moves itself. As bare consciousness, it intends the other; and this grasping of what is not itself differentiates self from other as an object of consciousness. The spirit which develops is differentiated into moments, each negating the other, which negation is then negated and brought to a higher level of consciousness. The negation of the original negation is the denial of the difference between an idea as it exists in itself and as it gets expressed for us in its aspects. The resynthesized form of the idea, as that now existing in and for itself as what it is, cancels the inner contradiction of the previous consideration of the Idea; the dialectical *Zwiespalt* is once again thought together as a unity: the universal

particularized becomes individual. In the working out of the contradictions of a simpler idea the form of our consciousness has the form
of a temporal becoming.

Consider the particular case. The "I" or ego is the initially pure
unity of self related to self—as abstracted from content as feeling,
dispositions, states, and the like, but which is still capable of "being
expressed" concretely in these. How? By the universal ego's fall into
individuality in the dialectical swing from idea-in-itself differentiated
from what it is *for us,* its aspects which are ultimately resynthesized
into the concrete idea existing in and for itself. That is, the formal
ego "falls" into individuality by falling into time.

The self manifests itself in its acts, and the process illustrates the
same dialectical structure as that existing between space and its
points, time and its moments: as indeed, between the points of space
having become moments of time. The dialectical split occurs when
the ego excludes itself from others, but this exclusion is overcome in
higher orders of social organization—the family, civil society, and
the state, for example. Developing in this way, consciousness exhibits
its dialectical derivation from sensuous awareness to the Absolute
Idea, which, as the entelechy of the bare, immediate consciousness,
has already been contained in it.

The restlessness of the Spirit continues until it knows only itself,
the notion grasping only the notion as expressed in all its component
forms. When the Spirit falls into time, under the impulsion of the
negation of negation, it becomes expressed as an historical event and
takes on the form of an object existing for us to be interpreted in the
universal history of consciousness.

And the Spirit must "fall" into history, or it will have no content,
nothing for itself to grasp for further conscious development. Without its content, the Spirit remains an abstract form needing that
content to become individualized. *Form* and *content* here are other
names for the dialectical division into two aspects of the same thing
that must be overcome in a resynthesized unity. Indeed, Hegel defines
this concretizing process of the idea of consciousness as "experience."
Such experience, which is the dialectical progress of the developing
consciousness, is the object of his *Phenomenology of Spirit.*

So, what is the relationship between Spirit and time for Hegel?
Let's look again. Time as the form of becoming is the purely self-
external, not grasped by itself, but only by us as we interpret the
process of the events developing in nature or history. Time's essence

is to become natural, that is, world-historical, in a process which is nothing more than the self-interpretation of the Spirit *in* time, just as in space the Idea expresses itself as nature.

Space, time, and spirit are united as an expressed Idea (analyzed into structural moments) that becomes recompressed back into itself in a form which overcomes the contradictions established in its expression. Because both Spirit and time are developed as the negation of a negation, that is, because they exhibit the same generative notion, the one is a natural symbol of the other. The only unfortunate feature is that the time which becomes expressed in this way is the withintimeness of the events in the world; and, as such, it is present to our observation as the form—the unsensuous form—of those events as sensed. The "being" of time thus is to be present, and it must "fall" into the time of the world that is likewise present to our observation through the use of calendars and clocks.

As for the Spirit, the universal substance and subject of history, its path is traced in the *Phenomenology of Spirit* from sensuous certainty to the level of the Absolute Idea. But there we read that this Idea, once it has been reached, must be referred to the conditions of actual time if we should like to understand how the development of Spirit in time creates history.

I HOPE to close this discussion by noting Heidegger's objections to Hegel's conceptual assimilation of the Spirit to time.

First, for Heidegger the concretion of a human existence is given in a "factically thrown self-projection into future possibilities of being." That's the human care-structure, whose meaning is temporality. The Spirit does not fall *(fallen)* into time; it exists according to the sructures of its primordial temporality. Ahead of itself, already in a world, and concerning itself with the entities of this world, it reckons with time. It may even lose itself in its concern for its items of equipment—including its clocks—and the objects of its natural environment. When it does so, it falls *(verfallen)* into inauthenticity from its authentic primordial temporality.

World-time, or the time of the events within the world, derives from the average understanding of the public world, but this understanding is derived from the more primordial ontological structure—the human temporality that temporalizes itself as the time of the world, thereby permitting history to historize itself into a set of world-historical events.

Like Aristotle and Augustine, Hegel missed the mark, first of all, for mislocating the context of interpretation as being fixed by the conception of nature, and then, for not possessing the proper method for making the interpretation. The search for a complete phenomenological account of the relationship between being and time must go on—in time.

Heidegger's projection of a continuation of the inquiry to ground this relationship phenomenologically is given in section 83 of the text—the last of the published work; so I have saved my commentary on that section to supply a basis for my next chapter—a summary evaluation of the cognitive claims made for an ontological understanding of beings, Being, and time, in Heidegger's first published version of *Being and Time*.

EPILOGUE

12

Beings, Being, and Time . . .

The question has been posed many times since the original publication of the text in 1927, by Heidegger and Heideggerians, without a conclusive answer. One of the reasons for my undertaking this reading of the text for the sake of other readers was to uncover the evidence for taking sides on this very issue. Is there a Heidegger II essentially different from the Heidegger I exposited in these pages? And if so, is the newer manner of philosophizing independent of the older? Heidegger himself claimed that there was indeed a second Heidegger but that one had to travel the path along the way opened up in *Being and Time* in order to grasp the significance of his later attempts to encapsulate, within the structure of language, the meaning of Being in general.[1]

Being and Time opens with an explanation of the structural meaning of asking any question whatsoever and proceeds by applying that structure to the question of the meaning of Being. The technique was to question beings as to their being and to project the concept of that being into the context in which an understanding might be said to have already been possessed. Thus, a human being is questioned for its being, interpreted, in the light of its preontological comprehension of itself, as temporality temporalizing itself into history.

283

True to his method throughout the published version of *Being and Time,* Heidegger returns the inquiry to the point of its origin, from the everyday condition of the person caring about its own identity, to that same person now fortified by the inquiry to the point of having the ordinary concepts of scientific investigation grounded phenomenologically within the structures of human being itself. The last return was to the ordinary concept of time, as derived from human temporality.

Previously, of course, similar "returns" exhibited the derivation of other concepts of the natural sciences from the existentials constitutive of human being: like space and signification, time itself derives from the world of transcendental significance to which the existential analytic has gained access primarily through the tracing out of those structures, which, as established by our a priori knowledge of them, constitute the conditions for the very possibility of those experiences that occasioned the inquiry in the first place. The Heideggerian ontology of *Being and Time* was grounded in the preontological, and therefore purely ontic, nature of human beings themselves.

Human beings as living entities were those entities with the possibility of fulfilling the requirements demanded by the ontic and ontological primacy of any questioning into the meaning of Being. Without the grounding of ontological inquiry in human existence itself, there would be no understanding either the question or its need. But given the fact that human beings, in their existence, question the nature of that existence, and hence exhibit at least the vague awareness of what it means to be, ontological inquiry is ontically grounded. The trick to be mastered is the ability to invert ontic and ontological significance, by carefully uncovering those ontological structures that make it possible for us to have ontical experiences.

The natural sciences are no guide here, since their inquiries are strictly ontical, interpreting phenomena of the natural or humane worlds in terms of concepts deriving from regular and repeatable conditions according to which they become present to our techniques of observation. But if the world (of nature) is an ontic concept, so are signification, space, person, time, history. Such concepts derive their human significance from the understanding we have of our being: worldhood, significance itself, spatiality, personality, temporality, and historicality. And after practicing the ontic-ontological reversal, we always come back to the original situation, realizing that we now possess the concepts necessary for understanding the nature of the real world, that one world in which we all live, and love, and die, along with others whose being is no different from our own.

Is this not enough? Can we now not get on with the business of learning more and more about the natural world, more and more about our selves and our social and political institutions, to settle the problems that plague our everyday existence? Another thinker, in another place at approximately the same time, argued that we could.

John Dewey's pragmatism came to its fullest development with the 1926 publication of *Experience and Nature.* The title itself suggests the grounds of the comparison: the concepts of nature derive from the experience of human beings in the double aspect of their activity—doing and undergoing, projecting ends while reacting to the forces of nature. The concepts for understanding nature itself are natural only because the human beings who construct them are natural; they do not present themselves to us readymade.

Dewey, of course, rejects any necessity of going beyond nature to establish a transcendental ground for it. And if we think clearly about the matter and the manner of his exposition, Heidegger can be interpreted in such a way as to have done the same. We must first limit ourselves to the published version of *Being and Time,* in which the question of Being was first given methodical investigation. The progression from human beings to caring to temporality and to time puts us in a position to concentrate on the problems of living in the cross section of two worlds, the natural and the humane. Is this not enough? Must we go beyond? And if so, how?

The difficulty in answering these questions stems from the Heideggerian text itself. Human beings question their being and discover their historicity. Who could fault such an inquiry? Who but positivists, like Carnap, for whom any questioning of being is nonsense,[2] and pragmatists, like Dewey, for whom nature is in no need of transcendental support? If the things of nature are considered as *pragmata,* items for our use, would not any ontology that makes such an interpretation of the being of entities resemble in some way or another that style of philosophizing we have come to know as pragmatism? If not, what enables our discourse to transcend the limitations placed upon it by nature? Heidegger's answer to this question is clear: the limitations of human discourse are not only natural but human as well; and only an investigation into the ontological grounds of discourse, as a specifically human behavior, will allow us to state what the human limitations are on the uses of language.

Heidegger's reasons for devising an ontological-existential analysis were not to ground the concepts of the natural sciences in some kind of effort to renew them or to allow them to grow out of the stage of crisis, although the need for such a grounding was explained as "the ontological priority of the question of Being" in Heidegger's introduction.[3] Such a project as this motivated the phenomenological research of Husserl, but his techniques were descriptive of consciousness and its acts. Ontology questions beings for an understanding of their being, and in this same place Heidegger is unequivocal: "Sein ist jeweils das Sein eines Seienden [Being is always the being of an entity]."[4] And therein lies the ground for the differences between interpretations of the Heideggerian ontology.

If being is at any time the being of an entity, no one need shy from the inquiry. Not the most hardened of positivists, who can see nothing beyond their protocol sentences; for them, the being of an object is its presence. Nor the softest of the pragmatists for whom truth is an idea that works, and whose "cash value" is its use in accommodating a human organism to its environment; for them, the being of an object is its power to generate a human reaction. For these latter individuals, however, pursuing scientific truth for its own sake is as barren as quietly contemplating the meaning of Being in general. But if Heidegger is right in his introduction, he has constituted the very grounds for questioning whether his grander scheme (the design of the originally projected version of *Being and Time*) could even have been accomplished.

In his *Vorbemerkung* to the seventh edition of the text, he informs us that, in the quarter century since *Being and Time* had been published in its original form, his own thought had changed so much that to complete the projected second part would necessitate a massive revision of the first half already published. Heidegger II talks here, and his speech refers us to another text, *Einführung in die Metaphysik,* which is the published version of his 1935 seminar in pre-Socratic philosophy. It is as if the vaunted "destruction of the history of ontology" were a dispensable portion of the Heideggerian project, provided one is capable of "dialoguing" with those earliest of philosophers whose thought was not bedeviled by the reification of logical or purely "ideal" entities.

But Heidegger II does not repudiate Heidegger I. In spite of the changes he thought he would have to bring into the original text, the investigation of the published text is still necessary: as indicating the way to be followed by anyone interested in reopening the question of the meaning of Being. The eighth edition of *Sein und Zeit* appeared in 1957, with the preface to the seventh edition unchanged. We read: "Deren Weg bleibt indessen auch heute noch ein notwendiger, wenn die Frage nach dem Sein unser Dasein bewegen soll. [The way (of the first half) remains even today a necessary one, however, if the question of Being is to move us as we exist]."[5] The questionable *"überhaupt"* does not muddy the waters here; whatever "Being" is meant here is still the being of some entity.

The positive sciences, whose purposes is to investigate all beings *(Das All des Seienden),* have done so by dividing the world into various areas of possible inquiry: history, nature, space, life, human existence, speech—in Husserl's terms all "material ontologies" whose phenomena are open to phenomenological description. But all these sciences—written history, chemistry and physics, geometry, biology, psychology and sociology, linguistics—remain groundless for Heidegger, until the question of Being has been sufficiently clarified.

The question forces itself upon us. Has the meaning of Being been sufficiently clarified in the published version of *Being and Time?* I shall divide my answer to this question into two parts, each devised as an answer to another question. First, what is meant by re-posing the question of the meaning of Being in general *(die Frage nach dem Sinn vom Sein überhaupt)?* And second, did Heidegger succeed in answering this question? Neither of these component questions has an obvious answer; so a good deal of textual analysis is in order.

1. Re-posing the question of the meaning of Being (in general).

Whether the vaguely suggestive *"überhaupt"* is stated as part of the question or not, there seems to be no doubt that the entire projected work of *Being and Time* was written to open anew the question of Being. What it means to reopen this question is another matter. Rereading the introduction to the published version of the work, however, makes it abundantly clear that Heidegger not only intended to reopen this traditional issue but also to indicate that his attempt to answer the question must take the form of any inquiry; that is, it must exhibit the form of questioning in general.

Following his analysis of what it means to question anything at all, Heidegger indicates for the first time that his own analysis will be "circular."[6] He could not question beings about their being in an effort to learn the meaning of that being if he did not already possess some kind of understanding of what it means to be. Putting the ·question presupposes at least a vague understanding of what could count as an answer to it. This vague understanding is preontological, of course, and so it is a part of our ordinary commerce with the entities of our worlds, a form of our own being as caring individuals.

There are two reasons not to consider the circularity of ontological investigation as logically vicious. First, asking the question does not ground something in the sense of deducing it from the question itself; that is, it is not a question-begging demonstration. Indeed, phenomenological ontology demonstrates nothing in the usual "logical" sense of the term. Asking the question of their being of beings is the preliminary step for laying bare the grounds of their existence, which are to be exhibited through the analysis of the conditions necessary for their being—or becoming—what they are. It was for this reason Heidegger began his inquiry with the data of his own being.

Nothing was involved there that did not concern the fact that wondering about one's existence is one way to exist, and finding answers to the questions deriving from human wonder is another way to exist. Beginning with existence as his own, the *Jemeinigkeit* of human being as existence, Heidegger merely sought to describe the existential structures ("the existentials," as I call them) that go to make up existentiality in general. The movement in thought is from a particular existence to its structural determination.

The grounds for the initial ontological question are found in the ontic condition of human beings. Although these grounds are preontological, any answer to the question will be couched in ontological terms. In this way, the move is from the vague and preontologically understood meaning of one's own being to an expected, precise ontological formulation of an answer to the question of the meaning of that being, which would presumably enable us to formulate a further description of the meaning of Being-in-general.

Ontological inquiry begins with the analysis of human existence since that is the only context in which the question can arise. The analysis itself is a complete, methodical attempt to work toward that postontological condition, which would still be ontic in that the analysis would have shown not only how it arose in the first place, but also would, in the second place, exhibit the structures of our human existence in interplay with the objects of our worlds as giving an opening for possible answers to the question.

Since the meaning of nonhuman entities is described in relation to that of human beings, when our ontological discourse has been completed, we should have described nonhuman being as well: such entities exhibit "being-disclosed"—either as present to our powers of observation and as parts of the real world, or as useful elements in a context of involvements by which we construct uniquely significant human worlds. As such, their being is complementary to our own, as "being-disclosing." Such, we recall from the actual analysis made, were the "secondary" and "primordial" senses of ontological truth.

Moreover, since all being is the being of some entity, and the entities of the world are either human or nonhuman, while these latter are merely present to us or useful for our purposes, a description of the three designated beings as existent, present, and useful would seem to answer the question that generated the inquiry. What is there to "Being-in-general" that is not covered in the concept of the being of all existent entities? Unfortunately, however, the matter did not seem to be resolved in this way by Heidegger himself, for whom the existential analytic—at least in some parts of his treatise—is merely a step on the way to answering the basic question of a more fundamental ontology.

Whatever is meant by "a fundamental ontology," however, the question for an ontology of human being is felt preontologically and can only be answered in careful analysis, where the implicit understanding of the meaning of being comes to explicit formulation. This last consideration, indeed, is the second reason for maintaining that the ontological inquiry, although admittedly circular, is not logically vicious. We cannot end with the same concept of being with which we started; and, in fact, Heidegger did not.

Stipulating the conditions under which the original question was to be worked out is the purpose of Heidegger's introduction to *Being and Time*. There we read that the work was undertaken to restate and supposedly answer the question of the meaning of Being; and that this task would be achieved in two steps: first, the preliminary analytic of existence, which would constitute the horizon for interpreting any further significance to the concept of Being; and, second, the destruction of the history of ontology, which would uncover once more whatever core of significance had been achieved in the earlier history of the subject before it had become hardened into a purely logical exercise.[7]

Here too Heidegger is talking about himself as a historian of philosophy, as someone benefiting from, while participating in, a tradition of inquiry whose purpose was to answer the question of the meaning of Being. His later attempts to ground historiography through the historizing of human historicality are relevant to this purpose. His own history of ontology was not to be merely monumental, in that it would come back to repeat a possibility by projecting its renewal; nor merely antiquarian, as merely reverently preserving the tradition of the pre-Socratic past as it was. Rather, it was to be critical, as viewing the present state of the art in terms of its having been handed down to us for the purpose of handing down a new answer for tomorrow, even while overcoming the oblivion in which the issue had become enshrouded in modern and contemporary philosophy.

The difficulty with this second project—the overturning of the history of ontology—is that it was left unfinished in *Being and Time.* The introduction retraces the historicity of the link between human subjectivity and the concept of time from the doctrine of Kant's schematism to Descartes' having begged the question in his substantial interpretation of the human ego, to Descartes' sources in medieval philosophy, and from there to the Hellenic tradition in which being and time were associated in the concept of *parousia*, that is, being as presence. Rather than pursue the ambiguities of this Greek term, however, which are as apparent in Aristotelian metaphysics as anywhere else, Heidegger chose Aristotle's *Physics* as the master source for the modern concept of time: as that which is measured through a change of position.

Heidegger practiced a similar "deconstruction" of the history of ontology in a 1927 seminar at the University of Marburg. The text of this seminar has recently been translated into English by Albert Hofstadter and published as *The Basic Problems of Phenomenology.* If, as the supporters of *The Basic Problems* would have it,[8] the seminar expounded Heidegger's position of four important ontological issues without reference to an existential analytic that had been exaggerated by his "existentialist" followers, it is likewise true that within the context of the seminar the destruction of the history of ontology lacks its foundation in the existential analytic, and so appears as a simple exercise in the history of philosophy. And if *Being and Time* failed to answer the question of the meaning of Being in general, *The Basic Problems of Phenomenology* did not even pose the question to be answered in a critical history of ontology and so left the notion of a fundamental ontology undeveloped.

What the two works have in common, besides a number of stages on the way back into the history of ontology, is the assumption of a methodological position. Both are phenomenological; and both consider phenomenology as the universal method of ontology. But it is in *Being and Time*, precisely in its introduction, that the connection between phenomenology as method and ontology as area of inquiry is explained.[9] And it is only in *Being and Time* that phenomenological analysis—qua hermeneutical expansion of the forestructure of human understanding—becomes itself a subject of inquiry.

In review, then, the introduction to *Being and Time* proposes a renewal of traditional ontological inquiry, one that is grounded through a destruction of the history of that subject to a newer, more firmly grounded understanding of the meaning of Being in general.

Giving phenomenological analysis his own characteristic hermeneutical twist, Heidegger was instrumental in founding a new school within the phenomenological movement. That certainly was one of the great achievements of the text under consideration. As a method, phenomenology in this newer manner still had to exhibit the phenomena by which an ontological significance is derived from ordinary ontic experiences; but, as shall be explained in what follows, the very greatness of this achievement is the cause of Heidegger's ultimate failure to answer the question of the meaning of Being in general. The phenomenological method certainly has its limitations, and Heidegger illustrated what these are in pushing it to the limits of rational discourse.

At present, it suffices to indicate that, even after the phenomenological analyses of *Being and Time*, it has not been made clear what this question asks; or whether what it asks, if this can be determined, is any different from those questions of being already answered in the description of human existence, of objects in their presence, and of tools in their use. More on this most basic of ontological conundrums follows.

2. Did Heidegger succeed in answering his question?

I have already indicated some reasons for believing that he failed to answer his question. But the evidence for my negative answer may be put in a clearer picture yet.

Not only was the larger project never finished, but the portion of it that was completed exemplifies a method that had reached a culminating point—interpreting the meaning of human being as temporality and deriving the ordinary concept of time from it—beyond which there was hardly any place to go. Recall that beings were to be questioned for their being in an effort to determine the meaning of that being. Time is not a being; and Being is not a being. How, then, were time and Being to be interpreted ontologically?

The last section of the projected first part, which Heidegger had entitled *Time and Being,* was to undergo a reversal in the original methodological plan. But how? Section 83 of the text, the last of the published version of *Being and Time,* contains little more than a list of unanswered questions, to be cited later. Rather than being brought to a conclusion, the text merely peters out, as if it were a discourse and the speaker had lost his voice.

Heidegger's usual excuse for this phenomenon is that the text was from his trembling hands untimely ripped. He was urged by Husserl to publish the manuscript as it was in order to strengthen his case as possible successor to Husserl in the chair of philosophy at Freiburg; and the scheme worked. But as a result of that decision the original text was not purified of its inaccuracies. I select as the primary example of such inaccuracies the very notion of a "fundamental ontology" it was Heidegger's intention to institute by stating the question of the meaning of Being. At times the fundamental ontology is identified with the existential analytic and at times the latter is only a step along the way.

An ontology would be fundamental if it grounded all other ontologies, such as those material and formal ontologies Husserl had described in his phenomenology or those various forms of ontological schemes that had developed in the history of the subject: from the *logos* and *nous* of the pre-Socratic philosophers, through substances of various sorts and Spirit throughout the ages, to the Nietzschean Will to Power in the nineteenth century. The destruction of the history of the subject was not to be a mere negation but would have the positive result of showing just what aspects or possible modes of being had been raised to the level of the "transcendent pure and simple," that is to Being itself.

We first run across the description of a fundamental ontology on pages 13–15 of the original text. Heidegger is there describing the ontical priority of the question of Being, which is grounded in the fact that as a human being exists it is concerned with its existence and possesses that by now famous preontological understanding of (its own) being. After making this case, Heidegger concludes:

> Daher muß die *Fundamentalontologie,* aus der alle andern erst entspringen können, in der *existenzialen Analytik des Daseins* gesucht werden.

> For this reason, *that ontology which is to be fundamental,* and from which all the others may be derived, must be sought in the *existential analytic of human being.*[10]

The case is not yet as clear as it might be: the fundamental ontology must be sought in the existential analytic, but it is not yet necessarily identical to it. Still, we have not read much further before we meet another statement:

> Jetzt hat sich aber gezeigt, daß die ontologische Analytik des Daseins überhaupt die Fundamentalontologie ausmacht, daß mithin das Dasein als das grundsätzlich vorgängig auf sein Sein zu *befragende* Seiende fungiert.

> But now it has been shown that the ontological analytic of human being makes up the fundamental ontology, so that consequently human beings function as those entities which in principle are to be *interrogated* for their being previously [to any other ontological investigation].[11]

Here it could be argued that the *"vorgängig"* is meant to indicate "in preparation for further inquiry," but the first part of the sentence precludes that this further inquiry be a fundamental ontology, since that is stated as being constituted by the existential analytic itself.

Passages such as these have predisposed some readers to suppose that the aims of Heidegger's fundamental ontology were achieved with the completion of the existential analytic. And according to one of the best of these readers, Heidegger produced an "existentialist phenomenology" in writing *Being and Time.*[12] If "Time and Being," the missing third part of the first half of the projected treatise, were to be a reversal of the published manuscript's theme, one should expect a familiar methodological gambit to reopen the missing sections: readjustment of the forestructure, possible selection of a new foresighted element or structure, interpretation, and return to the forehaving established *"grundsätzlich"* and *"vorgängig"* by a human being's prior knowledge of its existential situation. But that section of the originally planned treatise was published in another form, and its "method" is no longer recognizably phenomenological.[13]

Within the text of *Being and Time* itself, the two themes of a fundamental ontology begin to be separated, and very early.

> Sachhaltig genommen ist die Phänomenologie die Wissenschaft vom Sein des Seienden—Ontologie. In der gegebenen Erläuterung der Aufgaben der Ontologie entsprang die Notwendigkeit einer Fundamentalontologie, die das ontologisch-ontisch ausgezeichnete Seiende zum Thema hat, das Dasein.

> With respect to its subject matter phenomenology is the science of the being of entities—ontology. In the given explanation of the problems of ontology there arose a necessity for conceiving a fundamental ontology which has for its theme the ontic-ontological being par excellence, human being.[14]

The ontological problems referred to here are the two published parts of the treatise: an ontological analytic of human being as a horizon for posing the question of the meaning of Being-in-general, and the destruction of the history of ontology itself. Considering these two problems, we are told, convinces us of the necessity for working out a fundamental ontology with the ontic-ontological priority of human being as its theme. But we must recall one more thing: human being enjoys it ontic-ontological priority as the entity to be studied in a fundamental ontology because the being of nonhuman entities is relative to it—since without the understanding of being, there could be no "reality" as such whose being is to be described.[15] Understanding is simply a way for a human being to be in the world. Since the being of nonhuman entities is disclosed through the human self-projection, there would be no such being if there were no being-disclosing that projects itself and thereby discloses itself along with the entities it cares for in the natural or human environment.

Yet, both the existential analytic of human being and the destruction of the history of ontology were to be performed for the purpose of putting the ultimate ontological question: What is the meaning of Being-in-general? The last cited textual passage continues:

... so zwar, daß sie sich vor das Kardinalproblem, die Frage nach dem Sinn von Sein überhaupt bringt.

... so that it may consider the cardinal problem, the question concerning the meaning of Being-in-general.[16]

As the introduction progresses, then, the total treatise was to have settled two preparatory problems and then to have been capped off with an answer to the question of the meaning of Being. That is to say, the two-thirds of the first projected half of the larger treatise, which compose the entire manuscript we possess, and which develops only the existential analytic, and the entire second half, which is missing, but which would perform the required destruction of the history of ontology, call for a third, capping part of the originally intended treatise that does not even figure in Heidegger's sketch of its contents.[17] Presumably the "third missing part" might have been dedicated to solving the question with which Part I opens the inquiry. But that was not to be.

Under these circumstances it is reasonable to expect that the author of this text should have, somewhere within the eight editions through which it has been distributed, rewritten the introduction to fit the contents of the published version. Yet, it made no difference how untimely the original manuscript had been ripped from Heidegger's anxious grasp: it could not have been successfully completed by the method he chose to employ.

Indeed, when he explains how hermeneutical phenomenology was to approach its subject, he found only the four different applications: (1) uncovering the meaning of the being and the basic structures of existent human beings; (2) working out the conditions on which the possibility of any ontological inquiry depends; (3) developing an analytic of the existentiality of human existence; and (4) working out a methodology for those humane sciences that are historiological in character.[18] Each of these aims was achieved in the original published version that ended with the derivation of the ordinary conception of time.

Heidegger does consider, however, whether grounding the ordinary conception of time in the temporality of human being naturally ends his inquiry. In sketching out the range of his last chapter, he states:

Die Frage, ob und wie der Zeit ein "Sein" zukommt, warum und in welchem Sinne wir sie "seiend" nennen, kann erst beantwortet werden, wenn gezeigt ist, inwiefern die Zeitlichkeit selbst im Ganzen ihrer Zeitigung so etwas wie Seinsverständnis und Ansprechen von Seiendem möglich macht.

The question whether and how time is accommodated to a "Being," why and in which sense we refer to it as "being," can only be answered when it has been pointed out to what extent temporality itself in the totality of its temporalizing makes it possible for us to understand Being and address ourselves to entities.[19]

Meeting those conditions was the task of sections 79 through 80 of the text. What is intimated here is the reversal of ontological themes from Being and time to time and Being.

But instead of a smooth methodological transition to the reversed theme, Heidegger examines Hegel's suggested connection between time and the Spirit—which achieves nothing in the overall plan—before going on to consider the problem of relating the results of his own existential analytic with the question of the more fundamental ontology, which by this time means only posing and answering the question of the meaning of Being-in-general.

First, he gives a review of the analytic. Temporality has now been brought back into the forehaving of explanation, interpreted as the meaning of human being. If there is to be a fundamental ontology that would answer the question of the meaning of Being-in-general, that question must be shown to arise in existence, and once interpreted, it must be brought back into the forehaving already understood as part of a human being's concern for itself and its world.

And the method to be used is the same hermeneutical phenomenology explained in the introduction of the text and used throughout it to develop the existential analytic. Indeed, philosophy here[20] is itself defined as "universal phenomenological ontology." Philosophy in this manner takes its departure from existence and is brought back to clarify our understanding of existence. But to go beyond the existential analytic we need some clue, some point of access, and a clear sense of directedness toward some end. Which of the entities whose being is interpreted in the analytic should serve as the basis for the more fundamental inquiry? Human being or the real world?

Or perhaps both, as making-present implies both something that is present and something to which it is present.

Although the usual distinction between human being as conscious and the real world as the object of consciousness seems enlightening, upon inspection this seeming may be deceiving. Certainly the difference between consciousness and its objects leaves the question of their being unclarified. For example, why is consciousness itself usually reified in discussions of its being, at least from the time of Plato to that of Descartes and beyond?

The list of unanswered questions begins: What is signified when we say that consciousness is reified? How does consciousness come about? Why does "Being" get conceived as presence, rather than as handiness, when the latter is closer to our everyday understanding of being? Why does the question of Being always arise in consciousness?

And, on the other hand, if it is inappropriate to consider the being of consciousness as presence to self—as somehow having been reified—the list continues: What is the positive structure of human consciousness? Is the distinction between consciousness and things sufficient to establish a fundamental ontology? Can these be answered by the way that is opened up through the existential analytic? Can we even look for answers to these questions as long as the meaning of Being-in-general has not been clarified?

Although the analytic of human being has been developed for the purpose of supplying the horizon in which these questions might be asked and answered, it is only a step along the way toward the discipline that would answer them.

Something like Being has been disclosed in that inquiry, first of all in the preontological comprehension of their own being that human beings possess; this was then interpreted as care, whose meaning was shown to be temporality, from which the ordinary concept of time derives; by virtue of the understanding of being, human beings, before and after ontological inquiry, are able to comport themselves toward entities, including themselves as living—"beings."

Precisely what questions were left unanswered by the analytic of human being? The list goes on:

• If it is given, preontologically, as a fact of existence, how is the disclosive understanding of Being by human beings possible?

• Can this question be answered by reconsidering the primordial constitution of the being of that entity by which it is understood?

That is, by returning to the *"Da,"* the opening of a human being to its world that clears a region for ontological investigation?

• How is the way temporality temporalizes itself to be interpreted?

• Is there a way to move from an understanding of primordial time—human temporality—to the meaning of Being? That is, now that we have moved from human being to time, can we move from time to Being-in-general?

• Finally, does time itself manifest itself as the horizon for conceiving of Being?

And at this point in time—to quote the Watergate conspirators—*Being and Time* was itself made history; it merely ran out of time, and space, and words, and resoluteness to achieve a meaningful end.[21] The preceding two questions allow us to pose a third.

3. Has Heidegger succeeded in his personal quest for the meaning of Being-in-general?

The answer to this question depends upon a point of view.

By his own admission, *Being and Time* does not settle the "cardinal" problem of "fundamental ontology." The purpose of publishing the manuscript was to reopen that question and to provide an interpretive base for answering it. Those Heideggerian philosophers who disagree with the assessment of *Being and Time*'s achievement do so on the ground that, in their opinion, the book did settle the question of the meaning of Being-in-general.

Noting that the existential analytic designated different kinds of entities—beings—each of which displays a distinctive kind of being—caring, presence, and handiness—the question of the meaning of Being, or of being-in-general, seems fixed by a simple inductive argument. And since the technique describing these various modes of being was the unique application of the phenomenological method, it could be claimed that the central problem of the fundamental ontology Heidegger sought had already been answered in the existential analytic.

The more faithful Heideggerians, on the other hand, insist that *Being and Time* is nothing more than a prolegomenon to the real thing. Admitting that the published text does not settle the central issue of ontology in a definitive way, they study Heidegger's "reversal," from phenomenologist to "thinker,"[22] a part of whose activity—via the connection supposed to exist between *denken* and *danken*—is to give thanks for the "gifts" of Being.

There is a second Heidegger, to be sure; and he is a thinker who hearkens to the nuances of the mute resonances between the fixed sounding vocables of the German language. For some readers, that is his power.[23] But to find oneself in a position of having to change radically the method by which an inquiry was begun suggests an unsuspected weakness in the entire project. True, we must say *Sein* in pronouncing *Dasein;* but hyphenating this last expression, which may bring a visual aid to our artful understanding of the term as both an ontic and an ontological designation, does not enable us to visualize or to understand how the being of that being—its caring, if Heidegger is right—whose meaning is temporality, can be transcended in further ontological inquiry. The unanswered questions of section 83 of the text give ample justification of this claim.

But let's look—or listen—once more. Is the expression "Being-in-general" significant? Our positivistic friends claim it is the veriest of nonsense; the pragmatic, that it is the name for an idea that makes no difference; and the more recently analytic, that it is an expression without a use. And they may all be right. Consider.

If "Being-in-general" (as part of the expression "die Frage nach dem Sinn von Sein überhaupt") means to be a covering concept for all modes of being—such as existence, presence, and handiness—then we could express that idea in English merely by capitalizing the word, *Being.* It would still be open to the criticism of positivists, pragmatists, and analytic philosophers, but the mysterious *überhaupt* at least would have gone by the board. Its mission in a sentence is always expletive anyway, like the French *tout-court.*

What gets expressed in these expletives is the difference between the being of entities—be they persons, things, or tools—and being without further ado *(tout-court),* to which Heidegger refers as the transcendent pure and simple, that is, that which in every case transcends the entity that displays it, but which itself is not an entity and so cannot be treated as an object of ontological analysis in the same way entities were.

Presumably, Heidegger had forgotten his own suggestion that Being is always the being of some entity, along with the authority of Aristotle, who claimed that being could be said in many ways.[24] *Being, tout-court,* is an analogical term, used differently to designate substances or its attributes, creating or created substances, and the like. To search for a univocally determined meaning for the term would seem to be a paradigm case of a "category mistake."

Heidegger had already told us that although *Being* is a universal term, its universality does not stem from its being a genus. That direction, Aristotelian in source, leads to the hypostatization of Being itself, which is perhaps only a more distantly "transcendental" occasion of reifying the concepts of our language than that noted by Heidegger himself as the reification of consciousness. And he might have as well recalled the lesson of Hegel, who took exception to the transcendental nature of Schelling's "Absolute," calling it the dark of night in which all cows are black. To look for Being beyond the being of entities—however bovine—is to look in a place where there is nothing to be seen. Hegel's own absolute, we recall, was immanent within the course of history.

To explain the being of a being is to describe how we recognize it for what it is. Various beings are what they are for different reasons; so our ontological descriptions of the being of these beings will, and should, be as different as the things themselves.

But all this has been said by many other critics of Heidegger's personal quest for the meaning of Being, which in some manner lends its sense to the being of all those beings, which figure in the significance of our worlds. Far easier, it seems to me, to show that what we mean by the being of entities had already been achieved in that portion of *Being and Time* that was published in so untimely a manner in 1927; and that the value of the text is to be found in other areas than in its having grounded an unanswerable question.

STILL THERE IS that other point of view. If Heidegger's plight on publishing *Being and Time* in its unfinished state seemed to present still another figure of Hegel, in that his personal quest for the meaning of transcendental Being had ended with the separation of the inquiring consciousness from the object that was its truth, he came to embody "the unhappy consciousness" which must continue to suffer the conditions of that separation until once again it can screw up its courage to delve into the thickness of history, where alone the fates of individuals and the destinies of nations are decided at the higher levels of dialectical experience; his quest ended in tragedy. Having adopted his hermeneutical phenomenological method, he could neither deny his past nor continue repeating it indefinitely, neither go on nor renounce going on, for his own being was his historicity. As pointed out by Father Richardson,[25] he chose to go on by changing his method. To save Heidegger I, Heidegger I had to become Heidegger II, whose method was no longer phenomenological but "radical thought"—questioning and answering the appeal to being by continuing to care for beings, and in this way letting Being be.[26]

Heidegger II composed a "foreword" to Richardson's study of his philosophical career from its phenomenological base through the "reversal" and on into the thought of Being, warning readers that there would have been no Heidegger II if there had been no Heidegger I—a warning I interpret to mean that understanding the existential analytic is still necessary for understanding the man. That is, the horizon for making the interpretation of the new Heidegger had indeed been prepared in *Being and Time*.[27]

Although Heidegger's discourse in his later "philosophizing" became more and more metaphorical, we can understand those metaphors and outright neologisms on the basis of his prior philosophical explanations of worldhood, significance, disclosedness, and the like. Indeed, discourse is still the culminating structure of a human being's disclosive being in the world. When we later read that a world "worlds" ("Die Welt weltet")[28] or that a thing "things" ("Das Ding dingt")[29] or that nothingness itself nihilates ("Das Nichts selbst nichtet")[30] or that *Being* should be written "under erasure," as Jacques Derrida would have it, because considered with respect to things, Being is nothing,[31] a prior reading of *Being and Time* provides the forehaving for making an interpretation.

A world "worlds" in accordance with a human being's assignment of values to the entities found in its totality of involvements; and it is in this way that ontological significance is created by a human being's being in that world. A thing "things" as it "falls out" of a totality of involvements into a context where it is merely present to some observer's attention. Nothingness itself, and not a human being, holds the totality of entities *(das Seiende im Ganzen, which is not das Sein überhaupt)* into externality from itself; and the subjective correlative of our thinking the all of being, without reference to any particular being, is boredom, while that mood which is called out by our awareness of *das Nichts* is the anxiety we feel over our own nothingness.

Finally, when Heidegger comes to write Being as ~~Sein~~[32] which is *das Sein überhaupt,* he merely repeats that we have as yet found no accurate description for Being itself, that the designation is at best an approximation, and that if pushed, we should have to fall back on Hegel's description of an indeterminate Being as absolute non-

Being, the passage from one to the other or from the other to the one determining the context of becoming within which entities may come to be and pass away.

Later, Heidegger will describe this regioning of Being—still opened up by the clearing of an individual's being there—as the fourfold, a latter-day boxing of the compass, fixing the positions of those entities open to human ontological investigation—the heavens, the earth, the gods, and human beings; or, as he prefers, following Hölderlin, the "immortals" and the "mortals." Writing Being under erasure as S̶e̶i̶n̶ gives an added visual aid for conceiving Being as that context of all possible relationships that generates the significance of all those things standing in those relationships.

We need not follow Heidegger into the labyrinth of his later philosophy, since it is not my purpose here to explain all Heidegger's ontological metaphors by finding a basis for them in the existential analytic. But we should remember that writing in metaphor or more generally creating works of art that constitute indirect discourse is the only certain way of expressing one's authentic existence. Perhaps for this reason we should sum up the difference between Heidegger I and Heidegger II as that between an ontologist who conceived his task as shepherding Being and one who had learned in the process that language itself is the house of Being.

And one way of playing the shepherd to Being is to attend to the language of those who invented the concept. It is for this reason that Heidegger advises the readers of *Being and Time* to consult his *Introduction to Metaphysics*, the record of his "dialogue" with pre-Socratic philosophers.[33] The first of these, Parmenides, was both philosopher and poet, since his philosophy was written as a poem describing the two ways of achieving truth. Heidegger chose another way, to hearken to the language of all those poets whose works provide the best examples for the creation of significance.[34] Entering into dialogue with thinker and poet is one way of living in the house of Being; at any rate, he who would be a philosopher should always be *Unterwegs zur Sprache,*[35] even if along the way he discovers that it is language that speaks *(Die Sprache spricht!).*[36]

Could there be a better symbol for explaining why the Heideggerian search for the meaning of Being was continually fed by those meanings that have come down to us in history as encoded in the languages we speak? His own preferences were for Greek and German; Greek because the early Greek philosophers were the first to bring their wonder at being to a science of Being; and German, because only that language allows one to conceive why the thought of Being should call for our giving thanks. Why are there entities? Because *es (Sein) gibt Seiende.*

So runs the second option for reading significance into *Being and Time.*

But whether one adopts this or the earlier option, there remains a way out of the dilemma: we can go through the horns. When *Being and Time* was published, it entered into world history. As a world-historical event, it too was open to interpretation; and as a philosophical text, interpreting it constitutes a way for us to enter into dialogue with it. Moreover, interpreting a text in such a way as using its theses to give significance to other human or cultural involvements—even if one ignores the main thrust of its argument—only shows that a written text is a tool, whose being is to be useful for that purpose.

Consider the examples of how that text has been used. Sartre kept the aim of writing a phenomenological ontology but substituted the Hegelian categories to make his interpretation of the phenomena of existence; and his achievement was significant. There is perhaps no more insightful treatment of a fully human act than that depicted in part 6 of *Being and Nothingness.*[37] Bultmann turned the text into a method for de-mythologizing contemporary theology;[38] Tillich, for contructing his *Systematic Theology.*[39] Boss, Binswanger, and Carl Rogers turned the existential analytic into a methodology of psychotherapy.[40] Gadamer read the text as grounding all hermeneutical enterprises.[41] And Jacques Derrida turned it into a practical lesson in linguistics, allowing him to conceive of another relationship between signifier and signified than that explained in recent structuralism.[42] In a word, interpreting a text is not to explain a meaning, but to replace the original text with another set of signifiers.

And, lastly, I have myself just finished reading the text by following out its projection of a significance. If *Being and Time* does not reveal Being-in-general, it does show us how any text, including itself, must be read. If my reading has achieved anything, it has been to show that interpreting a text is one way we have for being in a world with an author. Heidegger's own being in the world was elaborated into the text read, and within that text it is shown how understanding progresses from mood through interpretation to expression. It was for this reason I claimed that the structure of the text itself contains the clue for its interpretation.

So, although Heidegger's original project reached a crisis point

and could not be continued to its imagined end as originally projected, he did provide us with a model for interpreting his failure.
We need only generalize on the lesson learned to establish a technique
for reading any written text. Derrida took that route, and I shall take
another in my final chapter.

WHAT, IN THE END, was the achievement of Heidegger's *Being
and Time?*

It invented a hermeneutical phenomenology and so broadened the
scope of phenomenological inquiry. It gave renewed impetus to the
existentialist movement begun by Kierkegaard, down to the details
of reviving the moment of vision and the necessity of repetition for
the conception of an original temporality; and in Heidegger's last
tragic end, as the Hegelian unhappy consciousness, he brought to life
once more Kierkegaard's depiction of the ultimate paradox—that
the Eternal should become historical—as stimulating both philosophical thought and religious commitment. Lastly, it provided a
schema for interpreting the significance of written texts, a basis for
an ontologically grounded literary criticism. But of this last, more in
my final chapter.

Being and Time, I hope it has been shown, is one of the truly great
books of the twentieth century; if not for the reasons I have stipulated,
at least as providing the horizon—or context of ultimate significance—for interpreting the works of Heidegger II.

It seems one always has the option of paying one's money and
taking one's choice; of using one's time to one's own best advantage,
or of losing it altogether. And writers of books are never in the
position of being able to decide that for their readers. All texts,
including this one, belong to their interpreters.

13

Being-in a Literary World: The Return to Worlding Significance

AS DEPICTED IN *Being and Time*,[1] A HUMAN being is left spanning three worlds, each with its own temporal determination: first, the world of nature, measured in eons of time, subtending ages of geological formation; next, the social world, of infinitely smaller duration, since it began with the evolution of *Homo sapiens sapiens*, whose time on this earth is measured by historians in epochs, and whose existence as a species we have only just begun to understand; and, lastly, the personal world of each individual, of shorter duration still, but whose time is measured both in years and days, sometimes in hours and minutes, but always by the spanned datability of those moments in its life between birth and death, those two outward limits of memory and expectation. But these considerations are only ontic, divulging an understanding of both space and time that, if Heidegger was right, had previously been ontologically ungrounded.

If the being of a human being is its caring, and the meaning of that being is its temporality, the time of the everyday world in which it began its ontological inquiry and to which it returned to establish its wholeness,[2] its integrity,[3] and its development,[4] is still measured by a change in position, as Aristotle had maintained; [5] only now, but not because of its "spatialization," infinite rather than finite, singular rather than plural, containing moments that are homogeneous rather than heterogeneous, continuous rather than discrete, universal rather than individual, a structure of the objective world rather than of one or more human existences thrown over into that world.[6]

The force of Heidegger's effort was to effectuate the ontological difference. Where, after the eons of time it took for nature to develop a hominoid animal, and still further millenia for that animal to become conscious,[7] one fine day one concretion sedimented from the universal gene pool of humanity could look out upon nature and be moved to write:

Le silence éternel de ces espaces infinies m'effraie,[8]

thereby bequeathing to us one of the most moving reports of a sensitive individual that found itself in the world as if thrown into a place as yet unknown and ultimately unknowable.

And as reflection deepened, that same conscious individual, already having discovered the mathematically sublime, would cast the image that reflects the power of consciousness to rise above even the most powerful forces of nature to destroy it. Disdaining the "spirit of geometry" to pit the infinitely small against the infinitely great, both of which beggar the imagination, Pascal drew upon that "spirit of finesse" we can all envy to liken himself to a reed buffeted by the wind, blown hither and thither, bending to the point of breaking, yet aware of itself as thus thrown about in midst of the world: a reed indeed, but a reed that thinks is man.[9] In this image, he registered that feeling of human ability to overcome even the most dynamically sublime power known to humankind, which, in its own natural environment, has witnessed straws driven through trees by tornadoes.

But, alas, these accounts too were only ontic. How are such events as human inherence in multiple worlds, including humanity's ability to characterize how it is to be there, to be understood ontologically? Heidegger wrote Being and Time in an effort to find out. I read that record as an account of his own being in the world that was aborted by the necessity he felt to reinforce his candidacy as replacement for Husserl at Freiburg by publishing an unfinished work, as well as by his exhaustion of the method he had devised to lead us to an unattainable goal: the solution of the problem of determining the meaning of Being in general. And whoever reads that still great work as the personal quest of its author will come away with still another image of human tragedy, described in Hegel's phenomenology as the "unhappy consciousness,"[10] as embedded within the objects of the world and looking for fulfillment in that one Being that was transcendent to every possible world—within medieval Christianity, the Everlasting God, upon whose face no human could look and yet continue to live.

Heidegger's existential analytic of human being did not replace our scientific understanding of the natural world by a pseudo-scientific account of the existentiality of human existence, which indeed was thought of as a replacement for the Hegelian dialectic; rather, it showed how the basic concepts of the natural sciences—space, signification, and time—were derived from a more primitive form of awareness, that of our being-in-the-world, disclosed to the human being existing there as its own spatiality, significance, and temporality.

In a word, Heidegger's work is not antiscientific; it is merely not scientistic; not ontic, but ontological; and, as such, *Being and Time* was limited to describing those structures of human being, *Existentialien* (which I have rendered as "existentials"), that make it possible for there to be human beings existing as we all do: thrown in and about a world, projected toward a future, and for the most part, in the present, absorbed in those entities we find around ourselves, somewhere in size between the infinitely great and the infinitely small.

Ontologically considered, the beings we find in our worlds, either in circumspective concern or in careful inspection of their natures, are either like unto ourselves or different; and if different, either serviceable to ourselves or to those beings like ourselves, or merely present to the powers of everyone's observation.

In short, if our own being is to exist, the being of those entities with which we concern ourselves as individuals or as groups is either their utility or their presence. And since all being is the being of some entity, the object of ontological disclosure was completed with the description of our being-in-the-world.

On this point, of course, Heidegger and the Heideggerians are not in agreement. For some of these, the existential analytic is precisely what Heidegger thought it to be, the projection of a horizon for restating and presumably answering the question of the meaning of Being in general; whereas, for others, less orthodox, the hermeneutical method of phenomenology reached its outward limit in *Being and Time,* with its return to the ordinary concept of time,[11] to that time of the everyday world in which the ontological question first arose. We can elect to stay there and make the best of it; or, as Heidegger did in his later writings, we can try to go beyond.[12]

But that attempt required a change in method, as illustrated by the "reversal" in Heidegger's thought that was left incomplete in *Being and Time.* For time and being we must consult other texts; and for the destruction of the history of ontology Heidegger left us with a double task, not only to make clear how that destruction was to be perpetrated, but to construct a written history that would record the very history he sought to "destroy."

If in the first wave the significations of science were traced to the significance of worlding worlds, in the new wave an attempt shall be made to capture the moment when significance becomes signification, when metaphor conveys a thought. Since the logic of the post-Aristotelian philosophers was thought to be responsible for the contemporaneous forgetfulness of being; or as, according to Nietzsche, it was the essentialism of Socrates that produced the decline of Attic tragedy, the new method was not to be a purely logical analysis of meanings, which can exhibit at best an effete *esprit de géométrie.*

In a word, within the new dispensation, where philosophy is to become thought once again, logic is to be replaced by dialogue—between philosopher and philosopher, or between philosopher and poet, struggling to convey meaning discovered in a personal existence wherein man still finds himself straddling two worlds, the natural and the human.

But the change brought on by the reversal in Heidegger's thought is not all that great. Although he continued to believe that no other problem of ontology would be settled until its fundamental problem had been answered, and his reading of Hölderlin's poems describes the poet as thinker, "creatively naming the gods,"[13] there is a common background to be found behind the two paths Heidegger's thinking actually took. It is found, in *Being and Time,* described as a structural item of human being as being-in-the-world: its "being-in," considered as such.[14] And to find out what that is, we must pose once again that rather simple-looking question: How is a human being in its world?

It will be worthwhile to review Heidegger's answer to this question. The question seems simple enough but immediately becomes complicated when we recall Heidegger's distinctions between the concepts of a world to which a human being may belong, the natural and the humane, the latter being both personal and cultural, and between "things" spread out in three dimensions and a human being whose essence is to exist, projected toward its potentialities of being.

If a human being were a thing, if its being were exhausted by the three-dimensionality of its body, then it could be in the world the way Dr. Seuss's cat was in the hat, or Dr. Wittgenstein's fly was in the bottle, that is, the same way a corpse is in its casket. Wittgenstein, of course, thought the philosophical problem was to get the fly out of the bottle, by clearing away the pseudoproblems of those muddle-heads whose metaphysics had put the fly there in the first place.[15] Open or break the glass container of the flytrap, and the fly can go on its merry way.

The things of this world, whose being is to be present, whose "reality" consists in their presence, may be contained in other things, and all the things containing things may themselves be conceived as being contained in another thing. That was indeed how Descartes conceived of the physical world, and Heidegger gave his "ontological" interpretation of that world in sections 19–21 of *Being and Time*.

Since the Cartesian concept of the world was contructed mathematically—as the summation of all three-dimensionally extended substances—it was something we could know very little about. Even the hardness of those substances had to be explained by a relationship to an experiencing subject who became aware of their resistance to touch. And without the subjects in this world, there could be no smells, or sounds, or tastes; no colors that were perceived; no values of any kind to be appreciated. Substances, even thinking ones, do not "ex-ist," and for this reason could be thought to be contained in the world—the soul in its body, and the body in its accustomed place, whether it be dead or alive.

The human world, on the other hand, is a context of involvements determined by instruments serving as equipment that permits human beings to achieve their ends, as they act to bring far near, and, as they orient their activity, to direct themselves through the things with which they are concerned toward others, toward this, toward that, and finally toward themselves as that for the sake of which the act had been projected in the first place.

The things of this world are not known in their presence but in their use. Their being is no longer that of a three-dimensionally extended object, but their serviceability; not their presence over against our consciousness to which they are present, whether in resistance or in resilience, but in their pliancy, their inconspicuousness, their inobtrusiveness, as being handy to human use.

The world itself, as the totality of one's involvements with the tools of the environment, does not come to closure through the application of a mathematical operation; it appears as a phenomenon. And the worlding of that world, its manner of permitting human action within its moving structures, is the most primordial sense of *significance,* itself a structure of human existence, one of those "existentials" going to make up the existentiality of our being in the world. That significance is felt in our every act of circumspective concern.

And it is only when the world turns badly, when our tools refuse to function, when they are no longer pliant but resistant, obtrusive, and conspicuous in their failure to respond to our attempts to use them that they fall out of the human world and into the natural world, where we can inspect them in order to determine the reasons for their malfunction. Only then does the thing "thing."

Growing old gives a vivid picture of creeping malfunction in the human body—a process, we recall, well enough understood by Oedipus to allow him to solve the riddle of the sphinx. His tragedy was in not knowing what else lay in store for him, not knowing whence he came, and, unfortunately for him and all his people, in not knowing just what he was doing in between. His fate was to suffer the consequences of his ignorance of self.

Our knowledge of our being-in-the-world, Heidegger tells us, is a founded mode of our being-in.[16] But this knowledge is not in the first instance conceptual; not descriptive, but acquaintive. And since our being is not that of a substance or essence of any kind, we can only be said to be the manner in which we live our attachment to our worlds. The existential analytic was written to allow us to describe, in ontologically appropriate terms, how we live those attachments, how we become acquainted with ourselves as we become acquainted with our worlding worlds.

To begin with, a human being is its existence. Here our English needs careful explanation. I have been translating *Dasein* as "human being" for reasons given elsewhere.[17] Ordinarily the term means existence, but Heidegger employs it to refer to that kind of existence exhibited only by human beings. Although his uses are primarily ontological, referring to that mode of being which is opposed to the being of things or tools, *Dasein* can be used in an ontical context as well, as when we refer to a human being, whose being is to be in the world in the way described above. All this, Heidegger claims, is contained in the *da* preceding the *Sein* of the human being.

The meaning of that being, we are told, is temporality, which permits the basic caring, the tripartite structure of thrownness into the world, existential projection upon possibilities of being, and falling, on the average, into a public world in which no one is oneself but always another; the human being temporalizes itself according to the three equiprimordial dimensions of the ekstatico-horizonal time: either remembering or forgetting the past while waiting for an inauthentic future, making present the objects of the public world, or retaining our pasts while anticipating a future that is our own in a moment of vision that illuminates our present situation.

Stretched spatially between the *here* and the *there* of the ambiguous *da*, a human being lives through the regioning of that opening region as being in between; between the real world wherein it is fixed by virtue of the position of its body and the world of its culture that enables it to transcend the limits of the physical by projecting novel significances into that world: institutions that permit it to regulate its being with others in the same worlds, and, not the least, works of art with which to communicate the most intimate of novel significances to those of us who have eyes with which to see, ears to hear, and worldly presence enough to understand what it is that we see or hear or read.

Being there, in the world, is always not to be closed off from the objects of that world, from our selves as projected from and into a personal world, or from those significant others with whom we share a common destiny. From the *Unverschlossenheit* ("unclosedness"), Heidegger moves on to *Erschlossenheit*, that essential openness of a human being to its world; and from there he will move on to the disclosedness by which a human being gives testimony to its being in the world, but not before dilating upon the light that is created by its being-there. Indeed, Heidegger's metaphor for the process by which "light" has been brought into the world—which it was by the evolution of the human eye and not merely by the length of a wave— is found in the expression *die Lichtung des Da,* "the clearing" of the here and there that has always been misinterpreted ontically as the *lumen naturale* that became our birthright as rational animals.

Actually, says Heidegger, the clearing is an opening as in a forest that has been thinned out to open up a space and allow the natural light of the sun to illuminate the paths to be followed to get from here to there. Sometimes, without the proper clearing we cannot see the forest for the trees, just as from a distance we cannot see the trees for the forest.

Heidegger refuses Husserl's gambit to pursue consciousness as the source of the light by which we claim to see whenever we understand anything at all because that term indicates an ontic function for our being in the world, retains many of the older substantive interpretations of that function (as did Descartes' description of the human soul as a thinking substance, which led Gilbert Ryle to caricature "mind" as a "ghost in a machine"),[18] and has misled other philosophers, such as Jean-Paul Sartre, to characterize consciousness in part as presence to self.[19]

We have already met the light in Heidegger's description of circumspection *(Umsicht)* by which the abandoned human being detects the significance of its thrownness, and we have seen it dimmed into indirection as his word for scientific inspection, *Hinsehen,* depicts the process rather than the medium that makes it possible; and we met it twice again in his description of our being with others as human solicitude expressed as considerateness *(Rücksicht)* and forebearance *(Nachsicht).* Obviously, we can see neither the forest nor the trees without the light of our being there in the world with them and the sun.

No, consciousness is not presence to self, even if the world of objects is thought to be present to it. That's the wrong sense of *world* again; the human world "worlds" into a phenomenologically disclosed significance. And in tracing out the development of human disclosedness into the equiprimordial structures of affectivity *(Befindlichkeit),* understanding *(Verstehen),* and discourse *(Rede),* Heidegger provided the basic ontological interpretation of conscious being that had eluded Husserl. What eventually gets understood by the techniques of interpretation in the application of the forestructure of understanding is a significance that had already been preontologically understood because ontically we always find ourselves attuned to our being in the world. The interpretation itself lays out the ground for reading something (a foresighted element of that world) as something we already understand (a foreconception).

It is for this reason that metaphor precedes concept, as Vico had pointed out many years earlier.[20] We can only explain the novel entities of our worlds in terms of what we already understand, the unknown by the known. The very form of our assertions exhibits the apophantical as-structure that reveals a sense to us. Those senses become significations for us, when they are embodied in speech; in the human speech that articulates and communicates a meaning in a logical semantics.

Language is a tool by which we communicate the significance of our being in the world. It is for this reason that Heidegger will later say that language is the house of Being; language is the medium for showing how it is to be in the world.[21] It is also a cultural product we inherit with the other institutions of our society; and it is for this reason that Heidegger claims that language, the one that already exists before we learn how to use it, modulating it to our own purposes, speaks through man.

Heidegger obviously used his own hermeneutical techniques to develop his existential analytic. *Being and Time* may be traced from preontological to postontoloical understanding via successive applications of the forestructure of the understanding considered as a constitutive structure of human disclosedness. I intend to show in what follows what happens to the field of disclosedness that opens out upon a purely literary world. It's still a matter of our being-in.

ENTERING A literary world is called reading, or writing, two apparently simple acts of our ontic existence. Together they constitute what I shall call "creative communication," a social act this, but still ontic, in which the experience of the one agent, the writer, illustrates the Heideggerian ontological category of being-with, as it calls out an appropriate response in the reader, whose own experience is guided by, indeed is constituted by, the system of signs going to make up the written text.

In a simple visual image, the world projected by the writer through the text—an imaginary world of the significations intended by the signs of the text—is mirrored on the other side of the text by the reader who projects his own understanding of that "worlding world" in terms of his own forehaving, his own background of knowledge (of the semantic and syntactic formation found in the text) and experience (his own worlding world and his being thrown into it as a being that projects "significance"). Such is the ontological structure of our being which permits our reading a fictional text as metaphor.

If the image is accurate, and if it can be given a more concrete explanation in Heideggerian ontological terms, we should have succeeded in giving an account of how a literary work of art comes to be and how it ultimately gets transmitted through the history of a culture.

But as we project this understanding of the literary process, a certain number of provisos must be kept in mind. I list them as they occur to me:

• The "idea" or the "feeling" expressed through a text is not something that is first "understood" or felt by the writer and then somehow translated into graphemic structures. I call this the "Platonic fallacy," since it assumes that an Idea preexists its expression in a text.[22] You can use Ockham's razor, if you like, and make a conscious decision not to multiply the entities of your universe beyond necessity; or you can merely attend to the phenomena involved, that is, to all those times when you were trying to say something but knew not what until you discovered in your own words what sense or nonsense you may have succeeded in uttering. Existentially considered, making sense is to dis-cover a significance. To be able to understand a phonemic context, we have to be able to hear and to project what we hear into an expression *(eine Aussage)*. And in context, that is, in their combinations, the individual words of a text have no fixed lexical meaning. Just say, "Their meaning is their use," and concentrate upon how they are used in the text.

• If in this way the ordinary semantical function of our words becomes "neutralized" (as if by phenomenological bracketing), the purpose of the expression is not to state a fact about the real world; neither is the "world" created in the context of expression uniquely of the order of "represented objectivities" in the Ingardenian sense.[23] In a literary context any kind of world may be represented: a realistic, a naturalistic; a surrealistic, a fantastic; a humanistic, an impressionistic; an idealistic, an existentialistic; and so on: however a world may be metaphysically conceived, that philosophical idea may become a "technique" for novelistic representation. Indeed, in some novels, such as those by Alain Robbe-Grillet, for example, the world represented may be reduced to the phenomenal "appearances" of the represented objects in a seemingly infinite series of multifaceted *Abschattungen,* to use Husserl's expression for the profiles or aspects of the perceptual objects given in perception.[24]

In order to avoid the confusion in the expression "literary world,"

I shall distinguish between the "world of the represented objectivities" and the "universe" of the literary creation, which always contains a world of represented objectivities, even if we possess no previously earned philosophical idea for such a world sedimented within our "forehaving," that is, in the context of the knowledge we already possess of our being-in-the-world by virtue of being it. In these latter cases, where we do not possess the sedimented idea, the represented world still comes to closure—its elements are perceived as making up a world; and it was this sort of closure that had constituted the basis for all those earlier discovered "philosophical ideas" by which we bring to closure our own interpretations of the objectivities represented in a text.

Elsewhere,[25] I have referred to such artificial closings of fictional worlds as exhibiting a distinctive genre in prose literature: call it "the philosophical novel," if you like; but interpret the genre as defined by a writer's technique for giving structure to his literary creation.[26] Still, representing a fictional world qua possible—i.e., qua imaginable—is only one strand in the texture of "the literary work of art,"[27] and elaborating the concept of "philosophical" novels is as external to our knowledge of their functioning in our experience as is the determination of historical epochs, the knowledge of which is still thought by some to explain "the significance" of artworks created within designated time spans of cultural history. It was this sense of historical explanation, which Heidegger had discovered in Dilthey, that needed ontological clarification so that a true historical account of human significance could be elaborated within the framework of his hermeneutical methodology.[28]

The knowledge we gain from a literary work is of the literary work itself, not of it in comparison to something else; if the figure were not too crude, one should call it carnal knowledge, after our knowledge of the flesh of another, since that knowledge is registered in a response of feeling to the literary work as a palpitating universe of significance. Such knowledge is always gained in an effort to bring things off at the right moment, and with the maximum of sensitivity. It is both a knowing that feels and a feeling that knows[29]—in Heideggerian terms, *eine Stimmung,* an affective state of a being thrown into its world that gets interpreted as revealing one's being in that world and is ultimately understood as such because that knowledge has been brought to discourse in the text expressing that feeling.

If we were to look for the basis of a general aesthetic theory in

Heidegger's ontology, we should find it already in *Being and Time* as the basic constitution of the existential-ontological *Da*, the here-there that both opens up a world and shows the human being as that dis-closedness by which there is a world. It is child's play to move from the general to the specific and show how the ontological structure fits the case of literature. The writer creates by projecting a significance through his text; and that text is interpreted as a modification of the reader's own being in the world.

But let us look closer. In addition to a set of signifieds constituting the "world" of represented objectivities, the literary universe contains an order of signifiers which bear some significance of their own. Ingarden refers to such significance as the "aesthetically valent" qualities found in each of the four constituent strata he has isolated within the polyphonic harmony of the literary work experienced as a whole interwoven texture,[30] not only that of the phonological elements but also of the semantical unities, the order of represented objectivities, and the schematized aspects under which those objects are imagined to appear.

So, when I speak of projecting a literary "world," I always mean that universe created by the relationship between the set of signifiers and the various orders of signifieds they may represent. Any reader will recognize here the postulate of linguistic structuralism: the phonological signifiers are related to an initial set of signifieds, which in their turn may become higher order signifiers, as in "symbolic" literature, for a higher order of signifieds.

My contention is that this relationship of signifier to signified may be brought to consciousness as a felt tension of significance—a phenomenon which seems as obvious in our conscious struggles to get things right, to bring them off with maximum sensitivity, if you will, whenever we express ourselves to find out what it is we mean, or interpret what another person has meant under similar circumstances, as in our experiences of successful works of art, which display the same ontological structuration.

Whenever an explanation or interpretation has been found for the expressiveness of a text, a German would say, "Das stimmt!" an ordinary Teutonic translation for the Archimedean "Eureka." What has been discovered in either case is a *fitting interpretation* for a problematic given.

Feeling the tensions of its text, however, is the knowledge we have, and the only authentic knowledge we can have, of the literary work of art. Such knowledge is always a return home in that it is gained by a modification of the forestructure of our understanding which begins with our awareness of a preestablished context of significance, and sights out an entity for projection back into that context on the basis of concepts already understood or upon the perceived similarities and differences by which we project novel meaning in terms of metaphorical congruence.

The spoken language may rely upon the concepts that lie like dead metaphors within our dictionaries; the speaking language, that is, the one which expresses a felt significance, may use such concepts but only in order to impart a new significance by creating a live metaphor. That indeed is the effect of using words and concepts to construct literary works of art. The expressiveness we feel in attending to the play of metaphorical meaning is the tension between the signifiers and the signifieds, at whichever level of interpretation they may obtain, within the expressive context created by the work.

• That work, lastly, represents nothing. Plato was wrong to have Socrates plead the superiority of a specialist's knowledge in interpreting works of art; not that there are no specialists qualified to practice that profession, but that a general's knowledge to lead an army or a physician's to heal the body, which may be relevant only to the intellectual content of an epic poem, is more appropriate than a rhapsode's knowledge of how best to perform such a work,[31] is a fallacious application of his own principle of the specialization of human knowledge and labor.

• Once the intellectual content of the literary work has been put into its place, that is, reduced to its functioning within the total expressive context, then the parts of a represented world may likewise be reduced to a level of functional elements in a larger structure. A fictional character, for example, is what he or she does in the context of the represented world. In order to "understand" how such an element functions in context, we may use any sort of intellectual device for interpreting such characters; we have only our forehaving of sedimented meaning structures with which to work; behavioristic psychology, as in *Clockwork Orange;* depth psychology, as in any modern surrealistic novel; Hegelian phenomenology, as in Beckett's *Watt;* humanistic psychology, as in the various novels of Willa Cather; and, since the expression *character* is loaded with moral connotations, any ethical description of a fictional character's behavior may be relevant as a device for interpreting the significance of that character's existence—again, within the context of the represented world, as an additional strand of the novelistic texture.

For this reason, any "ontological" interpretation of human being as represented in a fictional world cannot yield the significance we seek to explain: that felt significance of the literary context considered as a whole. We can interpret Beckett's characters in terms of their temporality and move to a higher level of meaning as that temporality is displayed within the structures of inauthentic existence, which in turn expresses the moral idea of human sublimity, the perception of which enables us to read the peripeteia of these characters as controlling the tragic lift we experience in their representation; but philosophical ideas, whether metaphysical (a "world hypothesis," for example) or moral, or both together, can never constitute the significance of a work, since they are themselves only a part of the expressive vehicle by which an author has projected his metaphor for HOW IT IS to be in a world.

What then gets created in a fictional universe? That universe itself. And, like Heidegger's "worlding world," a literary universe is experienced as a felt significance, as a phenomenologically registered tension, developing in time and expressing the psychic temporalities of—writer and reader.

Writer and reader both stand open to the universe of the literary work, in the disclosedness of their *Da*, because they both readjust their forestructures of understanding of how it is to be in the world by attending to the "discourse" *(Rede)* that lets the work be—merely what it is, the projection of a significance that we can experience if only we learn how to adjust or attune ourselves to the being of the work, by projecting its significance back upon the forehaving of a context of significance that is our own being-in-the-world.

In sum, then, the Heideggerian aesthetic gives an ontological explanation of those ontic structures by which we experience works of art in their expressiveness. The central phenomenon is the existence of works of art that are created and appreciated in structurally similar ways: primarily by a projection into the future that is brought "home" into the present that remembers its past as that past has been sedimented into a forestructured "understanding" of our being in the world. It is a general aesthetic theory, which, like Croce's,[32] is not based upon a more general theory of linguistics, but which itself constitutes one of the necessary elements within a general theory of linguistics: how novel significances are created by the uses we assign to the signs of our language and how they are communicated as determinative parts of our living cultures.

IF THE BASIS for a general aesthetic may be found in the Heideggerian account of the disclosedness of a human being's being-there in its world, the question arises as to why Heidegger himself failed to credit the hypothesis. But, upon reflection, nothing seems easier to understand. He failed to perceive the richness of his idea, and was carried away with the necessity of grounding all concepts used to depict the ontic occurrences of human experience in terms of the meaning still to be discovered for Being-in-general. Posing the problem in *Being and Time,* he could achieve no more than the preparatory analysis of human being to discover the horizon in which the moving question of a fundamental ontology could be posed.

But that work was left incomplete, and I have argued that the method to be used for describing the conditions under which Being itself could be disclosed to a living being would have to be changed from the hermeneutics of *Being and Time,* precisely because Being is not an entity that may be projected upon anything further to determine its meaning. Being itself is the transcendental, pure and simple. (As such, it is inaccessible to any form of phenomenological analysis.)

It is for this reason that Richardson has described Heidegger's career as tracing a path from phenomenology to thought, where thought is at least in part an act of giving thanks to that Being which gives *(Es [Sein] gibt)* the entities whose being we can understand through the techniques of hermeneutical projection. *Being and Time* leaves us with three modes of being: the existence of human subjects, the serviceability of their tools, and the presence of the objects with which the human subjects are concerned.

Beyond phenomenology, Heidegger claimed, was the method of asking questions for the purpose of showing a way to finding an answer. And what got questioned, in the period of Heideggerian philosophy after *Being and Time,* was the language of philosophers and poets, who best illustrated Heidegger's thesis that language is the house of Being. For this reason he refers the readers of *Being and Time* to his later work published as *Einführung in die Metaphysik,*[33] which contains his "dialogue" with the pre-Socratic philosophers, principally Parmenides and Heraclitus. That move was a return to the birth of ontological thought.

The second move was his interest in an ontological interpretation of writing poetry. His principal subject was Hölderlin, whose inspiration concerning the nature of creative writing was expressed in the famous line describing poetic thought as the creative "naming of the gods."

If the gods are symbols for what is transcendentally important in the lives of men, and if the gods reside always at a distance, naming them gives them at least that sort of presence; naming them brings them near, into the region opened up by the language of the poem wherein the poet and his readers are left to dwell: "Viel erfahren hat der Mensch / Der Himmlischen viele genannt / Seit ein Gespräch wir sind / Und hören können voneinander."[34] The lines are language about poetic language depicting the dialogue between poet and reader: the projection of a meaning to be grasped and an interpretation of that meaning as it has been grasped.

But nowhere, as far as I know, did Heidegger turn his talents of interpretation to the worlds created in prose fiction. Perhaps he was too interested in the connections between *dichten, denken,* and *danken* to have noticed how novels create a space and a time of their own within which we can appropriate our own being as attuned to their worlds. Yet he was aware of the possibility of generalizing his ontological interpretation of poetry to cover all cases of artistic creation. His essay on the subject was published as "Der Ursprung des Kunstwerkes," a questioning after the source of works of art.[35]

How does a work of art come to be? An answer to the question will depend upon what we consider a work of art to be. The usual aesthetics, which is formulated in terms of genius and taste, as it was for Kant, for example, is fit, said Heidegger, only for pastrycooks and their clients. To be taken seriously, as any other question, there must be an ontological answer. For this reason, Heidegger rejects the notion of a work of art as composed of matter and form: too naturalistic, this; or as a gestalt of the sensuous properties funding into a whole: too psychologistic, this.

A work of art, if it is to be known at all, is known through its manner of working. Ontological aestheticians should go about their tasks by observing and then describing what is at work in a work of art. Heidegger considers three examples: a painting by Van Gogh; a poem by the Swiss poet, C. F. Meyer; and a Greek temple. Although the painting and the poem are representational in nature, the temple is not; so the resulting description will not be prejudiced by either the presence or absence of any representational elements within the field of expression.

Consider first the painting, one of the series of peasant shoes painted by Van Gogh. What is at work in this work? The shoes, old and worn to the point of being worn out, placed in an open field where they had been worn into that condition under a dark, foreboding sky, painted in somber browns. Brought to our perception, says Heidegger, is the world of the peasant made visible on the surface of the painting. We can imagine the drudgery of the work that has put these shoes into their present condition, years of contact between ploughing foot and resistant soil, bringing to mind the totality of involvements in a peasant's working relationship with his natural environment: not the shoes in their presence, but the whole of a worlding world in which these shoes have come to be what they appear to be in the artist's depiction of them comes to expression, the whole of which is crowned in the foreboding, oppressive browns of the atmosphere.

Next the poem, entitled "Der Römische Brunnen." The subject of the poem is the rising and falling of the waters of the Roman fountain: jetting up *(Aufsteigt der Strahl)* and continually falling from the first through a third marble receptacle *(Und fallend gießt . . .)* where they come to rest while flowing still. In this work, too, something is depicted, no longer a world of utilitarian involvements, but of something that itself, if present, would have no purpose at all, a mere pattern of falling water.

But the poem is a verbal construct: its rhythms rise and fall in harmony with those that rise and fall and come to rest in the image of the falling waters. The surface of the poem constructed in kinaesthetic imagery harmonizes with the depth of the poem realized in visual imagery: again, an opening between the far and the near held in a taut tension binding the two "strata" of poetic expression. What is at work here? The conscious being of the reader whose intentional field is polarized by the perception of the surface and the imagination of the depth rhythms into a single, but tense, span of human temporality.

Consciousness is not represented in the poem—a fountain is; but our experience of the poem brings a specifically qualified consciousness into being. We read the words and experience a quality.

Lastly, the Greek temple. As merely present to our perceiving consciousness, it is a heap of stones, arranged into spaces where the gods are called to dwell. What is at work here? The stones rise and so thrust their weight against the counterweight of the enclosing roof, all suspended on an impressing and impressed entablature. At one pole here, the earth from which the temple takes its rise to create the world in which the faithful reach out to their gods. Building such a temple was itself an invitation for the god to descend. From the near pole here to that further pole yonder, within the ambiguity of the here-there of human existence, a tension is created within which the work has come to be. The building "expresses" the religious function of joining the spiritual to the one material world.

Earth and *world* are metaphors for expressing surface and expressed depth of a work of art. Whether they are the actual earthly stones of a Greek temple and the religious life they are arranged to accommodate, the kinaesthetic images of eidetic phonological sequences and the visual imagery presented through them, or the patterns of space, color, and line and the utilitarian world of an absent peasant, the earth and the world of a work of art, the surface and the depth of an expression, are held together by a tension felt within the field of our intentional awareness.

But we had seen all this before—in Heidegger's description, given in *Being and Time,* of the dis-closedness of a human being's being-there, in a world.

How strange, then, that Heidegger should wonder aloud in his final section of *Being and Time* why the ontological problem of reality has always been posed in terms of consciousness and its objects. Consciousness is no thing, and it is not present to itself as the things of its world are; he had known that already from the beginning of his existential analytic. So when he asks, "What *positive* structure does the being of 'consciousness' have, if reification remains inappropriate to it?"[36] he asked a purely rhetorical question, not one whose answer will lead us to an understanding of the meaning of Being in general.

If our aesthetic experiences of works of art reveal any ontological structures, they do so in the same way as any other of our ontic experiences, by exhibiting them in a concretely significant worldly context: not by representing them on the surface of some artwork, but by engaging the reader's ontological structures in the stretch between its here and its there, in that felt tension of being in its world that is brought to discourse in literary criticism. After all, no her-

meneutical interpretation has been completed until the thing interpreted is brought home again: until the original forestructural complex of human disclosedness has been modified to incorporate the
novel significance of the literary world.

The very purpose of an existential analytic is to dis-cover those
structures that make possible our existence in a world. Until the
existentials of the analytic are seen at work within the context of an
actual ontic experience of one sort or another, whether aesthetic,
practical, or theoretical, the explanatory loop which would complete
the hermeneutical process is left unclosed—even if those existentials
have been previously grounded in the temporality of human being.
To serve as an explanation, the abstracted structures of human temporality must be made concrete in time. Hegel had already reminded
us of this in the conclusion to his *Phenomenology of Spirit:* the
Absolute Idea can only manifest itself in history.[37]

Works of art temporalize and ultimately historize the being of
those humans who care enough to enter the world of the arts in their
own due times. This they can do as easily as by reading a literary
text. If the source of a literary work of art, like the painting, poem,
and temple whose working had been explained by Heidegger in "Der
Ursprung," is the writer's projection of a significance, it becomes
preserved in the lives of the community of readers who continually
reinvest that work with its living significance in the ongoing history
of our culture.

BASING THEMSELVES on another Heideggerian essay, "Die Zeit
des Weltbildes,"[38] a number of literary critics have discovered that
Heidegger's philosophy has heralded a new historical epoch in the
history of culture. Modern philosophers and modern prose-fiction
writers have occupied themselves with the task of presenting a picture
of the world, a general world view or hypothesis that would represent
within its projection the truth of the real world. That time changed
when Hegel's most ambitious philosophical world view—perhaps
the most grandiose ever—left philosophers with no place else to go:
his Absolute Idea encompassed all fragmentary human experiences,
from the mere act of pointing that is our sensuous certainty, to
consciousness of higher orders through self-consciousness and reason
to the spirit, where in its absolute form there is nothing left for the
notion to grasp but itself as developing from its beginnings.

But since history is the forum wherein the Spirit must reveal itself, there remained only history, and the temporality that temporalizes itself into history, as the object of philosophical study. The only thing lacking for that study was the ontological foundation for all the historiological, or humane, sciences, and Heidegger had written *Being and Time* in part to fulfill that lack.

According to "postmodernist" critics, however, not only have times changed and with them the "metaphysics" of the modern world, but postmodernist writers have begun to perpetuate a similar change, building their works without benefit of a convenient philosophical idea—although one of their number most often cited as fitting the bill propagated the notion that a philosophical idea was a device, available to any writer, for giving a structure to his literary world.[39] Others have eschewed plots and characterization altogether; such is the case for *le nouveau roman* of recent French history.[40] Robbe-Grillet's technique is to let the "represented objectivities" of his literary worlds present themselves as they engage his narrator's consciousness. Still others seem to be looking for ways not to tell a story, giving up the intent to fabricate the "supreme fiction," the better to involve themselves in the process of generating a fiction about fiction itself; such is the "metafiction" of contemporary writers like Barth and Barthelme,[41] for whom significance is not to be found beyond the text but in the act of constructing (or reconstructing) it.

But literary worlds have never been mere representations of the real world, despite the socialist realistic efforts to make them appear such. And if time were of the essence for a true postmodernist writer, no one has ever succeeded better than William Faulkner, in *As I Lay Dying,* to depict the time of the real world through the overlapping conscious moments of individual temporalities. That work is carried out in a form of temporal cubism in whose intersecting moments of subjective temporality there is depicted a naturalistic time line in which the courtship, marriage, family life, infidelity, adulterated family life, agony, death, and ultimate burial of Addie Bundren may be traced; but the only way to get at it is through the multiple points of view Faulkner has established through the interior monologues of his several characters. If it were a visual rather than a literary work, one would be tempted to say it sparkled like a diamond.

No matter which time is involved, the objectively universal time of the real world or the subjectively personal time of a fictional character's consciousness, or both together, if those times are only represented in the literary universe, they are not of the essence; for the simple reason that within the context of significance set up in such universes, all represented objectivities, and any hypothesis making a single idea of them all, are reduced to the role of counters of that context.

Such counters have no absolute significance and are recognizable only as a difference from other counters; and the significance that accrues to any of these counters is only by virtue of the relationships obtaining between them. Such, we remember, was the worlding of a Heideggerian world; the whole is what is ultimately significant, not the part, whether we are speaking of sentences, whole fictional works, or Hegel's absolute idea.

If the being of a literary work is the working of its counters, and if these in general may be grouped into two classes, surface and depth, *earth* and *world*, or signifier and signified, the temporality exhibited in works of art is not something represented, it is of the order of experience: an experience that registers within consciousness the tension of the pull between counters tending toward closure. That is what gets expressed in the notion of *an* experience: a single, qualitative slice of our conscious temporalities. The Heidegger of *Being and Time* called such a moment of our conscious lives *Befindlichkeit*, our being in tune with the way our worlds turn.

For this reason, those postmodern critics who claim Heidegger for their patron leave us with a quandary. It is admirable to seek a mode of criticism befitting the literary productions of our own age. But to refer to one's work as "postmodern" is to situate it with respect to the modern; and if the highest development of "modernist" criticism was formalism, then postmodernistic criticism should be postformalistic.

The irony of the situation is that in situating themselves within the development of contemporary culture as historically differentiated from their formalist predecessors, they view their own critical work in the same light as those preformalist critics had viewed the significance of works of art—as historically determined. This is not to say that the postmodernists have retreated to the galloping historicism of the pre–New Critical days, only that their call for a postformalist criticism needs stronger evidence than that presented for anyone to be convinced of the need for a change.[42] But change there was.

Structuralism was perhaps the first of the postmodernist schools, and it was devised to overcome the formalist overemphasis on represented worlds. It proposed a rule for gauging the signification of signs based upon the relationship between a set of signifieds within the history of a language that could be considered either synchronically or diachronically—upon a single act of speech if required to (synchronically), or upon the development of the language in which that act took place (diachronically)—but that did not depend upon a consciousness to interpret the relationship. The plan yielded signification in abundance but without any conscious significance. So. . . .

Structuralism gave way to poststructuralism, another of the schools touted to replace the older New Criticism that had taught us all how to read. The most vocal spokesman for this movement, the Frenchman Jacques Derrida, was moved to reject both formalism and structuralism on the grounds that both these earlier schools had suffered what Heidegger called the failure of the metaphysics of presence, that is, from the assumption that something is real insofar as it is made present to some observing consciousness.[43]

Not only did a set of signifieds not become present as a signification for the signifiers we read, not only were they not made present by our perception of the words of a text, but these signifiers themselves, which were at best blips on a preconscious screen, left only traces that could not be fine-tuned into a clear image, because behind every conscious moment of our existence there was only that outward bound of an unconscious, even prehistorical past, and before it, only the infinite tasks of future interpretation.

Thus, if Heidegger was right to replace Husserl's notion of consciousness as transcendental Ego with his description of a human being's disclosedness, he failed to make clear the extent of the signification of his discovery. In his own attempts to show how an artist created a world to allow Being to come to a stand within it, he too was a victim of the metaphysics of presence; Being, the transcendental pure and simple, cannot be brought to phenomenological intuition.

What the reader does who has learned the lesson of Heidegger's ontology is to replace a set of signifiers, not by a set of signifieds, but with another set of signifiers. The process of literary interpretation is the substitution of a new, critical text for the one the reader deconstructs in his reading. There is no surprise here: the highest point of human disclosedness is the achievement of creative discourse. But to the structural difference between the signifiers of our language, Derrida added a temporal deferral—an indefinite deferral of meaning, since for every written text there is another constructed to be further deconstructed.

The idea is not new for Americans, for American philosophers have been aware of it since Charles Peirce's theory of signs: what holds together a sign-vehicle serving as *representamen* and its object as represented is an *interpretant,* which itself may become an object for another sign, and will for that reason call for another interpretant.[44]

What happens to the text in this series of deconstructive interpretations? It virtually disappears; thus, Derrida:

> There is no present text in general, and there is not even a past present text, a text which is past as having been present. The text is not thinkable in an originary or modified form of presence. . . . Everything begins with reproduction.[45]

Or, as Heidegger had said, everything rebegins with our repetition of a past that steadfastly anticipates an authentic future; that is, our interpretations must be our own, based upon our own past experiences, upon our own present points of view, and upon our own projections of a future state of affairs.

The ultimate question is whether our aesthetic enjoyment must take place and time in the play of substitutive signifiers, or in the return to the significance of a worlding world, which behind any play of signifiers makes it possible for there to be anything signified. In other words, it has as yet to be shown that Heidegger's transcendental turn, looking for the possible in the actual, will not turn the trick.

What Heidegger had insisted upon retaining is the closure of a living being's personal world, since that world is determined by a context of involvements that are not open-ended but closed in the finite projection of a human existence for the sake of which those involvements are determined to be what they are by the self-projecting self. The human personal world does not appear as an object of perception; it is lived as a significance. And it is this significance that gets interpreted, in art and in science, in religion and in philosophy, each interpreting what is given according to a method appropriate to its own peculiar aims. And unless such significance were given, there could be no inquiry of any kind: artists would have nothing to express; scientists or philosophers, nothing to explain.

We need not linger too long on the ground for a human being's knowledge of its being in the world; it is preontological, and it is felt. And the same process of interpretation that links the preontological with the ontological links feeling with expression. And neither can be said to precede the other as they are "equiprimordial" structures of human disclosedness. To claim that we cannot be conscious of the quality of a present moment because consciousness itself cannot be made present is a simple fallacy of equivocation: true, no global conscious stream is ever present to one of its blipping moments, but to claim we are not aware of the blip is to equate the moment with the stream.

In the same way, to claim that we cannot be conscious of a present moment because each of our conscious moments is only one element of a tripartite Freudian psyche commits the same fallacy. Most assuredly the present form of human consciousness is an evolved characteristic of our being; [46] but how human beings were in their worlds prior to being conscious has no bearing on how one feels now, in this situation. The only closures we have to fear are those that are not a part of our personal worlds in their current temporalizing structures.

If there are no ideal texts, no finally closed texts, because every written text is a physical object and physical objects are present to us only in our perceptions of them, so be it; the texts we do possess give us ample grounds—even so—for entering into the literary universes they project. We have known for a long time, in phenomenological circles, that there are no objects-in-themselves hidden behind the profiles of the real objects we perceive. Criticism begins with the same sort of physical encounter: we see the marks we interpret as words that intend meanings and objects and images. As we attend to the tensions set up in this intentional field, we begin to experience the expressiveness of the object structured there.

In Heideggerian terms, that expressiveness is of the strife between the earth and the world of the expression. Criticism that is both phenomenological and structural attempts to bring to consciousness what is expressed in the literary universe: the felt tension of its closing counters. Hermeneutics is the tool for expanding the levels of signification, for calling attention to those structures of experience that permit the tension between earth and world—between the surface and the depth counters—to unfold.

Heidegger can claim that in this way we are merely letting Being come to stand in the region of our openness to the world, but that is what he claims for every perception, for every human act, whether aesthetic or not. It is for this reason that I find *Being and Time* more useful for aesthetics than his "Der Ursprung des Kunstwerkes." Although the latter is specifically about the creation and "preservation" of works of art, the former is more explicit on how this all comes about.

There are only two things to remember: first, that every hermeneutical expansion of a preontological significance must be brought back to the ontical circumstances that generated the ontological inquiry; and second, that the being of the investigator is modified in the process of making the expansion: that stage of knowledge to which it attains is different from that with which the inquiry had begun. Although what is known in its immediacy is the same in the two stages of the inquiry, the only change is from a status of an implicit to another of an explicit understanding, from a feeling undergone to a feeling understood.

As a clue for the aesthetic appropriation of the Heideggerian hermeneutic of disclosedness, then, a critic need only heed two prescriptions. First, let the work happen; read it. That will give you a feeling of the tension established within an intentional field. Call that a cognitive feeling, and do not apologize because it is yours; associate it with the preontological comprehension you have of your own being. Second, interpret the structures within that intentional field that govern this expressiveness. This process will end with a cognition that is felt, a stage of awareness equivalent to the ontic-ontological priority of the human being, exhibited in this very act.

Our postcritical awareness of the literary work is of its expressiveness under the control of its functioning counters—in Heidegger's terms, of the working of the work—where that working has been made explicit by an interpretation of the text, whatever its inner metaphysical constitution may be, and whatever the state of its outer physical imperfection.

In this way the circle is closed; and therein lies the closure of the work considered in its being as a functional world. If an interpretation of a text only brings us home again, what could we possibly have to fear from it? We interpret literary texts in a circle from a preinterpreted worldly experience of a text to a postanalytical comprehension of its worlding significance. And the long voyage into that world is only crowned by the safe return home again.

And to end this piece on a poetic note, remembering that we all live poetically on this earth, I shall cite that one line of DuBellay that celebrates all safe returns home,

Heureux qui, comme Ulysse, a fait un beau voyage.

The voyager returns to his point of departure, finding his wife there, still blooming and faithful, only to have his solitary being-in canceled yet uplifted in their renewed being-with each other.

Something similar transpires between the writer and the reader when they both know what they are about and, as consenting adults, enjoy the intercourse.

NOTES

Introduction

1. Martin Heidegger's *Sein und Zeit* was first published in spring 1927 as a volume in the *Jahrbuch für Phänomenologie und phänomenologische Forschung*, Band 8, edited by Edmund Husserl.
2. Jean-Paul Sartre's *L'Être et le néant: Essai d'ontologie phénoménologique* appeared in the collection *Bibliothèque des Idées.*
3. See Maurice Merleau-Ponty, *Eloge de la philosophie*, pp. 77–78.
4. See Jean-Paul Sartre, *L'Existentialisme est un humanisme.*
5. The lecture was first given before the "Club Maintenant" and later repeated in a private reading where his opponents were allowed to respond to his position. The originally published text of *L'Existentialisme est un humanisme* was derived from both these sources. See Sartre, *L'Existentialisme*, p. 143.
6. For Heidegger's original statement concerning the *Seinsvergessenheit* of our day, see his introduction to *Sein und Zeit*, chap. 1; for Sartre's "On ne fait pas à l'être sa part," see *L'Être*, p. 27.
7. Martin Heidegger, *Being and Time*, translated by John Macquarrie and Edward Robinson, p. 24 n. 3; p. 68 n. 3.
8. *Man and World* is edited by John Anderson and Joseph J. Kockelmans (Pennsylvania State University) and Calvin O. Schrag (Purdue University) and published by *International Philosophical Review Associates.* The first number appeared in February 1968.
9. *Studies in Phenomenology and Existential Philosophy*, general editor, James M. Edie; later transferred to the Indiana University Press.

10. Rudolf K. Bultmann, *Essays, Philosophical and Theological.*
11. Paul Tillich, *Systematic Theology.*
12. Paul Tillich, *The Courage to Be.*
13. Rollo May et al., eds., *Existence.*
14. Medard Boss, *Psychoanalysis and Daseinsanalysis.*
15. To wit, *Journal of Existential Psychiatry (Journal of Existentialism), Review of Existential Psychology and Psychiatry,* and *Review of Phenomenological Psychology.*
16. Most of Sartre's essays on American novelists have been assembled into his critical series, *Situations.*
17. Jean-Paul Sartre, *What Is Literature?* which is the greater part of *Situations* 2:20.
18. Jean-Paul Sartre, *Baudelaire; Saint Genet comédien et martyr; L'Idiot de la famille,* tr. Carol Gosman as *The Family Idiot: Gustave Flaubert, 1821–1857,* vol. 1.
19. Martin Heidegger, *Erläuterungen zu Hölderlins Dichtung,* pp. 39–40.
20. Martin Heidegger, *Holzwege,* pp. 7–68.
21. For the special reprint issue of *boundary 2* on Heidegger and literature, see William Spanos, ed., *Martin Heidegger and the Question of Literature: Toward a Postmodern Literary Hermeneutics.*
22. Martin Heidegger, "Der Ursprung des Kunstwerkes," p. 44 ff.
23. Ferdinand de Saussure, *Cours de linguistique générale.*
24. See Jacques Derrida's attempts in *L'Écriture et la différence* to "go beyond" the structuralist techniques of Roland Barthes in *S/Z.* For a readable secondary account of Derrida's "deconstructive" criticism, see Christopher Norris, *Deconstruction, Theory and Practice.*
25. The groundwork for Derrida's theory and practice of criticism was laid down in his *Of Grammatology.*
26. See Norris, *Deconstruction, Theory and Practice.*
27. See Hans-Georg Gadamer, *Wahrheit und Methode;* and "The Universality of the Hermeneutical Problem," in his *Philosophical Hermeneutics.*
28. See Paul Ricoeur, *The Conflict of Interpretations;* and *Interpretation Theory: Discourse and the Surplus of Meaning.*
29. See Paul Ricoeur, "Existence and Hermeneutics" in *The Conflict of Interpretations,* pp. 3–24.
30. David Hume, *A Treatise of Human Nature,* vol. 1, book 1, part 1.
31. See W. J. Richardson, S. J., *Heidegger through Phenomenology to Thought,* passim.
32. See Albert Hofstadter's translation of Heidegger, *The Basic Problems of Phenomenology,* the lexicon, pp. 348–50.

Chapter 1

1. Heidegger, *On Time and Being.*
2. Heidegger, *Die Grundprobleme der Phänomenologie* (1975), translated by Albert Hofstadler as *The Basic Problems of Phenomenology* (1982). The

four problems explained in this text—Kant's claim that being is not a real predicate, the medieval distinction between being as both essence and existence, the modern distinction between natural and moral entities *(res extensa* and *res cogitans),* the "being" of the copula, followed by Aristotle's doctrine of time—were actually covered in a course at Marburg in 1927, when Heidegger was asked to produce a publication to be considered for his chair at Freiburg.

3. Heidegger, *Sein und Zeit,* p. 477. Cf. Saint Augustine, *Confessions,* pp. 251–69.
4. See Paul Ricoeur, *The Conflict of Interpretations;* and Heidegger, *Being and Time,* p. 8.
5. See Edmund Husserl, *Ideas I,* pp. 57–59.
6. "Gott ist, aber er existiert nicht" occurs as an example to distinguish existence and being in *Was ist Metaphysik?,* p. 15. For Heidegger's account of philosophy as an "onto-theo-logical" conception of metaphysics, see *Identität und Differenz,* pp. 35–73.
7. For an introduction to the "death of God" theology, see T. J. J. Altizer and William Hamilton, *Radical Theology and the Death of God.* Heidegger discusses Nietzsche's dictum "Gott ist tot," in his "Nietzsches Wort 'Gott ist tot,' " in *Holzwege,* pp. 193–247.
8. See my introduction, pp. 10–12, above.
9. See Heidegger, "Die Zeit des Weltbildes," in *Holzwege,* pp. 69–104.
10. See Heidegger, "Der Ursprung des Kunstwerkes," in *Holzwege,* pp. 7–68.

Chapter 2

1. Heidegger, *Sein und Zeit,* p. 41.
2. Heidegger, *Being and Time,* trans. Macquarrie and Robinson, p. 65.
3. Heidegger, *Sein und Zeit,* p. 41.
4. Samuel Beckett, *Molloy, Malone Dies, The Unnamable,* p. 401.
5. Heidegger, *Sein und Zeit,* p. 56.
6. Ibid., p. 135.
7. See William H. Werkmeister, *Kant's Silent Decade,* pp. 123–24.
8. See Heidegger, *Being and Time,* trans. Macquarrie and Robinson, p. 584.
9. Heidegger, *Sein und Zeit,* p. 4.
10. Ibid., p. 111.
11. Ibid., p. 115; translation mine.
12. Heidegger, *Being and Time,* trans. Macquarrie and Robinson, p. 584.
13. Heidegger, *Sein und Zeit,* p. 101.
14. Ibid., p. 321.
15. Ibid., p. 229.
16. Ibid., p. 38, and n. 5.
17. Ibid., p. 362.
18. Heidegger, *Being and Time,* trans. Macquarrie and Robinson, p. 511.
19. Heidegger, *Sein und Zeit,* pp. 231 ff.
20. Ibid., pp. 232–35.

21. Ibid., p. 334.
22. Ibid., p. 17; translation mine.
23. Samuel Beckett, *Waiting for Godot.*
24. Samuel Beckett, *Comment c'est.*
25. Edmund Husserl, *Logical Investigations,* pp. 463–65.
26. See John Dewey, "The Need for a Recovery of Philosophy."
27. Heidegger, *Sein und Zeit,* p. 41.
28. See pp. 13–15, 27–29 above.
29. Heidegger, *Sein und Zeit,* p. 42; translation mine.
30. Ibid., p. 52.
31. Ibid., p. 54.
32. Ibid., pp. 56, 57; Heidegger, *Being and Time,* trans. Macquarrie and Robinson, p. 83.
33. Heidegger, *Being and Time,* trans. Macquarrie and Robinson, p. 83; Heidegger, *Sein und Zeit,* p. 57.

Chapter 3

1. See Ludwig Wittgenstein, *Tractatus Logico-Philosophicus,* 1–1.21.
2. Heidegger, *Sein und Zeit,* p. 67.
3. The expression is taken from a later essay by Heidegger, who wishes to express the nonsubstantive conception of a human world, as a process involving the system of references constitutive of the phenomenal "wherein" of the understanding that projects its own completion. See Heidegger, *Vom Wesen des Grundes,* p. 44.
4. Heidegger, *Being and Time,* trans. Macquarrie and Robinson, p. 114.
5. Heidegger, *Sein und Zeit,* p. 85.
6. See pp. 44–46 above.
7. See John Dewey, *Reconstruction in Philosophy,* pp. 74–75; and *Theory of Valuation,* in the *Encyclopedia of Unified Science,* vol. 2, no. 4.
8. Heidegger, *Being and Time,* trans. Macquarrie and Robinson, pp. 115–16.
9. Heidegger, *Sein und Zeit,* p. 86; translation mine.
10. See p. 56 above.
11. Heidegger, *Sein und Zeit,* p. 94.
12. Heidegger, *Sein und Zeit,* sec. 21, pp. 98–100; see also pp. 25–27 above.
13. Heidegger, *Being and Time,* trans. Macquarrie and Robinson, p. 138 n. 2.

Chapter 4

1. Arthur Koestler, *Darkness at Noon,* pp. 173 ff.
2. Jean-Paul Sartre, "La Transcendance de l'Ego."
3. One of the clearest expressions of this phenomenon is that of George H. Mead; see his *Mind, Self and Society from the Point of View of a Social Behaviorist.*
4. Heidegger, *Sein und Zeit,* sec. 27, p. 126; translation mine.

5. See Jean-Paul Sartre, *L'Être et le néant*, pp. 310–68, 431–84.

6. See Wilhelm von Humboldt, *Gesammelte Schriften*, Band 6, Abschnitt 1, pp. 304–30, cited by Heidegger, *Sein und Zeit*, p. 119.

7. See Heidegger, *Being and Time*, trans. Macquarrie and Robinson, their n. 4, p. 157.

8. See Heidegger, *Sein und Zeit*, p. 126, translation mine.

9. Ibid., p. 128, translation mine.

10. See Ernest Hemingway's short story, "A Clean, Well-Lighted Place," for a moving "existential" interpretation of consciousness as light.

11. Heidegger, *Sein und Zeit*, sections 29 and 30.

12. Heidegger, *Sein und Zeit*, p. 140, translation mine.

13. See Paul Ricoeur, *La Métaphore vive* (Paris: Editions du Seuil, 1975).

14. See Virgil, *The Aeneid*, book 2.

15. Heidegger, *Being and Time*, trans. Macquarrie and Robinson, their n. 2, p. 42. Although "forfeiture" captures the relationship between authenticity and inauthenticity in the choice of an impersonal world, the text plays on the various senses of falling to be associated with his usage and those to be excluded from it so much that to avoid using the latter terms seems perverse.

16. See pp. 95–97 above.

17. See Heidegger, *Being and Time*, trans. Macquarrie and Robinson, p. 191 n. 2.

18. Heidegger's preference for a genre of poetic composition seems to have been for Hölderlin's rather self-conscious "poetry to the second degree," that is, poetry about the writing of poetry, which dramatizes the plight of a poet in the throes of writing. See his *Erläuterungen zu Hölderlins Dichtung*, pp. 31–47.

19. Heidegger, *Sein und Zeit*, p. 169; translation mine.

20. For an effective creation of a scene depicting a mood determined by curiosity, ambiguity, and idle chatter see T. S. Eliot's *The Cocktail Party*. Eliot, of course, would have preferred to hear that his verse constituted an "objective correlative" for the feeling expressed through the incidents of his play.

Chapter 5

1. Heidegger, *Sein und Zeit*, p. 212; translation mine.

2. Ibid., p. 42; translation mine; see also pp. 12–14.

3. René Descartes, *Discours de la méthode* in *Œuvres et lettres de Descartes*, pp. 121–79.

4. Unlike Heidegger, Sartre selects shame as the grounding phenomenon for our knowledge of others; see Jean-Paul Sartre, *Being and Nothingness*, pp. 252–302.

5. Heidegger, *Sein und Zeit*, p. 190 n. 1.

6. For his objections to having been classified a "humanist" by Sartre, see his *Über den Humanismus*, pp. 10–21.

7. Heidegger, *Sein und Zeit,* pp. 196–98.
8. Herder's poem was entitled "Das Kind der Sorge" (Suphan XXIX, 75). Heidegger's source: K. Burdach, "Faust und die Sorge," *Deutsche Viertel-jahrschrift für Literaturwissenschaft und Geistesgeschichte* (1:1923,1 ff).
9. For the a priori character of all existentials, see pp. 46–49 above.

Chapter 6

1. Immanuel Kant, *Kritik der reinen Vernunft,* pp. 273–83.
2. See David Hume, *Treatise of Human Nature,* vol. 1, part 4, conclusion.
3. For the traditional opposition between skepticism and animal faith, see George Santayana's work by that title in *The Philosophy of George Santayana,* pp. 376–450.
4. See G. E. Moore, "Refutation of Idealism," in *Philosophical Studies,* pp. 1–30.
5. For example, see Edmund Husserl, *Ideas,* pp. 95–100.
6. Heidegger cites Wilhelm Dilthey's "Beiträge zur Lösung der Frage vom Ursprung unseres Glaubens an die Realität der Aussenwelt und seinem Recht" (1890) in *Gesammelte Schriften* 1:90 ff; and Max Scheler's lecture "Die Formen des Wissens und die Bildung" (1925), later published as a part of "Die Wissensformen und die Gesellschaft," in *Gesammelte Werke.* Scheler's "Erkenntnis und Arbeit" (pp. 233 ff) covers the same subject; finally, division 6 of "Die Wissensformen" (p. 455 et seq.) exposits Scheler's differences from Dilthey, as conceived by the former.
7. See Maine de Biran, *Mémoire sur la décomposition de la pensée* (Paris: Presses Universitaires de France, 1952), pp. 119–63.
8. Heidegger, *Sein und Zeit,* p. 210.
9. See Heidegger's letter *Über den Humanismus,* in which he quarrels with Sartre's classification of him as an "atheistic existentialist." One of their differences, he maintained, was the untranslatability of the German "Es gibt" into the French "Il y a."
10. Heidegger, *Sein und Zeit,* p. 212; translation mine.
11. H. Diels, *Die Fragmente der Vorsokratiker.*
12. See Heidegger, *Being and Time,* trans. Macquarrie and Robinson, pp. 256; 493 n. xx.
13. Aristotle *De Interpretatione,* 1. 16a.6. Macquarrie and Robinson note that Heidegger's quotation is inexact (*Being and Time,* p. 493 n. xxix).

Chapter 7

1. See Heidegger, *Sein und Zeit,* pp. 256 ff. He slides from the certainty of death as a phenomenon (*Gewißheit des Todes*) to the state of mind we would call "conviction" (*Gewißsein als Seinsart des Daseins*). The next step

to conscience is taken as the attestation of authenticity in the choice of a Self; cf. chap. 2, division 2.
2. Ibid., sec. 46.
3. Heidegger's judgment on theology and theodicy as interpretations of death should have sufficed for avoiding the kind of assessment made by George Steiner *(Heidegger,* pp. 86 ff) that Heidegger's ontology constitutes a meta-theology inspired by a pietistic background and his studies in medieval scholasticism and Luther's doctrinal reforms of the Roman Church.
4. See Evelyn Waugh, *The Loved One.*
5. I owe this account to Pierre D'Arcangues, *Le Destin de L'Espagne,* p. 58.
6. The motion picture by Herbert Vesely, entitled *Nicht Mehr Fliehen,* is constructed on the basis of Heideggerian existentialism. For a review, see my *Art and Existence,* pp. 297–304.
7. Heidegger, *Sein und Zeit,* p. 259; translation mine.
8. Sartre, *Being and Nothingness,* pp. 67–70.
9. Steiner, *Heidegger,* pp. 16–23, 169 ff.
10. *The Cassell's New German and English Dictionary* (New York: Funk and Wagnalls Co., 1939), p. 524.
11. Heidegger, *Being and Time,* trans. Macquarrie and Robinson, pp. 312 ff.
12. Steiner, *Heidegger,* p. 86.
13. Heidegger, *Sein und Zeit,* p. 287; trans. mine.
14. See Harvey G. Cox and Joseph Fletcher, eds., *The Situation Ethics Debate.*
15. See figure 6.
16. See Werner Marx, *Heidegger und die Tradition,* p. 17.

Chapter 8

1. Heidegger, *Sein und Zeit,* p. 306; translation mine.
2. See Kant, *Critique of Pure Reason,* pp. 213–30.
3. Heidegger, *Sein und Zeit,* p. 321; Heidegger's emphasis.
4. See Sartre, *Being and Nothingness,* pp. 102–5.

Chapter 9

1. Samuel Beckett, *Waiting for Godot.*
2. Søren Kierkegaard, *Philosophical Fragments,* pp. 30 ff.
3. Martin Heidegger, *The Basic Problems of Phenomenology,* translated by Albert Hofstadter, pp. 260, 306–7, 353.
4. See Søren Kierkegaard, *Repetition.*
5. Heidegger, *Sein und Zeit,* pp. 338–39.
6. Ibid., p. 344.
7. Ibid., pp. 362–63.
8. Ibid., p. 366.
9. Ibid., p. 368.
10. Shakespeare, *Macbeth,* 5.5.

Chapter 10

1. See the description of the Heideggerian style as a harmony between sense and form of expression, in which the technical aspects of the thought and the various shades of meaning are integrated into a formal unity possessing a kind of internal necessity, in George Steiner, *Heidegger*, p. 103. More familiar with literary objects than with the intricacies of philosophical reasoning, Steiner expresses his appreciation of the Heideggerian style in aesthetic terms, without demonstrating his claim. In my own terms for explaining the stylistic facts of the Heideggerian expression, I have throughout this commentary been attempting to show how the content of the treatise has been determined by the hermeneutical methodology.
2. Heidegger, *Sein und Zeit*, p. 384.
3. Ibid., p. 379.
4. In this way, Heidegger distinguishes between his own methodology and the method of "existential analysis" used by practicing psychotherapists. The difference is between the purely ontological (Heidegger) and the ontic-ontological analyses of the therapists (Boss, Binswanger).
5. Steiner seems obsessed with Heidegger's "Nazism" (*Heidegger*, pp. 153–66).
6. Heidegger, *Being and Time*, trans. Macquarrie and Robinson, p. 436.
7. Heidegger, *Sein und Zeit*, p. 385.
8. "*Nur Seiendes, das wesenhaft in seinem Sein zukünftig ist, so daß es frei für seinen Tod an ihm zerschellend auf sein faktisches Da sich zurückwerfen lassen kann, das heißt nur Seiendes, das als zukünftiges gleichursprünglich gewesend ist, kann, sich selbst die ererbte Möglichkeit überliefernd, die eigene Geworfenheit übernehmen und augenblicklich sein für 'seine Zeit'* " (ibid).
9. See Friedrich Nietzsche, "Nutzen und Nachteil der Historie für das Leben."
10. This was the generative notion of Hans-Georg Gadamer's monumental *Wahrheit und Methode*, which develops a hermeneutical methodology for textual interpretation, aesthetic appreciation, and the writing of history.
11. See Wilhelm Dilthey, *Briefwechsel zwischen Wilhelm Dilthey und dem Grafen Paul Yorck von Wartenburg*, 1877–97.

Chapter 11

1. See the opening gambit of Beckett's *Endgame*.
2. See *The Sound and the Fury*. The practical man referred to is Faulkner's character Jason Compson IV.
3. See ch. 6, pp. 135–40.
4. See ch. 6, pp. 140–42.
5. Heidegger, *Sein und Zeit*, p. 421.
6. Aristotle, *De Physica*, Δ 11. 219b1ff.
7. Plato, *Timaeus*, 37d; Heidegger, *Sein und Zeit*, p. 423.
8. For a similar derivation of the characteristics of "scientific" time, see A.

Cornelius Benjamin, *An Introduction to the Philosophy of Science*, pp. 281–96.

9. Aristotle, *De Physica*, Δ 14.223a–25.
10. St. Augustine, *Confessions*, X.1.26.
11. G. W. F. Hegel, *Encylopädie der philosophischen Wissenschaften im Grundrisse*, addendum to sec. 254.
12. Immanuel Kant, *Critique of Pure Reason*, pp. 21–43.
13. Ibid., pp. 100–109. See also Heidegger's *Kant and the Problem of Metaphysics*, which treats of Kant's doctrine of the schematism of the imagination as his principal contribution to the history of ontology. This book seems to have replaced division 2, part 1 of the originally planned *Sein und Zeit*.
14. Hegel, *Encyklopädie*, sec. 254.
15. For the development of consciousness according to the laws of the dialectic, see Hegel, *Phenomenology of Mind*.
16. Heidegger, *Sein und Zeit*, p. 430.
17. See Heidegger, *Kant and the Problem of Metaphysics*, passim.
18. Hegel, *Encyklopädie*, sec. 258.

Chapter 12

1. For an overview of Heidegger's change in philosophical style, see William J. Richardson, S. J., *Heidegger through Phenomenology to Thought*, with a foreword by M. Heidegger, pp. viii–xxiii.
2. See Rudolf Carnap, *Logical Syntax of Language*, pp. 277 ff.
3. Heidegger, *Sein und Zeit*, pp. 8–11.
4. Ibid., p. 9.
5. Ibid., p. v; translation mine.
6. Ibid., p. 8.
7. For an example, consider any work by W. V. O. Quine, whose doctrine of "logic without ontology" turns out upon closer inspection to be nothing more than a logicized ontology. See, in particular, *Word and Object*.
8. The claim that the *Basic Problems* would come to replace *Being and Time* was made by one of the reviewers of Hofstadter's translation of the *Basic Problems;* see the blurb by Hubert L. Dreyfus on the back flap of the dustcover.
9. See Heidegger, *Sein und Zeit*, pp. 27–39.
10. Ibid., p. 13; translation mine.
11. Ibid., p. 14; translation mine.
12. See Thomas Langan, *The Meaning of Heidegger: A Critical Study of an Existentialist Phenomenology*.
13. See *On Time and Being*.
14. Heidegger, *Sein und Zeit*, p. 37; translation mine.
15. See my discussion of this problem, above, pp. 27–29, 137–40.
16. Heidegger, *Sein und Zeit*, p. 37; translation mine.
17. Ibid., pp. 39–40.

18. Ibid., pp. 37–38.
19. Ibid., p. 406; translation mine.
20. Ibid., p. 436.
21. Ibid., p. 437.
22. See Richardson, *Heidegger through Phenomenology to Thought.*
23. As seen by George Steiner, *Heidegger,* pp. 19–20.
24. See Aristotle's *De Metaphysica,* p. 732.
25. Richardson, *Heidegger through Phenomenology to Thought.*
26. Heidegger develops this theme in *Gelassenheit.*
27. See Richardson, *Heidegger through Phenomenology to Thought,* pp. viii–xxiii.
28. See Heidegger, *Vorträge und Aufsätze,* p. 178.
29. See Heidegger, *"Das Ding,"* in *Vorträge und Aufsätze,* p. 176.
30. See Heidegger, *What Is Metaphysics?,* pp. 338–39.
31. For Heidegger's use of the device, see Heidegger, *Zur Seinsfrage,* pp. 5, 30–31; for Derrida's adaption of it, Jacques Derrida, *Of Grammatology,* pp. 23, 44.
32. Heidegger, *Zur Seinsfrage,* pp. 5, 30, 31, 34, 35, 41, 43.
33. See Heidegger, *Sein und Zeit,* p. v.
34. Although Heidegger has written commentaries on G. Trakl, R.-M. Rilke, Stefan George, Johannes Christian Friederich, Hölderlin, and others, his model for " the poet's poet" is Hölderlin. See his *Erläuterung zu Hölderlins Dichtung.*
35. *Unterwegs zur Sprache* is the masterwork of the later Heidegger; the text gives the clearest picture of the philosopher living in "the house of Being" (pp. 90, 166).
36. Ibid., p. 12.
37. Jean-Paul Sartre, *Being and Nothingness,* pp. 433 ff.
38. Rudolf K. Bultmann, *Essays, Philosophical and Theological.*
39. Paul Tillich, *Systematic Theology.*
40. For an explanation of Boss's and Binswanger's adaptation of the existential analysis, see Rollo May et al., eds., *Existence;* for Carl Rogers's, see his *On Becoming a Person.*
41. Hans-Georg Gadamer, *Truth and Method.*
42. Derrida, *Of Grammatology.*

Chapter 13

1. References to Heidegger's *Sein und Zeit* continue to be to the eighth edition (Tübingen: Max Niemeyer Verlag, 1957). The depiction intended in this chapter is a result of the unfinished nature of the originally intended work conceived under the same title.
2. See Heidegger, *Sein und Zeit,* secs. 46–53.
3. Ibid., secs. 54–60.
4. Ibid., secs. 61–66.

5. See Aristotle, *De Physica*, Δ 11.219b1ff; and Heidegger, *Sein und Zeit*, p. 421.

6. For a literary exploitation of the properties of universal and personal time, see William Faulkner, *As I Lay Dying*, published with *The Sound and the Fury*.

7. For a scientific, yet speculative, account of the evolution of consciousness, see Julian Jaynes, *The Origin of Consciousness in the Breakdown of the Bicameral Mind*.

8. See Blaise Pascal, *Pensées*, p. 88.

9. Ibid., p. 130.

10. See G. W. F. Hegel, *Phenomenology of Mind*, pp. 251 ff.

11. Heidegger, *Sein und Zeit*, sec. 83.

12. See W. J. Richardson, S. J., *Heidegger through Phenomenology to Thought*.

13. See Heidegger, *Erläuterung zu Hölderlins Dichtung*, pp. 36–38.

14. See Heidegger, *Sein und Zeit*, part 1, chap. 5, secs. 28–38.

15. See Ludwig Wittgenstein, *Philosophical Investigations*, p. 103.

16. Heidegger, *Sein und Zeit*, sec. 13.

17. See my introduction, pp. 15–16.

18. Gilbert Ryle, *The Concept of Mind*, pp. 15–16.

19. Jean-Paul Sartre, *Being and Nothingness*, pp. 73–79.

20. Giambattista Vico, *The New Science*.

21. Heidegger, *Unterwegs zur Sprache*, p. 166; Samuel Beckett's novel *How It Is* depicts this human predicament.

22. See Plato's *Ion*.

23. See Roman Ingarden, *The Literary Work of Art*.

24. For the correlation between philosophical idea and novelistic technique, see Jean-Paul Sartre, "A propos de *'Le Bruit et la fureur'*: la temporalité chez Faulkner," pp. 70–81; and for an analysis of Robbe-Grillet's technique, see Victor Carrabino, "The French *Noveau Roman:* The Ultimate Expression of Impressionism."

25. E. F. Kaelin, "What Makes Philosophical Literature Philosophical?" *Analecta Husserliana*, xix (1985), 451–67.

26. See Sartre "A propos de *'Le Bruit et la fureur,'* " and Samuel Beckett, "Dante . . . Bruno. Vico . . Joyce."

27. See Ingarden, *The Literary Work of Art*.

28. Heidegger, *Sein und Zeit*, sec. 77.

29. The notion of expressiveness as a cognitive feeling was introduced into American aesthetics by W. T. Stace; see his *The Meaning of Beauty*.

30. Ingarden, *The Literary Work of Art*.

31. See the *Ion*, in which the rhapsode, given the choice of being either a scoundrel (liar) or inspired, opts for the latter.

32. Note that the subtitle of Croce's *Aesthetic* is "the science of expression and general linguistic."

33. Heidegger's foreword *(Vorbemerkung)* to the seventh edition of *Sein und Zeit*.

34. "Man has learned of many things / And named many of the gods / Since we are a dialogue / And can hear from one another." Hölderlin's poetic lines are found in his third verson of *"Versöhnender, der nimmergeglaubt,"* *Samtliche Werke*, vol. 2, 1, p. 137. See Heidegger, *Erläuterungen*, p. 39. A similar view on the function of ancient poetry is maintained by Jaynes, *The Origin of Consciousness*, pp. 374–75. In Jaynes's version, however, poetry is the voice of the gods speaking to men, whose "bicameral mind" hallucinated the existence of the gods in the first place.
35. See Heidegger, "Der Ursprung des Kunstwerkes," in *Holzwege*, 4th ed., pp. 7–68.
36. See Heidegger, *Being and Time*, trans. Macquarrie and Robinson, p. 487; see Heidegger, *Sein und Zeit*, p. 437.
37. See Hegel, *Phenomenology of Mind*, pp. 807–8.
38. Heidegger's "Die Zeit des Weltbildes" was translated by Marjorie Grene and published as the lead article in *Martin Heidegger and the Theory of Literature*, ed. William Spanos, pp. 1–15.
39. See Beckett, "Dante . . . Bruno. Vico . . Joyce."
40. The case is made by Carrabino, "The French *Nouveau Roman*," and by Françoise Ravaux, "The Denial of Tragedy: The Self-Reflexive Process of the Creative Activity and the French New Novel."
41. The expression "metafiction" was the poetic coinage of Wallace Stevens; see his "Notes toward a Supreme Fiction." For the differences in structure between "metafictional" novels and the classified forms see Alan Singer, *A Metaphorics of Fiction*, p. 9.
42. See Spanos's introduction to *Heidegger and the Theory of Literature*, pp. ix–xix.
43. See Jacques Derrida, *Of Grammatology*, pp. 8–14.
44. For a handy compilation of Peirce's writings on the theory of signs, see *The Philosophy of Peirce, Selected Writings*, pp. 98–119.
45. Jacques Derrida, "Freud and the Scene of Writing," p. 92, cited in Lois Oppenheim, "The Field of Poetic Constitution," p. 49.
46. See Jaynes, *The Origin of Consciousness*.

BIBLIOGRAPHY

Altizer, T. J. J., and William Hamilton. *Radical Theology and the Death of God.* Indianapolis: Bobbs-Merrill, 1966.

Aristotle. *De Metaphysica.* Translated by W. O. Ross. In *The Basic Works of Aristotle,* edited by Richard McKeon. New York: Random House, 1941.

———. *De Physica.* In *The Basic Works of Aristotle,* edited by Richard McKeon. New York: Random House, 1941.

Augustine, Saint. *Confessions.* Translated by E. B. Pusey. New York: Modern Library, 1949.

Barthes, Roland. *S/Z.* Paris: Editions du Seuil, 1970.

Beauvoir, Simone de. *The Mandarins.* Translated by L. Friedman. Cleveland and New York: World Publishing Co., 1956.

Beckett, Samuel, *Comment c'est.* Paris: Editions de Minuit, 1961.

———."Dante . . . Bruno. Vico . . Joyce." *transition* 16–17 (1929): 242–53.

———. *Endgame.* New York: Grove Press, 1958.

———. *How It Is.* Translated by the author. New York: Grove Press, 1964.

———. *Molloy, Malone Dies, The Unnamable.* New York: Grove Press, 1959.

———. *Waiting for Godot.* London: Faber and Faber, 1955.

Benjamin, A. Cornelius. *An Introduction to the Philosophy of Science.* New York: Macmillan, 1937.

Bergson, Henri. *Mémoire sur la décomposition de la pensée.* Paris: Presses Universitaires de France, 1952.

Boss, Medard. *Psychoanalysis and Daseinsanalysis.* Translated by L. B. Lefebre. New York: Basic Books, 1963.

343

Bultmann, Rudolf K. *Essays, Philosophical and Theological.* London: SCM Press, Ltd., 1955.

Burdach, K. "Faust und die Sorge." *Deutsche Vierteljahrschrift für Literatur-wissenschaft und Geistesgeschichte* 1 (1923):1 ff.

Carnap, Rudolf. *Logical Syntax of Language.* Translated by Ametha Smeaton. London: Routledge & Kegan Paul, 1964.

Carrabino, Victor. "The French *Nouveau Roman:* The Ultimate Expression of Impressionism." *Analecta Husserliana* 18 (1984): 261–70.

Cox, Harvey, and Joseph Fletcher, eds. *The Situation Ethics Debate.* Philadelphia: Westminister Press, 1968.

Croce, Benedetto. *Aesthetic.* Translated by Douglas Ainslie. London: Macmillan, 1909.

D'Arcangues, Pierre. *Le Destin de l'Espagne.* Paris: Editions Denoël, 1938.

Derrida, Jacques. *L'Écriture et la différence.* Paris: Editions de Seuil, 1967.

———. "Freud and the Scene of Writing." Translated by Jeffrey Mehlman. *Yale French Studies* 48 (1972): 74–117.

———. *Of Grammatology.* Translated by G. Spivak. Baltimore and London: Johns Hopkins University Press, 1976.

Descartes, René. *Œuvres et lettres de Descartes.* Edited by André Bridoux. Paris: Gallimard, 1952.

Dewey, John. *Experience and Nature.* La Salle, Ill.: Open Court, 1926.

———. "The Need for a Recovery of Philosophy." In *Creative Intelligence.* New York: Henry Holt and Co., 1917.

———. *Reconstruction in Philosophy.* New York: Mentor Books, 1950.

———. *Theory of Valuation.* In *Encyclopedia of Unified Science,* vol. 2, no. 4. Chicago: University of Chicago Press, 1939.

Diels, H. *Die Fragmente der Vorsokratiker.* 6th ed. Rev. Berlin: Weidmann, 1952.

Dilthey, Wilhelm. *Briefwechsel zwischen Wilhelm Dilthey und dem Grafen Paul Yorck von Wartenburg.* Edited by S. v.d. Schulenburg. Halle-an-der-Salle: Niemeyer, 1923.

———. *Gesammelte Schriften.* Vol. 1. Leibzig and Berlin: Teubner, 1914–59.

Eliot, T. S. *The Cocktail Party.* In *T. S. Eliot, The Complete Poems and Plays, 1909–1950,* pp. 295–387. New York: Harcourt, Brace, 1952.

Faulkner, William. *The Sound and the Fury.* New York: Modern Library, 1946.

———. *As I Lay Dying.* New York: Modern Library, 1946.

Feick, Hildegard. *Index zu Heideggers "Sein und Zeit."* Tübingen: Max Niemeyer Verlag, 1961.

Gadamer, Hans-Georg. *Philosophical Hermeneutics.* Edited and translated by D. E. Linge. Berkeley: University of California Press, 1977.

———. *Truth and Method.* Translated by G. Barden and J. Cumming. New York: Seabury Press, 1976.

———. *Wahrheit und Methode.* Tübingen: Mohr, 1965.

Hegel, G. W. F. *Encyklopädie der philosophischen Wissenschaften im Grundrisse.* Edited by M. J. Petry. 3 vols. With English translation. Dordrecht: Reidel, 1978.

————. *Phänomenologie des Geistes.* 6th ed. Edited by Johannes Hofmeister. Hamburg: Meiner Verlag, 1952.

————. *Phenomenology of Mind.* Translated by J. E. Baillie. New York: Macmillan, 1961.

Heidegger, Martin. *The Basic Problems of Phenomenology.* Translated by Albert Hofstadter. Bloomington: Indiana University Press, 1982.

————. *Being and Time.* Translated by John Macquarrie and Edward Robinson. London: SCM Press, Ltd., 1962.

————. *Über den Humanismus.* Frankfurt am Main: Klostermann, 1947.

————. *Einführung in die Metaphysik.* 2d ed. Tübingen: Max Niemeyer, 1958.

————. *Erläuterungen zu Hölderlins Dichtung.* Frankfurt am Main: Klostermann, 1951.

————. *Gelassenheit.* Pfullingen: Neske, 1954.

————. *Holzwege.* 4th ed. Frankfurt am Main: Klostermann, 1963.

————. *Identität und Differenz.* 3d ed. Pfullingen: Neske, 1957.

————. *An Introduction to Metaphysics.* Translated by Ralph Manheim. New Haven: Yale University Press, 1959.

————. *Kant and the Problem of Metaphysics.* Translated by J. S. Churchill. Bloomington: Indiana University Press, 1962.

————. *Kant und das Problem der Metaphysik.* 2d ed. Frankfurt am Main: Klostermann, 1951.

————. *On Time and Being.* Translated by Joan Stambaugh. New York: Harper and Row, 1972.

————. *Sein und Zeit.* 8th unchanged edition. Tübingen: Max Niemeyer Verlag, 1957.

————. *Unterwegs zur Sprache.* Pfullingen: Neske, 1959.

————. "Der Ursprung des Kunstwerkes." In *Holzwege,* pp. 7–68. 4th ed. Frankfurt am Main: Klostermann, 1963.

————. *Vom Wesen des Grundes.* 5th ed. Frankfurt am Main: Klostermann, 1957.

————. *Vorträge und Aufsätze.* Pfullingen: Neske, 1954.

————. *Was ist Metaphysik?* 8th ed. Frankfurt am Main: Klostermann, 1960.

————. *What Is Metaphysics?* Translated by R. F. C. Hull and Alan Crick. In *Existence and Being,* edited by Werner Brock. Chicago: Regnery, 1949.

————. *Zur Seinsfrage.* Frankfurt am Main: Klostermann, 1959.

Hemingway, Ernest. "A Clean, Well-Lighted Place." In *The Short Stories of Ernest Hemingway,* pp. 379–84. New York: Scribner's Sons, 1966.

Hölderlin, J. C. F. *Sämtliche Werke.* Edited by Friedrich Bessner. Vol. 2, 1. Stuttgart: Kohlhammer Verlag, 1951.

Hume, David. *A Treatise of Human Nature.* London: Dent and Sons, 1911.

Husserl. Edmund. *The Crisis of European Sciences and Transcendental Phenomenology.* Translated by David Carr. Evanston: Northwestern University Press, 1970.

————. *Ideas.* Translated by G. Boyce Gibson. New York: Collier Books, 1962.

————. *Logical Investigations.* Translated by J. N. Findlay. New York: Humanities Press, 1970.

Ingarden, Roman. *The Literary Work of Art.* Translated by G. G. Grabowicz. Evanston: Northwestern University Press, 1973.

Jaynes, Julian. *The Origin of Consciousness in the Breakdown of the Bicameral Mind.* Toronto: University of Toronto Press, 1976.

Kaelin, Eugene F. *Art and Existence.* Lewisburg, Penn.: Bucknell University Press, 1970.

Kant, Immanuel. *Critique of Pure Reason.* Translated by J. M. D. Meiklejohn. London and New York: Colonial Press, 1900.

———. *Kritik der reinen Vernunft.* Edited by Raymond Schmidt. Hamburg: Meiner Verlag, 1952.

Kierkegaard, Søren. *Philosophical Fragments.* Translated by D. Swanson. Revised by H. V. Hong. Princeton: Princeton University Press, 1962.

———. *Repetition.* Translated by W. Lowrie. New York: Harper and Row, 1964.

Koestler, Arthur. *Darkness at Noon.* 7th printing. New York: Signet Books, 1955.

Langan, Thomas. *The Meaning of Heidegger: A Critical Study of an Existentialist Phenomenology.* New York: Columbia University Press, 1959.

Marx, Werner. *Heidegger und die Tradition.* Stuttgart: Kohlhammer Verlag, 1961.

May, Rollo, et al., eds. *Existence.* New York: Basic Books, 1958.

Mead, George H. *Mind, Self and Society from the Point of View of a Social Behaviorist.* Edited by Charles Morris. Chicago: University of Chicago Press, 1934.

Merleau-Ponty, Maurice. *Eloge de la philosophie.* Paris: Gallimard, 1953.

Moore, G. E. "Refutation of Idealism." In *Philosophical Studies.* Paterson, N.J.: Littlefield, Adams & Co., 1959.

Nietzsche, Friedrich. "Nutzen und Nachteil der Historie für das Leben." 2d essay of *Unzeitgemässene Betrachtungen.* 1874. In *Nietzsches Werke,* vol. 2. Leipzig: Naumann Verlag, 1906.

Norris, Christopher. *Deconstruction, Theory and Practice.* London and New York: Methuen, 1982.

Oppenheim, Lois. "The Field of Poetic Constitution." *Analecta Husserliana* 18 (1984): 47–59.

Pascal, Blaise. *Pensées.* Edited by Léon Brunschvicg. Paris: Editions de Cluny, 1934.

Peirce, Charles S. *The Philosophy of Peirce, Selected Writings.* Edited by Justus Buchler. New York: Harcourt-Brace, 1940.

Plato. *Ion.* In *The Dialogues of Plato,* translated by B. Jowett, vol. 1. New York: Random House, 1937.

———. *Timaeus.* In *The Dialogues of Plato,* translated by B. Jowett, vol. 2. New York: Random House, 1937.

Quine, Willard Van O. *Word and Object.* Cambridge, Mass.: MIT Press, 1960.

Ravaux, Françoise. "The Denial of Tragedy: The Self-Reflexive Process of the

Creative Activity and the French New Novel." *Analecta Husserliana* 18 (1984): 401–6.

Richardson, W. J. *Heidegger through Phenomenology to Thought.* Vol. 13 in *Phänomenologica.* The Hague: Nijhoff, 1963.

Ricoeur, Paul. *The Conflict of Interpretations.* Translated by K. MacLaughlin, et al. Evanston: Northwestern University Press, 1974.

———. *Interpretation Theory: Discourse and the Surplus of Meaning.* Fort Worth: Texas Christian University Press, 1976.

Rogers, Carl. *On Becoming a Person.* Boston: Houghton Mifflin, 1961.

Romains, Jules. *La Mort de quelqu'un.* Paris: Gallimard, 1923.

Ryle, Gilbert. *The Concept of Mind.* New York: Barnes and Noble, 1949.

Santayana, George. *The Philosophy of George Santayana.* Edited by Irwin Edman. New York: Modern Library, 1936.

Sartre, Jean-Paul. "A propos de '*Le Bruit et la fureur*': la temporalité chez Faulkner." In *Situations* 1:70–81. Paris: Gallimard, 1947.

———. *Baudelaire.* Paris: Gallimard, 1947.

———. *Being and Nothingness.* Translated by Hazel Barnes. New York: Philosophical Library, 1956.

———. *L'Être et le néant: essai d'ontologie phénoménologique.* Paris: Gallimard, 1943.

———. *L'Existentialisme est un humanisme.* Paris: Nagel, 1946.

———. *The Family Idiot.* Translated by Carol Gosman. Chicago: University of Chicago Press, 1981.

———. "Question de méthode." *Les Temps Modernes* 13 (1957): 338–417, 658–98.

———. *Saint Genet comédien et martyr.* Paris: Gallimard, 1952.

———. *Situations.* 3 vols. Paris: Gallimard, 1947–49.

———. "La Transcendance de l'Ego." In *Recherches Philosophiques* 6 (1936): 85–123.

———. *What Is Literature?* Translated by B. Frechtman. New York: Philosophical Library, 1949.

Saussure, Ferdinand de. *Cours de linguistique générale.* Edited by Ch. Bally, A. Sechehaye, A. Riedlinger. Paris: Payot, 1949.

Scheler, Max. *Gesammelte Werke.* Vol. 8. Berne: Francke Verlag, 1954.

Singer, Alan. *A Metaphorics of Fiction.* Tallahassee: Florida State University Press, 1983.

Spanos, William, ed. *Martin Heidegger and the Question of Literature: Toward a Postmodern Literary Hermeneutics.* Bloomington and London: Indiana University Press, 1976.

Stace, W. T. *The Meaning of Beauty.* London: At the Cayme Press, 1929.

Steiner, George. *Heidegger.* Spanish translation by Jorge A. Mora. Mexico City: Fondo de Cultura Economica, 1983.

Stevens, Wallace. "Notes toward a Supreme Fiction." In *The Collected Poems of Wallace Stevens,* pp. 380–408. New York: Knopf, 1964.

Tillich, Paul. *The Courage to Be.* New Haven: Yale University Press, 1952.

————. *Systematic Theology.* 3 vols. Chicago: University of Chicago Press, 1957–63.

Vico, Giambattista. *The New Science.* Translated by T. G. Bergin and M. H. Fisch. Ithaca: Cornell University Press, 1948.

Virgil. *The Aeneid.* With introduction, notes, vocabulary, and grammatical appendix by Clyde Pharr. Book 2. New York and London: D. C. Heath and Co., 1930.

von Humboldt, Wilhelm. *Gesammelte Schriften.* Band 6. Berlin: Preussische Akademie der Wissenschaft, 1829.

Waugh, Evelyn. *The Loved One.* New York: Modern Library, 1958.

Werkmeister, William H. *Kant's Silent Decade.* Tallahassee: Florida State University Press, 1979.

Wittgenstein, Ludwig. *Philosophical Investigations.* Translated by G. E. M. Anscombe. New York: Macmillan, 1953.

————. *Tractatus Logico-Philosophicus.* Translated by D. F. Pears and B. F. McGuinness. London: Routledge & Kegan Paul, 1964.

INDEX

(914) 271 7585

Lucia Lieb   6842686

NYU Student